A Concise History
of Modern Korea

A Concise History of Modern Korea

From the Late Nineteenth Century to the Present

Volume 2

Second Edition

Michael J. Seth

ROWMAN & LITTLEFIELD
Lanham • Boulder • New York • London

Published by Rowman & Littlefield
A wholly owned subsidiary of The Rowman & Littlefield Publishing Group, Inc.
4501 Forbes Boulevard, Suite 200, Lanham, Maryland 20706
www.rowman.com

Unit A, Whitacre Mews, 26-34 Stannary Street, London SE11 4AB, United Kingdom

British Library Cataloguing in Publication Information Available

Library of Congress Cataloging-in-Publication Data

Names: Seth, Michael J., 1948– author. | Seth, Michael J., 1948– Concise history of Korea.
Title: A concise history of modern Korea : from the late nineteenth century to the present / Michael J. Seth.
Description: Second edition. | Lanham : Rowman & Littlefield, 2016. | "Volume 2." | Includes bibliographical references and index.
Identifiers: LCCN 2016000109 (print) | LCCN 2016000775 (ebook) | ISBN 9781442260467 (cloth : alk. paper) | ISBN 9781442260474 (pbk. : alk. paper) | ISBN 9781442260481 (electronic)
Subjects: LCSH: Korea—History. | Korea (South)—History. | Korea (North)—History.
Classification: LCC DS907.18 .S424 2016 (print) | LCC DS907.18 (ebook) | DDC 951.9—dc23
LC record available at http://lccn.loc.gov/2016000109

∞™ The paper used in this publication meets the minimum requirements of American National Standard for Information Sciences—Permanence of Paper for Printed Library Materials, ANSI/NISO Z39.48-1992.

Printed in the United States of America

Contents

Primary Source Readings

Preface

Korea until recently has been a country little known to most of the world. Several decades ago it was possible to place almost all the scholarly literature on Korean history in English on a single shelf. Indeed, Korea was so little understood that when it appeared at all in Western textbooks it often was restricted to developments related to the Korean War and the Cold War. In recent years this neglect of Korean history has been replaced by a rapidly developing interest by Western academics, and the historical scholarship available to non-Koreans has grown enormously. Most of the recent historical literature is on modern Korea. In the six years since publication of the first edition of this book, enough new scholarship has emerged to warrant a number of revisions, as well as to add thirty titles to the select bibliography. At least some of this scholarship has been incorporated into each chapter.

Chapters 1 and 2 make reference to the insights from recent scholarship that attempt to provide a more complex and nuanced view of Korea under Japanese colonial rule. Increased interest in North Korea has resulted in a flood of books and articles. Most have been by political scientists viewing the country as a security issue, but there have been some excellent historical studies and enough information from defectors and careful analysis of what information is available to be able to construct a better picture of that state's history. Based on this new information, parts of Chapter 3 and much of Chapters 4 and 7 have been substantially revised. Chapter 8 has been updated to incorporate new developments as well as some insights provided by recent scholarship.

While this edition has attempted to be as up to date as possible, Korean history in the West is an expanding field that constantly generates new information and insights. And Korea itself is a dynamic society capable of amazingly rapid change. As it evolves so will our understanding of its history.

Acknowledgments

Among the people who have assisted me in some way I would like to thank Professor Lee Yoon Suk of Yonsei University, artist Lee Sang-guk, and Choi Soo-ok. Kirk Larson carefully read the manuscripts for the first edition, offered many suggestions, and caught some embarrassing mistakes. The Korea Foundation and the Academy of Korean Studies have partially sponsored some of my visits to Korea. The patience and help of Susan McEachern and the staff of Rowman & Littlefield helped me with both the first and second editions of this book. The comments of reviewers of the first edition were helpful for this second revised one. My colleagues in the area of Korean studies whose work is cited in the text as well as in the endnotes and bibliography of this book have done most of the hard research on which this book is based. My students at James Madison University have been guinea pigs for the early drafts of this text, as they were for my previous book. Their questions guided me in deciding what to include and how to make it comprehensible to non-specialists. The History Department at James Madison University provided some relief from a heavy teaching load to complete the manuscript for the first edition.

This book is the product of years of being around people who aided me in various ways in my pursuit of understanding Korean history. I want to express my gratitude to them, especially to the many Koreans who over the years have shared their love and knowledge of their culture and who have encouraged me to continue in my attempt to make Korea a bit better known to non-Koreans.

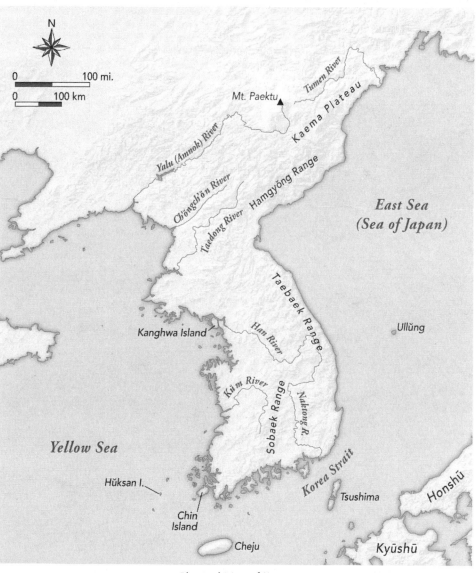

Physical Map of Korea

Physical Map of East Asia

Chosŏn Korea

Modern Korea

Introduction

Korea has a history unlike any other modern nation. In the late nineteenth century, few if any states could match Korea's territorial and institutional stability, its historical continuity, its ethnic unity, and its isolation. The last earned it the sobriquet "the hermit kingdom." As with so much of the non-Western world, Korea became a victim to the great age of imperialism. Its colonial experience was atypical, however, in that it was ruled by Japan, another non-Western society, a familiar neighbor with which it shared many cultural affinities. But what makes Korea's modern history unique was its division in 1945 by the United States and the Soviet Union at the thirty-eighth parallel. Korea was divided along a totally arbitrary line that had no historical, geographical, cultural, or economic logic; just a line that conveniently separated the country into roughly two equal halves—dividing provinces, valleys, and families. A nation that was arguably the most ethnically homogeneous in the world, with thirteen centuries of political unity, with national and provincial boundaries older than any almost any other state, was abruptly severed by the two superpowers.

While in theory this was only a temporary measure, almost immediately two separate regimes emerged. In 1948, the United States and the Soviet Union set up their client states: the Republic of Korea, better known as South Korea, and the Democratic People's Republic of Korea, or North Korea. The two "Koreas" had different leaders, different political and economic systems, and different external orientations. Both saw the division as an unacceptable and temporary condition, but the attempts to unify the country led to one of the bloodiest conflicts since the end of

1

World War II. Despite horrific destruction and loss of life, both regimes survived and continued on their markedly different trajectories of development. North Korea evolved into one of the world's most totalitarian and militant states, ruled by a family with a cult of personality unequaled in its extreme intensity. It is the world's most closed, and for many, most enigmatic state, with a leadership busy developing missiles and nuclear weapons while millions of its children were stunted from malnutrition. South Korea, by contrast, after a rocky and uncertain start evolved into an open, democratic society, whose spectacular economic growth and internationally competitive industries made it an outstanding success story among the postcolonial states.

Nowhere else was a nation so arbitrarily divided and the peoples of the two halves so effectively isolated from each other; nowhere else did such radically different political and social systems emerge.[1] The boundary between the two Koreas is not only the world's most heavily armed and until recently most hermetically sealed but marks two dramatically different living standards and lifestyles. Nowhere else is there such a sharp contrast between two contiguous states—one rich, democratic and cosmopolitan; the other impoverished, totalitarian, and isolated. And arguably the history of no other society in the past century offers such contrasting examples of how societies can undergo modern development. Korea's modern history is both a remarkable story and an incomparable example of how the interplay of historical contingency, policy choices, and cultural heritage can shape societies so distinctively.

Korea is also a fascinating land with a rich and distinctive culture that continues to evolve in interesting and even surprising ways. Yet, Korea and its history have often been overlooked in the past. Except for the Korean War it has not, at least until recently, drawn much attention from the rest of the world. Partly this is due to the fact that it has been overshadowed by its larger neighbors, China and Japan. Next to China, the world's most populous nation and second-largest in area, Korea looks small. And it is overshadowed by a larger, wealthier, and dynamic Japan. It also borders another giant, Russia. Koreans themselves sometimes call their country a "shrimp between whales." But it is not so small. North and South Korea together have approximately the same area as Great Britain. Their combined population of around seventy-five million is a little larger than France, a little smaller than Germany. Nor is it culturally insignificant. Korea not only has a long cultural tradition but it is among the better-recorded ones. Koreans have been avid compilers of history and produced an impressive body of historical scholarship. They also possess a rich literary and artistic heritage. Historically, Korea was a largely rural, agricultural society with a less-vibrant urban and commercial life than its neighbors, but it had a complex, sophisticated system of government and education. Nor was it technologically backward. The Koreans were the first to use rain gauges and keep records of rainfall, the first to use moveable metal type, and the first to build ironclad ships; and the oldest known printed materials have been found there. Today Korea is emerging from its past obscurity. Besides the notoriety of Kim Jong Un and the North Korean nuclear threat, South Korea has become a major world economy whose corporate names—LG, Samsung, and Hyundai—are globally recognized and whose popular culture has a huge audience among its Asian neighbors and is beginning to be known beyond Asia. Yet its remarkable modern history with its important implications is still not widely known nor appreciated.

Geographically, Korea is a mountainous peninsula about 600 miles long and an average 120 miles wide with a mixture of maritime and continental climates. The mountains are not high, reaching only 9,000 feet with Mount Paektu on the border between North Korea and Manchuria. Yet no place in Korea is not within sight of them. Arable land is limited but well watered and fertile. Winters vary from short and mild in the south to long and bitter cold in the north; summers are wet and humid almost everywhere. The muggy summers and dry autumns are ideal for rice cultivation, and except in the far north where it is too cold to grow rice, this plant has been the staple crop for several millennia. Wet rice agriculture is labor intensive but produces high yields per acre. Therefore, despite the limited amount of land suitable for farming, Korea has been for centuries a densely populated country and until quite recently an overwhelmingly rural, agricultural one. No part of Korea is far from the seas. The seas, however, while filled with abundant fish and seafood, important components in the Korean diet, are not friendly to navigation. The east coast on the Sea of Japan (or "East Sea" as the Koreans call it) has few good harbors and is cut off from the major population centers by rugged mountains. Navigation on the western Yellow Sea coast is made difficult by shifting sandbars and some of the world's highest tides. Confined to a geographically well-defined peninsula with ample resources to support a fairly populous agricultural society, Korea developed its own distinctive society and identity while borrowing heavily from China.

Korea entered the twentieth century as one of the world's oldest and most ethnically and culturally homogeneous societies. Except for one brief period in the early tenth century, the country had remained politically unified since 676.[2] Before then, three states occupied the Korean peninsula: Koguryŏ governed most of what is now North Korea and good parts of adjacent Manchuria, Paekche ruled the southwestern portion of the peninsula, and Silla the southeastern. All emerged in the fourth century as Chinese-influenced states that eventually adopted Buddhism introduced by Chinese missionaries. Silla unified most of the peninsula, stamped its culture on it, and ruled to the tenth century. In 935, it was replaced by the Koryŏ dynasty and in 1392, the Chosŏn (sometimes called Yi) dynasty, which ended in 1910. The last two dynasties together spanned a millennium; both were unusually long-lived by historical standards.

Korea was an aristocratic society dominated by a hereditary class of landowners and government officials that came to be known as *yangban*. The *yangbans'* economic base was their agricultural holdings—not large estates but usually scattered patches of rice paddy, barley fields, and other lands worked by tenants or slaves or rented by free peasants. Their social status was confirmed, the families' prestige enhanced, and access to important political positions acquired by success in civil service exams. Borrowed from China, these exams were the major means by which government posts were allotted to the elite. Powerful aristocratic families shared power with a king whose authority theoretically came from the Chinese emperor. The Korean king held considerable power over his kingdom but this power was often limited or checked by officials representing the *yangban* class. An elaborate bureaucracy administered a highly centralized state with little local autonomy. During the Chosŏn dynasty the state appointed the governors of the eight provinces and the administrators of the roughly three hundred counties and other subprovincial units. A law of avoidance meant the officials could not serve in their home provinces.

Under the aristocracy was the peasant majority mostly living in small villages of mud and thatched-roof dwellings. They had little access to power. Under them were certain outcaste groups such as leather workers and shamans. These outcaste groups were also hereditary, as was a small class of government clerks and technical specialists such as lawyers, doctors, and astronomers called *chungin*. At the bottom of society were slaves who may have made up close to a third of society at one point but whose numbers were declining in the nineteenth century. There were also peddlers and wholesale merchants, but a geography of rugged mountains and a traditional disdain of merchants inhibited commerce.

During this time Korea enjoyed considerable stability and continuity. The changes of dynasties marked neither radical cultural nor social breaks with the past. The same institutions with modifications served as the organs of government and many of the same families dominated political, social, and cultural life for more than a millennium. After the tenth century there were only modest changes in the political boundaries of the kingdom, and only minor adjustments in its provincial boundaries after the eleventh century. Geography played a role in this, as the peninsula formed a natural geographical compartment, but so did the success by which Koreans developed a set of institutions and values that held the society together. From time to time the country's larger and militarily more formidable neighbors invaded Korea. Yet each time, the political and social order displayed an impressive resiliency.

In the distant past, various groups of peoples from northeast Asia entered the peninsula; some went on to become the ancestors of the Japanese and others mixed and merged to become a single Korean ethnic group sharing one language and culture. Indeed, by the fifteenth century and perhaps earlier, ethnicity, language, and polity were largely coterminous. This is uncommon in world history; one has only to think of the ethnic and linguistic kaleidoscope of India, or the problems of nation-building among diverse groups divided along ethnic, linguistic, or sectarian lines in Pakistan, Iraq, Indonesia, or the nations of Africa. Germany was unified only in 1871, but even then the country did not include all German-speaking people. France has a longer history of unity, to give another example, but the boundaries of France never included all French-speaking people and contained small ethnic minorities: Bretons, Basques, and German-speaking Alsatians. Or one can point out Arab countries or those of Latin America to appreciate the fact that a state generally does not coincide with a distinctive language, ethnicity, or cultural identity. Korea was different—when Korea began to enter the modern world in the late nineteenth century there were no significant populations of Korean speakers outside the political boundaries of Korea and no ethnic or linguistic minorities within. In this respect only Japan, perhaps, is comparable.

Korea's culture was derived in large measure from China. For centuries Koreans had patterned their political institutions, legal concepts, literature, and art after the Chinese. From China arrived Buddhism and Confucianism. Confucianism had an especially strong impact, shaping the way people thought about government, society, and ethics. Confucian concepts and terminology date from the days before unification; however, it was the newly reinvigorated form known by Westerners as Neo-Confucianism that had the most impact. From its arrival in the fourteenth century on, waves of firm adherents insisted that Korea model political and social institutions on Confucian tenets; and this in fact is what happened. By the seventeenth century if not earlier, Korea became more Confucian than China; in fact, no society ever made greater efforts to conform to its principles. Confucian values such as loyalty to kings, respect for parents, obedience of women to men, leadership by moral example, and the importance of education as a means of moral perfection sank deep roots in Korea.

Korea's worldview was firmly lodged in the Sinocentric tribute system. In theory, China, the "Middle Kingdom," was the center of civilization, and the emperor of China, nominally at least, ruler of all that is under

Heaven. From the emperor flowed all legitimate political authority. Those societies that adhered most closely to Chinese norms were the most civilized and least barbarian. Neighboring states did not maintain diplomatic relations but instead sent tribute missions to the emperor with gifts. These missions were often a cover for trade. Korea was proud to be a loyal tributary and was regarded by the Chinese as one of the most civilized and reliable subject states. In practice Korea was quite independent, and the tributary relationship was mainly ceremonial. It was an enormous source of pride for Koreans to be part of the great cosmopolitan civilization centered in China, and the Koreans shared the Chinese contempt for barbarians outside of this civilization and for the semi-barbarians on its periphery such as the Japanese.

Yet Korea was not China. Geographically it was separate, with the two states permanently bordering each other only with the establishment of the Qing (Manchu) dynasty in the mid-seventeenth century. The language was different. Korean is a highly inflected, non-tonal language unrelated to and radically different from Chinese.[3] The folk customs, shamanism, domestic architecture, dress, and cuisine were distinctive. In the fifteenth century Koreans developed their own writing system, the *han'gŭl* alphabet, although they continued to use Chinese characters as well. The educated elite were proud to be part of this Sinocentric world. But Koreans were also conscious of being part of a land with its own history and traditions.

Long stretches of peace were broken from time to time by invasions. The seminomadic Khitans from what is now Manchuria invaded in the tenth and early eleventh centuries, the Mongols launched a series of particularly devastating invasions in the thirteenth, the Japanese paramount leader Hideyoshi invaded in the 1590s, and the Manchus in the mid-seventeenth century. None of these invasions radically altered the course of Korean history, and the society usually made a speedy recovery. The invasions, however, instilled a wariness of outsiders. With China under the rule of the "barbarian" Manchu or Qing dynasty after 1644, late Chosŏn dynasty Koreans began to regard their own land as the truest bastion of Confucian civilization. The kingdom pursued a strict policy of isolation. Except for official tributary missions to China and the occasional diplomatic mission to Japan, Koreans were prohibited from leaving the country. All foreigners were barred entry, except for official Chinese on diplomatic missions and Japanese, who were allowed to trade only at a small walled compound, the Waegwan, in Pusan.

Under the benevolent umbrella of China, off the world's major trade routes and with little contact with foreigners, Koreans lived in a comfortable isolation that ended with their abrupt entry into the Western-dominated world of the late nineteenth century. Korea's first modern century, from its "opening" by Japanese gunboats in 1876, was a troubled one. Ill prepared, Koreans struggled with competing variants of modernity while the major powers fought over influence. The nation was annexed to Japan; then it went through thirty-five years of wrenching change and social upheaval caused by the transition to a new modern society, made worse by exploitative and inconsistent policies of the Japanese colonial administration. The real turmoil began with the mobilization of the population by Japan during World War II. This was followed by liberation and the division into two Koreas.

Yet despite this similar traditional and colonial heritage, North and South Korea moved in very different directions. Each state's development was unusual and poses many questions. How can we account for the extraordinary transformation of South Korea from a nation with a per capita income below Ghana or Haiti in 1960 to one of the only developing nations to "graduate" to developed status? How did a nation where the majority of the adult population in 1945 was illiterate and only 5 percent had a secondary education become one of the most literate societies in the world by 2000, a country whose students consistently score at or near the top in international tests of learning competencies? How can we account for the development of an internationally competitive economy in a society that had previously lacked a vibrant commercial life? What accounts for the emergence of one of Asia's most lively democracies in a society that had known only authoritarianism? Meanwhile, why did North Korea evolve into such a totalitarian state? How can we explain the bizarre cult of personality associated with Kim Il Sung and his family? Or how can we understand the regime's extreme militancy and hostility to the West? Or explain the regime's continual survival despite the collapse of its economy, mass famine, and global isolation?

The most fundamental question is why the courses taken by the two Koreas were so different. That is, how is it possible that such a culturally and ethnically homogeneous people could have evolved so differently in seven decades? Korea's modern history challenges us to rethink the way we look at history and culture. The success or perceived lack of success of modern nations to develop well-functioning political, social, and economic systems is often judged, at least in part, by their cultural heritages. Japan's success, for example, has been attributed to its strong sense of unity, traditions of craftsmanship, competitive samurai spirit, and respect for learning; Singapore's to its Confucian culture. In some cases, religious heritage—for example, Islam—or the legacy of autocracy are pointed out as explanations for failures to achieve political freedom or economic prosperity. Korea's recent experience provides evidence that a nation's heritage can be the basis for very different outcomes. It suggests that historical contingencies and public policies, as well as cultural legacies, are extremely important in shaping a nation's history.

Chapter 1 looks at the entry of Korea into the modern world and the age of imperialism in the late nineteenth century and traces its loss of independence to Japan. Chapter 2 surveys the thirty-five-year period of colonial rule, from 1910–45, and its impact on later Korean history. Chapter 3 narrates the division of Korea, the development of two separate regimes, and the horrendous Korean War. Chapter 4 examines the evolution of North Korean society from the end of the Korean War in 1953 to the early 1990s. Chapters 5 and 6 cover South Korea's development during this time. More attention is given to South Korea than to the North since not only does it contain a majority of the Korean people, but also its history is far better documented. Chapters 7 and 8 deal respectively with North and South Korea from the early 1990s to 2015.

The creation of two Koreas and the radically divergent paths they followed offer many insights for understanding economic, social, and political development. Korea is also an important part of the global community with a rich and dynamic culture. That alone makes its history worthy of study.

NOTES

1. See chapter 3 for comparisons with Germany and Vietnam.

2. Some historians regard Korea as not achieving unity until the tenth century. For this as well as discussions on the emergence of ethnic homogeneity see Michael J. Seth, *A Concise History of Premodern Korea: From Antiquity through the Nineteenth Century* (Lanham, MD: Rowman & Littlefield, 2016).

3. Noting the structural similarities of Korean to Japanese, some scholars have suggested the two languages are related. Others have placed both into a larger Altaic family of languages that includes Turkish and Mongolian. More likely, Korean is an isolate, a language not related to any other.

1

❧

Korea in the Age of Imperialism, 1876 to 1910

It could hardly have been obvious to any Korean in the early nineteenth century that their society was to undergo a relentless series of upheavals and radical transformations. Theirs was a twelve-century-old kingdom with a social and political system that had evolved but not drastically changed in more than a millennium. Korean leaders and elites were confident in the virtuousness of their state and society, considering it a bastion of truly civilized values, the most faithful adherent of correct ethical norms derived from the Chinese Confucian tradition. Except for a tiny number of Christians, the world outside East Asia was of little concern for them. All this changed radically as the world of Western imperialism began to intrude upon Korea.

EARLY CONTACTS WITH THE WEST

The world Koreans inhabited was dominated by China, the vast continental empire that contained one of the world's wealthiest, oldest, and most sophisticated societies. Then there was Japan to the east, a participant in the broader East Asian cultural world but also a warlike and dangerous society. To the northwest were the seminomadic peoples that had so often invaded. Koreans maintained sporadic contact with Vietnamese, Siamese, and other Southeast Asian people. Beyond this was the world of distant barbarians that Koreans had little contact with, knowledge of, or interest in. Among these remote peoples were the Europeans. Early in the sixteenth century reports of the presence of "Pullanggi" (Franks) in

Southeast Asia reached Korea, and in 1597 a Jesuit, Gregorio de Cespedes, arrived in Korea accompanying the Japanese troops, but there is no Korean record of his presence. Some Korean captives in Hideyoshi's invasions were brought back to Japan and converted to Christianity. One, baptized as Antonio Corea, arrived in Italy in 1606 and married a European woman. Antonio Corea never made it back to Korea to report on what he saw. Not until the late nineteenth century did a Korean visit a Western country and come back to relate his experiences to his compatriots.

Direct contact with the West came in the seventeenth and eighteenth centuries. The Jesuits under the talented polymath Matteo Ricci (1552–1610) established a small mission in Beijing at the end of the sixteenth century. While they made few converts, they did attract admiration for their skills in perspective painting and mapmaking, their knowledge of mathematics and astronomy, and their curious mechanical devices, especially clocks. The Chinese emperors employed Jesuits to help them maintain an accurate calendar. Koreans traveling on diplomatic missions encountered these Jesuits and shared the Chinese admiration for their technical and mathematical skills. An early reference comes from Yi Sugwang (1563–1628), who wrote the *Chibong yusŏl* (*Topical Discourses of Chibong*) in 1614, an encyclopedic work with 3,500 entries. Included in his entries were brief descriptions of Western maps, self-striking clocks, ships, prisms, grape wine, Western religion, and Matteo Ricci. Among his descriptions of the countries of the world he mentioned Portugal, which he placed southwest of Siam, and England, which he confused with the Kirghiz tribe in central Asia.[1]

A number of other scholars and officials on diplomatic missions met Jesuits and picked up some knowledge of Western science and religion. One of these, Chŏng Tu-wŏn, in 1631 brought back with him a telescope, a clock, a Western gun, maps of the world and the heavens, and books in Chinese by Western missionaries on astronomy and world geography. For the most part Koreans were dismissive of Christianity, which they viewed as nonsensical and indicative of the low cultural level of Westerners despite their technical skill. Westerners' skills at calculating an accurate calendar were another matter, since one of the most important functions of a ruler was to be able to determine when his people could plant and harvest crops. Prince Sohyŏn, while being held hostage in Beijing by the Manchus, met Adam Schall (1591–1666), one of the most learned of the Jesuits in China, and invited him to send a Jesuit to Korea. Although nothing came of this, the Koreans did adopt Western calendrical methods to determine the position of heavenly bodies over Seoul and thus make a more reliable calendar. Previously they had relied on a calendar based on the positions of heavenly bodies over Beijing.

In the eighteenth century Korean visitors to China continued to stop by the Jesuit mission, which, as historian Donald Baker has noted, became part of the standard tour of exotic sights in the imperial capital. Jesuits even complained about the Korean visitors who handled their musical instruments and wandered around the cathedral in Beijing, spitting on the floor and ignoring its sanctity. Some Koreans were impressed by Western painting, especially its mastery of linear perspective. Pak Chi-wŏn in his *Yŏlha ilgi* wrote how he and his companions when entering a Jesuit church stretched out their arms to receive babies falling from clouds on the church ceiling. The clouds looked real, and humans appeared to be alive and moving.[2] Western realism even had some influence on eighteenth-century Korean artists, but as in Qing China, the interest in Western painting techniques was a fad that waned in the nineteenth century.

Few Koreans seemed to take the Europeans very seriously as bearers of a great tradition, rather seeing them as just clever barbarians. One of the early reported exchanges between a Korean and a Westerner is preserved in the correspondence of Yi Yong-ho, a young Korean diplomat who met Joao Rodriques (1561–1633), in which Yi challenged the Jesuit scholar on his explanation of the universe.[3] China is the center of the universe, Yi informed the Jesuit. Rodrigues replied that there is no center of the world. Western cosmology, he further argued, is far superior to the Chinese view, for the Chinese astronomers did not know why celestial bodies moved but the West had an explanation. The Jesuit then went on to explain Catholic cosmology, linking the knowledge of celestial spheres with the broader cosmology of heaven, hell, and God. Yi was impressed with the Westerner's science, but found his cosmology unconvincing.[4] A few took Western knowledge seriously. Yi Ik, for example, although he never met any Europeans, read Chinese translations and extracts of Western mathematics, geography, and medicine, for all of which he had great respect. However, nothing the Koreans learned of the West shook their belief in the superiority of East Asian civilization or their Sinocentric views of the world. In fact, Yi Ik noted that Western world maps show China in the center of the world dominating its largest continent, which he regarded as evidence of China's centrality. Mostly Westerners were strange creatures with round eyes, big noses, and sometimes red hair, who as it was frequently repeated, urinated like dogs by lifting one leg.[5]

In 1627, three shipwrecked Dutch sailors washed up on the shores of Korea. They were employed building guns for the Korean military. Two died in the Manchu invasion of 1636; a third, Jan Janse Weltevree, who married a Korean woman and adopted a Korean name, survived to greet the arrival of thirty-six of his countrymen in 1653 when their ship wrecked on Cheju. These Dutch sailors too were forcibly detained in

Korea and employed for their technical skills. Eight later escaped, and one, Hendrick Hamel (1630–1692), wrote the first account of Korea in a Western language. An accurate observer, Hamel provided a useful outsider's view of seventeenth-century Korea. Hamel reported that Koreans treated Westerners as objects of curiosity but that even educated Koreans showed little knowledge or curiosity about Western countries. "When we nam'd some Countries to them, they laugh'd at us, affirming we only talk'd of some town or village; their Geographical Knowledge of the coasts reaching no farther than Siam by reason of the little Traffick they have with Strangers farther from them."[6] After Hamel, no more Westerners are known to have arrived in Korea for nearly two centuries.

This changed dramatically in the nineteenth century as the expansive West of the nineteenth century began to intrude upon Korea. In 1832, the *Lord Amherst* of the British East India Company appeared along the coast, offering to trade, but the Koreans explained it was against their law to trade with outsiders. In 1845, the British warship *Samarang*, surveying Korean waters, visited Cheju and other Korean ports and again inquired about trade. Korean authorities again explained that they had no desire to open their country to trade. The Koreans then requested the Qing government to make it clear to the British that it did not seek trade. But the Koreans were not to be left alone. In 1846, three French warships arrived on the coast and sent a letter to be forwarded to the king and left. In 1854, two armed Russian vessels sailed off the northeast coast and clashed with Koreans.

Koreans, through their diplomatic missions in China, were aware of more disturbing events. The British went to war with China from 1839 to 1842 in what is known as the Opium War, in which they defeated the Chinese and forced them to open ports to trade on British terms. Britain and France went to war with China again from 1858 to 1860, inflicting another defeat and extracting more concessions. The Opium War could be dismissed as merely a successful pirate attack by barbarians, but the capture and pillage of Beijing in 1860 by an Anglo-French force was a truly alarming development. Koreans through their diplomatic missions in Beijing kept informed of these disturbing events. At the same time, Korea acquired a new neighbor, as the Russians expanded south, annexing territory on China's northern frontier and advancing to Korea's Tumen River border in 1860. During 1864–1865, a number of Russians came to the border town of Kyŏnghŭng insisting on trade, while in 1863, Koreans living in the northeast began to migrate across the border into Russian territory.[7] To the east, the United States forced Japan to open itself to trade with the West in 1854.

Even before these alarming events took place a small number of Koreans became attracted to Christianity, which became known as *Sŏhak*

(Western Learning). It was introduced to Korea rather indirectly through written texts. A handful of Koreans on diplomatic missions to China met with Western missionaries in the seventeenth and eighteenth centuries. Most Koreans were highly dismissive of Christianity for many of the same reasons they objected to Buddhism: it promoted selfishness, honored celibacy, and gave credence to miracles. Even an admirer of Western learning such as Yi Ik dismissed these religious beliefs, which he called the "grains of sand and pieces of grit" amidst their scholarship.[8] Only in the late eighteenth century did a few Koreans become genuinely drawn to the religion. In 1784, Yi Sŭng-hun (1756–1801) accompanied his father on a diplomatic mission to Beijing and was baptized by a Western Catholic priest. A small number of *yangban* converted, mostly from the Namin faction that was out of power and tended to produce dissidents. Some *chungin*, however, converted as well. The converts included the scholar Tasan and his two brothers, Chŏng Yak-chŏn and Chŏng Yak-chong. In many ways Christianity's progress in Korea was unique for it was not spread directly by missionaries but by intellectuals who were attracted to Catholicism through their readings of Christian tracts in translations and through sporadic contacts with Christians in China. The beginning of Christianity in Korea was thus unusual in world history in that early converts largely converted themselves. Lacking any ordained priest, they even baptized themselves with only a vague idea of how baptism should be performed.

In China the Rites Controversy had weakened the Catholic mission the Jesuits established there in the seventeenth century. The pope had ruled in 1742 that ancestor worship and belief in Christianity were incompatible. This angered the Chinese authorities since the rites honoring a family's ancestors were central to Confucian practice. As Korean officials became aware of Catholicism they too condemned it. Chŏngjo declared it a heresy in 1785; the following year all importation of books of any kind from Beijing was banned lest they contain Christian writings. In 1791, Yun Chi-ch'ung, from a *yangban* family in the southwestern province of Chŏlla, was sentenced to death for failing to prepare an ancestral tablet for his mother. Four years later, however, the first priest from China, Zhou Wenmo, entered Korea in response to appeals from the small Christian community and began making a great number of new converts. By 1801, there were an estimated 4,000 Christians in the peninsula. That Catholicism could grow was in part due to the protection given by Ch'ae Che-gong, a Namin who held great influence during King Chŏngjo's last years. But with Chŏngjo's death and the ascension of Queen Dowager Kim (Yŏngjo's queen) as regent for the youthful King Sunjo, suppression of Catholicism resumed. This was intensified when a convert, Hwang Sa-yŏng, sent his "silk letter" to the French Catholic bishop in Beijing. In it he asked the pope to request that the Chinese emperor require the Korean king to grant religious freedom and to have Western nations send naval forces of 50,000–60,000 men to compel the Korean government to do so. It was to be delivered by another convert who was scheduled to go on a tribute mission. This only confirmed what many feared, that Catholicism was a dangerous heresy. Furthermore, that many converts like Hwang were from prominent, well-educated families was alarming. In the Catholic Persecution of 1801, 300 converts were put to death, including the scholars Yi Sŭng-hun and Chŏng Yak-chong, along with Zhou Wenmo. Chŏng Yak-chong's brothers Chŏng Yak-chŏn and Tasan were exiled to remote places. This persecution became entangled in factional disputes, since the Pyŏk branch of the Noron faction that was coming to power charged its Si branch of the Namin opponents with heresy. Religion became enmeshed with factional politics.

A few years later, however, with the royal in-law Andong Kim lineage securely in power, the persecution of Catholics eased. Meanwhile, the Vatican had appointed a vicar apostolic for Korea, and in 1836, the French priest Maubant, and in 1837, two others, Chastan and Imbert, surreptitiously entered the country. The number of converts reached 9,000 by the late 1830s. But when the P'ungyang Cho came to power they began the Catholic Persecution of 1839 in which the three foreign priests and seventy-five converts were executed. A few years later the first Korean priest, Kim Tae-gŏn (1821–1846), was ordained in Macao and then smuggled into the country. His arrival was shortly followed by the arrival of three French naval ships to investigate the massacres of 1839. Assuming a connection between Kim and the arrival of foreign ships, the court executed him along with eight converts in 1846. With King Ch'ŏlchong on the throne in 1849 and the Andong Kim in power again, the persecutions let up. Twelve French Catholic priests entered, and Catholic books and pamphlets were published. The number of converts reached 20,000 by 1864. In the nineteenth century many converts were from the urban poor; many were women. Most were from the Seoul area. Christianity was by no means sweeping the country, but the presence of a Christian minority with its foreign links was troubling to Korean conservatives.

THE OPENING OF KOREA

The growing menace Westerners posed, along with internal financial problems, contributed to a growing sense of crisis. Korea responded with a vigorous reform effort led by the Taewŏn'gun. When King Ch'ŏlchong (r. 1849–1864) died without an heir, the second son of a relative, Yi Ha-ŭng, was selected to succeed as Kojong (r. 1864–1907). As Kojong was a minor, his father became regent, taking the title of Taewŏn'gun (Grand Prince). The Taewŏn'gun's program of reform was designed to strengthen the monarchy and the power of the central government. He rebuilt the main royal palace and restored royal tombs, instituted a new currency, and carried out measures to increase the state's tax revenue. Among the latter was a new household tax that was levied on the previously tax-exempted *yangban*, the hereditary aristocracy that dominated Korean society, as well as on commoners.

Initially the Taewŏn'gun was tolerant of the Christian community in Korea. The growing foreign crisis in East Asia fed fears that Christianity was a dangerous Western doctrine that would undermine the political and social order. The connection between Catholicism and the French presence in Asia resulted in a belief that Catholic missionary activities were part of hostile French designs on Korea. The regent launched a major persecution in 1866 on the advice of many of his officials. In March 1866, nine French priests who were illegally in the country were ordered to leave; when they refused, six were executed while three others fled. Forty Korean converts were also executed. The Qing government in Beijing warned Korea against hostile actions against foreign missionaries, but the regent's belief in the need for strong measures against any Western threat was only reinforced by the U.S.S. *General Sherman* incident. In August 1866, a heavily armed U.S. merchant ship with a crew of Americans, Malays, British, and Chinese entered Korean waters and sailed up the Taedong River to Pyongyang seeking to open trade. Ignoring orders to leave, the crew fired upon a hostile crowd and burned nearby boats. A few days later when the ship was caught in a receding tide, the local governor, the distinguished scholar Pak Kyu-su, ordered it destroyed. The *General Sherman* was burned and its crew killed. Although little known to Americans, the *General Sherman* incident would be later celebrated in North Korea as the beginning of the Korean people's resistance to American imperialism. The Taewŏn'gun then carried out further persecutions of the small Catholic minority in Korea in which several thousands of converts died—which became known as the Catholic Persecution of 1866.

In October 1866 the French sent seven ships and 600 men on a punitive expedition to Korea in response to the execution of its missionaries. After capturing a fort on the strategic island of Kanghwa near the mouth of the Han River, the French Admiral Roze delivered a letter to the capital court in the Korean capital of Seoul demanding that those responsible for the murder of the missionaries be punished. The Taewŏn'gun's response was to mobilize thousands of available forces. When the French tried to seize a fortified Buddhist temple on the southern end of the island in November they were driven back by Korean troops. With winter coming on, the French left. Meanwhile, news of the disappearance of the *General Sherman* eventually reached the Americans in China. The United States instructed Admiral Shufeldt to investigate. The admiral sent a ship to Korea in 1867 and another in 1868 to make inquiries, but the Koreans refused to deal with either one. Tensions with foreigners were further aggravated by a bizarre incident in May 1868. In an effort to open trade, the German merchant Ernest Oppert landed on the coast of Korea and desecrated the grave of the Taewŏn'gun's father in a failed attempt to use his father's bones as a bargaining chip for trade concessions.

Gradually the United States became aware of the fate of the *General Sherman*. In 1870, the newly appointed U.S. minister to China, Frederick Low, began preparations to take firm action against the "semi-barbaric and hostile" Koreans.[9] In May 1871 Low led five ships and 1,200 men under Admiral John Rodgers on a punitive expedition. When on June 1 the Koreans fired upon a survey party, the Americans destroyed the shore batteries. The Americans waited for a reply to a letter demanding an account of the missing ship, but the Korean government replied that it was not interested in negotiations. The Americans then attacked the city of Kanghwa and forts on the island. The Koreans fought to the death, inflicting some casualties on the U.S. forces. Not authorized to proceed further, and frustrated by the Koreans' refusal to talk and their fierce resistance, Low and Rodgers decided to withdraw. The Taewŏn'gun proudly put up stone signs proclaiming, "Western barbarians invade our land. If we do not fight we must then appease them. To urge appeasement is to betray the nation."[10] It appeared to him that the Westerners, like all pirates, could be dealt with best by uncompromising resistance.

To the east, Japan posed another threat to Korea. Japan underwent a sweeping change with the collapse of the Tokugawa shogunate and the creation of the new reform-minded Meiji government in 1868. In January 1869, an envoy from the Japanese island of Tsushima arrived in Pusan to announce the new government. The Korean officials refused to receive the letters. They were offended by the idea of an imperial restoration. Koreans had never recognized the Japanese ruler as an emperor, since that would place him on a basis of equality with the Chinese emperor. Furthermore, the new Western-style uniforms of the delegation from Tsushima were also offensive, reinforcing the old attitude that the Japanese were semi-barbarians. This impression was confirmed when in June 1870 the German chargé d'affaires in Japan arrived in Pusan with Japanese aboard his ship and with another Western request that the country open itself to foreign trade. The Korean refusal to receive the notification of the restoration of imperial rule was highly offensive to the new leaders of Japan, who were in any case concerned about securing their periphery. The Japanese began a vigorous colonization of the northern island of Hokkaido, brought Okinawa under direct rule in 1873, and secured the Kurile Islands in an agreement with Russia in 1875. The strategic importance of Korea, as well, was not lost upon the leaders of Meiji Japan, who conducted heated debates on how to deal with Korea. In 1873, some Meiji officials seriously discussed provoking an incident that would lead to an invasion of Korea, but cooler heads prevailed, and the idea was dropped.

Although the Japanese leadership decided not to invade Korea, they were determined to open diplomatic relations with their neighbor. In May of 1875, they sent the warship *Unyō* to Pusan, joined two weeks later by a second ship. The Japanese showed off these modern Western-built ships by inviting Koreans aboard and by firing their guns in demonstration. The *Unyō* and other ships then sailed along the coast of Korea, surveying the waters. When they entered the prohibited area off Kanghwa Island, they were fired upon by shore batteries. The *Unyō* returned fire, destroying the Korean guns. Japanese troops then overran a small fort on an island off Inch'ŏn, killing and wounding a number of defenders. Other warships were dispatched to Pusan with the excuse of protecting the Japanese residents there. In February 1876, Kuroda Kiyotaka landed on Kanghwa Island with a substantial military force and demanded an apology for what he claimed was an unprovoked attack on Japan's ships. Japan wanted more than an apology; it insisted that Korea open diplomatic and trade relations with its new government.

The Korean court was now in crisis. In December 1873, the Taewŏn'gun had been forced to resign, and the young king, Kojong, took personal control. Shortly after assuming power, Kojong faced this serious challenge. Most officials opposed negotiations, but some, such as Pak Kyu-su, the same official who had ordered the destruction of the *General Sherman,* argued for negotiations, as did the Chinese government. Kojong supported the latter view, and in February 1876 his government signed the Treaty of Kanghwa. In the treaty, Korea recognized the new administration in Tokyo and agreed to open Pusan and two other ports within twenty months to the Japanese. The twelve articles of the treaty had profound implications that few Koreans at the time probably understood. Korea was recognized as an independent state possessing the same sovereign rights as Japan. This contradicted the traditional view of Korea as a Chinese tributary state. The concept of an international community of equal and sovereign nations was alien to the East Asian order as Koreans had always interpreted it. The other articles permitted the Japanese to survey Korean waters, allowed Japanese to reside in treaty ports, and gave the Japanese the right of extraterritoriality; that is, Japanese in Korea would be subject to Japanese law and courts. In accordance with Article 11 of the treaty, a further agreement on trade was signed a few months later that gave additional economic privileges to the Japanese.

The Treaty of Kanghwa proved a turning point in Korean history. It ended its isolation, undermined the tributary system that had framed Korean foreign relations for centuries, began the Japanese penetration into Korea that would eventually undermine its economic and political order, and it brought Korea into the imperialist rivalries of the late nineteenth century. Korea's vigorous efforts to insulate itself from the changing world around it came to an end. It is not likely, however, that many Koreans in 1876 were aware of just how momentous a step they had taken.

EARLY REFORMS, 1876–1884

From a modern historical perspective, the years after 1876 mark a radical departure from Korean history. They may not have appeared so to Koreans at the time. The Korean state was simply adjusting itself to deal with menacing neighbors, as it had before in its history. However, the Koreans were entering a world for which their past experience had ill prepared them. It was the world of the high imperialism of the late nineteenth century, when nearly every corner of the globe was faced with the unbridled expansionist ambitions of the Western powers. Korea's situation was especially complex, since it not only had to deal with the forces of the West—Britain, France, the United States, and especially Russia—but also with its two traditional East Asian neighbors, China, which was determined to consolidate control or influence over its periphery, and a rapidly modernizing, expansionist Japan.

After the Treaty of Kanghwa was signed, the court dispatched Kim Ki-su, a respected scholar and official, to head a mission to Japan. Korean kings had sent emissaries to Japan in the past to keep an eye on their troublesome neighbor, although this was the first such mission since 1810. Kim met a number of officials who showed him some of Japan's reforms carried out to "enrich the nation" and "strengthen the military."[11] After reluctantly meeting with the Japanese emperor, Kim left without Japan's modernization having made much of an impression on him. Rather than using the trip as an opportunity to introduce Korea to the rapidly changing world heralded by Japan's reform efforts, it was treated as one of the occasional missions sent to Japan in the interests of "neighborly relations" (*kyorin*). It was another four years before Seoul sent another mission. When the king sent a mission in 1880, it was headed by Kim Hong-jip, who was a keener observer of the reforms taking place in Japan. While in Japan, the Chinese diplomat Huang Cunxian presented him with a study called *A Strategy for Korea* (*Chaoxian Celue*). The work warned of the threat to Korea posed by Russia and recommended that Korea maintain friendly relations with Japan, which was at present too economically weak to be an immediate threat, work closely with China, and seek an alliance with America as a counterweight to Russia. Upon returning to Korea, Kim presented the work to Kojong, who was so impressed with it that he had copies made and distributed to his officials. Many conservatives were outraged by the proposal to seek alliance with Western barbarians or even to maintain friendly relations with Japan. Some even plotted a coup. Kojong responded to this opposition by executing one prominent official and banishing others. The document became the basis of his foreign policy.

After 1879, China's relations with Korea came under the authority of Li Hongzhang, who had emerged as one of the most influential figures in China after playing an important role in putting down the Taiping Rebellion, 1850–1864. Li was an advocate of "self-strengthening," by which China would selectively borrow elements of Western technology, especially military technology, and maintain correct relations with Western countries while adhering to traditional core values. He was appointed by the Qing in 1879 as governor-general of Zhili Province (in the Beijing area) and imperial commissioner for the northern ports. Li urged Korean officials to adopt China's own self-strengthening program to strengthen the country in the face of foreign threats. Kojong was receptive to this advice.

In 1880, following Chinese advice, Kojong decided to establish diplomatic ties with the United States, a true break with tradition. Admiral Shufeldt came to Tianjin, and in 1881–1882 negotiated with Korea through Chinese officials a Corean-American Treaty of Amity and Commerce, which was signed on May 22, 1882. In the treaty, the United States offered its "good offices" in the case of a threat from a third power. It fixed tariffs on imported goods and gave extraterritorial rights to Americans. Several elements made the treaty more acceptable to conservatives: it kept tariffs high, made extraterritoriality provisional upon the reform of Korean laws and judicial procedures to conform to America's, and it did not mention permitting missionary activity. Kojong seems to have thought it offered American protection in time of external threat. In the spring of 1883, an American minister arrived in Seoul, and an eight-man diplomatic mission was sent to the United States under Min Yŏng-ik and his deputy Hong Yŏng-sik, where they performed the traditional kowtow before a rather surprised President Arthur.

Kojong took several other steps toward reform. In early 1881, he set up an Office for the Management of State Affairs (T'ongni Kimu Amun) modeled on a similar institution created in China as part of the self-strengthening program, the Zongli Yamen. The new institution was in charge of the various areas needed to deal with the new international environment: foreign affairs, international trade, foreign language instruction, military affairs, and weapons manufacturing. Kojong also created a special Skills Force of eighty cadets under a Japanese army lieutenant to learn modern warfare. In the same year, Kojong sent twelve officials, averaging a comparatively young age of thirty-nine, to Japan on a so-called "Gentlemen's Observation Mission" to spend ten weeks studying the new modern institutions and technologies in use there. Two members of the mission stayed on in Tokyo as students, while the others reported back on what they had seen and learned to an interested monarch and his court. Later that same year, an official, Kim Yun-sik, led a group of about forty students and artisans to China where they studied the modern weapons facilities in Tianjin.

None of the efforts proved highly effective. The T'ongni Kimu Amun underwent constant reorganization without actually accomplishing much. The Special Skills Force was small, incurred the jealousy of regular soldiers, and was abolished in 1882; and the study mission to Tianjin ran out of funds, the students became homesick, and it was abandoned before there was enough time to absorb the new technologies. For all their limitations, these activities, especially the trips to Japan, exposed a small number of Koreans to new ideas and institutions. These Koreans gradually formed a reform party sometimes known as the Progressive Party (Chinbo-dang) or more often as the Enlightenment Party (Kaehwa-dang), a small group committed to major reform efforts. In the meantime, the Japanese pressed Korea to open up two more ports, as required in the treaty. Wŏnsan on the east coast was opened in 1880, and only after considerable pressure was Chemulp'o (now Inch'ŏn) opened in 1883.

Although modest in scale, the reforms instituted by Kojong were too much for conservatives, who rallied around the Taewŏn'gun. An opportunity for his return to power came soon. In 1882, regular soldiers who had not been paid in months revolted when they found their grain rations had been adulterated with chaff. The soldiers, resentful of the privileged position of the special guards, murdered the Japanese officer and attacked and burned the Japanese legation. Japan's minister to Korea, Hanabusa Yoshimoto, and his staff barely escaped. After the soldiers called upon the Taewŏn'gun for support, Kojong brought his father back to help restore order. The former regent was given full authority, which he used to abolish the Special Skills Forces and the T'ongni Kimu Amun. Ominously, the military incident brought about the open rivalry between China and Japan for influence in Korea that would cause so much trouble. Hanabusa returned with Japanese military troops, but the Chinese, in their first intervention in Korea since the sixteenth century, sent a much larger body of troops, about 4,500, under General Wu Changqing. Chinese troops were now stationed at various points in Seoul. The Chinese took the Taewŏn'gun captive and brought him to exile in Tianjin. Japan then worked out the Treaty of Chemulp'o, which allowed them to station some troops at their embassy in Seoul.

The military uprising was a setback for the early reform efforts. It also brought the Chinese into Korea, where they now began to directly interfere in the country's internal affairs. The Chinese took several measures to gain a certain amount of control over Korea. They negotiated the Regulations for Maritime and Overland Trade Between Chinese and Korean Subjects in October 1882. This permitted Chinese merchants to trade in Seoul and along the border, and allowed Koreans to trade in Beijing. Thus Korea was opened to Chinese merchants. Significantly, this agreement was not a treaty but was issued as a regulation for a vassal.[12] Under Chinese advice, the monarch created the Office for the Management of Diplomatic and Commercial Affairs, better known as the Foreign Office, to handle foreign affairs and an Office for the Management of Military and National Affairs, usually referred to as the Home Office, to deal with internal matters. Also at the recommendation of the Chinese, the king appointed two advisors to the Foreign Office: the Prussian Paul Moellendorff, who had served in the Chinese Maritime Customs Service, and the Chinese diplomat Ma Jianchang. The Chinese also supervised the creation of a Korean Maritime Customs Service in 1883 with Moellendorff as its head. Again on the advice of China, Korea established a Capital Guards Command, which was to be trained by a young Chinese officer, Yuan Shikai.

In addition to the Chinese-instigated reforms, the Korean government continued on its own initiative with some modest attempts to reach out to other nations and institute further reforms. It sent Pak Yǒng-hyo to Japan in October 1882 on an apology mission. He was accompanied by Kim Ok-kyun (1851–1894), who had come under the influence of Japanese modernizers and by Sǒ Kwang-bǒm, another young scholar interested in Japan's reforms. In 1883, the king sent a mission to the United States, while American diplomats arrived in Seoul. At the recommendation of Pak Yǒng-hyo and others, the state created an Office of Culture and Information, which published a thrice-monthly gazette, *Hansǒng Sunbo*, Korea's first newspaper. Forty students were sent to Japan to study military and technical subjects, and a postal administration was established.

The small group of reformers who constituted what became known as the Enlightenment (Kaehwa) Party became frustrated at the small scale and erratic pace of progress. These youthful, well-educated Koreans, most from the *yangban* class, were impressed by the developments in Meiji Japan and impatient to emulate them. They were strongly influenced by Japanese writer Fukuzawa Yukichi (1835–1901), who used the term "enlightenment" to refer to the Western ideas of social, political, and economic progress. In late 1884, they plotted to carry out a coup that would bring them to power so they could carry out sweeping reforms, much as a group of young samurai had done in Japan in 1867–1868. Its

members included Kim Ok-kyun, Pak Yŏng-hyo, Hong Yŏng-sik, Sŏ
Kwang-bŏm, and Sŏ Chae-p'il (1864–1951). It was a very young group.
Pak Yŏng-hyo, who came from a prestigious lineage related to the royal
family, was twenty-three. Hong was twenty-nine, Sŏ Kwang-bŏm was
twenty-five, and Sŏ Chae-p'il only twenty. All had spent some time in
Japan. Kim Ok-kyun, at thirty-three, was the oldest. While studying in
Japan he had cultivated friendships with influential Japanese figures and
was the de facto leader of the group. Some of their thinking was a radical
break with Korean tradition. They began to view civilization as measured
not by adherence to Confucian norms but the new criteria of modern political and economic institutions and by the adoption of modern technology. They looked not to China as a model but for the first time in Korean
history to Japan and to the West.

Their reform efforts were intertwined with factional politics in Korea.
The Min clan of the royal consort, Queen Min, had been able to use the
newly created institutions as bases for power. Their growing monopoly
of key positions frustrated the ambitions of the Enlightenment Party.
Furthermore, the Min were pursuing a pro-Chinese policy. This was
partly a matter of opportunism, but it also reflected an ideological bent
toward the more comfortable and traditional relationship as a tributary
of China. The Min had become advocates of the "Eastern Ways, Western
Machines" idea of Chinese moderate reformers. This emphasized the
need to maintain the superior cultural values of the Sinocentric world
while recognizing the importance of acquiring Western technology, especially military technology, in order to preserve autonomy. Thus, rather
than the major institutional reforms and the adaption of new values
such as legal equality or introducing modern education, the advocates of
this stream of thought sought a piecemeal adoption of institutions that
would strengthen the state while preserving the basic social, political, and
cultural order. Most Korean adherents of this "Eastern Ways, Western
Machines" school saw their aim as containing the threat of the Western
barbarians. But some saw some clear practical benefits in a selective adaptation of Western technology. This was exemplified by Pak Ki-jong, a
lecturer at the State Confucian Academy, who proclaimed that Western
Learning (*Sŏhak*) should be rejected but that Western technology was
useful for improving living standards. This could be done in accordance
with the Confucian tradition of "enriching the well-being of the people by
taking advantage of the useful" (*iyong husaeng*).[13]

In late 1884, the more radical reformers of the Enlightenment Party under the leadership of Kim Ok-kyun began plotting the removal of the Min
clan and other obstacles to sweeping reform. The Japanese minister to Korea, Takezoe Shin'ichiro, promised to provide Japanese legation guards
to support the coup plotters, although these numbered only about 200

men. The coup attempt is known as the Kapsin Chongbyŏn (the Political Disturbance of the Year Kapsin [1884]). On the night of December 4, 1884, during a banquet for the opening of the new postal administration hosted by Hong Yŏng-sik, its director, the plotters set fire to a house near the royal palace and set off some explosions in and around the palace. Taking advantage of the confusion, the leaders then entered the Ch'angdŏk Palace and removed the royal family to the Kyŏngu Palace, where they were protected by the forces of the Japanese legation. They then murdered six top officials and the leaders of the military units stationed in Seoul.

The next day, Kim Ok-kyun and Pak Yŏng-hyo proclaimed a new government and issued a fourteen-point reform program. The program called for the abolition of class distinctions, including the official ending of *yangban* status. To alleviate the plight of the poor, it called for tax reform, the punishment of avaricious and evil officials, and the permanent cancellation of debts. The program also called for the creation of a modern police system, a unified modern military through merger of the existing four military units, placing all financial affairs under the Ministry of Finance, and giving full responsibility to the State Council to formulate all laws and regulations. Reforms such as the institution of a land tax, the abolition of class distinctions, and the modernization of the police and military paralleled the early reforms of the Meiji government. The new government lasted only two days, collapsing on December 6, when 1,500 Chinese troops accompanied by Chinese-trained Korean troops intervened under the command of Yuan Shikai. They quickly overwhelmed the Japanese soldiers protecting the royal family in a brief fight. Hong Yŏng-sik and a number of the progressives were killed. Kim Ok-kyun, Pak Yŏng-hyo, Sŏ Kwang-bŏm, and Sŏ Chae-p'il fled with the retreating Japanese to Japan. All told, 180 died, including 38 Japanese and 10 Chinese. The clash between Chinese and Japanese troops was an ominous development. Eager to ease tensions between the two powers, Japanese leader Itŏ Hirobumi went to China and negotiated the Convention of Tianjin on April 18, 1885. Under this agreement, both nations agreed to withdraw their troops from Korea, neither would send military instructors, and if one party found it necessary to send troops to Korea it would notify the other.

As historian Choe Yong-ho has pointed out, the Kapsin coup was a setback to the reform movement. It left many of the leaders in exile. Yu Tae-ch'i, who was important in introducing enlightenment ideas to others, disappeared. Pak Che-hyŏng, author of a reform tract, *Mirror of Modern Korean Politics* (*Kŭnse Chosŏn chŏnggam*), was murdered by a mob. Kim Ok-kyun's and Pak Yŏng-hyo's fathers were executed. Hong Yŏngsik's wife and elder brother committed suicide.[14] It alienated many Koreans from Japan, which as a result could less effectively serve as a model for

Korea. The coup leaders sought to limit the growing involvement of China, but ironically the coup only strengthened China's role in Korea.

THE CHINESE DECADE, 1885–1894

In the decade following the failed coup, the Chinese exercised considerable influence in Korea. China's policy was one of cautious reform. Its main concern was to keep Korea from falling into the hands of another power. Beset in every direction by aggressive imperial powers, China, like Japan, was concerned with protecting its periphery. Korea's tributary relationship had long been as much symbolic as real; in all practical matters Korea was an autonomous state. However, the Chinese now exercised a direct interference in Korean affairs. Although China withdrew its troops from Korea following the Convention of Tianjin, it appointed the ambitious military commander, Yuan Shikai, to act as a sort of proconsul in Korea. He was given the vague title of commissioner of trade, which became translated by Westerners as "Resident," implying a sort of proconsul role.[15] His main concern was to limit the influence of Japan in Korea, advance the interest of Chinese merchants, make sure that in foreign affairs Korea remained subordinate to China and did not act in a way that was threatening to China, and ensure that pro-Japanese individuals were kept out of positions of authority in Korea.[16]

From 1885 to 1894 China took control over the customs service and the telegraph system. An American, Henry Merrill, a protégé of Robert Hart, the British director of the Chinese Customs Service, took over the management of the Korean Customs Service in October 1885. Since the tariff on the growing volume of foreign imports was becoming a major source of revenue for the Korean government, this gave China considerable leverage over its finances. Li Hongzhang arranged for Korea's first telegraph line, linking Inch'ŏn and Seoul; this was extended to Ŭiju, and from there it was linked with Chinese telegraph lines. When the Seoul-to-Pusan telegraph was completed in 1888, it too was placed under Chinese control. Meanwhile, Yuan, only twenty-six years of age when appointed "Resident," showed a skill at making Korean friends. However, he repeatedly interfered in Korean politics. The young official strove to keep a watch on Kojong, whom he did not trust, and to prevent officials thought to be pro-Japanese from obtaining key positions. Seeking to counter the growing Chinese influence, Kojong sought to strengthen ties with Western countries, opening diplomatic relations with Russia in 1884, Italy in 1885, and France in 1886. The king more than once requested the United States to dispatch military advisors and teachers. A small number of Americans sympathetic to Korea and concerned about maintaining its independence from China became close to the monarch. These included Horace Allen, a Presbyterian missionary and doctor attached to the U.S. legation since 1883; George Foulk, the military attaché to the legation; Hugh Dinsmore, the American minister to Korea from 1887 to 1889; and Owen N. Denny, an advisor on Korean foreign affairs. Concerned by this American influence, Yuan in 1886 plotted to remove the king, but he was not supported by Li Hongzhang. He did succeed, however, in removing a number of officials who were in favor of closer ties to Russia that year. As a result of the removal of these officials, the power of the Min clan increased.

Korea's link with the outside world was obstructed by the Chinese, who guarded against any sign of an independent foreign policy that might place the country outside of its orbit. Following Denny's advice, the king appointed Min Yŏng-jun as the first Korean resident minister to Tokyo in 1887 as a prelude to opening up a permanent legation there. Shortly afterward, two envoys were sent to Washington and the capitals of the five European nations with whom Korea had established relations, with the purpose of opening up permanent legations in those countries. The Chinese did not object to the legation in Tokyo but tried to block the opening of Korean missions in Western countries. When the United States objected to this interference Korea was permitted to open a legation in Washington in 1888, but Beijing successfully prevented others in Europe. The effectiveness of Korea's first overseas diplomatic outposts in Tokyo and Washington, however, was limited by Chinese interference. The Chinese also sought to check foreign influence in the country by blocking several attempts by the Korean government to seek foreign loans to finance development projects. It is significant that during this period Korea did not send any major cultural mission abroad comparable to those that had been sent to Tianjin in 1881 and Japan in 1882. The Chinese, with the collusion of Korean conservatives, were able to keep Koreans from traveling abroad, thereby contributing to the country's intellectual and cultural isolation. A rare exception was a ten-member musical troupe sent to the Chicago World's Fair in 1893. All students sent abroad by the government prior to 1885 were ordered to return home.[17] While isolating Korea from other countries, Resident Yuan promoted Chinese trade in Korea to counter the rapid expansion of Japanese mercantile activities in the country. The Chinese merchant community was large enough to cause resentment among Koreans. Anti-Chinese riots broke out in 1888 and 1889 in Seoul, and Chinese shops were burned. However, the Japanese remained the largest foreign community and Korea's largest trading partner.

Very few reform efforts were carried out during this period. In 1886, the Yugyŏng Kongwŏn (Royal College) was established for sons of the elite who were to be instructed in a modern Western education. Instruction was in English, and three Americans, including the missionary Homer Hulbert, later an eloquent spokesman for Korean sovereignty, were hired as instructors, but this received little financial support. The state closed the *Hansŏng Sunbo*, a vehicle for disseminating Western ideas, in 1885, but the following year Kim Yun-sik, with the assistance of a Japanese, Inoue Kakugorŏ, began publishing *Hansŏng Chubo* (*Seoul Weekly*). This too was closed in 1888 under Chinese pressure. In the same year, American general William Dye and three others were hired to modernize the military, but they received little support, so not much was accomplished.

China was trying to reassert its role as Korea's suzerain, ignoring that the country's relationship as a vassal had been largely ceremonial. Direct Chinese intervention into Korean affairs had been rare; in fact, not since the Mongols ruled China as the Yuan dynasty in the fourteenth century had it so directly interfered in Korean affairs. China's role in Korea was not entirely negative; it provided loans, assisted in building telegraph lines, and in other ways promoted modernization. Overall, however, the attempt by Beijing to put Korea firmly under its guidance limited Korea's contact with the outside world, hindered reform efforts, weakened the position of reformers, and in general contributed to the country's lack of preparedness for the challenges to its sovereignty. By being protected by China, Korea had its fate attached to a declining power whose own failure to carry out necessary reforms was dramatically demonstrated in its clash with Japan in 1894.

While successfully hampering Korean access to outside knowledge, the Chinese were not able to isolate Korea from international intrigue. Moellendorff, who had been appointed by Li Hongzhang, soon decided that Korea needed another power to balance that of China. He worked toward establishing closer ties with Russia. In 1885, Moellendorff suggested to the Russian representative in Korea that the country be made a Russian protectorate. Russian diplomats also expressed a willingness to send military advisors to Korea. Russia's interest in Korea was growing. As Russia expanded into the Pacific region, Korea offered the possibility of ice-free ports; especially tempting was Wŏnsan on the east coast. In that year, Kojong dispatched a secret mission to Vladivostok seeking Russian assistance. Russia's growing interest in Korea alarmed the British. As a warning to the Russians, in April 1885 the British occupied the small island of Kŏmundo off the south coast of Chŏlla Province, which they called Port Hamilton. Their presence on an island the Russians had once considered for use as a coaling station met with a threat from the tsarist government in St. Petersburg to occupy some Korean territories, possibly some northern ports. Eventually Russia gave assurances that it would not occupy any part of Korea, and in 1887 the British withdrew from Kŏmundo.

The United States played a more modest role in Korea. A small community of American diplomats and missionaries in Seoul were concerned about threats to Korea's sovereignty. However, they received little support from Washington. The U.S. government, with no special interest in Korea, was largely indifferent to requests by the Americans in Seoul to become actively involved in guaranteeing its independence.

Japan, in contrast, remained very much concerned with Korea, fearing both Chinese domination and Russian involvement in the peninsula. Japan was developing considerable economic ties with Korea, which it saw as a source of agricultural produce, but it was facing Chinese competition. Tokyo's concerns about protecting its economic interests in Korea are revealed by the "Bean Controversy." In 1889, the governor of northeast Hamgyŏng Province, fearing a food shortage caused by a drought, issued an embargo against soybean exports to Japan. The Japanese protested the embargo and demanded an indemnity to compensate its importers. The "Bean Controversy" was finally settled in 1893 when Korea agreed to pay the indemnity and end the embargo.[18] Japanese merchants and manufacturers focused on the Korean market. Paying close attention to the needs of Korean consumers, they out-competed local, Chinese, and Western merchants in capturing much of the textile trade with their cheap cotton cloth.[19] But Japan's greatest interest in Korea was strategic. As one leader remarked, it was "a dagger pointed at the heart of Japan." As it built up its Western-modeled army and navy, and as its economy grew, Japan became more inclined to act upon its anxieties over the Chinese position in the peninsula.

THE TONGHAK REBELLION

While political intrigue went on in the capital, the bulk of the population, the peasantry, was also feeling the changes brought on by Korea's entry into the international economy. Peasants suffered the burden from tax increases to pay for the country's reforms. The countryside was being penetrated by Chinese and especially by Japanese merchants, a disturbing development in a society neither used to outsiders nor experienced in a modern commercial economy. These developments contributed to peasant unrest that led to the Tonghak Rebellion, a conflict that became entangled with the rivalries of China and Japan in Korea.

The primary cause of this uprising, however, was the chronic resentment of the corruption of local officials. Peasant uprisings were not uncommon in Korea. A major uprising took place in northern Korea in 1811–1812 and in southern Korea in 1862. The Tonghak Rebellion differed in that it had its roots in the new religious movement known as Tonghak

(Eastern Learning) founded in 1860 by Ch'oe Che-u (also known as Suun). Ch'oe's new line of teachings seems to have been as a response to the unsettling new ideas and developments taking place, including the spread of Christianity. Ch'oe's teaching appeared to show a Christian influence, including a belief in a Lord of Heaven, an omnipotent God. It also drew heavily from shamanism and Korean folk religions, including the practice of healing rites in which the spirit that intruded into the body and caused illness was stabbed with a sword. Paper talismans were burned and their ashes drunk, another folk religion custom. But its main roots were in Confucianism.[20] Drawing from the teachings of Mencius, who considered government an instrument for the welfare of the people, Ch'oe called for an end to corruption, the punishment of evil officials, and a more egalitarian social order. It is clear, though, that his new faith had incorporated some Christian concepts too. For this reason and because of his call for sweeping social reform, the court saw the new religion as a threat. Fearing rebellion among his followers, the state arrested and executed Ch'oe in 1864. But the new religion did not die out. He left behind a few hundred followers, and out of these a second leader emerged, Ch'oe Si-hyŏng (Hyewŏl), a man from a poor commoner family. Based on a few poems and essays the founder Suun had left, he compiled a holy book of Tonghak thought and a hymnbook. His followers gradually grew in numbers during the 1880s. Following a time-honored Korean custom of honoring one's ancestors and teachers by seeking to posthumously exonerate them if they had been disgraced or purged, Tonghak leaders urged Ch'oe Si-hyŏng to petition the court to restore the founder's good name as well as those of other victims.

In 1892, several thousand followers gathered in Samnye in Chŏlla demanding Suun's exoneration and calling for the end of persecution of Tonghak. They negotiated with the governors of Chŏlla and Ch'ungchŏng provinces, who agreed to stop the persecutions but explained they had no authority to exonerate the spiritual founder. Ch'oe Si-hyŏng then agreed to assemble with his believers outside the royal court at the Kwanghwa Gate in Seoul. Three days later, on March 31, a messenger vaguely promised their petition would be accepted if they dispersed and went home. But the persecution of members continued. On the thirtieth anniversary of the execution, Ch'oe Si-hyŏng called a mass meeting in Poun in Ch'ungchŏng. This assembly in April 1893 was attended by 20,000 followers from all over the country. Despite Ch'oe Si-hyŏng's attempt to take a more moderate position, the Tonghak members were becoming more radicalized. Displeasure with continual persecution of the church and defamation of its founder was linked to the peasant unrest over the new taxes, local grievances with corrupt officials, resentment at the Japanese merchants, and anxiety over the growing foreign presence in the country.

Members called for the punishment of corrupt officials and the expulsion of Japanese and Westerners from Korea.

The next spring, protests over taxes in the southeastern region of the country erupted into violence. The leader of the movement was Chǒn Pong-jun, the son of a local clerk, who had supported himself by private teaching and had become a recent convert to Tonghak. Peasants were angry with Cho Pyǒng-gap, the magistrate of Kobu County, who was accused of extorting excessive taxes and forcing peasants to build a reservoir without compensation and then levying a water tax on them. With Chǒn leading, the peasants, wearing headbands and armed with clubs and bamboo poles, attacked the magistrate's office and destroyed the reservoir. Under Chǒn's leadership the rebellion grew. The Tonghaks were careful to express loyalty to the king but called for the elimination of the *yangban* class, punishment of all corrupt officials, and the end of grain exports to Japan. While the government commander in the region negotiated with the rebels, a panicky government in Seoul requested Chinese assistance on June 4. The Chinese government quickly ordered naval and land forces to go to Korea. By the time Chinese forces began to arrive, the government had negotiated a truce with the Tonghak. An office was set up in Chǒlla Province to investigate complaints, and Tonghak members were allowed to participate. The Tonghak forces were allowed to have an overseer in every county of the province. The leaders decided to wait until after the autumn harvest before deciding on further action.

With the situation apparently under control, the Chinese forces were not needed. Meanwhile, in accordance with the agreement worked out in 1885, China informed Tokyo of its intention to dispatch troops, done, it was added, "in conformity with China's ancient custom of sending troops to protect vassal states."[21] The Japanese then decided to send troops to Korea under a new minister, Ōtori Keisuke, who arrived at Inch'ǒn with eight Japanese warships on June 9 and proceeded to Seoul with 400 marines. Another 3,000 Japanese troops landed at Inch'ǒn four days later. The Chinese requested that the Japanese withdraw, but instead the Japanese government decided that it was time to bring about change in the Korean government. They proposed that the two powers take joint actions to bring about reforms in Korea, which China rejected. The Japanese ignored the Korean government's request that it withdraw its troops. On July 13, Ōtori presented Korea with a plan to reform its government. The Korean government evaded the Japanese proposal and asked their forces to leave.

Japan then took direct action to bring about political change in Korea. Its troops, now with reinforcements outnumbering the Chinese, occupied the Kyǒngbok palace, where the king resided, and disarmed the Korean forces. The king agreed to form a new government headed by Kim Hong-jip. The next day, on July 25, the Japanese attacked the Chinese warships at Asan Bay. The Sino-Japanese War, as this conflict became known, was a complete victory for Japan. Chinese forces were routed at the battle of Pyongyang in mid-September, and in October were driven back to the Yalu River. Japanese forces overran the Liaodong Peninsula at the southern tip of Manchuria, capturing the strategic ports of Lushun (Port Arthur) and Dalian. China's northern fleet was destroyed, and the major port of Weihaiwai in Shandong fell. On April 17, 1895, Li Hongzhang negotiated the Treaty of Shimonoseki, in which China recognized Korea as an independent state, surrendering all claims as its suzerain; ceded Taiwan and the Liaodong Peninsula to Japan; and agreed to pay a war indemnity. China was no longer able to play a role in Korean affairs; a dramatic shift in power had occurred in East Asia.

Meanwhile, after the autumn harvest, Tonghak leaders called for resistance to the corrupt officials and the Japanese Army. An estimated 100,000–200,000 peasants participated. Japanese Army officers led Korean forces in an attack on the rebels, inflicting crushing defeats on the huge but poorly equipped peasant troops, who were armed mostly with bamboo spears. Chŏn was betrayed and captured. When questioned by prosecutor Sŏ Kwang-bŏm and the Japanese consul, he insisted his only aim was to remove corrupt officials. He was executed at age forty-one along with other leaders of the rebellion. Ch'oe Si-hyŏng and his appointed successor, Son Pyŏng-hŭi, escaped to Kangwŏndo, where they hid in homes of followers.[22] Ch'oe was arrested in 1898 and died in prison, but Son lived to reorganize the Tonghak movement, which was renamed Ch'ŏndogyo. It still exists today as an organized religion. The Kabo Peasant War, as the rebellion is sometimes called, failed in its immediate aims of redressing peasant grievances. Instead, it strengthened the Japanese presence in Korea.

KABO REFORMS

From July 1894 to February 1896, Korean reformers under the sponsorship of the Japanese enacted a sweeping series of laws and regulations that marked a sharp break in the country's historical traditions. Although these efforts by some of the most talented and progressive of Korea's leaders were of great importance in bringing about necessary steps toward modernization, the fact that they were carried out under Japanese military pressure and the heavy-handedness of the Japanese interference left an ambiguous legacy.

When the Japanese troops occupied the palace, the king became a virtual prisoner under the direction of the Japanese minister, and a new government was placed in charge. In late July 1894, the Japanese-directed reformers created a Deliberative Council (Kun'guk Kimuch'ŏ) with seventeen and later twenty-three members. Until it was abolished in December, it was the principal organ for carrying out the sweeping restructuring of government and society. The new government was staffed by the leading reformers in the country. To appease conservatives and the Tonghak, the Japanese installed the aging Taewŏn'gun as the nominal head of the new government. He was also a foe of the pro-Chinese Min clan. Important conservative officials were appointed to a largely powerless Privy Council. The State Council was replaced by a cabinet-style organization with a prime minister. New ministries were created to deal with foreign affairs, home affairs, finance, justice, education, defense, agriculture and commerce, and industry. Much of the authority of the king was removed to the new cabinet and to a prime minister. The affairs of the court were separated from the rest of the government and administered by a Department of Royal Household Affairs. The government was rationalized with clear separations of judicial and military functions from civil ones. It enacted laws that established a separate hierarchy of courts, and issued decrees outlawing the torture of suspects, guilt by association, and the punishments of family members of criminals. The government created a new capital and provincial police system, and made plans to rationalize the tax system as well. It abolished arbitrary taxes and merchant monopolies.

A series of measures brought about significant social reforms. An official 1886 ban on the sale of slaves was confirmed; now, thirty-one years after the United States had done so, the government legally abolished slavery in all forms. The new administration officially eliminated social distinctions of all sorts; the *yangban* no longer had a legal status. Outcaste distinctions were also legally abolished. The council enacted the radically new principle of equality of law, opening all positions to men of talent regardless of social background. It increased the marriage age for men and women to twenty and sixteen respectively, outlawing child marriage. A long legal prohibition against widows remarrying ended. It relaxed sumptuary laws that had emphasized social distinctions. One of the most momentous actions by the council was its abolition of the civil service exams that had been central to recruiting officials and confirming elite status. To signal a break with the old Chinese tributary system, it proclaimed June 6 as Korean Independence Day; it used the Korean alphabet, *han'gŭl*, in government documents; and decreed that Korean history was to be taught in school. The old Ming Chinese calendar was replaced with the Western one. A new Ministry of Education promulgated a series of ordinances creating a Western-style education system. The Hansŏng (Seoul) Normal School was established, along with five primary schools in the capital, with plans to establish others throughout the country. The ministry created a new modern curriculum and compiled textbooks for it.

The whole program is known as the Kabo Reform (Kabo Kyŏngjang) after the year Kabo (1894). The Deliberate Council issued over 200 reform bills in total. In December, Japan sent a leading political figure, Inoue Kaoru, to supervise the reform effort. To eliminate threats to the new government, he removed the Taewŏn'gun, who had been secretly plotting with the Chinese, seeking to dethrone his son, Kojong, who was now cooperating compliantly with the Japanese. Inoue had also ordered Japanese troops to destroy the Tonghak. Pak Yŏng-hyo and Sŏ Kwang-bŏm returned from exile in Japan and joined the "Coalition Cabinet," which replaced the Deliberate Council and continued with the reforms. Another exiled participant in the Kapsin Coup, Sŏ Chae-p'il, and the American-educated reformer Yun Ch'i-ho (1864–1945) later joined the cabinet. It is interesting to note that the latter two were Protestant converts, the first to serve in Korean government.

Japan's victories over China only strengthened its prestige, aiding those Koreans who wanted to use the Meiji reforms as a model. It now seemed inevitable that Japan would be Korea's new big brother. But all this changed rather suddenly with the diplomatic setback that almost immediately followed the Treaty of Shimonoseki. In the treaty of April 17, 1895, China agreed to lease the Liaodong Peninsula, with its potential naval base at Port Arthur, to Japan. This alarmed Russia, which had its own designs on Port Arthur as a possible warm-water port in the region. Russia quickly gained the support of France and Germany to issue a joint demand by the three powers that Japan cancel the lease. Facing what was called the Triple Intervention, Japan complied. This humiliation coming shortly after its victory was interpreted by Koreans as evidence of Japan's weakness. Opponents of the pro-Japanese government gained courage. Min clan members forced Pak Yŏng-hyo back into exile in July, and the Kabo reform effort seemed threatened. A new Japanese minister, Miura Gorŏ, arriving in September, sought to reverse this shift in power by eliminating Queen Min, around whom many of the pro-Russian, anti-Japanese Korean officials rallied. Following his plan, on October 8, Japanese thugs and some Korean collaborators broke into the palace and murdered Queen Min, two ladies-in-waiting, and a court official. Queen Min's body was then covered with kerosene and burned. This brutal and shocking affair, once it became known, led to a wave of anti-Japanese feeling. It also brought international condemnation. The Japanese government recalled Miura, promising to punish those involved, and sent Inoue Kaoru back to Korea along with a new minister, Komura Jutarō, to salvage the situation. But they were unable to reverse the anti-Japanese sentiment, and with the collapse of Japanese influence, the Kabo reformers were unable to maintain themselves in power. The first comprehensive effort at restructuring Korean government and society ended.

Even if the Japanese influence had not waned, it is not clear how the Korean reformers would have been able to implement so many radical changes. One last event symbolized both the depth of the reform effort and the degree to which the reformers had moved ahead of most ordinary Koreans. On December 30, Kojong, following the instruction of the reform government, dutifully issued a decree (*tanballyŏng*) requiring Koreans to cut off their topknots and adopt Western-style haircuts. He himself, did so. Korean men had long worn the hair long, tying it up at the top. This was a proud custom; in fact, Korean travelers to China and Japan sometime made disparaging reports about the haircuts of their neighbors. It was an issue that both conservative *yangban*, smarting over their loss of legal privileges, and ordinary peasants could rally behind. Riots took place throughout the country; in some provincial towns government officials announcing the decree were attacked by mobs and killed. Nonetheless, the Kabo reforms were a step in the transformation of Korean society, brought on by the new international environment.

THE RUSSIAN ASCENDENCY AND THE INDEPENDENCE CLUB

The decade from 1895 to 1905 was marked by the rivalry between Russia and Japan for influence in Korea, the last Korean-initiated attempts at major reform, and the establishment of a Japanese protectorate over Korea, effectively ending Korea's independence.

In late November 1895, a group of pro-Russian officials, including Yi Pŏm-jin, attempted to remove the king from the palace and spirit him off to the Russian legation for protection. A second attempt on February 11 was successful, beginning a rather bizarre episode in which the king and crown prince reigned from the Russian diplomatic compound in Seoul for one year. Now under Russian protection, Kojong, surrounded by conservative advisors, ignored the cabinet government established by the Kabo reforms and directly appointed and dismissed ministers. Tensions between the Japanese and the Russians were eased when on May 14, 1896, Komura Jutarō and Karl Waeber, the Russian envoy, worked out an agreement in which the countries would advise the Korean king on appointment of ministers. Japan would be allowed to use military police to guard the Seoul-Pusan telegraph; both countries agreed on the number of troops stationed in Seoul, Pusan, and Wŏnsan, and to limit the number of troops in the country. Shortly afterward, the Japanese senior official, Yamagata Aritomo, went to Russia and signed the Moscow Protocol (Lobanov-Yamagata Agreement) with Russian foreign minister Lobanov, confirming this agreement. Both powers recognized the independence of Korea; any loans and assistance for internal reform would be done by mutual agreement.

The Korean court sent an envoy, Min Yŏng-hwan, to Russia in the spring of 1896 to attend the coronation of Nicholas II with the intention of obtaining an alliance with Russia. Having safely contained Japanese influence in Korea, the Russians eventually agreed only to send a few military advisors to Korea. Meanwhile, during the post-Kabo period, the king and his officials approved a number of concessions to Russians and other Westerners. The right to build a Seoul–Inch'ŏn railway that had been given to Japan in 1894, for instance, was revoked and given to an American, James Morse, who also received a concession to operate a gold mine at Unsan in North P'yŏngan Province. A Russian, Jules Bryner (the grandfather of actor Yul Brynner), received a concession to cut timber along the Tumen River and on the island of Ullŭngdo. In a reaction to these concessions, the Japanese sought to discredit the Russians by making the Komura-Waeber Memorandum public. When the king returned to his palace in February 1897, the Russian influence in the government was strong; Russians were even employed as palace guards.

Russian and Japanese interference in Korea, and the country's continued weakness, led to the creation of the Independence Club (Tongnip Hyŏphoe) in 1896 by a group of Koreans eager to disseminate and implement new social and political ideas. Its leader was Sŏ Chae-p'il. The youngest of the Kapsin coup leaders, Sŏ fled to the United States, where he earned a medical degree from Johns Hopkins and became a U.S. citizen under the name of Philip Jaisohn. He returned to Korea early in 1896, accepted a position on the Privy Council, and founded a newspaper, *Tongnip Sinmun* (*The Independent*). This was the first newspaper to be published solely in *han'gŭl*, the Korean alphabet, rather than in the more prestigious Chinese characters, itself a statement of Korean cultural independence. The paper became a vehicle for the promotion of the concepts of representative government, national sovereignty, and modern reforms. The paper was launched in April, and in July Sŏ assisted in the organization of the Independence Club whose active members included Yun Ch'i-ho, Yi Sang-jae, and a young American missionary school graduate, Yi Sŭng-man (1875–1965; better known to Americans as Syngman Rhee). The club carried out educational and cultural campaigns and sponsored lectures and debates, using every format to promote the ideals of individual freedom and national independence. The club campaigned to have the Yŏngŭn Gate in Seoul, where the Chinese envoys traditionally arrived, torn down and replaced with an Independence Gate. The China Adoration Hall in Seoul was renamed Independence Hall. These symbols of subservience to a foreign power were thus converted into symbols of national independence. The Independence Hall became a forum where public debates sponsored by the club were held every Sunday on issues of national concern. A major campaign was the return of the king from the Russian legation. When he did so in February 1897, he declared himself emperor, giving himself the name Kwangmu ("Glorious Military"), and renamed the country Taehan Cheguk (the Great Han Empire). This, too, was of symbolic importance, since it made him and his country equal to China and, of course, Japan. In a new campaign, the Independence Club demanded the government stop granting leases to foreigners. A mass meeting was held at Chongno in central Seoul on February 20, 1898, to pressure the government and to arouse the interest of the public on this issue.

Conservatives in the government were concerned about the growing influence of the club and of Sŏ Chae-p'il. When in the spring of 1898, under pressure from these conservatives, Sŏ returned to the United States, the club lost its most important leader. Yun Ch'i-ho took over the leadership of the club and seemed to get some support from the king. In October, the club brought about a new organization, the Ten Thousand People's Cooperative Association, also called the People's Assembly. It held a mass rally in central Seoul. With this new tactic, the Independence Club attempted to pressure the government to stop granting concessions to foreigners, to reform the tax system, and to convert the royal Privy Council into a parliamentary assembly, among other reforms. The king and conservative officials were able to work with or at least tolerate the Independence Club when it served their purposes of asserting Korean sovereignty, but the public rallies and the proposed creation of a parliament threatened their monopoly of power and they turned against the club. The government created an Imperial Association consisting of members of the peddlers' guild to break up meetings and beat and intimidate club members. Cho Pyŏng-sik, a conservative official, arrested seventeen members of the club. The club held daily rallies demanding the release of its jailed members. The king, vacillating, released them and permitted the Independence Club to elect twenty-five members to the Privy Council. Then, changing his mind again, perhaps bowing to conservative officeholders, he ordered the club dissolved. Its leaders fled the country, and this spasm of the reform movement came to an end.

The Independence Club failed to bring about significant institutional change, but this organization, led mostly by young intellectuals and political activists, was important in the emergence of a new conception of the Korean state. While most historians have argued that nationalism is a modern concept born in the West in the late eighteenth and nineteenth centuries, Koreans have long had an awareness of living in a society with clear physical and cultural boundaries, of having a shared language and shared customs, of being a people united by a ruling dynasty. New to Koreans in the late nineteenth century was the concept of national sovereignty and of a state existing within an international community of sovereign states. The name "Independence" taken by the club and its newspaper was an assertion of this concept and a rejection of the Sino-centric tribute system or any other orientation that would subordinate Korean sovereignty to another power. The leaders of the Independence Club in their effort to enlist popular support and participation in govern-ment were also introducing the beginnings of the concept of citizenship, the state being more than subjects loyal to a dynasty, but as consisting of active citizens participating in and willing to sacrifice for their state.

For the next few years the Korean government drifted, making only modest efforts at self-strengthening. In the last two decades of the nineteenth century most of the country's most energetic and talented reformers had left the country or withdrawn from public affairs, and some had been killed. The government at its center had an indecisive king who erratically shifted positions. Conservatives held the top posi-tions, and incompetent and often corrupt officials made up the staff. The reform movement was also weakened by its failure to find a suitable foreign protector and model to follow. China had failed in both these purposes. Japan was the obvious model, but its usefulness had been undermined by the fact that it had emerged as the most serious threat to the nation's sovereignty. Pro-Japanese reformers could not extricate themselves from Japan's often heavy-handed and ruthless designs on the country. The United States, through its missionaries, had won a great deal of goodwill among some Koreans, but it was too distant and different to serve as a useful model and too indifferent to act as a pro-tector. The same was largely true of Western European countries such as Britain or France. Then there was Russia. It was useful as a counter to Japan, but it too had imperialist designs on northeast Asia, including Korea. In the end, the greatest threat to Korea proved to be the swift rise of a dynamic, modernizing Japan, determined to secure its peripheries by gaining control of the Korean peninsula.

THE RUSSO-JAPANESE WAR AND THE PROTECTORATE

The end to Korea's effective independence came not suddenly but as a gradual process that began with the outbreak of the Russo-Japanese War in 1904. From then on its autonomy was stripped away in steps un-til its annexation by Japan in 1910 ended only the nominal appearance of sovereignty.

A major imperialist power in the age of imperialism, Russia took ad-vantage of the retreat of Japan in 1895 to advance in northeast Asia. It con-cluded a secret treaty with China to build part of the Trans-Siberian Rail-way it was constructing across Manchuria. The Russians also acquired twenty-five-year leases on Port Arthur and Dalian, and began a program to build a rail line linking these warm-water ports to the Trans-Siberian. In 1900, Russian forces entered Manchuria during the Boxer Rebellion. These forces were supposed to be withdrawn after the rebellion ended, but in fact they remained there, alarming Britain as well as Japan. In 1902, to counter Russian expansion in the East, Britain abandoned its long-held policy of avoiding formal alliances by concluding the Anglo-Japanese Alliance. Britain agreed to acknowledge Japan's interest in Korea in exchange for Japan's recognition of British rights and interests in China. With its position strengthened, Tokyo demanded the withdrawal of Russian troops from Manchuria. Russia, however, reneged on promises to do so. Instead, in July 1903, a small group of Russian soldiers entered Korea at Yongnamp'o, a trading port at the mouth of the Yalu, and started constructing a fort. At Japanese insistence, they withdrew. Many Japanese had hoped to work out an agreement with Russia—a free hand in Manchuria for Russia in exchange for a Japanese free hand in Korea—but nothing came of this. Instead Russia's provocations were such that Japan decided to take military action to prevent Korea from falling into Russian hands. In February 1904, the Japanese carried out a surprise attack on the Russian naval facilities at Port Arthur.

Korea declared its neutrality in January 1904 in the wake of rising tensions between the two imperialist powers. When hostilities broke out, Japanese troops entered Seoul, as they had done at the start of the Sino-Japanese War, and compelled the Korean government to bow to its wishes. The Korean foreign minister signed a protocol in February that in effect made Korea a protectorate of Japan. It gave the Japanese government the right to take any necessary action to protect the Korean imperial house or the territorial integrity of Korea if threatened by a foreign power and gave the Japanese the right to occupy certain parts of the country. In another agreement signed in August 1904, Korea agreed to appoint a Japanese advisor to the Ministry of Finance and a non-Japanese foreigner recommended by the Japanese government to advise the Ministry of Foreign Affairs. It also required Korea to consult with Japan before signing any treaties or agreements with other countries, or any contracts or concessions to foreigners. A Japanese, Megata Tanetarō, became financial advisor, and an American, Durham White Stevens, became the foreign affairs advisor. In effect, the Korean government had conceded control of its financial and foreign affairs to Japan. Meanwhile, a pro-Japanese association called the Ilchinhoe (Society for Advancement), under the leadership of Song Pyŏng-jun, was actively advocating the union of Korea and Japan. This group received support from nationalist, pro-expansionist groups in Japan. Often dismissed as a front for Japanese expansionists, recent research suggests its members had were admirers of the progressive, modernizing nature of the Japanese empire.[23] Nonetheless, it served Japanese purposes to give an impression that the Japanese takeover of Korea had popular support among Koreans. Many Japanese nationalists became involved in the project to bring Korea under Japanese rule, sometimes working in tandem with their government, sometimes running ahead of it. Later Koreans would find it difficult to understand how at least some Koreans could support or at least accept Japan's takeover of their country. One reason was that a number of Koreans were influenced by Pan-Asianism, the concept promoted by the Japanese that all East Asians should unite under Japan's leadership to resist Western domination. While a rationalization for Japanese imperialism, it also reflected a new racial-cultural identity among some East Asian people that they did indeed belong to a "yellow race," as well as the idea that Japan represented the vanguard of progress among Asians.

To the surprise of many observers and largely to the delight of the British and Americans, Japan emerged victorious in the war. Facing overly extended supply lines and revolt at home, Russia concluded the Treaty of Portsmouth with Japan in September 1905, with President Theodore Roosevelt acting as mediator. Russia withdrew from Manchuria, and Japan acquired Port Arthur and was now unchallenged in its efforts to achieve domination over Korea. The United States tacitly accepted the transfer of Korea to Japan in the Taft-Katsura Memorandum of July 1905. In this exchange of views between American secretary of war William Howard Taft and the Japanese prime minister Katsura Tarō, the United States recognized Japan's right to take appropriate measures for the "guidance, control, and protection" of Korea; in exchange, Japan recognized America's position in the Philippines. Britain, renewing its alliance with Japan in 1905, also tacitly accepted Korea as being in Japan's sphere. The way was diplomatically prepared for Japan to take a free hand in Korea.

In November 1905, Itō Hirobumi, one of the principal architects of Meiji Japan, came to Seoul to conclude a treaty establishing a protectorate. On November 17, 1905, with Japanese troops displaying a show of strength on the streets of the capital, the Korean foreign minister, Pak Che-sun, signed what has been called the Protectorate Treaty of 1905. The acting prime minister, Han Kyu-sŏl, refused to sign it. This agreement transferred all foreign relations to Japan. A Japanese resident-general (*tōkan*) was to be stationed in Seoul with direct access to the Korean emperor. According to the treaty, his role was to manage diplomatic affairs, but his authority soon expanded to include most aspects of the country's administration. Beginning with the Americans, the international community closed its legations in Seoul, and the country was now only nominally independent. Most Korean officials such as Pak Che-sun, who became prime minister, simply accommodated themselves to the new reality. A few were despondent. Diplomat and official Min Yŏng-hwan committed suicide in protest; others went into exile. In reality, Korea had been under Japanese control since the start of the Russo-Japanese War in early 1904, so the formal protectorate was not a sudden change or traumatic event but simply one in a series of steps by which Japan consolidated its rule over Korea. The process, however, did not end with the protectorate; rather, it was another step in Japan's absorption of Korea.

THE PROTECTORATE, 1905–1910

In the spring of 1906 Itō returned to Korea to take up the position as resident-general. He was able to find enough Korean officials to work with him—men such as Yi Wan-yong, the minister of education—but he had some problems with Kojong, who had never signed the protectorate treaty. In 1907, Kojong sent the American missionary Homer Hulbert to Washington to gain U.S. support for Korea. Hulbert made two trips but was ignored by the Roosevelt administration, which had accepted Japan's position in Korea. In 1907, the king secretly sent three representatives to the Second Hague Peace Conference with a petition requesting international assistance in recovering Korea's sovereignty. The Western powers refused to recognize and seat them. Their petition was ignored, but it did generate publicity in the Western press. Embarrassed and annoyed, the Japanese, using a combination of pressure and trickery, got Kojong to abdicate and made his mentally challenged son Sunjong emperor. Angry Korean mobs stormed and burned the residence of Yi Wan-yong, who had become prime minister. Pak Yŏng-hyo, who held the position of minister of the imperial household and who plotted a coup to replace the pro-Japanese cabinet with those who would resist further efforts to erode Korea's sovereignty, was exiled to the southern island of Cheju. Following the abdication, Yi Wan-yong signed a new agreement requiring the resident-general's approval for virtually all laws, regulations, and appointments and removals of high officials. The protectorate issued a press law that banned books that were considered anti-Japanese and tightened control over the press. Several newspapers were closed. On July 31, 1907, the resident-general ordered the small 9,000-man Korean Army disbanded.

When the protectorate was established in 1905 a few members of the *yangban* class organized what were called "Righteous Armies" (*ŭibyŏng*). When the Korean Army was ordered disbanded in 1907, the commander of the First Infantry Guard committed suicide. Many of his troops along with the troops of the Second Infantry Guards responded by revolting. Retreating to the countryside, they were joined by some provincial units to become the core of a widespread resistance movement. Some civilians, both *yangban* and non-*yangban*, also took up revolt, forming more Righteous Armies. An example was Hŏ Wi, who had taken up a small resistance group in 1896 that was disbanded. He now organized another. In 1907 Hŏ and another resistance fighter, Yi In-yŏng, each leading over 1,000 fighters, reached within eight miles of Seoul but were then driven back with heavy losses.[24] Guerrilla bands were organized in many parts of the country from Chŏlla in the southwest to Hamgyŏng in the northeast. The scale of this resistance movement and the number of casualties is not known for certain. They were large enough to require a major military operation by the Japanese. By some estimates 50,000 Korean insurgents participated, and more than 10,000 of these were killed. The resistance was divided into many small bands, mostly from 100 to 500 in number. There was little overall coordination, and for the most part the insurgents were poorly trained and equipped. Activity peaked in 1908; by 1910 the guerrillas had been defeated or driven across the border to Manchuria or Siberia.

At some point the Japanese government decided to annex Korea. There was little opposition to this from Britain and the United States, since both had largely given their approval to Japan to act as it saw fit in Korea. In 1907, Tokyo also reached a secret agreement with Russia in which the latter accepted the annexation in return for Japanese recognition of Russia's special interests in Outer Mongolia. Itō Hirobumi, who had doubts about whether the time was right for annexation, resigned as resident-general in 1909 and was succeeded by the vice-resident-general, Sone Arasuke. But Itō continued to assist in the preparation for annexation by negotiating a treaty abolishing the Korean ministries of justice and defense. Shortly after, he went to Harbin, China, to confirm Russian acceptance of annexation. There on October 26, 1909, he was assassinated by An Chung-gŭn (1879–1910), a Korean Catholic, motivated by Christian and Asianist-influenced nationalism.[25] He was not the only victim of angry Koreans. When Durham White Stevens, the Japanese-nominated advisor to the Korean government, went to the United States in 1908 to promote the benefits of Japanese rule in Korea, he was shot and killed in San Francisco by two Korean students, Chang In-hwan and Chŏn Myŏng-un.

In July 1910, Terauchi Masatake, a former war minister, arrived in Seoul as the new resident-general. He banned all political discussion and assembly, imposed tight press censorship, and arrested Koreans deemed a threat to the authorities. On August 16, Terauchi presented a draft of the treaty of annexation to Korean ministers. Prime Minister Yi Wan-yong, to the condemnation of later Korean nationalists, signed it. On August 29, the Japanese government issued edicts in the names of Emperors Meiji of Japan and Sunjong of Korea announcing the merger of the two countries.

The Korean kingdom established in the seventh century and the Chosŏn dynasty that had ruled it since 1392 came to an end.

The Japanese takeover has been viewed by most Koreans as one of the two great tragedies of their modern history, the other being the division of the country. Could the colonization of Korea have been avoided? Historians often assign blame to the king, to recalcitrant conservatives, to a *yangban* elite that could not rise above self-interest, and to mistakes by reformers. All are blamed for their failure to maintain Korean sovereignty by carrying out the institutional changes that would have strengthened the state and enabled it to operate more effectively in the new international environment. But Koreans had little time to absorb and adjust to the new world into which they had been thrust. For centuries Korea maintained its autonomy within the East Asian world order dominated by China. The experience of Koreans with the tributary system, their proud adherence to Confucian values and institutions, and their limited experience with the West did not prepare them well for the challenges of late nineteenth-century imperialism. The intrusion of the West came rather suddenly and left them with little time to develop adequate responses.

Nonetheless, some educated Koreans were quick to grasp the realities of a changing international environment and pushed for institutional changes that would strengthen their state. Significant measures were carried out to adjust the Chosŏn state to the new realities. Many of these, such as the Kabo reforms, were taken at the prompting of the Japanese, but they were embraced with enthusiasm by many officials. Although many scholars have viewed the attempts by the state to carry out needed reforms in its late decades as pathetically inadequate or carried out only by Japanese intervention, some recent research has suggested that the late Chosŏn state at times acted independently to rationalize administration and carry out social change.[26] The modernization that took place under Japanese colonial rule can be seen as a continuation of these earlier efforts. However, Chinese interference, Japanese expansionism, and Russian intrigue, along with the indecisive leadership of the king and the petty self-interest of many members of the elite all hampered these attempts to carry out reform and maintain sovereignty. Furthermore, as has been pointed out, it was difficult to find an appropriate model for Korea. Japan was the most obvious, but its aggressive policies undermined its advocates.

More significantly, Korea's geopolitical situation was a most precarious one. Surrounded by three major expansionist powers, all of which had identified Korea as strategically important, it is difficult to see how it could have easily navigated its way safely toward modernization without inviting the intervention of its neighbors. Nor is it easy to conceive how a poor, overwhelmingly agricultural nation of perhaps 15 million could have resisted its much larger and more powerful neighbors. Few nations escaped colonization in this era, including other long-standing states such as Vietnam and Burma. Among the small number of exceptions were states such as Thailand, Afghanistan, and Persia, which did so partly as buffer states between empires, but Japan's victories over China and Russia ruled out this possibility.

KOREA IN TRANSITION

Despite the country's loss of independence, this period brought about important changes that marked the birth of a modern Korea. Korea's entry into the world of imperialism profoundly altered society. By the early twentieth century, the forces of modernization were being felt throughout the country. Railway construction, financed by Japanese and American companies, began in 1896; Seoul was being electrified. The first electric streetcar opened in 1898 and by 1902, 3,000 electric lamps were lighting the streets.[27] Western-style buildings were changing the face of the city. Port cities such as Pusan and Inch'ŏn were taking on a cosmopolitan atmosphere. In the countryside, where the great majority of the population lived, farming was increasingly oriented toward the export of rice, soybeans, and other agriculture products for the Japanese market. The old rigid social structure of Korea, based on inherited status, was starting to break down. The legal privileges of the dominant *yangban* class had ended. The examination system that had been a principal vehicle for reaffirming status and gaining access to powerful government positions was abolished, as was slavery.

It would be wrong to see Koreans as the passive victims of external forces. Many ordinary farmers, as well as large landowners, took advantage of the opportunities presented by the new markets for their produce. Some poor farmers found opportunities in the new mines that were opening, such as the American-owned gold mine at Unsan in the northwestern part of the country. Many sought positions in the new post offices, customs posts, telegraph offices, and the new government departments. They sent their children to the new schools, and a few took the opportunity to travel abroad. Mission schools provided a new means for social advancement for people of humble status. Members of sub-elite groups such as *chungin*, the heredity class of technical specialists, and rural clerks were able to enter higher bureaucratic positions that would have been previously closed to them. And a new small entrepreneurial class was emerging. Some of these entrepreneurs came from the small group of wholesale merchants that emerged in the eighteenth and nineteenth centuries, others came from varied backgrounds. Although most of these changes were only just starting before 1910, the old social order was coming to an end.

As educated Koreans sought to make sense of the changing world around them, they were assisted by American missionaries, who played an important role as agents of change and reform. Especially active were the Presbyterians under the leadership of Horace N. Allen and Horace G. Underwood, both arriving in the 1880s. The latter was able to draw on the wealth from his typewriter business to build schools and hospitals. A number of Korean intellectuals became Christian, including: Sŏ Chaep'il, Yun Ch'i-ho, Yu Kil-chun, the first Korean to travel around the world and write an account of his travels, and a young Yi Sŭng-man (better known to Americans as Syngman Rhee). Korean Christians admired the United States for its strength and for what they considered its enlightened political and social concepts. However, America's usefulness as a model was limited by the racism they also found there.[28]

A small class of intellectuals started publishing newspapers, forming discussion groups, establishing educational associations, and opening up new private schools with modern curricula. Koreans had always associated education with moral perfection, and under the civil exam system it served as a means for advancement. With the end of civil examinations, the elite were increasingly attracted to Western-style education. Young men and some women were attending these new private schools or those established by Western missionaries, and going to Japan and the West for advanced schooling. Japan, because of its proximity, lower costs, and cultural similarities, was becoming a popular destination for education among the small number of Koreans who could afford it. A flood of new ideas about government, society, and science flowed into the country as Koreans read Western works, often in Chinese or Japanese translations. Members of the educated elite formed educational and patriotic organizations inspired by Western ideas. Women who were attending some of the Western-style schools became involved in these organizations. The very fact that many women were attending the new schools was a sign of the radical changes in Korean society that were starting to take place. Women's education was pioneered by American missionaries such as Mary Scranton, who founded the first Ewha Girls School in 1886; by 1910 many Koreans had accepted the importance of schooling for girls.

Changing too was the sense of identity that was emerging among Koreans. As Andre Schmid has pointed out, in the years after 1895 the new journals, newspapers, and various educational associations were starting to create a community of educated Koreans who argued over how to protect the nation, and after 1905 how to revive it.[29] It was a community drawn from both the old *yangban* class and from commoners exposed to modern education and ideas, a community that began to think of themselves as belonging to what should be a sovereign state. The Independence Club had been an early manifestation of this new conceptualization. This feeling of being a nation, of being a people with a shared culture, history, and common destiny, when combined with the concept of national sovereignty, marked the beginning of modern Korean nationalism. Historians and political thinkers such as Pak Ŭn-sik (1859–1923) and Sin Ch'ae-ho (1880–1936) were reexamining Korea's place in the world and what it meant to be Korean. In 1908, the young Sin published an especially important essay, "A New Reading of History" (*"Toksa Sillon"*), in which he borrowed the concept of "folk" (Korean: *minjok*) from Japanese and Chinese writers and placed it at the center of history. The history of Korea became a history of a Korean people with their unique cultural tradition. Other scholars were standardizing and promoting the Korean alphabet, *han'gŭl*, which was becoming a symbol of a modern, national identity.

Koreans, with their long history of borrowing abroad, began a new process of adopting and adapting foreign culture. By the time of the annexation of the country by Japan in 1910, Koreans had already begun laying the foundation for a new society with a new sense of national identity.

KOREA IN GLOBAL PERSPECTIVE: KOREA IN THE AGE OF IMPERIALISM

Many historians have challenged the older interpretations of history that see this period as one in which events are driven by the challenge of imperialism, and in which the actions of Koreans are judged in terms of how well they responded to that challenge. Instead they point to the importance of appreciating the internal changes that were taking place before 1876. Government slavery was abolished in 1801, and private slavery was declining. There were signs that the society was becoming more commercial as a result of changes in the tax system in which tribute was replaced with cash payments, and with the emergence of a new class of wholesale merchants. They point to the peasant rebellions in the nineteenth century and to the restlessness among people from more marginalized northern provinces, as well as to the emergence of the Tonghak religious movement and the growth of the small Christian community from the late eighteenth century as signs of social unrest and cultural change. Korea, as these historians have maintained, was not intellectually, economically, or socially stagnant in the nineteenth century, nor is there any clear evidence that it was in a state of decline. Nonetheless, it is not obvious that Korea was set for a major transformation or upheaval in the mid-nineteenth century; and it is clear that forces of imperialism altered the course of its history, as they did in most of the world.

How does Korea's experience with imperialism compare to other nations? In many ways it was a typical victim of the imperialist powers of the late nineteenth and the early twentieth centuries. Yet certain aspects were distinctive. As was the case with other states, such as Morocco, Korea was an object of competing imperial rivalries. Unlike most societies in the non-Western world, it was colonized by a neighboring nation, not a distant foreign power. Korea itself differed from most colonies. It possessed a greater coherence as a cultural and historical unit and a longer history of territorial stability than almost all other nineteenth-century states. It had clearly defined borders, and a distinctive ethnic culture and language not shared by any other peoples. It was a state that was an ethnic group, or an ethnic group that was a state. And it had many centuries of autonomy. China was theoretically its suzerain, but for all practical purposes Korea had been an independent state with little outside interference since the Manchu incursions of the first half of the seventeenth century. Few other states had such stability, such a long period of self-government, or such a homogeneous ethnicity and culture.

Furthermore, Korea had many attributes that gave it a foundation for making the transition to a modern state: a long tradition of rational bureaucratic government; a fairly high literacy rate, at least among men; a common shared set of values and customs that gave the country a sense of unity and purpose; and not least, a tradition of borrowing from abroad. In fact, considering the isolation of the country and the suddenness of its forced opening to outside intercourse, educated Koreans were quick to learn new customs. Western missionary schools after an initial slow decade became very popular from the 1890s; by the end of the nineteenth century, Koreans were establishing many private schools offering new Western-style curricula. Despite the many barriers, hundreds made it overseas to acquire learning. The enthusiasm with which Korean intellectuals became absorbed in new ideas, despite the enormous linguistic hurdles, is impressive, especially when contrasted with the much slower response of Chinese or Muslim intellectuals. Indeed, the speed with which Koreans began appreciating the strength of Western nations and the value of Western learning is more comparable with Japan.

Yet the country's modest level of commercial development, the social gap between the elite and commoners, the traditional disdain for the military, and the stubborn sense of Confucian righteousness among many of the governing class also hindered its ability to respond effectively to the imperialist threat. And the institutions of government proved woefully inadequate to the challenges that it faced. Nor was Korea a nation in the modern sense. As made clear in the work of contemporary scholars such as Gi-Wook Shin, one of the major challenges educated Koreans faced was deciding who they were, and where their society fit into the world.[30] Some, such as Kim Ok-kyun, identified Korea as being, along with China and Japan, one of the three Asian *hwa* (cultures or societies) that had to unite against Europe and America. He and others looked to Japan as the country that could lift up its neighbors to a level of civilization that could compete with the West. Some Koreans began to see race as a category and themselves as part of an Asian race. Many of these, too, looked to Japan for leadership. This became mixed with Pan-Asianist ideas of the unity of the East Asian peoples. And Pan-Asianism was influenced by Social Darwinism, the application of natural selection to societies. In Korea Social Darwinism was referred to as *yakyuk kangsik* (the weak are meat, the strong eat) and lent urgency to both the reform of Korea lest it fall prey to stronger societies and to the hope that Japanese leadership would enable Asia to be strong enough to compete in the struggle for survival.[31]

But by 1910, intellectuals such as Sin Ch'ae-ho and Pak Ŭn-sik, influenced by Western writings on race and nation, began to see Korea as a unique land with its own history and tradition, as a member of an international community of nations with its own "folk," its own traditions, and its own history. They were establishing the basis for a new Korean nationalism that no longer saw itself as firmly rooted in a Chinese-centered Confucian civilization but as a distinctive nation. Thus, if Korea was unusual in its cultural homogeneity, its long history as a self-governing state, and the stability of its political institutions, it was typical in the process by which it struggled to create a sense of how it fitted into the new Western-dominated world of nation-states.

Inaugural Message of the *Independent*, April 7, 1896

As we publish the first issue of *The Independent* today, we shall declare to everyone in Korea, foreigners and natives alike, what we believe.

> We are impartial and nonpartisan and recognize no distinction between upper and lower classes; everyone shall be treated equally as a Korean. We shall speak only to benefit Korea, and we shall be fair. We shall speak not only for the people in Seoul but for everyone throughout the country on every subject.
> We shall communicate to the people what the government does and convey the conditions of the people to the government, thereby benefitting both sides who need not feel uncomfortable or suspicious.

Since we are not publishing the paper for the sake of profit, the price of a copy is low. We write in the vernacular (*han'gŭl*) to enable men and women of all social classes to read; we also insert space between the words to make reading easier.

We shall be truthful, we shall report on those government officials who may misconduct themselves; we shall let the whole nation know about any corrupt and self-enriching officials; we shall investigate and publicize any private persons who may violate the law.

We are for His Majesty, the government of Korea, and the Korean people; there shall not be any partisan discourse nor words to benefit only one side printed in our paper.

We have a page written in English because foreigners are not well informed on the Korean situation and, therefore, are liable to be misguided in their thoughts by relying solely on biased words. In order to give them correct information we shall prepare a section in English.

It will become evident, then, that this newspaper exists only for the interests of Korea. Foreigners and Koreans, men and women, people of diverse social classes and stations, all will become informed about Korea. We will also report from time to time on the situations in foreign lands so that those Koreans who cannot travel to foreign countries may learn about them.

As today is our first day of publication, we have outlined where we stand. We believe that by reading our paper the opinions and wisdom of the Korean people will be improved.[32]

Chang Chiyŏn, "We Wail Today"

Author Note: The Korean-Japanese Protectorate Treaty was signed on the night of November 17, 1905 and was announced on November 18. This well-known editorial was printed in the November 20 issue of *Hwangsŏng sinmun* (*Imperial Capital News*), a newspaper that first appeared in September 1898.

When Marquis Itō came to Korea the other day, the innocent people of Korea said to one another that, since he had hitherto devoted himself to bringing about stability and peace among the three nations of the East, his visit this time would surely be for the purpose of recommending measures for strengthening our nation's independence. Therefore, officials and civilians alike gave him a big welcome all the way from the port to Seoul. There are, however, many unpredictable things in this world. How could these five totally unexpected articles of the treaty be proposed? Since the proposed provisions will not only affect Korea but also cause division among the three nations, one wonders about Marquis Itō's ultimate intention.

Due to the strong objection of His Majesty the emperor, we may surmise that Marquis Itō could have known of the eventual defeat of the treaty and have withdrawn it. Nevertheless, the so-called ministers of our government, who are not even worthy of being compared to dogs and swine, sought their own rewards and gains, got frightened by momentary threats, and, to our consternation, became traitorous criminals. They handed over to foreigners a nation with a four-thousand-year history and a dynasty that has lasted five hundred years, thereby reducing twenty million souls to being the slaves of foreigners. Foreign Minister Pak Chesun and other ministers are beneath the level of dogs and swine and do not even deserve the honor of serious censure.

The man whose official title is supposed to be prime minister is the head of the government, yet he only cast a negative vote as if that alone were enough to discharge his official responsibility and save his honor. Unlike Kim Sanghŏn who tore up the document and wailed or Chŏng On who disemboweled himself in protest, the prime minister is still alive and moves about. How dare he face His Majesty and his twenty million fellow countrymen?

Alas! How deplorable! Fellow countrymen, now slaves to foreigners, are you dead or alive? Should we let the national spirit that has been preserved for four thousand years since the days of Tangun and Kija (Chi Tzu) disintegrate overnight? How deplorable! How deplorable! Fellow countrymen! Fellow countrymen!

—from the newspaper *Hwangsŏng sinmun*
(*Imperial Capital News*), November 20, 1905[33]

NOTES

1. Donald Baker, "Cloudy Images: Korean Knowledge of the West from 1520–1800," *B.C. Asian Review* 3, no. 4 (1990): 51–73.
2. Yi Sŏngmi, "Western Influence on Korean Painting of the Late Chosŏn Period," in *Proceedings of the 1st World Congress of Korean Studies: Embracing the Other: The Interaction of Korean and Foreign Cultures*, The Academy of Korean Studies (Seoul: July 2002), 576–84.
3. Donald L. Baker, "Jesuit Science through Korean Eyes," *Journal of Korean Studies* 4 (1982–1983): 207–29, 213.
4. Baker, "Jesuit Science through Korean Eyes," 217.
5. Baker, "Cloudy Images," 68.
6. Gari Ledyard, *The Dutch Come to Korea* (Seoul: Royal Asiatic Society, 1971), 223.
7. Key-Hiuk Kim, *The Last Phase of the East Asian World Order* (Berkeley: University of California Press, 1980), 44–45.
8. Baker, "Cloudy Images," 63.
9. Key-Hiuk Kim, *The Last Phase of the East Asian World Order*, 56.
10. Ki-baik Lee, *A New History of Korea*, translated by Edward W. Wagner with Edward J. Shultz (Cambridge, MA: Harvard University Press, 1984), 266.

11. Martina Deuchler, *Confucian Gentlemen and Barbarian Envoys: The Opening of Korea, 1875–1885* (Seattle: University of Washington Press, 1977), 53.

12. Deuchler, *Confucian Gentlemen and Barbarian Envoys*, 141.

13. Deuchler, *Confucian Gentlemen and Barbarian Envoys*, 151.

14. Yong-ho Ch'oe, "The Kapsin Coup of 1884: A Reassessment," *Korean Studies* 6 (1982): 105–24.

15. Jerome Ch'en, *Yuan Shih-k'ai* (Stanford, CA: Stanford University Press, 1961), 33–34.

16. Young-ick Lew, "Yuan Shih-kai's Residency and the Korean Enlightenment Movement (1885–1894)," *The Journal of Korean Studies* 5 (1984): 63–107.

17. Lew, "Yuan Shih-Kai's Residency," 63–107.

18. Andrew C. Nahm, *Korea: Tradition and Transformation* (Elizabeth, NJ: Hollym International, 1988), 173.

19. Kirk W. Larsen, "Trade, Dependency, and Colonialism: Foreign Trade and Korea's Regional Integration, 1876–1910," in *Korea at the Center: Dynamics of Regionalism in Northeast Asia*, ed. Charles K. Armstrong, Gilbert Rozman, Samuel S. Kim, and Stephen Kotlin (Armonk, NY: M.E. Sharpe, 2006), 51–60.

20. Susan Shin, "The Tonghak Movement: From Enlightenment to Revolution," *Korean Studies Forum* 5 (Winter–Spring 1978–1979): 1–79.

21. Nahm, *Korea: Tradition and Transformation*, 176.

22. Shin, "The Tonghak Movement," 51–52.

23. See Ken Uchida, *The Great Enterprise: Sovereignty and Historiography in Modern Korea* (Durham NC: Duke University Press, 2011).

24. Carter J. Eckert, Ki-baik Lee, Young Ick Lew, Michael Robinson, and Edward W. Wagner, *Korea Old and New: A History* (Cambridge: Korea Institute, Harvard University, 1990), 243.

25. Franklin Rausch, "Visions of Violence, Dreams of Peace: Religion, Race, and Nationalism in An Chung-gŭn's 'A Treatise on Peace in the East,'" *Acta Koreana* 15.2 (December 2012): 263–291.

26. Kyung Moon Hwang, "Citizenship, Social Equality and Government Reform: Basic Changes in the Household Registration System in Korea, 1894–1910," *Modern Asian Studies* 38.2 (2004): 355–387; Marie Song-Hak Kim, *Law and Custom in Korea: Comparative Legal History* (Cambridge, UK: Cambridge University Press, 2014).

27. Min Suh Son, "Enlightenment and Electrification: The Introduction of Electric Light, Telegraph and Streetcars in Late Nineteenth Century Korea," in Dong-no Kim, John B. Duncan, and Kim Do-hyung, eds., *Reform and Modernity in the Taehan Empire* (Seoul: Jimoondang, 2006), 267–298.

28. Hahm Chaibong, "Civilization, Race or Nation? Korean Visions of Regional Order in the Late Nineteenth Century," in Charles K. Armstrong, Samuel S. Kim, and Stephen Kotlin, eds., *Korea at the Center: Dynamics of Regionalism in Northeast Asia* (Armonk, NY: M.E. Sharpe, 2006), 35–50.

29. Andre Schmid, *Korea between Empires, 1895–1919* (New York: Columbia University Press, 2002).

30. Gi-Wook Shin, *Ethnic Nationalism in Korea: Genealogy, Politics, and Legacy* (Stanford, CA: Stanford University Press, 2006).

31. Vladimir Tikhonov, *Social Darwinism and Nationalism in Korea: the Beginning (1880s–1910s): "Survival" as an Ideology of Korean Modernity* (Leiden, Neth: Brill, 2010).

32. Yŏng-ho Ch'oe, Peter H. Lee, and William Theodore de Bary, eds., *Sources of Korean Tradition*, volume 2, *From the Sixteenth to the Twentieth Centuries* (New York: Columbia University Press, 2000), 279–89.

33. Ch'oe, Lee, and de Bary, *Sources of Korean Tradition*, vol. 2, 312–13.

2

Colonial Korea, 1910 to 1945

Korea's modern history was profoundly influenced by its thirty-five years (1910 to 1945) as a colony of Japan. The Japanese colonial regime established the basis of many of the economic, educational, and governmental institutions of Korea, while its authoritarian rule, its mass mobilization campaigns, and its attempt at forced assimilation touched the lives of almost every Korean, often in disturbing and even traumatizing ways. As Koreans responded to the demands, opportunities, and challenges presented by the colonial regime, they developed the ideological divisions that would be so important in determining the course of their history after 1945.

Japanese colonial rule was top-down, centralized, direct, and intensive. The centralized nature of colonial government, Government-General of Korea (*Chōsen Sōtokufu*), as it was called, can be seen in the power concentrated in the hands of the governor-general (*Sōtoku*). Appointed by the Japanese emperor and directly responsible to the prime minister, he possessed an enormously broad authority, including the right to issue laws, ordinances, and regulations and to appoint various officials. All governors-general were military men, generals or admirals, and possessed the power to mobilize and command the troops stationed in the country. Assisted by a centralized police apparatus, they ruled with powers Adrian Buzo has likened to "a general in a theater of war."[1] A symbol of his authority was the Government-General building in front of the throne-hall of the Kyŏngbok Palace, the major royal residence. Under the governor-general there was a director-general of administration (*Seimu Sōkan*), the second-most-important position, who was appointed by the Japanese prime minister. The colonial regime maintained Korea's administrative division of thirteen provinces, which were subdivided into over 200 counties and municipalities. Counties, in turn, were subdivided into districts, villages, and hamlets. The governor-general appointed all the provincial governors and county superintendents. These officials appointed the district and village heads. Thus, although Korea under the Chosŏn dynasty had been a centralized state with a government that appointed officials down to the county level, the colonial regime penetrated even further to the township and village level. Commanding the military forces in the peninsula, controlling a highly centralized police system, appointing all important local officials, and possessing broad legislative power as well as executive power, the governor-general was a new authoritarian figure in Korean political history. Not even the kings had had so much power concentrated in their hands.

Not only was it highly centralized, but colonial rule also became increasingly intrusive as it grew to become a vast apparatus. To administer the country, the Government-General in 1910 had about 10,000 officials. This number was to grow until it reached 87,552 in 1937, comprising 52,270 Japanese and 35,282 Koreans. If all members of the military, state, and semi-government banks and companies are included, the figure is closer to 246,000 Japanese and 63,000 Koreans. By 1940, there were 708,418 Japanese residents of Korea, amounting to 3.2 percent of the population. About 40 percent directly and indirectly worked for the government. To impose its authority, the Japanese employed 6,222 military and civilian police in 1910, half Korean. This grew to 20,771 in 1922 and 60,000 by 1941.[2] The police had the power to judge and sentence those arrested for minor offenses. But their role went beyond that to include: tax collecting, supervising irrigation and water controlling, overseeing road construction and maintenance, enforcing health regulations, and acting as public information officers. It was a comprehensive system that grew to over 2,500 substations and one officer for every 800 households.[3]

The first decade of colonial rule was particularly harsh, what Koreans have called the "dark period" (amhŭkki). It was characterized by harsh political repression that stifled cultural as well as political life. The press was under tight control, police permits were required for any public gathering, and all organizations and meetings deemed political in nature were prohibited. To emphasize their authority, Japanese officials, even schoolteachers, wore swords, although Koreans were not allowed to own any type of weapon.

This harsh administration took place in an atmosphere of troubled and tense relations between Koreans and their Japanese rulers. The most publicized incident took place in December 1910 when the Japanese announced the discovery of a plot to assassinate the new governor-general, Terauchi Masatake, led by An Myŏng-gŭn, brother of An Chung-gŭn, who assassinated Itō Hirobumi. Some 700 Koreans were detained, 123 arraigned, and in 1911, 105 were convicted. Three others died during interrogations. Most of the arrested were Christians, including the prominent Protestant leaders Yun Ch'i-ho (1864-1945) and Yi Sŭng-hun. The trial, which became referred to as the "Case of 105 Persons," generated considerable international publicity, not least because it seemed to focus on Christians. Furthermore, many of the defendants gave highly improbable confessions that implicated the members of the foreign mission community.[4] Few of these confessions seemed plausible, and the heavy-handedness of the Japanese proved an embarrassment. Many were re-tried, given lighter sentences, and eventually released. The trial was a clear warning to Koreans that the colonial government would not tolerate any anti-Japanese activity. There were many other similar sweeps and waves of arrest by the colonial administration. Tens of thousands of Koreans were arrested from 1910 to 1919 for political reasons.

Under these repressive conditions, resistance to Japanese rule took place mainly among the exile community. During most of the long Yi dynasty period (1392–1910) very few ethnic Koreans lived outside Korea. This began to change in the late nineteenth century. From the 1860s, small numbers of Koreans began to cross the Yalu and Tumen Rivers into Manchuria and Siberia. Originally this migration was motivated by economic distress near the border regions, beginning with a drought in the 1860s. Most of the Koreans in Manchuria settled in Kando (Jiandao in Chinese), a sparsely populated area adjacent to the border. Kando had a population of 65,000 in 1894 and 109,000 in 1910. Koreans left mainly fleeing poverty, but after 1905 the desire to flee Japanese rule added to the migration. A wave of 60,000 poured into the area during the first two years of colonial rule. Their descendants formed the Yanbian Korean Autonomous Region in China today. Tens of thousands of Koreans also migrated to the Russian Maritime Province for both economic and political reasons. Another 7,000 Koreans migrated to Hawaii from 1902 to 1910 to work on the sugar and pineapple plantations until U.S. authorities restricted the migration. Small Korean communities emerged in Shanghai after 1910, mostly political exiles. In Japan there was a growing student population numbering several thousand in the 1910s. A small handful of Koreans lived in the United States and Europe, mainly as students. These Korean communities became the homes of a number of small nationalist groups, some of which later played an important role in Korean politics.

THE MARCH FIRST MOVEMENT

Although there were small nationalist exile groups and dissidents within Korea from the time of the protectorate, a truly nationwide Korean resistance movement to Japanese occupation first took place in March 1919. The end of World War I and the Versailles Peace Conference inspired hopes for colonial peoples throughout the world. In part, this was sparked by the peace settlement, and in particular by President Wilson of the United States, who in his Fourteen Points called for the principle of "national self-determination." While this was meant only to apply to European people, the Korean diaspora, like so many non-Western colonial subjects, was greatly excited by these events. An exile group led by Kim Kyu-sik (1881–1950) went to Paris to argue for Korean independence. An attempt by the small Korean community in Hawaii, through its Korean National Association (Taehan Kungminhoe), tried to dispatch a delegation led by Syngman Rhee for the same purpose, but it failed when they were denied passports. The most significant of the developments outside Korea was among Korean students in Japan. They organized a Korean Youth Independence Corps (Chosŏn Ch'ŏngnyŏn Tongniptan). In Tokyo over 600 Korean students attended a meeting on February 8, 1919, where they passed a declaration written by intellectual and writer Yi Kwang-su (1892–1950) calling for immediate independence. The group then sent members to Korea in order to agitate for independence there. In Korea, several different groups were discussing independence in early 1919: a group of Ch'ŏndogyo members including Son Pyŏng-hŭi, a group of Presbyterians based in Pyongyang led by Yi Sŭng-hun, Methodists in Seoul, and a group affiliated with Chungang High School that included Kim Sŏng-su (1891–1955) and Song Chin-u (1890–1945), both to later play a prominent role in Korean political life. The arrival of Korean students from Tokyo with news of their calls for independence and about activities of exile groups stimulated them into action. But the catalyst for major action came with Kojong's death on January 21, 1919. Rumors that the Japanese had poisoned him or that they had forced him to commit suicide added to unrest. Taking advantage of the large crowds that were expected to arrive in Seoul for the scheduled funeral on March 3, representatives of the various groups decided to issue a declaration of independence in Pagoda Park in Seoul on March 1. Thirty-three signed it: sixteen Christians, fifteen Ch'ŏndogyo members, and two Buddhists. A petition was to be sent to the Japanese and U.S. governments and to the Paris peace conference. The signers were careful to emphasize the nonviolent nature of their protest. They do not appear to have intended to create a mass uprising. The reading of the declaration was moved to a restaurant on February 28 for security reasons. Nonetheless, crowds met to hear the declaration on the afternoon of March 1. There, a person who happened to have a copy read it to an enthusiastic crowd that began marching down the main street in downtown Seoul. In the following days, demonstrations took place throughout the country.[5]

What is most interesting about the demonstrations that took place beginning March 1, 1919, was the large number of participants and how widespread they were. It has been estimated that 500,000 to 1 million people participated in the demonstrations that continued throughout the spring. There were 667 reported peaceful demonstrations along with hundreds of violent incidents that took place in every province and city.[6] A small radical group known as the National Congress (Kungmin Taehoe) called for more violent action, but for the most part leaders attempted to keep what became known as the March First Movement peaceful. The Japanese authorities reacted by attempting to suppress the demonstrations, often quite violently. All assemblies and street demonstrations were banned, and reprisals were taken against groups that participated. One sixteen-year-old girl, Yu Kwan-sun, who was arrested and tortured and who died in prison, became an icon of the independence movement. Much of the suppression was directed at the Christians, who, along with members of the Ch'ŏndogyo, were heavily represented in the movement; over 400 churches were destroyed. In one notorious incident a church was burned with its congregation perishing inside. Officially 553 were killed, 1,409 injured, and over 14,000 arrested during the months that followed. Korean nationalists claimed the figures were much higher, up to 7,000 deaths and tens of thousands arrested.[7]

The March First Movement was a major turning point in Korean history. It has been regarded by some historians as the birth of modern Korean nationalism. Others have seen it as not the beginning of Korean nationalism but its transformation from a small movement of isolated and scattered intellectuals and of tiny exile groups abroad to a mass movement that cut across class lines. An impressive number of women, peasants, and non-elite urban and small-town residents participated in it. A vision of Korea as a nation appeared to have emerged among many Koreans at this time. Koreans were seeing their land as one of an international community of nations, a nation that had lost its independence. The movement encouraged exiles abroad to combine efforts to achieve national independence, an effort that was centered in Shanghai. Domestically, the demonstrations were suppressed without achieving independence, but they embarrassed the Japanese government and led it to change its policy toward Korea.

THE POST–MARCH FIRST PERIOD

The March First Movement was an embarrassment to the Japanese government and resulted in a call by some political leaders for a reform of its harsh military rule in Korea. It also coincided with a more liberal atmosphere in Japan. The Japanese government had been partly modeled on the Prussian/German one. With the victory of the more democratic Allied powers in World War I—the United States, Britain, and France—there was a call for liberal democratic government at home. Thus Japan entered what is called "Taisho Democracy," a period ending after 1930. Japanese policy reflected this liberal trend. Japan's liberalism in the 1920s, however, was modest. Even more modest was its liberalism in Korea. Nonetheless, the government of Prime Minister Hara Takashi issued the Revised Organic Regulations of the Government-General of Korea in August 1919, which marked a change in policy under the new slogan "Harmony between Japan and Korea" (*Nissen yūwa*). He appointed as governor-general Admiral Saitō Makoto from the more liberal navy, with a mandate to make major administrative changes.

Saitō quickly received a reminder of the discontent in Korea—a bomb went off in Seoul Station the day of his arrival. To carry out his reform, he appointed Mizuno Rentarō, former home minister (1916–1918) to assume the duties of director-general of political affairs, the number two position, and a talented young Maruyama Tsurukichi as the head of his police. A number of changes were made. The gendarmerie was abolished, replaced by a regular police force. Many of these reforms were symbolic. Japanese teachers and civil officials no longer wore military uniforms and carried swords. Minor offenses were no longer punished by whippings. Laws regulating burials, slaughtering of animals, and peasant markets that interfered with traditional customs and were greatly resented were abolished or modified. Korean government workers were to receive the same wages as Japanese, although they still did not receive the bonuses that their Japanese counterparts did. Saitō created an advisory council with provincial Korean representation. Koreans were appointed to serve on city, county, and provincial councils. Business and trade was also liberalized. The Japanese government eliminated the tariff barriers between Japan and Korea, the Korean market was now open to Japanese trade and investment. In 1921, the Japanese invited key Korean businessmen to participate in the Chōsen (Korea) Industrial Commission.

In the spring of 1920, the Korean crown prince married Japan's Princess Nashimoto. This symbolic merger of the two royal houses was accompanied by an amnesty of several thousand political prisoners and the inauguration of what the government called its "culture policy" (Japanese: *bunka seiji*). There was a new, more tolerant attitude toward Korean cultural activities. The ban on Korean newspapers was lifted, and in that year prominent Koreans established the *Chosŏn Ilbo* and *Tonga Ilbo*, still South Korea's two leading papers. With restrictions on publishing reduced, hundreds of popular magazines and specialized publications appeared. Beginning in 1920, the lifting of harsh restrictions on organized activity resulted in an explosive growth in the youth, religious, social, educational, intellectual, labor, and farmer organizations. Many were small and local; some were large and countrywide.

This freer atmosphere was accompanied by efforts of the colonial regime to maintain tight control. The colonial administration expanded the police force and opened hundreds of new police stations throughout the country. To provide better intelligence and surveillance capabilities Maruyama created the High Police (Kōtō Keisatsu). The police presence was conspicuous in Korea with policemen stationed throughout the country, half being Japanese. These policemen assumed many roles, from enforcing detailed regulations to collecting taxes and supervising the collection and transport of rice, becoming a ubiquitous presence in the lives of ordinary Koreans. The new administration may have reflected some more liberal thinking in the Japanese government, but it also represented a more sophisticated attitude toward control. The Government-General in the 1920s co-opted Korean nationalists by providing intellectuals and others an avenue to legally express themselves, showing a greater sensitivity to Korean culture, and removing the most hated symbols of Japanese authority, while increasing the size and efficiency of the colonial administrative and police organs. Allowing Korean activists to move about more openly also made it easier to observe them.

There were limits to the freedom allowed. Koreans were not allowed to openly advocate independence; their criticisms of the administration had to be very circumspect. Failure to adhere to this resulted in the banning of organizations, the closing of publications, and arrests. A rigorous censorship was still carried out, and publications were frequently shut down. Freedom of expression began to tighten with the passage of the Peace Preservation Law in Japan in 1925, which gave police much greater latitude in imposing restrictions on any speech or activity deemed subversive. Still, compared to the years before and after, the early 1920s was a fairly liberal period.

CULTURAL FERMENT OF THE 1920s

The 1920s was an especially important time in Korean cultural history. Not only did the years immediately after World War I and the March First Movement see a burst of creative energy among artists and intellectuals who laid the foundations for modern literary and artistic expressions, but the main split among nationalists on how they envisioned a modern Korean nation took shape. Indeed, it could be argued that the intellectual foundations of the two Koreas were established at this time. External events stimulated the movement: the excitement over the Versailles Peace Treaty, the Bolshevik Revolution, and the growth of anticolonial movements around the world. The more liberal policies of the Japanese colonial administration facilitated the intellectual ferment. Furthermore, the young people who grew up after the traditional political and social order had fallen, and who were educated in modern-style schools, were coming of age.

There was an explosive burst of creative energy, as artists and intellectuals explored new ideas and new literary and artistic forms. New literature flowered in the journals *Creation* (*Ch'angjo*, 1919), *Ruins* (*P'yehŏ*, 1920) and *White Tide* (*Paekcho*, 1922). The novelists Kim Tong-in (1900–1951) and Yŏm Sang-sŏp (1897–1963), and the Buddhist poet Han Yong-un (1879–1944) pioneered modern Korean literature. Leftists wrote proletarian literature. Modern theater, which had begun with the Wŏn'gaksa Theater in Seoul in 1908, flourished. A new avenue of artistic expression, the cinema, began in the 1920s. One of the early works was the film *Arirang*, directed and acted by Na Un-gyu in 1926. The colonial authorities banned it for its nationalist theme. A number of silent films were produced from 1926 to 1935, sometimes called the golden age of Korean cinema; unfortunately few of these films have survived.

MODERATE AND RADICAL NATIONALISM

This period of cultural ferment in the early 1920s saw a division among Korean nationalists that would profoundly shape Korean history: between the moderate, Western-looking cultural nationalists, and the more radical nationalists who tended to look toward the Soviet Union and Communist movements abroad for inspiration. Modern Korean nationalism, which can be traced to the 1890s, came to maturity at this time. Nationalists held a strong sense of loyalty to a Korean nation that was defined by its distinctive culture, its language, history, and heritage. They regarded the loss of sovereignty to Japan as a great tragedy and sought eventual independence. By the 1920s, many Korean intellectuals looked to the West as a model for civilized behavior, much as the Korean intellectuals in the past had looked to China. Ironically, many of these were educated in Japan, where they read Western works in Japanese translation, although in some cases they studied Western languages, usually English or German. They were highly critical of Korea's cultural backwardness, which they saw as responsible for the fall of their country to the Japanese. Other nationalists turned to anarchism, socialism, and after 1917 to Communism.

Many advocated a moderate agenda, working within the limitations of the colonial framework. The focus of these moderate nationalists, whom historian Michael Robinson calls "cultural nationalists," was on culture, not politics. This was partly based on pragmatism, since any call for independence would result in arrest and harsh repression, and therefore be ineffective. But it was also based on a sincere conviction that Korea must develop spiritually and culturally before it could be ready for independence. It was their duty to work on uplifting society first. Cultural nationalists advocated a gradual approach to development, seeing education as a key. They propagated their ideas through the newspapers, a host of new magazines, and through various youth, women's, educational, and cultural associations. Especially important vehicles for expressing their ideas were the two major newspapers and the new intellectual magazines that emerged in the early 1920s.

Among the leaders of these moderate nationalists was Kim Sŏng-su. Kim came from a wealthy *yangban* family in North Chŏlla. Educated in Japan, Kim combined a bright intellect with a keen business sense. He took advantage of the Japanese demand for Korean rice to consolidate and expand his holdings over some of Korea's richest rice paddies. Then he invested much of this into new industrial enterprises, eventually becoming one of Korea's richest businessmen. A strong promoter of Korean education, he founded the Posŏng foundation, which supported Korean-owned schools, one of which was to become Koryŏ (Korea) University. He also established the *Tonga Ilbo* newspaper. Closely associated with Kim Sŏng-su was Song Chin-u, a prominent moderate leader and the president of *Tonga Ilbo*.

Another key figure in the moderate nationalist movement was Yi Kwang-su. Born in P'yŏngan in 1892, Yi was educated at a village school. After his parents died he lived with relatives associated with the Tonghaks. Through various connections, he received a scholarship from the Ilchinhoe to study at Japanese secondary school in 1905. Later he traveled to Shanghai and the Russian Far East. Then with financial support from Kim Sŏng-su he went back to Japan to study at Waseda University, where he earned a degree in philosophy. Yi was the principal author of the Tokyo Korean Student Declaration in February 1919. He then joined other political exiles in Shanghai but returned to Korea under the more liberal conditions in 1921. Already well established as a novelist as well as political activist, Yi, not yet thirty years old, was probably Korea's leading writer and thinker. In May 1922, he wrote a long essay in *Kyebyŏk*, "Minjok Kaejoron" ("Treatise on the Reconstruction of the Nation"), that articulated the agenda for moderate nationalists. It advocated working within the colonial system, not violently opposing it; and it argued for the need for national development prior to political independence.[8]

Many of these moderate nationalists were Christians. Some were from the *yangban* class, but many were of more humble background. Whatever their background, and however critical they were of Korea's cultural heritage, they tended to assume much the same role as the old premodern intellectual elite had in being the guardians of knowledge, whose role was to lead the masses. As with the old Confucian elite they often despised, they placed the highest value on moral and spiritual development through education. They criticized what was called *sadaejuŭi*, or the blind cultural subservience to China, as a source, if not the main source, of Korea's backwardness, and they looked for a distinctive Korean cultural tradition. Yet they advocated for the adoption of many aspects of Western culture, with a similar admiration for foreign models.

Many Korean intellectuals, however, began to look at their own cultural heritage with pride. Some were angered by the work of state-sponsored Japanese scholars that found Korean history characterized by stagnation in contrast to the progressive societies of Japan and the West. To counter this idea, scholars such as Ch'oe Nam-sŏn (1890–1957) sought to create national histories that pointed to the unique and dynamic nature of their nation's past. In 1934, a group of scholars established the Chindan Hakhoe (Chindan Society) to publish historical scholarship from this nationalist point of view. Another significant project by nationalists was the effort to promote and standardize the Korean written language. Since the 1890s the Korean alphabet, *han'gŭl*, had become a symbol of Korean cultural distinctiveness and was promoted by many. The pioneer in the work of standardizing the rules of grammar and spelling was Chu Si-gyŏng (1876–1914), who believed language was a fundamental form of the expression of national identity. Chu died young, but his disciples, taking advantage of the more liberal atmosphere after 1920, created the Korean Language Research Society (Chosŏnŏ Yŏn'guhoe) in 1921. Their work was made easier by the fact that Korea was a homogeneous country where everyone spoke the same language and by the fact that the regional dialects were not so marked that they posed a problem in creating uniform rules of orthography. This was in contrast to the problems encountered by the similar *baihua* movement that was going on in China. The society led mass literacy campaigns in the late 1920s and produced a *Unified Orthography* (*Matchumbŏp t'ongil an*) in 1933. In the 1930s, the society's main task was the compilation of *The Big Dictionary* (*K'ŭn sajŏn*). The principal editor of this work was arrested by the Japanese during World War II for the crime of compiling a dictionary, and he died in prison, but the society continued on and completed the dictionary after 1945. There emerged, then, among many moderate nationalists, an ambiguity toward their cultural traditions, which they viewed with both shame and pride.

One of the major attempts by moderate nationalists to rally the people in a national cause, while still working within the framework of legality, was the Korean Production Movement. It was begun in the summer of 1920 in Pyongyang by Cho Man-sik (1882–1950). Cho was a Presbyterian elder who studied at Waseda University in Japan, where he read about and became an admirer of Gandhi's nonviolent, noncooperation nationalist movement in British India. His own deep religious and ethical convictions, belief in nonviolence, simple lifestyle, and modest personal demeanor earned him the sobriquet "the Gandhi of Korea." Influenced by Gandhi's effort to raise national consciousness and self-sufficiency by encouraging the use of homespun cloth, Cho established the Society for the Promotion of Korean Production to encourage Koreans to buy locally made products and boycott imported Japanese goods. The idea was not entirely new; during the protectorate period some Koreans launched a National Debt Movement, a similar campaign of economic self-sufficiency. Cho's movement became national when the Society for the Promotion of Korean Production was created in January 1923. An impressive array of leaders joined the campaign, from the writer and intellectual Yi Kwang-su to the businessman Kim Sŏng-su. Christian, Buddhist, and Ch'ŏndogyo leaders; youth; and women's groups all actively participated. It had a permanent headquarters with branches in every province and published a monthly journal, *Industrial World* (*Sanŏpkye*). There was an auxiliary women's association, T'osan Aeyong Puinhoe, to assist. The main aim was to encourage people to shop at Korean-owned stores and buy Korean-made products, even if more expensive and of lesser quality. Consumer cooperatives were established as alternatives to the Japanese-dominated commercial markets. The Government-General banned major rallies, especially in Seoul, and censored announcements and pamphlets for nationalist references but otherwise tolerated the movement. The Korean Production Movement rallied people throughout the country and was greeted by great enthusiasm that had not been seen since the March First Movement. From 1923 to 1924 it appeared to be somewhat effective, but then the movement ran into problems. Korean manufacturers could not meet demands for many products, while Japanese merchants were able to weather the campaign and offer lower prices. Furthermore, the colonial authorities began offering subsidies to Korean businessmen, something they had been requesting since 1920, thus weakening their support. Korean merchants also worried about competition from the consumer cooperatives the movement organized. After the initial wave of excitement, public enthusiasm waned and the movement declined. It did not disappear, but was periodically revived. With the more repressive political atmosphere after 1931, its political activities were limited. Still, it survived until 1937, when the organization and its journal were ordered closed.[9] More radical nationalists dismissed the whole movement as led by capitalist collaborators; in any case, its effectiveness was limited.

Moderate nationalists established the Society for the Establishment of a National University (Minnip Taehak Kisŏng Chunbihoe). Koreans had always valued education, but the lack of higher educational opportunities in their own country was very frustrating, especially to members of the elite who were forced to seek it in Japan or elsewhere. A movement in the early 1900s to create a university had not proceeded far. This time the movement was very popular, resulting in a nationwide fund-raising campaign. It was led by Yi Sang-jae and Song Chin-u, editor-in-chief of *Tonga Ilbo*. The society established offices for the fund-raising campaign in provincial cities and sent representatives to Manchuria and the United States. Despite the widespread enthusiasm, the movement was plagued with mismanagement, infighting among chapters, and the withdrawal of radical nationalists, including the All Korean Youth League, from the movement, part of the growing split between moderates and leftists. The troubled campaign suffered perhaps a fatal blow when the Japanese government announced it would establish a Keijō (Seoul) Imperial University by 1926.

In contrast to the moderate nationalists and their program of gradualist reform, a number of Koreans took a more radical view of nationalism. They saw their role less as cultural reformers bringing the masses up to modern standards of civilization than as part of the vanguard of the "people." Under the influence of socialism, especially in its Marxist form, they looked to the common people as embodying the essence of the nation and their own role as leaders of the people. They rejected cooperation with the colonial regime, were suspicious of both the old landowning and the newly emerging Korean entrepreneurial classes, and saw the overthrow of both the colonial regime and the elite as their aim. Most of these radicals in the 1920s became associated with the fledgling Communist movement.

The Korean Communist movement reflected the fractured, geographically dispersed, complex nature of Korean nationalism during the colonial period. The first Communist groups appeared among the exile communities in Siberia that had a large Korean community that became caught up by the Bolshevik Revolution of 1917. The Bolsheviks, seeking support in the region, offered aid to Korean exiles in regaining their independence. In 1918 the first Communist organization was formed in Khabarovsk, the Hanin Sahoe-dang (Korean Peoples Socialist Party), by Yi Tong-hwi (1873–1945). Yi did not have a likely background for a Communist. A major in the royal army of Korea, he resigned in protest in 1905 at the Japanese takeover of Korea and was arrested in 1910 for an alleged involvement in an assassination plot against the Japanese governor-general; after being released he joined the exile community in the Kando region of Manchuria.[10] Shortly afterward, he went to Shanghai to participate in the Korean Provisional Government, becoming its prime minister. About the same time, other more assimilated Koreans in Russia, led by Nam Man-ch'un, formed a Korean section of the Bolshevik Party in the Siberian city of Irkutsk, where they established a military academy. The two Communist groups became rivals. The Irkutsk Communists were critical of Yi Tong-hwi with his Ŭibyŏng (Righteous Army) and Christian past, regarding him as not a true Communist but simply a nationalist who was taking advantage of Soviet assistance. Their attempt to assert control over Yi's group led to an armed clash at Alekseyevsk in Siberia in June 1921 in what was called the "Free City Incident," killing and capturing hundreds of them. The Irkutsk faction became part of the Bolsheviks, with their own Korean regiments in the Red Army. In the 1930s, Stalin, becoming distrustful of the loyalty of the Koreans, disbanded these regiments, and purged Korean army cadres. The Korean community in the Soviet Union no longer played an active role in the nationalist movement, but they would be important in the creation of the North Korean state after 1945.

The domestic Marxist movement was born among students in Japan. In contrast to the moderate nationalist movements, the Communist movement in Korea never attracted prominent cultural figures but mainly consisted of young, educated, but not well-known activists. In 1922, one group of young people, the Friends Society of Tokyo, issued the first known public call for class struggle in Korea. About a month later, the Proletariat League (Musanja Tongmaeng-hoe) was created in Seoul to champion the rights of the working class. A public lecture in Seoul in December of that year drew 1,500 to hear speeches denouncing capitalism.[11] In 1923 some members of the Proletariat League formed the New Thought Study Society (Sin Sasang Yŏng'gu-hoe), with ostensibly all new ideas. On the birthday of Karl Marx, November 19, 1924, it was renamed the Tuesday Society; and on April 17, 1925, the Tuesday Society merged with another group, the North Wind Society, to form the Korean Communist Party (Chosŏn Kongsandang). Most of the group were arrested by the Japanese later that year. A second KCP was organized in 1926, but soon its leaders were arrested as well. A third party was organized in December 1926, but most of these were arrested in January 1928. A fourth attempt that February led to another wave of arrests in August 1928.[12] In December 1928, the Comintern leaders issued the December Theses analyzing the causes of the failures of the Korean Communists. They complained that they consisted of only intellectuals and students, that they were weakened by their factionalism, that they failed to attract industrial workers and poor peasants, and that they needed to develop a clearer understanding of Marxist-Leninist principles.

Meanwhile, secondary students became involved in nationalist protests. A number of student incidents, such as school strikes, occurred in the 1920s. From 1920 to 1926 some 386 recorded school strikes occurred. Many of these, in fact a majority, had anti-Japanese overtones, often directed at teachers thought to be pro-Japanese. An example took place in

May 1927, when some 400 pupils at Sukmyŏng Girls School, a secondary school, went on strike, demanding the dismissal of Japanese administrators. They were joined by the students at Chinmyŏng Girls School. Leftist organizations sometimes infiltrated the student bodies at secondary schools. This happened at the three secondary schools in the provincial city of Kwangju. These schools had histories of student protests. In the fall of 1929, the students at all three went on strike over the alleged mistreatment of female Korean students by Japanese male students. This spread throughout Korea as secondary students in protest boycotted classes and sometimes attacked Japanese students. By the spring of 1930, 54,000 Korean students in 194 schools had joined what had become an anti-Japanese movement. Students demanded the end of police interference in school activities, the release of arrested students, the reinstatement of expelled students, and the reform of the educational system. Student pamphlets with slogans such as "Down with Imperialism" and "Long Live the Proletarian Revolution" indicate the leftist influence in the movement.[13] The movement was crushed by authorities, with many students arrested or expelled. Sporadic student strikes and protests occurred after that date, but these became increasingly difficult with the imposition of a harsher colonial policy after 1931. However, the colonial period left a tradition of student activism that would be taken up again in South Korea after 1945.

Despite the split between the moderates and radicals in the nationalist movement, the two groups united in 1927 to form the Sin'ganhoe (New Shoots Korea Society). The leadership consisted of moderate nationalists, but it was supported by Communists and other leftist groups who gained control over many of its branches. The Sin'ganhoe was a broad-based organization consisting of youth, labor, farmer, intellectual, and women's groups. By 1928, according to nationalist sources, Sin'ganhoe had 143 branches and more than 20,000 members. Korean Communists, having difficulty operating due to constant Japanese repression, found the organization a way to become involved in nationalist activities. Ironically the Japanese found it useful as well, as a means of bringing leftist activities into the open, and therefore they tolerated it. The organization struggled with disputes over whether to support the Kwangju Student Movement in 1929 but survived to 1931. In that year, following Comintern directives, it was dissolved after moderates unsuccessfully fought to save it.[14]

A shift to a more repressive policy by the colonial regime in 1931 meant that open nationalist activities became largely confined to the exile communities. The scattered Korean diaspora was involved in the nationalist movements. Their numbers were small and their activities were largely ineffective, but they influenced the developments in Korea after 1945. Some in Japan joined nationalist groups. There was also an anarchist organization, the Black Comrades Society, whose leader, Pak

Yŏl, attempted to assassinate Crown Prince Hirohito on his wedding day. Police uncovered the plot, and Pak and many members of his group were arrested. Tight police surveillance made such activities increasingly difficult. A special "student section" of the Ministry of Education kept watch on Korean students in Japan. More important were fragmented nationalist groups and individuals located in China, Manchuria, Russia, and the United States. Many of these were Communists, some anarchists, and others, such as Syngman Rhee in Hawaii, were staunchly anticommunist and pro-Western. Communists were the more numerous of the active nationalists outside Korea. As was the case with other exile groups, they were never united under a single leader or organization. Some Korean Communists fought with the Chinese Communist Party. Among them were Kim Chŏng, better known by his revolutionary name, Mu Chŏng, who made the 1934–1935 Long March with Mao Zedong and the other Chinese Communist to their new base at Yanan. When war broke out between China and Japan in 1937 some Koreans joined the anti-Japanese struggle. Some fought with the Guomindang and others with the Chinese Communists. Mu Chŏng formed a Korean military unit with several hundred Koreans that was engaged in battle with the Japanese from 1939. As they found out about this military unit, many Koreans in China joined it. In 1942 it became known as the Korean Voluntary Army. Other Koreans fought with the Chinese Communist–led anti-Japanese guerrilla units that sprang up in Manchuria after its annexation by the Japanese in 1931. Most of these Koreans were drawn from the Korean communities of southern Manchuria just north of the Korean border. One of these guerrilla fighters, who achieved some fame, was the young Kim Il Sung (Kim Il-sŏng, born Kim Sŏng-ju) (1912–1994). Kim Il Sung and the other guerrilla leaders fought in small units of 50 to 100, rarely more than 300. Kim's claim to fame was a successful raid into northern Korea and brief occupation of the Korean town of Poch'ŏnbo in June 1937. Japan began a determined effort to clear the Manchurian border areas of guerrillas in the late 1930s, and succeeded in driving Kim and the other guerrillas out of Manchuria into the Soviet Union by 1940. There the ex-Chinese and Korean Manchurian guerrillas were organized into a brigade of the Soviet Army but saw no action during the war.

The largest non-Communist nationalist resistance movement was the Korean Provisional Government. Originally based in Shanghai, during World War II it was headquartered in Chungking (Chongqing). It had a small force of troops, the Korean Restoration Army (Han'guk Kwangbokkun). Under the leadership of Kim Ku (1876–1949), it had about 3,000 or so resistance fighters. But this was still a modest-sized group. Like the Communists, the non-Communist nationalist resistance movements were fragmented and ineffective.

Both internally and among the exile groups, a strong ideological divide split Korean nationalism. This division between the moderate "cultural" nationalists and the more radical, mostly but not exclusively Marxist nationalists contributed to the radically different directions the two Koreas would take after 1945.

ECONOMIC DEVELOPMENT

Korea's economy grew considerably under colonial rule, although the extent to which the colonial period laid the foundations for its economic transformation after 1945 is controversial. The record is complex and ambiguous. Japan did build an elaborate infrastructure and industrial base in Korea and modernized agriculture, but it did so in ways that often minimized the benefits for Korea and created structural problems. And at the end of colonial rule, Korea still remained mostly rural, with the majority of Koreans very poor, arguably, in some ways more impoverished than at the start of colonial rule.

The period around 1919–1920 marked an important turning point in South Korea's economic development. Japan emerged at the end of World War I from a debtor to a creditor nation. Capital-rich Japanese companies now sought to invest in Korea and pressured the Japanese government to abolish the tariffs in 1920 that had largely closed Korea to investment. The rice riots that broke out in Japan during 1918 protesting the soaring prices of this staple also acted as an incentive to promote rice production in Korea. The period was also a turning point because merchants and landlords in Korea who had accumulated capital began to actively participate in modern industry. The Kabo Reforms ended the legal prohibition of retired government officials who were members of the landowning *yangban* elite from participating in commerce. More significantly, attitudes were changing. By the early twentieth century, the traditional disdain of the elite for business was dissipating. Instead, many formed societies for the promotion of industry and commercial activity. Most Korean intellectuals and reformers saw commerce and industry as a source of national strength, and regarded Korea's traditional disapproval of these occupations as a source of its weakness and backwardness.

Among the pioneer Korean-owned industries was the Kyŏngsŏng Cord Company, founded in 1910 by the aristocratic Yun family and becoming a joint-stock company in 1911.[15] Also prominent were the Koch'ang Kims from Kobu (now Koch'ang) County in the rich rice-growing lands of North Chŏlla Province in southeast Korea. An old *yangban* family, the Kims took advantage of their location near the port of Kunsan to expand their holdings and produce rice for export. To this they added rice mill-ing and other subsidiary businesses. Already by 1920 they emerged as a wealthy and prominent family. The leading members were Kim Sŏng-su and his brother Yŏn-su, both Japanese educated, who combined the traditional role of the scholar-gentry, being active in intellectual, cultural, and political affairs, with the new role as entrepreneurs. Their Kyŏngbang Textile Company became one of the largest and most successful Korean-owned industries. Other prominent entrepreneurs were Min Kyu-sik, of the Korean-owned Hanil Bank, and Pak Hŭng-sik (1903–1994), who owned a chain of retail stores including the Hwasin department store in Seoul. Pak, of humble background, became the richest man in Korea by the 1940s. This small Korean entrepreneur class worked closely with their Japanese counterparts. They needed access to Japanese capital, permits for establishing shops and factories, and access to Japanese suppliers. A significant point of contact was the Keijō (Seoul) Chamber of Commerce and Industry (Keishō) established in 1888 to serve the Japanese business community. Korean participation became mandatory when, in 1915, the Government-General prohibited separate chambers of commerce for Koreans. This small class of modern entrepreneurs, fluent in Japanese and accustomed to working closely with their Japanese counterparts, formed the basis of South Korea's business community after liberation.[16]

Despite the emergence of a Korean entrepreneur class, the economy was dominated by Japanese firms. These worked closely with the Government-General, which provided it subsidies and loans through state-owned banks. All of Japan's major *zaibatsu* (industrial-financial conglomerates) became involved in Korea. The Noguchi *zaibatsu*, founded by Noguchi Jun, was based entirely in Korea. The Nippon Chisso plant in Hŭngnam was owned by Noguchi's Chōsen Nitrogenouso Fertilizer Company, one of the largest chemical complexes in the world.

To accompany this industrialization, an impressive infrastructure was built. Before 1910, the Japanese completed the Pusan-Ŭiju railway. After 1910, railway construction continued and was coordinated with the development of the Japanese-owned South Manchurian Railway Company in northeast China, which took over the management of Korea's railroads in 1933. By 1945, Korea had one of the most extensive rail networks in Asia. Most of the cities and ports in Korea were linked by rail. The total kilometers of track was a quarter that of Japan's well-developed rail system, but considering that Korea had only half the area and a third the population of Japan, this is quite impressive. Yet it carried only a tenth as much freight and less than 3 percent as many passengers as the Japanese rail system. This is because the rail network was built as much for military purposes as for economic ones. To a large measure, it was designed to facilitate the movement of troops in Korea and, especially after 1930, to link Korea to the empire on the Asian mainland. It was, however, a stimulus to economic development.[17] There was considerable mining, mostly in the northern part of the country: gold, silver, iron, tungsten, and coal were all mined. American interests were involved in the gold mines until the Japanese bought them out in 1939; otherwise mining was largely done by Japanese companies. Originally the mines primarily served to supply Japan with raw materials, but by the late 1930s much of the output of the mines supported Korea's own growing iron and steel, chemical, and other industries.

During the 1930s, with the Japanese conquest of Manchuria and then the invasion of China, the industrialization of Korea accelerated. New industrial cities sprang up in the north. Najin, a village of 500 people in 1927, had a population of 26,000 a decade later, while Ch'ŏngjin grew from a village of 100 in 1900 to a city of 72,353 in 1938, when it was the leading port on the Sea of Japan.[18] The economic activity during the colonial period had some unfortunate ecological consequences. A particularly tragic development was the deforestation of the country. A combination of aggressive logging by Japanese companies and the pressure of a growing population for firewood and land for subsistence farming resulted in a denuded mountainous landscape. Efforts by the authorities to reforest lands were not successful. A similar tragedy afflicted the nation's fisheries. Fishing, as always in Korea, was a major economic activity. Koreans had continued to rely on fishing as an important source of food, but most of the seafood caught was by larger Japanese commercial operators who through overfishing depleted the country's fisheries.

MODERNITY AND SOCIAL CHANGE

While Koreans have often been portrayed in modern histories as either passive victims of imperialism or engaged in a nationalist struggle against their Japanese oppressors, it is perhaps more accurate to see them as embracing elements of change and taking advantage of the opportunities available to them. Colonial-era Koreans were presented two versions of what it means to be modern: Japan's own version and the one from the West. If the Soviet Union is considered, it could be argued that Koreans were presented with at least three ways a society and individuals could be modern and successful. Koreans eagerly embraced them all. Intellectuals were quick to adopt liberal democratic ideals from Western Europe and America, socialist ideas from the Soviet Union, and concepts of state and society from Japan, while people of all backgrounds moved into new occupations and adapted to new institutions.

Educational development under colonial rule provides a good example of such adaptation. Koreans were hardly reluctant to accept new styles of schooling, seeing it as a way of advancing in a changing society. Education was flourishing by the last two decades of the Chosŏn period, from 1890 to 1910. Hundreds of new schools were established by Koreans and by foreign missionaries, while the state was beginning to create a national system of public education. The colonial regime sought to gain control over schooling and to channel it toward serving Japanese aims—primarily to provide basic schooling for unskilled and semiskilled laborers. In 1911 the Japanese administration created a new educational system that provided up to fourteen years of schooling for Japanese residents but limited public education for most Koreans to four years of "common school" with a few four-year "higher common schools" mostly focused on vocation education. According to the Educational Ordinance, the purpose of the educational system for Koreans was "to give the younger generations of Koreans such moral character and general knowledge as will make them loyal subjects of Japan, at the same time enabling them to cope with the present condition existing in the Peninsula."[19] Tight restrictions were placed over the hundreds of private modern-style schools that mushroomed in the early twentieth century. Many Korean-run schools were forced to close because they were unable to provide the education in the Japanese language the colonial authorities required.

With the new more liberal "culture policy," a major reform of educational policy took place in 1922 that extended elementary education from four to six (sometimes five) years and secondary education to five years, while adding a three-year college preparatory or advanced technical school. Expansion of the school system, however, proceeded very gradually. As late as the mid-1930s less than one in six Korean children of elementary school age were enrolled in officially recognized schools. The pace of educational expansion failed to meet the public needs. In response, Koreans established hundreds of unlicensed schools; many of these were night schools taught by young graduates of public or mission-run educational institutions. Traditional village schools known as *sŏdang* flourished; generally they consisted of little more than children meeting in the house of a literate but untrained teacher. Although maintaining a more traditional curriculum, they remained the principal form of schooling for most Korean children; in fact, these village schools increased in number, with enrollment peaking in the 1930s. The increase in these traditional schools and hundreds of other unlicensed institutions reported to be supplying basic education indicated a rising demand for schooling that the deliberate pace of educational expansion pursued by the Japanese was not satisfying. But unlicensed private schools could not issue certificates, and *sŏdang* were, as far as a means of social advancement was concerned, dead ends, since only a modern-style education could provide opportunities for success in the new society.

Frustration at the gradualist approach to educational development was felt most keenly by members of the elite and the small but growing urban middle class. A central issue for upper-class and upwardly mobile Korean families was higher education. Keijō Imperial University, established in 1925, remained the sole university in Korea until after 1945. The faculty was overwhelmingly Japanese, and the student body contained a disproportionate number of Japanese students. The Japanese colonial authorities did not monopolize schooling in Korea. Private schools, many operated by American missionaries or by American-trained Koreans, survived. Since the Japanese state invested little in higher education for Koreans, private institutions were important at that level. In 1935, 73.6 percent of postsecondary education was carried out by private schools and non-university institutions. These private colleges were regarded with suspicion by Japanese authorities, and most were eventually closed down. Overall, the Japanese record on providing opportunities for higher education for Koreans compares unfavorably with the British in India or the Americans in the Philippines. Because the expansion of higher education was too slow to meet demand, an increasing number of Korean students sought schooling in Japan. In 1925, 13.8 percent of Korean students in higher education were in Japan. By 1935, the figure was 47.3 percent, and in 1940, 61.5 percent. In 1942, there were 6,771 Koreans attending institutions of higher education in Japan, but only 4,234 in Korea. Also impressive was the number of Koreans attending secondary schools in Japan; in 1940, 71.6 percent of the 20,824 Korean students in Japan were enrolled at secondary schools. The Japanese government gave little assistance or encouragement to this educational exodus, and the higher living costs were a heavy burden for most. Yet rapidly increasing numbers of Koreans were overcoming linguistic handicaps and making financial sacrifices to achieve education because in their own country the rising demand for education was outstripping opportunities at all levels.

Limited access to the higher reaches of education was paralleled by the limited opportunities for Koreans to serve in administration and teaching. The bureaucracy remained dominated by Japanese. In 1922, 29 percent of the instructors in public schools were Japanese; ten years later, 30 percent of all teachers in public schools were Japanese, a figure that rose to 44 percent in 1938. This created serious problems after liberation in 1945, when these teachers returned to Japan. But the most serious problem for many individual Koreans and their families was being blocked from taking the traditional route to honor and privilege, advanced education, and appointment to government office. This frustration was aggravated by wartime policies after 1938 that further limited the number of schools of higher education, even as it expanded primary education, and that redirected the curriculum away from literary to less prestigious technical education and vocational training. The result was an unsatisfied desire for schooling at all levels, but especially at the higher levels, that became evident immediately after liberation in both North and South Korea. The Japanese may have established a comprehensive modern education system, but the popularity of mission schools and of village schools during the colonial era suggest, as Seong-cheol Oh and Ki-seok Kim have pointed out, that Japanese policies may not have been crucial to the expansion of education.[20]

The rising demand for modern-style schooling reflected the social changes in Korea. The country's old order began to crumble with the Kabo Reforms of 1894–1895 that legally abolished the rigid and heredi-tary social structure of Chosŏn-dynasty Korea. It accelerated during the colonial period with the rise of an industrial working class and a new middle class, the emergence of social movements among women and outcastes, and acceleration of social mobility. The new industrial working class grew slowly at first. Although there was an increase in industrial production in the 1920s, as late as 1928, 80.6 percent of the labor force was employed in agriculture, while only 2.1 percent was in mining and factory work.[21] In the 1930s, the numbers grew dramatically. There were 99,000 factory workers in 1933 and 390,000 in 1943. The number of mine workers during the same period grew from 70,000 to 280,000. Along with transportation and construction workers, the Korean working class num-bered about 1,750,000 in 1943. The industrial workforce included large numbers of women, generally confined to menial and repetitive sectors of industry such as silk reeling and cotton fabric production. Female la-borers were mostly young, unmarried girls working to help their families and to save for marriage.

This growth in industry is reflected in the urban population. Between 1935 and 1944 the urban population (living in cities over 20,000) went from 7 percent to 13.2 percent of the population. This, it should be pointed out, was far less than in Japan, which in the early 1940s was about 42 per-cent urban; it was, in fact, about the same as Japan in 1908. The population of Seoul increased nearly three times from 1925 to 1942, from 342,000 to 1,114,000. The greatest increase in the labor class was in Kyŏnggi Prov-ince, the area around Seoul, and in the northeastern Hamgyŏng Province. In general, industry and mining were concentrated in the northern areas while the southern provinces remained overwhelmingly agricultural. Japanese workers in Korea made up about 10 to 11 percent of the work-force until 1937. With the huge increase in Korean workers, they declined to only around 7 percent of the workforce in 1943.[22] Japanese were mostly skilled workers and were paid much better than Koreans. However, by the early 1940s an increasingly larger number of Koreans entered more skilled positions. Korean workers enjoyed few protections, since there was little regulation of working conditions and business practices. They also suffered from sharp disparities in wages with Japanese workers in the same plants and firms. Korean workers in the employ of Japanese firms not only made much less than Japanese workers but also had wages well below those of Japan's other major colony, Taiwan. In 1937, Japanese workers earned 2 yen a day, Taiwanese 1 yen, and Koreans .66 yen.

Yet Korean workers, rather than being passive victims, often showed a surprising militancy participating in labor agitation. After 1920 labor strikes increased. Most of the strikes involved day laborers on the docks, on construction projects, and in other nonfactory jobs. The most famous was the Wŏnsan General Strike that took place in 1929. Communists following Comintern directives made serious efforts to organize "red" labor unions during 1930 to 1931 with some success. Among these was the Hamhŭng Committee of the Chosŏn Red Labor Unions created in February 1931. But the police arrested more than 1,800 members of this and other red unions in the early 1930s. By the mid-1930s labor union activity continued only tenuously as an underground movement. In 1938, the government launched the Campaign for National Protection Corps of Industrial Workers (Sanpō); this included a labor-management council to make sure all worked together for the war effort. These wartime industrial relations programs, Soon-won Park has argued, profoundly shaped later South Korean labor practices. The politicization of labor movements in South Korea, the intervention into labor-management relations by the government, and the prevalence of company unions were all influenced by wartime colonial practice.[23]

A small modern middle class emerged in colonial Korea. This class included professionals such as teachers, doctors, accountants, businessmen, bankers, and civil servants in the colonial bureaucracy. More than any other group, they were a group open to new ideas and often eagerly embraced the modern world. They wore Western-style clothes; sent their children to modern schools; and read newspapers, magazines, and modern literature by foreign writers in translation or by Korean writers such as Yi Kwang-su. Many came from yangban backgrounds, some were from the old chungin class, but many were of humble family origins. The latter represented the new social mobility in Korea. A key to their new status was education, and access to education would be a central concern to all those who aspired to or sought to maintain this status. Members of the middle class were urban, cosmopolitan, and open to new ideas. The members of the newly emerging middle class may have made up no more than 5 to 10 percent of the population, but they were to form the political, economic, and cultural leadership of colonial Korea.

Few social changes marked a greater break with tradition than those that concerned women. Many Korean women embraced new ideas and opportunities presented by a modernizing society. Korean progressives in the late nineteenth century saw the humble status of Korean women as symptomatic of the country's low level of civilization. The Kabo Reforms had abolished some of the legal restrictions on women. They also abolished child marriages and ended the prohibition on widows to remarry. The issue of establishing greater equality for women, begun by the tiny number of Koreans exposed to the outside world in the 1890s, was embraced by much of the intellectual community in colonial times. Many Koreans blamed the Confucian concept of *namjon yŏbi* (revere men, despise women) as emblematic of both the country's backwardness and its past uncritical adoption of Chinese customs. Of particular concern was the exclusion of women from formal education. They noted that girls attended schools in Western countries and that Japan had drawn up plans in the 1870s to make basic education universal and compulsory for girls as well as boys. An early proponent of women's education was Sŏ Chae-p'il, whose editorial in the *Tongnip sinmun* on April 21, 1896, called for equal education for men and women to promote social equality and strengthen the nation. In another editorial in September that year, he argued that gender relations were a mark of a nation's civilization. Conservatives in the late Chosŏn government were less sympathetic to the need for women's education. A petition to the king by a group of women from *yangban* families to establish a girls' school was ignored.[24] Women's education was established by American missionaries, not Koreans. After an initial slow start, many families began sending their daughters to these new schools, and the enthusiasm for education among Korean women was commented on by foreign missionaries. Women graduates of these schools became active in patriotic organizations, and thousands of women participated in the March First Movement. It was only, however, during the 1920s that the women's movement became a major force in Korea. One of its important figures was Kim Maria. Educated in Tokyo, she formed in April 1919 the Taehan Aeguk Puinhoe (Korean Patriotic Women's Society), an organization to promote national self-determination. The organization worked with the Korean Provisional Government in Shanghai and in 1920 claimed some 2,000 members. The activities of this and other, mostly Christian, women's groups helped win respect for women among Korean intellectuals.

In the 1920s men and women participated in discussions about the role of women and gender relations. Feminists included Kim Wŏn-ju, who published *Sin yŏja* (*New Woman*); artist Na Hye-sŏk (1896–1948), who wrote for *Yŏja kye* (*Women's World*); and the poet Kim Myŏng-sun. Some members of this small class of women led lives daringly defiant of tradition. They wore Western-style clothes with short skirts and bobbed hair, socialized in public, advocated free love and the right to divorce, and rejected the confinement of women to the roles of housewife and mother.

These ideas, however, were too radical for Koreans, including male intellectuals. Moderate nationalists called for an educated, healthy woman whose role in society was very much like the "wise mother, good wife" (hyŏnmo yangch'ŏ) ideal promoted by the Japanese government; meanwhile, leftist male nationalists argued for the need to subordinate gender issues to those of class.

Two individuals exemplify this new small class of "modern" women. One is Kim Hwal-lan, known to Westerners as Helen Kim. Born in 1899 to Christian parents in Inch'ŏn, she attended mission schools, became active in the YWCA, went on to Boston University, and received a PhD from Teachers College of Columbia University in 1930. After returning, she became president of Ewha College, the most prestigious school of higher education for women in Korea, a position she held from 1939 to 1961, except for a brief period (1944 to 1945) when the school was shut down by the Japanese. Pak Kyŏng-wŏn (1901–1933), daughter of a rich farmer, attended an industrial arts school in Japan and took a job as a technician in the silk reeling industry, an industry dominated by women workers. She then returned to Japan to learn to become a driver, a rarity for a woman, and then became one of the few women to attend an aviation school. Korea's first woman aviator, she won a number of flying competitions in Japan before perishing in a flight back to her home in Korea.[25]

The women's movement was quite political, since most writers linked the liberation of women with national liberation. While this may have made the belief in women's rights and equality more acceptable to educated Koreans, it meant that feminists subordinated their own social agenda to the national political agenda. It also meant that the women's movement followed the general split between moderate, gradualist reformers and radical leftists that characterized most political and intellectual activity from the early 1920s. Moderate women reformers were associated with the YWCA and various church and moderate patriotic associations, while some thirty women with socialist and Communist leanings established a more radical group, Chosŏn Yŏsŏng Tonguhoe (Korean Women's Friendship Society) in 1924. As part of the united front, in 1927, moderate and radical women worked together to organize the Kŭnuhoe (Friends of the Rose of Sharon). By 1929, the Kŭnuhoe had 2,970 women, including 260 in Tokyo.[26]

The colonial legacy for Korean women was mixed. In many ways the "wise mother, good wife" concept promoted by the Japanese and embraced by much of society reinforced the traditional ideas of a sharply defined domestic "inner" sphere for women and "outer" sphere of public life for men. Yet as Sonja Kim writes, this domestic space for women was "infused with new conceptualizations of equality, rights, and humanity."[27] For the vast majority of Korean women, their traditional subordinate social status remained unchanged, but the emergence of a small number of politically active and assertive women among the educated was an important precursor of more radical changes that would take place after 1945.

Another marginalized group that took advantage of new opportunities were the *paekchŏng*, a low-status hereditary group in Korea who lived in their own villages. While most were farmers, they also worked in the "unclean" professions such as butchers, leather workers, and sometimes executioners, as well as other less obviously undesirable jobs such as ferrymen and wicker craftsmen. Very much like the untouchables (or *dalits*) of India or the *eta* (or *burakumin*) of Japan, they were socially shunned by ordinary citizens, possessing a legal status as "mean people" (*ch'ŏnmin*) below the ordinary peasants or even slaves. They were not allowed to wear the clothes and hats of nonoutcastes, and marriage between *paekchŏng* and commoners was legally prohibited, although it did occur. Even their names distinguished them, since they were not allowed to include Chinese characters with noble meanings. The status was legally abolished in the Kabo Reforms, but this did not result in any effective change in their position, since their legal rights were ignored. During the colonial period many *paekchŏng* became workers in state slaughterhouses, where, although shunned, they became exposed to new ideas and lifestyles. A few managed to achieve a modern education and some prosperity. In April 1923, *paekchŏng* social activists formed the Hyŏngp'yŏngsa (Equalization Society) in Chinju. This became a national organization that at its peak in the 1930s claimed over 400,000 members, most probably an inflated figure. It campaigned for the end of discrimination in the schools, workplaces, and society at large; the end of segregated grave sites; and their inclusion in local meetings. As was so often the case, education was a major concern. Ordinary Koreans sought to exclude them from public schools; an example was the Ikchang incident in 1924, in which non-*paekchŏng* protested about their children sharing classrooms with outcaste members.[28] Despite deep-seated prejudices, their social status improved, and during the social upheavals of the 1930s through the 1950s they became assimilated into the general population. The ferment among the outcastes, like the growing movement among women, reflected a change in the old hierarchical social order of Korea and the growth of egalitarian ideals that would emerge so strongly after 1945 and shape the history of North and South Korea.

RURAL SOCIETY

Korea remained an agricultural land. During most of the colonial period, three out of four Koreans were farmers. One of the first major tasks of the new colonial administration was to carry out an accurate survey of land. Korea was an agricultural society; the great majority of the population consisted of farmers, and wealth derived from agricultural rents was the principal economic basis of the *yangban* class. Agriculture was the basis of the colonial order as well. Tokyo regarded Korea as an important supplier of food, a rice producer for an industrializing Japan. The Korean state had derived much of its revenue from taxing farmers. This was true of the colonial regime as well but with a difference. Traditionally the Korean state taxed agricultural production, the colonial government taxed land. The importance of Korea as an agricultural producer and the reliance on a land tax made the need for a careful survey and codification of land-ownership a high priority of the colonial government. The Korean state undertook what became known as the Kwangmu Land Survey from 1898 to 1902, but it was highly unreliable, so the Government-General carried out a comprehensive survey of land from 1910 to 1918. With a thorough-ness that Korea had not seen, at least in recent times, every plot of land was carefully recorded and classified according to type, such as dry field and wet paddy land. Each plot was also graded by productivity.

The land survey has become a subject of controversy. Many ordinary Korean farmers were unable to produce the formal documentation neces-sary to show ownership of their land. Many peasants held partial own-ership or certain customary squatters or tenant rights that could not be documented. No doubt many were simply confused by the new unfamil-iar legal procedures and did not register their lands. It is widely believed that as a result of these problems many Korean farmers lost their lands to the Japanese. However, recent research indicates that while many poor Koreans lost land or the customary use of lands, the chief beneficiaries were members of the old *yangban* class, who were able to take advantage of the survey to increase their landholdings. Indeed, Carter Eckert has described this period as part of the "halcyon era for the Korean landlord class" that began in the late nineteenth century.

But the Government-General became the largest landowner. It took possession of the lands owned by the Korean state and the Yi royal house-hold—in short, all public lands including forests and riverbeds. In 1930, the colonial government owned 40 percent of all land. Japanese individu-als and corporations also acquired a great deal of land. Some of this was purchased from the Government-General at bargain prices as part of an effort to encourage Japanese settlement in Korea. As early as 1907, Tokyo created a semigovernmental Oriental Development Company for the pur-pose of acquiring land and then offering it to Japanese farmers at bargain prices if they would settle in Korea, but few came.

With the industrialization of Korea in the 1930s agriculture's share of the economy declined. Yet the great majority of Koreans were still peasants. While some land did fall into Japanese hands, most landlords were Koreans, generally from the former *yangban*, who benefited from the rationing of land because it provided opportunities to consolidate their holdings. The majority of landlords owned less than 50 *chŏngbo* (123 acres) and these were mostly Koreans. In 1942, of landlords with more than 50 *chŏngbo*, 2,173 were Korean, 1,219 Japanese. Only among the very largest landowners, possessing more than 500 acres, did Japanese outnumber Koreans: 184 Japanese and 116 Koreans.[29]

Most peasants worked for landlords as tenant farmers. But the picture is complicated, since tenants sometimes owned some land that was insufficient to support their families, so they also served as tenants on additional fields. One report found that 538,000 farmers owned some land and rented some; 1,073,000 were tenants; and 971,000 were sharecroppers. About 2.5 percent of families owned 64 percent of the farmland. Overall, the majority of Korean farmers owned no land or not enough to support their families. Tenancy rates in the agriculturally rich southwest approached 80 percent. Their life was hard. On average, half the harvest went to the landowner. Tenant conditions were made more difficult by the tendency of landowners to make the cultivators pay for the costs of irrigation projects, fertilizers, tools, and seeds. Farmers were forced to borrow and often were victims of usury. Population growth also increased pressure on the land and drove up rents. Land taxes, which before the 1930s were the main source of revenue for the colonial administration, were also burdensome. Consequently, many Koreans moved into the mountains, where they cleared public forestlands to create fire fields. Land would be burned, a crop then sown, and then the farmer would move on to another field. It was a precarious, hard, uncertain way to survive and contributed to deforestation.

A major change was the commercialization of agriculture, a change that began with the opening of Korean ports after 1876 and accelerated during colonial rule. Farmers grew for the market, which often meant that rice farmers could not eat their own rice. The per capita consumption of rice actually declined even though rice production increased 140 percent from 1910 to 1939.[30] Many Koreans ate millet, mixed rice and millet, or other less desirable grains. In the 1930s, Korea imported millet to feed itself even while it was exporting rice to Japan. For a people for whom the words *meal* and *rice* are synonymous, this was a bitter hardship. Farmers had always suffered from the unpredictability of the weather. As farming became commercial, the fluctuating market prices and the often unexpected changes in government agricultural policies added to their worries. Changing market prices contributed to the growing indebtedness that burdened both landlords and peasants. Indebtedness increased with the Great Depression, forcing many owners to mortgage their cultivated lands.

Landlord-tenant disputes were frequent. In the late 1910s and 1920s there were many well-organized, reform-minded peasant groups aimed at rent reduction and securing tenancy tenure. Many of these were successful. But an agriculture depression in the late 1920s followed by the Great Depression made the position of peasants less secure. Rural Korea was hit hard by the Depression; the price of rice, the most important cash crop, fell in 1931 to 39 percent of its 1925 level.[31] Landlords, many also facing debt, began evicting tenants. Tenant disputes became more defensive, with many arguing for their right to subsist, and in a traditional Confucian manner calling upon the benevolence of the landlord. These were less successful, and many landless farmers immigrated to Manchuria, to Japan, or to the new industrial centers in the north looking for work.[32] A number of Red Peasant Unions were organized, especially in the northern part of the country. Although linked with the Communists and often brutally suppressed by the Japanese, recent studies show these to have been more concerned with local tenancy disputes than with fomenting revolution. Nonetheless, a tradition of peasant radicalism began, especially strong in the north, as well as a legacy of bitterness and frustration among tenant farmers that reemerged after the end of colonial rule in 1945.

Alarmed by peasant unrest, the Government-General in the 1930s attempted to ameliorate conditions. It enacted the Arbitration Ordinance of 1932 and the Agricultural Lands Ordinance of 1934, which attempted to reduce landlord-tenant disputes through government intervention, sometimes at the expense of the landlords. In 1932, the colonial government inaugurated the Rural Revitalization Campaign aimed at improving the economic conditions of the peasantry, made worse by the Depression, by reducing debt and promoting self-sufficiency. Modeled on a similar program to aid the plight of Japanese peasants, the campaign focused on gathering information and finding ways to better utilize labor and get villages to work together for mutual assistance. Local youths, both men and women, with some schooling, and those between the ages of eighteen and twenty-five were recruited as village leaders to promote rural improvements; 9,000 were trained between 1936 and 1940. This program achieved only modest success, but it proved useful after 1937 as part of the general mobilization of the Korean population for the war effort.[33]

All the commercialization of Korean agriculture and the various programs for rural development might be misleading. Despite the commercialization of agriculture, in many ways life for the majority of Koreans living in villages did not change radically, at least not until the 1930s. Customary dress, diet, and habits of everyday life remained the same. Much of the countryside was still economically and socially dominated by *yangban*, although they now often lived in the more exciting world of the cities, leaving stewards behind to manage their properties. When the colonial period ended, the common farmers revealed themselves to be restless, seeking to get out of indebtedness and tenancy.

WARTIME COLONIALISM, 1931–1945

Korea's colonial experience changed profoundly after 1931. Two aspects of this change deeply impacted Korea's historical development. One was a great uprooting of people. Massive dislocations took place by the wartime mobilization. Koreans were uprooted from their homes, either voluntarily or by compulsion, and they migrated to the industrial cities of the north, to Manchuria, to Japan, or to other parts of the empire to supply labor needs. Few Korean families were not affected by this mobilization and dislocation. The other feature of wartime colonial rule was Japan's effort to forcibly assimilate the Korean people, to remake them into Japanese.

The relatively liberal policies inaugurated by the colonial authorities after 1919 were replaced by a reassertion of a harsher, more repressive rule. The crackdown on Korean cultural, social, and political activities came in three steps: in 1926, in 1931, and in 1937. The Government-General began a tightening of freedom in 1926. Partly this reflected worries about Communism in the home country that resulted in the 1925 Peace Preservation Law, which gave domestic police in Japan greater authority to root out radicals. Authorities also feared a repeat of the March First demonstrations. In June 1926, the funeral of Sunjong, the last Chosŏn monarch, resulted in widespread demonstrations known as the June 10 Incident. Soon there was a crackdown on political activities; many suspected leftists were arrested and many publications shut down. The Korean press would never be as free again. A concern of the police was the effort by leftists to organize tenant farmers and labor unions. The police became increasingly effective in undermining efforts to establish these unions.

While 1926 saw a tightening of Japanese control over Korea, a much more significant change occurred in 1931. The Great Depression hit Japan hard in 1930 and tilted Japanese politics away from the more liberal and pro-Western-minded to those who advocated a more ultranationalist, militarist direction, and who viewed the Western powers, especially Britain and the United States, more suspiciously. As military and ultranationalist circles gained influence in Japan, the country resumed its imperialist expansion in Asia with a new vigor. In September 1931, the Japanese Kwantung Army created an incident as an excuse to seize control over the vast northeast Chinese region of Manchuria. In 1932, Tokyo formed a nominally independent state of Manchukuo, but the new territory was controlled by the Japanese Army and became an agricultural and industrial base for further expansion into China. The new orientation of Japan away from cooperation with the West and toward imperial expansion in Asia greatly impacted Korea. Korea was now a link between Japan and Manchuria and a strategic base for the further expansion of the Japanese Empire. To implement changes in colonial administration in view of Korea's new position in the empire, Tokyo appointed a new governor-general, the army general Ugaki Kazushige, in 1931. His policy was to mobilize Korea for the benefit of the empire by increasing the production of food and other needed products. As Japan moved toward greater economic self-sufficiency within its empire and less reliance on world trade, which had greatly contracted with the Great Depression, its colonies became a more significant source of raw materials, investments, and trade. The colonial authorities made efforts to mediate landlord-tenant disputes, to stabilize the countryside, and to increase rice production for exports. Korean rice exports, however, were depressing prices of the rice production of the Japanese, and from 1933, the Government-General began an agricultural diversification program. Agricultural production shifted away from food to fabrics under the slogan "cotton in the south, sheep in the north."

With the outbreak of war between Japan and China in 1937, colonial rule took a radical turn toward mass mobilization of the Korean people for the war effort. The Government-General began to shut down Korean organizations of all types. In their place were a large number of state-sponsored organizations designed to control the activities of the population and direct them toward the war effort. In 1938, for example, it formed the Korean Federation of Youth Organizations as an umbrella organization to control and utilize all the country's youth groups. The authorities ran Local Youth Leadership Seminars and Training Institutes for Children's Organizations. Writers were organized into the All Korean Writers Federation, and there were similar nationwide associations for laborers, tenant farmers, and fishermen. Among the other organizations that the colonial authorities established were the Korean Defense Association, the Association for the Study of Policy Dealing with the Critical Situation, and the Korean Association for Imperial Rule Assistance. The colonial government established a Korean League for General Mobilization of the National Spirit in 1937 with branches in every county and township. In 1938, it created another all-embracing organization, the Korean Anticommunist Association, which also had branches in every province. There were local offices in police stations and associated groups in villages, factories, and other workplaces. Almost every Korean became associated with some mass organization. Beginning in September 1939, the first day of each month was Rising Asia Service Day, on which people were required to perform tasks for the sake of developing the new Asia.[34]

In 1940, the entire colony was organized into 350,000 Neighborhood Patriotic Associations, each with ten households. These became the basic units for collections of contributions, imposition of labor service, maintenance of local security, and rationing.

Education became highly militarized and regimented. Compulsory military drills were introduced to all middle and higher-level schools. Political rallies became a part of schooling, as did mass mobilization of Korean youth for the war effort. In incremental stages, the colonial government brought the students into the war. In April 1938, the Japanese government organized a Special Student Volunteers unit for selected Korean students who wanted to participate in military duty. Then in May 1943, the state permitted all Korean students to volunteer for service in the army, and in October of that year for the navy. Because the numbers volunteering proved to be modest, the state made registration for military service compulsory in November 1943.[35] In October 1940, all student organizations automatically became branches of the Citizen's Total Mobilization League. Students found their time increasingly occupied by extracurricular activities, such as collecting metal for the war effort and attending patriotic rallies. College students were sent to the countryside to explain the war effort to farmers and rural folk. In the early 1940s, the school term was shortened and students of secondary schools were required to work on military construction projects. After 1942, many students were conscripted to work in Japan, while at home the *kinrōtai*, student labor groups, were formed to do "voluntary" work such as building airstrips and defense works. By the spring of 1945, virtually all classroom instruction above the elementary level was suspended and students were fully involved in labor and military service.

In 1938 Japan set up a Korean Special Volunteer Soldier System for Koreans to enlist in the war effort. But the Japanese felt ambivalent about Koreans fighting in the Imperial forces, which in part reflected a continual contempt for Koreans. Only 17,000 out of 800,000 applicants were accepted over the next five years.[36] A few Koreans were admitted into the Japanese Military Academy in Tokyo during the 1930s and early 1940s, and a larger number into the Manchurian Military Academy. Although the total number of Korean officers in the Japanese Army was small, they were to provide the nucleus for the officer corps of the postwar South Korean Army. Most Koreans who joined or were conscripted into the Japanese Army did labor duty on airstrips or served as prison guards.

An extreme form of coercion was the comfort women, or comfort girls. These were young Korean girls who were either recruited or forcibly enrolled as sex slaves to serve the Japanese troops. The so-called comfort girls included Filipinas and Chinese, but most were Koreans. Many of these girls were recruited under false pretenses. They or their parents were told that they were to be given well-paying jobs. In practice, they were treated miserably. After the war, these girls returned home disgraced and were forced to hide their past or live lives as unmarried and unwanted women. Between 100,000 and 200,000 Koreans became comfort women. One example was Mun Ok-ju, an eighteen-year-old woman from a poor family of casual laborers in Taegu, in southwestern Korea, who was offered "a good job in a restaurant," by two civilian recruiters. Lured by the promise of a good salary to support her family, she went along with a group of seventeen other young women between the ages of fifteen and twenty-one who were shipped off to Burma, where she "serviced" thirty men a day under conditions of virtual imprisonment. Five of the girls in her group died or committed suicide.[37]

The abuse of the comfort women has become one of the most contentious issues in colonial history. In many ways it symbolizes the brutality and exploitation of Japanese colonialism at its worst. It was only one way Koreans were victimized. Koreans also suffered from Allied bombing while working in Japan, for example. Among the more than 2 million Koreans working in wartime Japan, at least 10,000 died from the atomic bombs on Hiroshima and Nagasaki.[38]

FORCED ASSIMILATION

During World War II a vast, unprecedented experiment in mass assimilation began. The new governor-general, Minami Jirō (1936–1942), pledged to end discrimination and promote reconciliation between Japan and Korea under the slogans "Japan and Korea as one body" (*Nai-Sen ittai*) and "harmony between Japan and Korea" (*Nissen yūwa*). All Koreans were required to register at Shinto shrines, even though this was an alien religion to all Koreans and especially offensive to Christians. The authorities required students and government employees to attend Shinto ceremonies. Then in late 1939, the government issued the Name Order, which set in motion the process by which Koreans were to change their names to Japanese ones. Generally, this was done by having people select Chinese characters that could either be the same or similar to their names, but pronounced in a Japanese way, or they could select entirely new names. From 1940, all government employees, families with children in school, and others affiliated with the state were more or less pressured to adopt new Japanese names. Eventually, about 84 percent of Koreans complied and adopted new names. In a society where ancient family lineage was prized, this loss of names was a particular humiliation. Korean-language newspapers were ordered closed in 1940; except for the Korean edition of the official government daily, all remaining twelve newspapers were in Japanese. By the early 1940s, the publication of all Korean books ceased.

Korean language use in the schools was extremely restricted after 1938, and by 1943 students could be punished for speaking Korean at school.

Yet the colonial regime was ambiguous about this policy, insisting that Koreans were now Japanese but also maintaining their distinct identity and status as subordinate and inferior subjects. All public documents, school records, and job applications listed the original family name as well as the place of birth and the clan. Official reports made a clear distinction between "peninsular" people and "homeland" Japanese. Japanese leaders themselves had no clear, consistent idea of exactly what the relationship between Koreans and Japanese was. There was some debate among Japanese political leaders as to whether Koreans could be allowed to participate directly in the Japanese government. From 1921 the House of Representatives, or Diet, introduced resolutions calling for extending the franchise for Koreans and allowing Korean representation in parliament. Some Koreans actively campaigned for the franchise. In the 1920s the writer Ch'oe Rin led a home-rule movement demanding that the political rights guaranteed to Japanese in their 1889 constitution be extended to Korea. A number of pro-Japanese associations flourished in the 1930s; in 1937 Minami created the National Association of Koreans to unite them. A resolution in 1939 and another in 1940 to grant the franchise to Koreans passed, but both were vetoed by the cabinet.[39] Only in December 1944 did Tokyo approve of Korean (and Taiwanese) representation in the Diet, which was to begin in 1946.

Koreans, however, were far from assimilated into Japanese culture. Most Koreans could not speak Japanese, did not have any social interaction with Japanese people, and did not identify with Japan. One Japanese source in 1943 stated that 23 percent of Koreans comprehended Japanese, 12 percent without difficulties.[40] Some Koreans may have genuinely been attracted to Japanese culture. Among the small professional class, there were many who enjoyed Japanese literature, films, and music and enjoyed the opportunity to visit Tokyo. Yet assimilation failed. Japanese and Koreans remained two separate peoples who did not mix socially. By the early 1940s out of some 750,000 Japanese living in Korea, most of them men, fewer than 1,000 were married to Koreans. Rather than leading to assimilation, the presence of a privileged alien minority in this historically homogeneous society, and the clumsy and inconsistent efforts at erasing their culture, created a strong collective sense of ethnic and national identity among Koreans of all social classes.

A SOCIETY IN TURMOIL: THE LEGACY OF COLONIAL RULE

Historians debate over how to evaluate Japanese colonial rule. To what extent did Japan establish the foundation for modern Korea? How much credit or blame Japan can take for developments in the history of North and South Korea is still debated, but there is no doubt that Japan's colonial rule left a complex legacy. In so many ways, the bases for a modern society were established during colonial rule. Recent scholarship has given a great deal of attention to "colonial modernity," the process by which Korea was modernized under Japanese rule. Japan provided high standards of government efficiency, established much of the infrastructure for a modern industrial society, and laid the foundations for a modern school system. However, as as Taylor Atkins and many Korean scholars have pointed out, it was a modernization within a colonial context designed to benefit the colonizer not the colonized.[41] Furthermore, scholarship on colonial Korea, often based on Japanese sources, perhaps underestimates the degree to which modernization was initiated by Koreans themselves. Some historians have pointed to the fact that many of the steps toward establishing a national education system, creating a sense of legal equality, rationalizing the administration of the country, and other aspects of creating a modern state and society began under the last two decades of the Chosŏn dynasty.

The colonial administration saw the erosion of the old social order, the emergence of a modern middle class, and the beginnings of an industrial working class. The Japanese provided a model of a closely related people who had appropriated Western science, technology, and some institutions and values, and had established a nation that could successfully compete in the world. The Japanese introduced a government both more efficient and more authoritarian than Koreans had previously known. Korean society was most profoundly impacted by the last years of Japanese rule. The state became more coercive, and every aspect of life more politicized and militarized when Japan's imperialist adventure in China put the colony on a wartime basis.

The lives of almost all Koreans were deeply affected by the colonial experience. Many of the leaders of postwar Korea—industrialists such as Chung Ju Yung (Chŏng Chu-yŏng) (1915–2001), the founder of Hyundai, and Lee Byung-chul (Yi Pyŏng-ch'ŏl) (1910–1987), founder of Samsung, and leaders such as Park Chung Hee (Pak Chŏng-hŭi) (1917–1979), who as South Korean president oversaw the big push for industrialization in Korea, and the North Korean dictator Kim Il Sung—were profoundly shaped by their experiences growing up in colonial Korea. The impact of Japanese rule upon Korea was especially traumatic after the occupation of Manchuria in 1931 and the creation of the puppet Manchukuo state the following year. Korea's position in the Japanese Empire changed from peripheral to central, as the peninsula became a bridge from the Japanese archipelago to the Chinese mainland. Industrial development in Korea increased, particularly in the north, and jobs in the newly industrializing centers in northern Korea and in Manchuria became available to many

Koreans, setting into motion a great social migration as hundreds of thousands left their villages to take advantage of these new opportunities. This process accelerated in 1937, when war broke out between Japan and the Republic of China. At first the movement of farmers and laborers was mainly voluntary on the part of many poor Koreans, who left their villages in search of employment in the mines and factories that were mushrooming in the northern part of the country and in Manchuria, but this soon involved a forced mobilization of millions of Koreans to work where needed in Korea, Japan, China, and elsewhere in the expanding empire.

The scale of this great social upheaval, which continued to accelerate in the early 1940s, is extraordinary. The Korean population of Manchuria swelled after 1931 to perhaps 1.5 million. The fastest-growing immigrant community during the colonial period was in Japan. Korean population in Japan increased from 26,000 in 1919 to 276,000 in 1929 and 543,000 in 1934.[42] These included students, some of whom settled in Japan, and laborers working in factories and mines. Life for them in Japan's homogeneous and often xenophobic society could be harsh. Koreans in Japan were not assimilated but remained outsiders. Thousands of Koreans were murdered by hysterical Japanese mobs in the aftermath of the Kantō (Tokyo region) earthquake of September 1923. Then, after 1937, a huge number of Koreans came to work in the mines and factories, most voluntarily; some were simply conscripted as laborers. In 1945 there were 2.4 million Koreans in Japan, making up a quarter of the industrial labor force. By 1944, as Bruce Cumings has pointed out, 11.6 percent of all Koreans were residing outside of Korea, and 20 percent were living abroad or in Korea but outside their home provinces.[43] According to Cumings, "forty percent of the adult population was part of this uprooting."[44] This mass movement of people served to break down routines of ordinary life and open up new experiences and possibilities to millions of Koreans. The last years of colonial rule, especially, had shaken up traditional Korean society. This society would be further shaken by the political turmoil and civil war that followed liberation.

Japanese rule, especially its last years, would provide both North and South Korea with a model of state-directed economic development, with the examples of mass mobilization of the population for national purposes, and massive propaganda campaigns. The cult of the Japanese emperor and the many Shinto shrines was to have an echo in the cult of the ruling Kim family of North Korea. The incessant propaganda, the mass mobilization, the use of images of violence and heroism to inspire citizens to sacrifice themselves for the leader (the emperor in colonial Korea) bear striking similarities methods employed in North Korea.[45] Thirty-five years of Japanese rule also helped to foster and shape a powerful sense of Korean nationalism. Significantly it also resulted in an ideologically divided nationalist movement.

KOREA IN GLOBAL PERSPECTIVE:
THE KOREAN NATIONALIST MOVEMENT

The colonial period saw the emergence of an intense Korean national-ism. Chronologically, the growth of nationalist movements within and outside the country coincided with nationalist movements elsewhere in the colonial world, but was perhaps embraced more widely and more passionately than was the case in many other countries. The strong sense of Korean cultural identity, the homogeneity of Korean society, and the intrusive and intense nature of Japanese colonial rule help account for this. The exclusive nature of Japanese culture and their presence in a land that was unaccustomed to foreigners contributed to the sense of Koreans as a distinct and different group. Some Koreans did accept an identity as members of a greater Japanese Empire, but discriminatory practices only reinforced the fact that they were not Japanese. Even the efforts at assimilation were contradicted by all sorts of legal distinctions that were still imposed on Koreans.

In many ways, the nationalist movement in Korea was a typical one among colonial peoples in the first half of the twentieth century. Japan's rule, while allowing some scope for activities expressing ethnic and cultural sentiments, placed severe limits on overt political activity. Fur-thermore, the colonial authorities often were able to involve prominent Koreans in the public life of the colony, undermining the nationalist credentials of many leading figures in Korea. In its suppression of any calls for independence, and with its insistence on the active participation of everyone in the war effort during the 1930s and 1940s, the Japanese weakened the ability of most of the members of the professional class to serve as effective and credible national leaders. As a result, it was mostly the exiled members of the independence movement that emerged in 1945 with the most unblemished reputations. These included both conserva-tives such as Syngman Rhee and radicals such as the Communist guerrilla Kim Il Sung. In this way, the Japanese colonial administration resembled the Dutch in the East Indies and the French in Indochina more than the British in India. As with Vietnam, the Communists proved to be highly effective organizers. Korea, however, lacked vast remote regions that could provide guerrilla strongholds, and the Japanese police and military establishment was more formidable and effective than those of most other colonies. The exile community was also at a disadvantage, since it was so geographically fragmented. Unlike many independence movements, there was no logical base or center for opposition. However, in contrast to many independence movements—Burma, Indonesia, India, or much of Africa—Korean nationalists did not have to deal with separatist move-ments; the boundaries and unity of Korea were taken for granted.

KOREA IN GLOBAL PERSPECTIVE:
KOREA'S COLONIAL EXPERIENCE

How unique was Korea's colonial experience? In many ways it was a typical colony. The Japanese modeled much of their colonial administration on those of the major European powers. As Mark Caprio has pointed out, even their assimilationist polices were at least partly influenced by German and French examples.[46] In fact, Japanese colonialism can be seen as a late, imitative form, part of that nation's efforts to achieve parity with the great Western powers. The Japanese promoted industrial development in Korea far more than was the usual case for a colonizer. As a result, Korea in 1945 was industrialized to a greater extent than most colonies, more than any in Asia or Africa. But the nature of the industrialization and economic development in general fit a typical colonial mold. It was designed to produce raw materials and products needed by the mother country, which directed and controlled its development. And in spite of this industrialization, Japan, until World War II at least, saw Korea primarily as a producer of commodities for the home country. The push to grow rice and soybeans and later cotton and wool for the Japanese market, for example, conformed to the conventional pattern of colonial development.

Yet Korea's colonial experience differed from most others in that Korea was neither a contiguous appendage to a land empire nor ruled by a distant overseas power. Only 115 miles from Japan's shores, Korea had a long history of interaction with its colonizer, including the sixteenth-century invasions and attempted conquest. It was a familiar, often menacing neighbor. But Japan shared a common East Asian cultural heritage with Korea. Like Korea, much of its legal, literary, political, and artistic traditions were derived from China. Although Confucianism was not the all-embracing ideology that it was in Korea, Japan remained throughout the colonial period a society profoundly influenced by Confucian values and concepts. Its rule reinforced some of these values, including emphasis on rank, hierarchy, authority, and respect for education, and it married them to Western concepts of science, industry, technology, and bureaucratic efficiency. Japanese propaganda often touted the nation as the vanguard of modern progress for the rest of East Asia, and to some extent it was. Korea could and did often follow Japan's lead in adapting to Western institutions and values—a task made easier by the fact that their languages were similar, not just in grammatical structure but in the commonly shared vocabulary borrowed from Chinese.

Yet few people have shown more bitterness toward their former occupier than have the Koreans. Contemporary Koreans, both in the North and South, almost universally condemn the Japanese rule of Korea as a cruel, brutal occupation. There is little of the open sentimentalism that is sometimes found in other countries toward former colonial rulers. In few former colonies has there been such lingering hatred. Both North and South Korea, to a degree uncommon among postcolonial states, consciously attempted to rid their societies of Japanese influences. The Shinto shrines that dotted the countryside and cities were completely destroyed almost immediately after liberation. In both Koreas, Japanese films, videos, and books were banned after 1945. Japanese words were purged in "language-purification campaigns," despite the fact that modern Korean, especially as used in South Korea, has absorbed a vast number of foreign loan words, mostly from English.

There are many reasons for this lingering animosity: not the least is that governments in North and South Korea have made anti-Japanese sentiment a rallying point for patriotism. The Koreans have historically been not a little xenophobic and especially wary of the Japanese. The bitterness toward the Japanese was also a result of the intense nature of Japanese rule. In the late 1930s nearly a quarter of a million Japanese served in Korea as bureaucrats; police; garrison soldiers; and employees of state banks, companies, and schools. By way of comparison, the French colony of Vietnam, with a slightly smaller population of 17 million versus 20 million for Korea, in 1937 had 2,920 French administrative personnel; 10,776 French troops; and about 38,000 indigenous personnel.[47] The Japanese personnel in Korea were equal in number to that of the British in India, which had twenty times the population. The vast bureaucracy and police system penetrated down to the village level. While most European colonies were administered by a fairly small number of officials who governed through native underlings and pliant local elites, Japanese colonial rule was direct all the way down to the local neighborhood policeman. Especially important in generating a legacy of hatred were the last years of the colonial regime, which witnessed coercive mass mobilization of the Korean people and the strange attempt at forced assimilation. And it was this wartime aspect of Korea's colonial experience that was historically unique.

Son Pyŏnghŭi et al., Declaration of Independence

We hereby declare that Korea is an independent state and that Koreans are a self-governing people. We proclaim it to the nations of the world in affirmation of the principle of the equality of all nations, and we proclaim it to our posterity preserving in perpetuity the right of national survival. We make this declaration on the strength of five thousand years of history as an expression of the devotion and loyalty of twenty million people. We claim independence in the interests of the eternal and free development of our people in accordance with the great movement for world reform based upon the awakening conscience of mankind. This is the clear command of heaven, the course of our times, and a legitimate manifestation of the right of all nations to coexist and live in harmony. Nothing in the world can suppress or block it.

For the first time in several thousand years, we have suffered the agony of alien suppression for a decade, becoming a victim of the policies of aggression and coercion, which are relics from a bygone era. How long have we been deprived of our right to exist? How long has our spiritual development been hampered? How long have the opportunities to contribute our creative vitality to development of world culture been denied us?

Alas! In order to rectify past grievances, free ourselves from present hardships, eliminate future threats, stimulate and enhance the weakened conscience of our people, eradicate the shame that befell our nation, ensure proper development of human dignity, avoid leaving humiliating legacies to our children, and usher in lasting and complete happiness for our prosperity, the most urgent task is to firmly establish national independence. Today when human nature and conscience are placing the forces of justice and humanity on our side, if every one of our twenty million people arms himself for battle, whom could we not defeat and what could we not accomplish? We do not intend to accuse Japan of infidelity for its violation of various solemn treaty obligations since the Treaty of Amity of 1876. Japan's scholars and officials, indulging in a conqueror's exuberance, have denigrated the accomplishments of our ancestors and treated our civilized people like barbarians. Despite their disregard for the ancient origins of our society and the brilliant spirit of our people, we shall not blame Japan; we must first blame ourselves before finding fault with others. Because of the urgent need for remedies for the problems of today, we cannot afford the time for recriminations over past wrongs.

Our task today is to build up our own strength, not to destroy others. We must chart a new course for ourselves in accord with the solemn dictates of conscience, not malign and reject others for reasons of past enmity or momentary passion. In order to restore natural and just conditions, we must remedy the unnatural and unjust conditions brought about by the leaders of Japan, who are chained to old ideas and old forces and victimized by their obsession with glory.

From the outset the union of the two countries did not emanate from the wishes of the people, and its outcome has been oppressive coercion, discriminatory injustice, and fabrication of statistical data, thereby deepening the eternally irreconcilable chasm of ill will between the two nations. To correct past mistakes and open a new phase of friendship based upon genuine understanding and sympathy—is this not the easiest way to avoid disaster and invite blessing? The enslavement of twenty million resentful people by force does not contribute to lasting peace in the East. It deepens the fear and suspicion of Japan by the four hundred million Chinese who constitute the main axis for stability in the East, and it will lead to the tragic downfall of all nations in our region. Independence for Korea today shall not only enable Koreans to lead a normal, prosperous life, as is their due; it will also guide Japan to leave its evil path and perform its great task of supporting the cause of the East, liberating China from a gnawing uneasiness and fear and helping the cause of world peace and happiness for mankind, which depend greatly on peace in the East. How can this be considered a trivial issue of mere sentiment?

Behold! A new world is before our eyes. The days of force are gone, and the days of morality are here. The spirit of humanity, nurtured through the past century, has begun casting its rays of new civilization upon human history. A new spring has arrived prompting the myriad forms of life to come to life again. The past was a time of freezing ice and snow, stifling the breath of life; the present is a time of mild breezes and warm sunshine, reinvigorating the spirit. Facing the return of the universal cycle, we set forth on the changing tide of the world. Nothing can make us hesitate or fear.

We shall safeguard our inherent right to freedom and enjoy a life of prosperity; we shall also make use of our creativity, enabling our national essence to blossom in the vernal warmth. We have arisen now. Conscience is on our side, and truth guides our way. All of us, men and women, young and old, have firmly left behind the old nest of darkness and gloom and head for joyful resurrection together with the myriad living things. The spirits of thousands of generations of our ancestors protect us; the rising tide of world consciousness shall assist us. Once started, we shall surely succeed. With this hope we march forward.[48]

NOTES

1. Adrian Buzo, *The Making of Modern Korea: A History* (London: Routledge, 2002), 20.

2. Bruce Cumings, *Origins of the Korean War*, vol. 1 (Princeton, NJ: Princeton University Press, 1981), 53–61; Carter J. Eckert, Ki-baik Lee, Young Ick Lew, Michael Robinson, and Edward W. Wagner, *Korea Old and New: A History* (Cambridge: Korea Institute, Harvard University, 1990), 259; Andrew J. Gradjanzev, *Modern Korea* (New York: Institute of Pacific Relations, 1944), 75–76.

3. Ching-chih Chen, "Police and Community in Control System in the Empire," in *The Japanese Colonial Empire, 1895–1945*, ed. Ramon H. Myers and Mark R. Peattie (Princeton, NJ: Princeton University Press, 1984), 213–34.

4. Kenneth M. Wells, *New God, New Nation: Protestants and Self-Reconstruction Nationalism in Korea, 1896–1937* (Honolulu: University of Hawaii Press, 1990), 76.

5. Frank Baldwin, "Participatory Anti-Imperialism: The 1919 Independence Movement," *Journal of Korean Studies* 1, no. 1 (1979): 123–62.

6. Baldwin, "Participatory Anti-Imperialism," 135.

7. Gradjanzev, *Modern Korea*, 55–56.

8. Michael Robinson, *Cultural Nationalism in Colonial Korea, 1920–1925* (Seattle: University of Washington Press, 1988), 64–65.

9. Robinson, *Cultural Nationalism in Colonial Korea*, 100.

10. Chong-sik Lee, *The Korean Workers' Party: A Short History* (Stanford, CA: Stanford University, Hoover Institution Press, 1978), 3–4.

11. Lee, *The Korean Workers' Party*, 19.

12. Lee, *The Korean Workers' Party*, 28–29.

13. Andrew C. Nahm, *Korea: Tradition and Transformation* (Elizabeth, NJ: Hollym International, 1988), 286–88.

14. Kim Ch'ang-su, "How the Shin'ganhoe Society Came to Be Dissolved," *Korea Journal* 27, no. 9 (September 1987): 23–33.

15. Carter J. Eckert, *Offspring of Empire: The Koch'ang Kims and the Origins of Korean Capitalism* (Seattle: University of Washington Press, 1991), 29.

16. Dennis L. McNamara, "The Keishō and the Korean Business Elite," *Journal of Asian Studies* 48, no. 2 (May 1989): 310–23.

17. Gradjanzev, *Modern Korea*, 185–86.

18. Bruce Cumings, *Korea's Place in the Sun: A Modern History* (New York: W.W. Norton, 1997), 166.

19. Government-General of Chosŏn, *Annual Report on Reforms and Progress in Chosŏn 1910–1911* (Keijö [Seoul]: Sötokufu, 1911), 201.

20. Seong-cheol Oh and Ki-seok Kim, "Expansion of Elementary Schooling under Colonialism: Top Down or Bottom Up?" in Hong Yung Lee and Clark W. Sorensen, eds., *Colonial Rule and Social Change in Korea 1910–1945* (Seattle: University of Washington Press, 2013), 114–139

21. Soon-won Park, "Colonial Industrial Growth and the Emergence of the Korean Working Class," in *Colonial Modernity in Korea*, Gi-wook Shin and Michael Robinson, eds. (Cambridge, MA: Harvard University Press, 1999), 128–60, 133.

22. Park, "Colonial Industrial Growth," 135–41.

23. Park, "Colonial Industrial Growth," 155–57.

24. Kenneth M. Wells, "The Price of Legitimacy: Women and the Kŭnuhoe Movement, 1927–1931," in *Colonial Modernity in Korea*, Gi-wook Shin and Michael Robinson, eds. (Cambridge, MA: Harvard University Press, 1999), 191–220, 198–99.

25. Theodore Jun Yoo, *The Politics of Gender in Colonial Korea: Education, Labor, and Health, 1910–1945* (Berkeley: University of California Press, 2008), 192–94, 202–4.

26. Wells, "The Price of Legitimacy," 200–207.

27. Sonja Kim, "Women, Gender and Social Change in Colonial Korea, Michael Seth, editor, *Routledge Handbook of Modern Korean History* (London: Routledge, forthcoming).

28. Joong-Seop Kim, "In Search of Human Rights: The Paekchŏng Movement in Colonial Korea," in *Colonial Modernity in Korea*, Gi-wook Shin and Michael Robinson, eds. (Cambridge, MA: Harvard University Press, 1999): 311–35.

29. Cumings, *Origins of the Korean War*, vol. 1., 46.

30. Gradjanzev, *Modern Korea*, 295.

31. Gi-wook Shin and Do-Hyun Han, "Colonial Corporatism: The Rural Revitalization Campaign, 1932–1940," in *Colonial Modernity in Korea*, Gi-wook Shin and Michael Robinson, eds. (Cambridge, MA: Harvard University Press, 1999), 70–96, 78.

32. Gi-wook Shin, *Peasant Protest and Social Change in Colonial Korea* (Seattle: University of Washington Press, 1996), 174–89.

33. Shin and Han, "Colonial Corporatism," 70–96.

34. Nahm, *Korea: Tradition and Transformation*, 233.

35. Michael J. Seth, *Education Fever* (Honolulu: University of Hawaii Press, 2002), 27.

36. Brandon Palmer, *Fighting for the Enemy: Koreans in Japan's War, 1937–1945* (Seattle: University of Washington Press, 2013), 184.

37. George Hicks, *The Comfort Women: Japan's Brutal Regime of Enforced Prostitution in the Second World War* (New York: W.W. Norton & Company, 1995), 12–15.

38. Cumings, *Korea's Place in the Sun*, 183.

39. Nahm, *Korea: Tradition and Transformation*, 231.

40. Gradjanzev, *Modern Korea*, 269.

41. Taylor Atkins, "Colonial Modernity," in *Routledge Handbook of Modern Korean History*, Michael Seth, ed. (London: Routledge, forthcoming).

42. Nahm, *Korea: Tradition and Transformation*, 324.

43. Cumings, *Origins of the Korean War*, vol. 1, 53–61.

44. Cumings, *Korea's Place in the Sun*, 177.

45. Michael Kim, "The Aesthetics of Total Mobilisation in the Visual Culture in Late Colonial Korea," *Totalitarian Movements and Political Religions*, 8.3–4 (September–December 2007), 483–502.

46. Mark Caprio, *Japanese Assimilation Policies in Colonial Korea, 1910–1945* (Seattle: University of Washington Press, 2009).

47. Cumings, *Origins of the Korean War*, vol. 1, 53–61.

48. Peter H. Lee, ed., *Sourcebook of Korean Civilization*, vol. 2, *From the Seventeenth Century to the Modern Period* (New York: Columbia University Press, 1996), 432–34.

3

❧

Division and War,
1945 to 1953

The liberation of Korea from Japanese rule was accompanied by its great national tragedy—the division of the country. Several developments during the closing days of World War II proved crucial in creating this division. Most important of these were: the contingencies of the allies as the war was coming to an end, the emerging rivalry between the Soviet Union and the United States, and the scattered and divided nature of the Korean nationalist movement.

The Korean Provisional Government (KPG), which had become virtually moribund by the mid-1920s, revived during Japan's invasion of China and had become closely associated with its sponsor, the Nationalist regime. The Nationalist regime of Chiang Kai-shek in Chungking (Chongqing) promoted the KPG. Chiang wanted a friendly, reliably anti-communist, independent Korea. In April 1942, Chungking proposed that all the allies recognize the KPG as the government of Korea. But this was ignored by the United States. Instead, in early 1943 President Roosevelt and the British foreign secretary, Anthony Eden, agreed that Manchuria and Taiwan (or Formosa, as it was commonly called in the West at that time) would be returned to China and that Korea would be placed under a trusteeship with China, the United States, and one or two other countries.[1] Later that year when Chiang Kai-shek, Franklin Delano Roosevelt, and Winston Churchill met in Cairo to discuss the future of Asia, they issued a communiqué on December 1, in which they stated that China, the United States, and Britain, "mindful of the enslavement of the people of Korea, are determined that in due course Korea shall become free and independent."[2] Roosevelt's plan was for a long trusteeship. Stalin appeared

93

to have gone along with the plan for a trusteeship at the Teheran Conference, which followed the meeting at Cairo.[3] Roosevelt's idea was for a forty-year tutelage, but this was reduced to twenty or thirty years at Yalta.

The Cairo Declaration was important because it was the first public statement on what the allies were planning for Korea. Korea was not of great interest or concern for the United States or Britain, but Roosevelt did have the idea that it should be placed under a trusteeship. The idea may have been influenced by the model of the U.S. role in the Philippines, where Americans saw themselves as tutors preparing that colony for its full independence, which was scheduled for 1946. It was not based on any real knowledge of Korea, its history, culture, or the strong nationalist aspirations of its people. Most Koreans who became aware of the declaration interpreted the phrase "in due course" to mean immediate independence, totally unaware of Roosevelt's well-meaning but, as history would prove, unrealistic plans.

While the idea of some sort of U.S. and other Allied-power occupation of Korea had been for a long time part of the plan for the postwar settlement, the division of Korea was the product of expediency. On August 6, 1945, the United States dropped an atomic bomb on Hiroshima; on August 8 the Soviet Union declared war on Japan and immediately began an offensive along Japan's northern frontier in Sakhalin, Manchuria, and along the extreme northeast corner of Korea that borders Siberia. On August 9 the second atomic bomb was dropped on Nagasaki. The Japanese government began signaling its desire to surrender, and on August 15 it did so unconditionally. This rush of events leading to the final surrender of Japan came with an unexpected suddenness. Urgently, the State-War-Navy Coordinating Committee assigned Colonel Dean Rusk and Charles Bonesteel on the night of August 10–11 to draw up a line for the occupation of Korea by Soviet and American forces. While Soviet forces were already entering the northeast of Korea, the closest American forces were 600 miles away in Okinawa and would not be able to reach Korea for several weeks. It was therefore urgent that the United States work out an agreement to prevent the entire peninsula from falling into Soviet hands. As they later explained, Rusk and Bonesteel looked at their map and saw that the thirty-eighth parallel split the country into roughly equal halves but kept Seoul in the southern half. They decided that was where to draw the line. George M. McCune, chief of the Korean section in the Office of Far Eastern Affairs in the U.S. State Department, wrote that it was "an arbitrary line, chosen by staff officers for military purposes without political or other considerations."[4] Truman approved the proposal on August 13, and it was sent to Moscow. To the surprise of many, the Soviets almost immediately accepted the line, even though they were in a position to occupy all of the country. Perhaps Stalin hoped by agreeing to a joint military occupation that the door would be left open for a Soviet role in the occupation of Japan and perhaps Europe as well. Recent research suggests he was also concerned about avoiding a potential conflict with the United States in Korea.[5]

It is important to note that the thirty-eighth parallel was an arbitrary line on the map and did not correspond to any geographical, cultural, or historical division of the country. It cut across the two provinces Kyŏnggi and Kangwŏn, across counties, and across natural geographic features. Korea had been a unified country since the seventh century; no Korean had ever proposed a division of their land. Interestingly, outside powers had made similar proposals before. In the 1590s the Japanese military hegemon Hideyoshi had proposed a division of Korea following his unsuccessful attempt to invade and conquer the peninsula in 1592. His offer to the Chinese, who had come to Korea's rescue during the invasion, was that the four southern provinces would be ceded to Japan and the northern provinces would be made a sort of buffer kingdom under the Korean monarch. Japan again in 1896 proposed a division, at the thirty-eighth parallel, into a Russian and Japanese sphere, but Russia rejected this. As Japan's position in Korea grew stronger, Russia proposed a division at the thirty-ninth parallel in 1903. It is unlikely that the Americans were aware of these earlier precedents.

The Korean nationalist movement, as discussed earlier, was divided ideologically, fractured organizationally, and geographically dispersed. The Communist movement in Korea had fallen victim to relentless and effective repression by the colonial government. Most of the Communists had been killed, jailed, or driven underground. Yet, while no organized party structure existed, there was a loose network of underground Communists, largely isolated from the internationalist movement and often from each other. The head of the Korean Communist Party was Pak Hŏnyŏng (1900–1955), who had been arrested in 1933 but released in 1939 because he was thought to be insane and harmless. All moderate nationalist movements in Korea had also been repressed during the war. Virtually every prominent Korean had been forced to support the war effort and the Japanese imperialist cause, so there were few non-Communists in Korea with an untarnished nationalist record.

Outside of Korea, the Korean Provisional Government in Chungking had a small force of troops—the Korean Restoration Army (Han'guk Kwangbokkun) under the leadership of Kim Ku. It had about 3,000 or so resistance fighters, who were geographically far removed from Korea. After 1942, these Koreans had been cooperating with U.S. military intelligence officials and advisors in China. In the north of China, a few thousand Koreans were fighting with the Chinese Communist Party, most notably those serving in the Korean Volunteer Army led by Mu (Kim)

Chǒng (1905–1952). He had joined the Chinese Communists in 1928, participated in the legendary Long March, and operated out of the CCP headquarters in Yanan. Other Korean communists with the Chinese Communist Party included Kim Tu-bong and Ch'oe Ch'ang-ik. Besides these two groups of Koreans in China, there were the former Manchuria-based guerrillas that had retreated into Siberia by 1939–1940 and were serving with the Soviet Army. There were also some Korean exiles in the United States; most prominent was Syngman Rhee, who spent the war in Washington promoting Korean independence among any American officials who would listen. But none of these exile groups were regarded very seriously by the great powers or consulted by them, nor did they play much of a role in the events at the immediate end of the war.

THE END OF COLONIAL RULE IN KOREA

As these events were taking place abroad, in Korea the Japanese governor-general, Abe Nobuyuki, aware of the gravity of the situation, began to look for prominent Koreans to work out some sort of postwar transition. On August 9 he started contacts with Song Chin-u, discussing the postwar situation and the possibility of heading a transitional body of prominent Koreans to ensure domestic order and prevent anti-Japanese violence until the occupation forces arrived. Song seemed an ideal candidate to lead a transition, since he was well respected, and was less tainted with collaboration activities than most of his contemporaries. He was also conservative and therefore less threatening to the Japanese. Song, however, refused to work with the colonial authorities, so on August 15 they turned to Yǒ Un-hyǒng (1886–1947). Yǒ agreed, but only after insisting that the Japanese release all political prisoners, allow Koreans to carry out peacekeeping and independence-preparation activities without interference, and ensure food supplies.[6] Yǒ had unblemished nationalist credentials that few Koreans not in exile could match. Well educated, a charismatic speaker, he was a leftist but not a Communist, a man of socialist leanings, a proponent of democracy and equality, but an opponent of violent revolution. His choice to head some sort of interim Korean authority might have seemed appropriate, especially as at the time no one in Korea or Japan was aware of the decision by the United States to divide the peninsula into two occupation zones. Soviet forces had begun amphibious landings in Korea by August 14 and quickly overran the industrial northeast of the country; on August 16 they landed at Wǒnsan farther down the coast. It was probably assumed that all of Korea would be under Soviet occupation. From that point of view, the Government-General saw in Yǒ someone who could work with the Communists but who could be trusted to oppose violence against the Japanese. Yŏ then set up the Committee for the Preparation of Korean Independence.

The emperor's August 15 radio announcement of Japan's surrender came to most Koreans as a shock, followed almost immediately by joyous celebration. Koreans fondly recall these first days; people danced, partied, and wept with joy. Symbols of Japanese authority such as the Shinto shrines were destroyed, and everywhere the long-banned Korean flag was displayed. It appears that almost all Koreans felt that independence was imminent; none suspected Allied plans for a trusteeship. Local people of all political persuasions met to plan for independence. People's committees (*inmin wiwŏnhoe*) were organized throughout the country. In a little over two weeks Koreans set up people's committees in every one of the country's thirteen provinces, as well as local people's committees in cities and counties. A controversy over these people's committees has arisen among historians. The speed by which they emerged has suggested to some that there was a secret network throughout the country, perhaps led by the Communists. However, it appears that they were in most cases spontaneous responses to the liberation. Many Communists released from prison or emerging from hiding actively participated in the committees, but they do not seem to have dominated or directed them.

On September 6 several hundred delegates from the people's committees met in Seoul and declared the Korean People's Republic (KPR). Syngman Rhee was named the chair, and Yŏ Un-hyŏng and the conservative businessman Kim Sŏng-su were given prominent positions. The Korean People's Republic appears to have been a broad coalition with Communists and non-Communist leftists being the most active participants. Six days later, the delegates of the KPR drew up a program calling for confiscation of land owned by Japanese and national traitors. They also called for the limiting of rents to 30 percent, an eight-hour workday, a minimum wage, and other reforms. It is interesting to note just how pressing the issue of land reform was. While the KPR may be a good indication of the hopes for quick independence and the demands of tenant farmers, agricultural and industrial laborers, and others, it was a powerless organization, since the authority resided with the U.S. military occupation forces, which never recognized it.

NORTH KOREA UNDER SOVIET OCCUPATION

Local people's committees were organized throughout northern Korea as they were in the southern area. In Pyongyang, the local committee was associated with the Committee for the Preparation of Korean Independence (CPKI) that was based in Seoul and headed by the well-known Presbyterian leader Cho Man-sik. The committee was dominated by Christians, although it did contain two Communist members. This is not surprising. While only 2 or 3 percent of Koreans in 1945 were Christians, Pyongyang was a center of Christian activity. Cho, probably one of the most respected leaders in the north, was a natural choice to lead the government there. On August 26, the headquarters of the Soviet Twenty-fifth Army arrived at Pyongyang. The Soviets worked with the CPKI, appointing a number of Communists, while maintaining the conservative Cho as its head. On October 19, the Soviets organized a Five Provinces People's Committee with a Five Province Administrative Bureau to administer the country with Cho Man-sik as head. As the Communists took effective control of the organization and the local people's committees, Cho and other Christian leaders organized a Korean Democratic Party in November. In February 1946, Ch'ŏndogyo members organized a Friends Party. The existence of these two parties gave the illusion of a multiparty government in the north, but in reality all power fell into the hands of the Communists.

The Soviets, by working with the people's committees, were able to carry out a relatively smooth and peaceful transfer of power. Moscow brought in several hundred Soviet-Koreans (Koreans of Soviet citizenship who were the descendants of earlier migrants to Siberia), to assist them in their administration. Initially they had a problem finding appropriate Communist leaders. The local Communist leader, Hyŏn Chun-hyŏk, was too independent, and most of the Communist exiles were in China, far removed from Soviet control. Therefore, they turned to the ex-guerrilla soldiers of the Eighty-eighth Reconnaissance Brigade of the Twenty-fifth Red Army, which included Kim Il Sung and sixty-some others, which had entered North Korea at Wŏnsan on September 19.

Kim was born in 1912 into a family of modest means near Pyongyang. His mother was Christian, he seemed to have grown up in a Protestant Christian household, and his father was an active nationalist. In 1919 the family moved to Manchuria, perhaps to escape poverty, as was the case of many others, although Kim claimed it was due to their anti-Japanese activities. His education stopped after completing middle school in Manchuria. As a young man, he became involved in anti-Japanese nationalist groups and joined the Northeast Anti-Japanese Army in the early 1930s. After leading a small guerrilla band, Kim, like most of the guerrillas fighting along the Manchurian border, was forced by the Japanese to flee to Siberia. There, from 1940 to 1945, he sat out the remainder of the war. In September 1945 he was one of several prominent guerrilla leaders, such as Kim Ch'aek (1903–1951), Ch'oe Hyŏn, and Kim Il (1910–1984), who became his close associates. Exactly why the Soviet occupation forces decided to support him is not clear. He had achieved some notoriety for his successful raid at Poch'ŏnbo in 1937 and was familiar to some Soviet officers, while the local domestic Communists were weak and largely unknown to the Russians. For whatever reason, in October the Soviets eventually decided to promote him as the Communist leader in the North. He was publicly introduced on October 14 when the Soviets chose him to lead the welcoming ceremonies for the Soviet troops. As the Soviets promoted Kim Il Sung, they removed local Communists who opposed him. On October 1945, the Soviets created the North Korea Branch Bureau of the Korean Communist Party, still headquartered in Seoul. In December of that year Kim Il Sung was appointed to its chairmanship.

SOUTH KOREA UNDER U.S. OCCUPATION

Neither the Soviets nor the Americans had planned for the occupation of Korea. Both began as military occupations without clear instructions and both initially lacked Korean interpreters. However, the Soviet occupation was orderly and well organized compared to the American occupation, which was marked by confusion of purpose, lack of preparation and planning, mixed signals from Washington, and the more open and chaotic politics of the South.

General John R. Hodge, commander of the XXIV Corps in Okinawa, was selected to head the occupation force. Hodge was assigned the task simply because his forces were closest to Korea and Washington felt it was important not to wait too long before establishing a presence there. Still it was not until September 6 that the Americans arrived. Hodge was a competent and honest military man with little background or knowledge of Korea. In fact, the United States in general was not well prepared for the occupation; it had made plans for the occupation of Japan but not Korea. As historian Bruce Cumings has pointed out, South Korea got the occupation meant for Japan. This was demonstrated almost from the beginning, when a number of serious errors were made, and by the lack of translators and interpreters, making the Americans heavily dependent on the few Koreans who were competent in English.

U.S. forces arrived, landing at Inch'ŏn, on September 8. Acting under instructions from Washington, Hodge ignored a delegation from the KPR that sought to meet him at Inch'ŏn. The Americans received an enthusiastic greeting from the jubilant Koreans, who regarded them as liberators. While the role of the United States in defeating Japan left a residual goodwill, the enthusiasm quickly dissipated when the U.S. authorities ordered Koreans to obey Governor-General Abe and his 70,000 Japanese officials. Realizing this was an error, the Americans removed Abe on September 12 and gradually over the next three months the Japanese officials were re-patriated back to Japan. Power was transferred to the United States Military Government in Korea (USAMGIK). This awkward start reflected the woeful unpreparedness of the U.S. military for the occupation of Korea. American military and civilian officials lacked clear orders from Washington, especially in the early days, and they found the situation in Korea confusing and chaotic. U.S. military officials were highly suspicious of the local people's committees that were springing up throughout the fall of 1945 and were effectively taking control of much of the countryside. The Americans feared or suspected Communist infiltration and subversion, and most simply did not fully appreciate the depth of the Korean desire for independence. The Japanese occupation, especially during its last years, was a bitter, hateful experience; it was now the time, Koreans felt, to govern themselves without foreigners.

Meanwhile, conservative landowners and businessmen, many linked to Kim Sŏng-su and Song Chin-u, formed the Korean Democratic Party (KDP) on September 16. Looking for Koreans he could work with, Hodge found this group reasonable and, of course, anticommunist. On October 5, he created a Korean Advisory Council with Kim Sŏng-su as head. As Hodge began working with conservatives, he criticized the KPR, declaring on October 10 that it had no authority. This helped to undermine the organization. As conservatives and moderates then left, it became an increasingly radical, Communist-dominated organ. On December 18, Hodge outlawed KPR and it collapsed, although some local people's committees survived for a while. Adding to the political turmoil was the return of two prominent anticommunist exiled leaders. On October 16, Syngman Rhee arrived in Seoul, managing to finagle a ride on MacArthur's private plane. Four days later, General Hodge introduced Rhee to the Korean public, giving an air of official American endorsement to the longtime U.S.-based exile. At Hodge's request, Kim Ku, the president of the Korean Provisional Government in China, and its vice president, Kim Kyu-sik, returned to Korea in November.

By the late fall, the South Korean political scene included: the Communists under Pak Hŏn-yŏng, still hoping to work with non-Communists to bring about an eventual socialist revolution; the conservatives of the KDP, representing the landowners, businessmen, and wealthy elite; moderate leftists such as Yŏ Un-hyŏng; moderate conservatives such as Kim Kyu-sik; the radical rightist Kim Ku; and Syngman Rhee, who while conservative preferred not to ally with anyone but had his own organization, the Committee for the Rapid Realization of Korean Independence. Then there was the U.S. occupation authority, both fearing the spread of Communism and looking for moderate democrats with a political agenda comprehensible to and comfortable for the Americans.

TRUSTEESHIP

Meanwhile, the Allied powers met at the Moscow Conference that began on December 27, 1945, to discuss the postwar settlement. There it was agreed that a four-power trusteeship of the United States, the USSR, China, and Britain would be set up for four to five years. This was a considerable and more realistic reduction from the earlier twenty to thirty years agreed to at Yalta, but it was still four to five years too long for most Koreans. Koreans of all political persuasions, who were still expecting immediate independence, were outraged at the news of a planned trusteeship. Massive demonstrations took place, with all major groups participating. Koreans were united in their opposition to the trusteeship idea. In the midst of the agitation, a potential leader of high standing, Song Chin-u, was assassinated on December 30. The unity of all Koreans in their opposition to the trusteeship was short lived. The Soviet Union ordered the Communists to support the trusteeship, which they dutifully did by switching their position on January 3, a move that cost them much popular support in the South. In North Korea, Cho Man-sik, who criticized the trusteeship, was removed from office on January 4, 1946.

At the conference, an American-Soviet Joint Commission was created to work out details of the trusteeship. Before it met in March 1946, preliminary talks were held in Seoul in January. A number of basic issues were brought up, such as the problem of electricity. Most of the South's electricity came from the North, and the USAMGIK wanted to guarantee its supply; it also wanted to allow free movement across the thirty-eighth parallel where the Soviets had set up roadblocks, but no progress was made on this or on other issues. When the Joint Committee met in March, the Soviets refused to allow representatives of any organization that did not support the proposed trusteeship to participate. This, in practice, meant that almost all political groups in the South other than the Communists were excluded from any consultative role in the trusteeship. Deadlocked, the talks were postponed indefinitely on May 8.

By early 1946, the outlines of separate occupational zones, with their own administrations, had already appeared. This was an unintended outcome of the military occupation. No Korean wanted or foresaw such a development. Nor does it appear to have been the initial intention of either the USSR or the United States to create two separate states.

ESTABLISHING A SEPARATE REGIME IN THE NORTH

In retrospect, it is clear that a Communist regime was rapidly being put in place in the Soviet zone by early 1946. There is no clear evidence that the

Soviet Union had initially planned to create a separate state in their zone; evidence suggests that Moscow entered the occupation unprepared and with no clear plan.[7] The Soviets appeared to have been interested in the trusteeship and preferred to work through a National Front government with the Communists in ultimate control. It is even possible that Moscow would have settled for a neutral and united Korea.[8] But with the opposition of Cho Man-sik and other non-Communists to the trusteeship during the Moscow Conference, the Soviets began rapidly pushing for a communization of the North. On February 8, 1946, the Soviets created a North Korea Provisional People's Committee to carry out a number of reforms. It was supposedly a broad coalition of all political groups, but in reality it was dominated by the Communists, who were rapidly consolidating their control over the country. The Provisional People's Committee carried out the nationalization of Japanese industry. The most important reform, the Law on Land Reform, was enacted in March. It confiscated all lands owned by Japanese and national traitors and limited all other holdings to 5 *chŏngbo* (12.25 acres). This was, in effect, a redistribution of land from large landlords to individual farm families. The land reform addressed an important concern of millions of rural poor who made up a majority of the population. Although there were not as many large landlords in the North it was still a sweeping change. Its implementation was also made easier by the fact that thousands of rich landlords, fearing repression, had already fled south of the thirty-eighth parallel. The regime carried out a number of important measures in the spring and summer of 1946, creating large-scale social organizations that aimed at mobilizing women, peasants, workers, and other groups that had previously had little power in Korea, and granting legal equality to women.[9] The provisional government also announced plans for universal primary education. At the same time, movement across the border was further restricted and the rudiments of a defense force established.

In the summer of 1946 the North Korean Branch Bureau of the Korean Communist Party headed by Kim Il Sung became the North Korean Workers' Party. It merged with another Communist party, the Sinmindang (New People's Party), made up of Korean Communists returning from China and led by Kim Tu-bong. The North Korean Workers' Party held its first party congress in August of 1946. Then in December 1946, a Korean National Democratic Front (KNDF) consisting of all northern parties, plus representatives of all southern workers' parties, was formed. Shortly afterward, elections were held for local people's committees and the KNDF received 97 percent of the vote. Delegates from these people's committees met in February 1947 as a Congress of People's Committees, which elected a People's Assembly. Thus, step-by-step, a centralized government with branches at every local level took shape. This new government organized women, youth, labor, and intellectuals in support of a new social and economic order under the guidance of the North Korean Workers' Party. Meanwhile, the Soviets continued to promote Kim Il Sung as the leader, placing his picture in public places alongside that of Stalin. In October 1946 they named the main university Kim Il Sung University.

THE BEGINNINGS OF A NEW REGIME IN THE SOUTH

In the South, the USAMGIK had a less sure sense of the direction than the Soviets, but it too moved toward setting up a separate, centralized regime acting under U.S. guidance. On February 14, 1946, a Representative Democratic Council was formed with the intention of representing various points of view, but it was dominated by conservatives and had little power. In August, the USAMGIK announced plans to establish an Interim Legislative Assembly. This had ninety members; forty-five elected and forty-five appointed by the USAMGIK. Elections were held, but these were boycotted by leftists. Kim Kyu-sik, a moderate conservative, was made the head. This assembly was riddled with factionalism and accomplished little. Political problems were complicated by economic ones. Economic conditions in the South were a major challenge. One and a half million refugees from China, Manchuria, Japan, and North Korea arrived from August 1945 to August 1946.[10] Inflation was a serious problem, undermining savings and adding to economic uncertainty. Industries were idle and much of the population unemployed.

To maintain law and order the USAMGIK created the Korean National Police (KNP) headed by KDP member Chang T'aek-sang (1893–1969). Its members were mostly Korean police who had served under the Japanese. Unfortunately, they employed the same brutal methods that they had learned from their former colonial masters. In January 1946, the USAMGIK created a 25,000-member constabulary force, a paramilitary force that became the nucleus for the South Korean Army. To train officers, the USAMGIK established a Korean Military Academy. Initially it selected twenty veterans of the Japanese Army, twenty from the Kwantung Army, and twenty from the Restoration Army to serve as the first class. However, most of the members of the Restoration Army refused to serve with those who had participated in the Imperial Japanese cause, so that the new officer corps was largely composed of those who had served in the Japanese forces during World War II. Thus, in the view of some Korean nationalists, both the police and the emerging military forces were staffed with collaborators, not true Korean patriots.

A major problem for the USAMGIK was the shift in tactics by the Communists from an attempt to work with other groups in the South to one of attempting to disrupt the military government. Those angry over the proposed trusteeship joined the Communists and other leftist groups. Discontent from workers suffering from inflation and economic hardships and peasants impatiently waiting for land reform contributed to the tensions and disorder that characterized the American occupation zone. In June 1946, the military banned trade unions but strikes continued. On September 24, a Pusan railway strike spread and led to large uprisings in Taegu, the South's third-largest city. The uprising was put down with much loss of life, and afterward, most of the Communist leaders were jailed or fled to the North.

The most effective political leader was Syngman Rhee, who used the anti-trusteeship movement to advance his political stature. Rhee started out with his impeccable nationalist credentials, his personal prestige, and the impression that he was somehow the favorite of the Americans. As the Koreans were losing patience with the U.S. occupation, he was able to become a champion of immediate Korean independence over American trusteeship. The United States found him too nationalistic, too antileftist, too authoritarian, and too difficult to work with. They looked for more moderate leaders with strong anticommunist credentials. In October, Yŏ Un-hyŏng and Kim Kyu-sik formed a Coalition Committee of Rightists and Leftists to create a moderate center away from the increasingly repressive conservatives manning the police and constabulary and the leftist agitators. Hopes by some Americans that this organization would emerge as a new force were dashed when the charismatic Yŏ was assassinated by an unknown assailant on July 19, 1947. The rightists, who controlled the police, made no real effort to find the assassin. Desperate to find a moderate leader, Hodge welcomed the return to Korea of Sŏ Chae-p'il, a participant in the 1884 Kapsin Coup and the leader of the Independence Club in the 1890s. Hodge wanted Sŏ to take a leadership role and challenge Rhee. But Sŏ, a very old man, arrived in Seoul in July 1947 dying of cancer and soon returned to the United States.

TOWARD DIVISION

The American-Soviet Joint Committee met again from April to July 1947 in another attempt to work out ways to cooperate on establishing a unified independent Korea. The Soviets continued to insist that those organizations or parties that opposed the trusteeship must not be allowed representation. The U.S. government did not want to stay in Korea for long, and the talks with the Soviet Union were not making any progress, so in September it turned to the UN. The United Nations created a UN Temporary Committee on Korea (UNTCOK) to move the country toward independence. The UN plan was to hold elections throughout Korea for a unified National Assembly no later than March. Power would be transferred to this new political authority, the Soviet and American forces would then withdraw, and Korea would achieve its full sovereignty. In retrospect this plan seems to have been doomed, since it was clear that two separate political systems were already taking shape on the peninsula. It was unrealistic to think that the U.S.-supported regime in the South that had been repressing the Communists would accept a Communist victory or that the Soviets would accept a non-Communist government on their side of the border. The Communists who dominated the government in the North and the conservative anticommunists who dominated the South were moving along very different paths.

Since the Soviet Union did not recognize the authority of UNTCOK, there was no way it could sponsor elections in the North. It therefore decided on February 26 to hold elections in "accessible" areas, in other words in the South. Many southern Koreans worried that such elections would in fact create a separate government in the South. They still did not give up hope of unity. Nonetheless, elections were held May 10 for a 200-member National Assembly. Many people boycotted it, as they realized the elections meant the end of achieving a unified government. Although there were more than 300 registered political parties, nearly half the members were independents. The largest party, the conservative Korean Democratic Party, received only twenty-nine seats. Syngman Rhee was made chair of the Assembly. On July 17, the National Assembly adopted a constitution, which required elections for the National Assembly every two years. Every four years the Assembly elected a president, who had strong executive powers. Three days later it elected Rhee by an overwhelming margin as the Republic of Korea's first president. The only other person to receive any votes was Kim Ku; sixteen Assemblymen voted for him. On August 15, 1948, the Republic of Korea (ROK, Korean: Taehan Min'guk) was proclaimed.

The U.N. General Assembly on December 12 accepted the UNTCOK report that the elections were "a valid expression of the free will of the electorate" of that part of the country where they could be monitored; and it declared that the ROK was not only a "lawful" government but also "the only such government in Korea."[11] Authorities in the North then went ahead with their own elections to a new Supreme People's Assembly, which included delegates representing the South as well as the North, the former supposedly chosen through secret "illegal elections." The new assembly declared the Democratic People's Republic of Korea (DPRK, Korean: Chosŏn Minjujuŭi Inmin Konghwaguk) on September 9, 1948. Thus what came to be called in the West North Korea and South Korea came into being as sovereign states.

THE REPUBLIC OF KOREA

The new Republic of Korea began in a precarious state. The North Koreans had cut off the electric power supply, contributing to an already shattered economy. It was an economy that had been geared toward supplying Japan with its needs. Japan, however, was no longer importing Korean products. The South had been the rice basket, but there were no external markets for its production. Most of the industry was in the North. What was located in the ROK was in a sorry state. With its Japanese suppliers and markets gone, the Japanese technicians repatriated, erratic power supplies, and the confusion that followed the government takeover of Japanese enterprises, the meager industrial base was in shambles. Half the country's industries had ceased to operate; the remainder were working at only 20 percent of capacity. South Korea, instead, was heavily reliant on U.S. aid, which amounted to $116 million in 1948–1949, but the Americans were wary of a heavy economic commitment and cut the aid in half during the 1949–1950 period.

President Syngman Rhee governed the state in an authoritarian style. Despite his American education and his decades spent in Hawaii and the U.S. mainland, his manner was autocratic rather than democratic. He carried an antagonistic attitude toward the National Assembly, where his supporters numbered hardly more than a quarter of the 200 seats. To maintain his authority, he relied on the bureaucracy, the police, and the military, all dominated by members who had loyally served in their posts under the Japanese. All six divisions of the ROK Army formed to replace the constabulary had commanders who had served in the Japanese forces. One, Kim Sŏk-wŏn (1893–1978), had headed a special unit to hunt down Kim Il Sung in the late 1930s.[12] Thus the government was open to charges that it was staffed by collaborators, which the many independents in the National Assembly were quick to point out. Since Rhee's own nationalist, anti-Japanese credentials were impeccable, he was able to shield his officials, and they in turn served him. This he had to do when in September 1948 the Assembly passed a National Traitors Act and began investigations of those guilty of serving the colonial authority. Rhee resorted to intimidation and the arrests of assemblymen to protect his base.

To maintain his government's grip on power Rhee made use of the various youth organizations that flourished after the war. Among these was Yi Pŏm-sŏk's (1899–1972) Korean National Youth Corps. Yi himself had an interesting career. Born in Kyŏnggi Province in 1899, he fought as a guerrilla on the Sino-Korean border in the 1920s. In 1933, he went to Germany to study and then to China, where he became an admirer of the Nationalist leader Chiang Kai-shek and of his paramilitary Blueshirts (modeled after the Italian Fascist Blackshirts and the Nazi Brownshirts).[13]

Under the slogan *"minjok chisang, kukka chisang"* (nation first, state first), Yi's Korean National Youth Corps became the largest and most impressive of the many youth groups after the war. In order to keep Yi under control and to utilize his youth corps, Rhee made him his prime minister. There were other youth groups as well, such as the Sŏbuk (Northwest) Youth, a violent anticommunist group containing many refugees from the North. Thus the politics of South Korea was dominated by fear of Communist subversion, a desire and intent to unify the country by force if necessary, and by quarrels and tensions over the question of collaboration during Japanese rule. The presence of so many who had served and even profited under the Japanese threatened to undermine the legitimacy of the government. Compounding all these problems were the severe economic slump, the difficulty of absorbing huge numbers of refugees, and continual clashes along the border.

An example of the new state's instability was played out tragically on Cheju, now a popular resort island off the southern coast of Korea, "Korea's Hawaii." Cheju was the scene of perhaps the most horrendous civil conflict in Korea. There in May 1948, protests against the holding of separate elections in the South became a violent insurrection. The islanders were able to utilize caches of small arms and the miles of defensive tunnels left by the Japanese, who had prepared to make a stand there against Allied invaders. A long campaign in which the population was herded into fortified villages or concentration camps took place before the rebellion was subdued in April 1949. Estimates of casualties vary, but according to historian Kim Hun Joon, about 10 percent of the island's 300,000 people perished.[14]

A further example of the fragility of the new regime became apparent only weeks after the Republic of Korea was proclaimed. On September 13, 1948, the American military completed the transfer of administration to the Koreans, and on October 13, the United States began its withdrawal of troops. A week later, units of the newly formed Army of the Republic of Korea, which were assembled in the southern port of Yŏsu on their way to put down the rebellion on the island of Cheju, themselves rebelled. After a few days of heavy fighting, the revolt was quelled, although some soldiers and supporters continued to hold out in nearby mountains. The Yŏsu Rebellion, occurring almost immediately after responsibility for national security was transferred from the U.S. military to the republic's forces, was a powerful blow to the confidence of the new government, which reacted with a heightened emphasis on internal security.

On October 27, 1948, the National Assembly passed a Law for Special Punishments for Rioters, and on November 20, a more sweeping National Security Law was issued; both gave the National Police, which had proven itself a reliable instrument of control at Yŏsu, broad authority to arrest those who were endangering the security of the state. This law worded antistate activities in such a vague way that it could be used against all kinds of real and perceived enemies. It would remain as one of the most often used and controversial laws in South Korea. Almost every administration for the next half century used it at times for its political advantage. Consequently, a staggeringly large number of Koreans became victims of these measures. More than 700 persons were arrested as subversives in the first week of November alone. American sources estimated that by mid-1949 there were more than 30,000 political prisoners in South Korean jails. Rumors of North Korean infiltrators and conspiratorial activity by subversives were a pervasive part of the South Korean scene in late 1948. On December 1, 1948, for instance, the Seoul chief of police had posters placed on the city streets proclaiming "the North Korean People's Army has already begun its invasion of South Korea. . . . Persons inciting civil disturbances will be shot on sight."[15]

Purges were carried out in the schools, where hundreds of teachers were arrested; in government offices; and in every institution. By some estimates, in the spring of 1950 the number of people in jail had swelled to 60,000, the majority for violating the National Security Act. Meanwhile, the National Assembly elections of May 1950 resulted in only 31 incumbents winning another term. A new, less educated and less politically experienced Assembly was elected. Of these only 57 were Rhee supporters, 27 came from minor parties, and 126 were independents, many anti-Rhee. Anticipating an unfavorable outcome, Rhee attempted to postpone the elections but was forced to hold them as scheduled due to U.S. pressure. Such was the troubled and unstable situation of South Korea on the eve of the Korean War.

THE DEMOCRATIC PEOPLE'S REPUBLIC OF KOREA

North Korea during the 1948–1950 period was a contrast to the instability of the Republic of Korea. The Communist regime was firmly in command. The North Korean Workers' Party, renamed in 1949 the Korean Workers' Party after its merger with the South Korean Workers' Party, consisted of Kim Il Sung and his partisans, who shared key positions with the Yanan Communists such as Kim Tu-bong, some prominent Soviet Koreans, and Pak Hŏn-yŏng and other southern Communists who had fled north. The North Korean government had begun to carry out sweeping reforms. The regime launched massive programs to promote adult literacy. It nationalized major industries and made a start at developing a viable economy under the 1949–1950 two-year economic plan, the product of Japanese-trained economists. North Korea benefited from the array of

Japanese-built industrial plants it inherited, its rich mineral resources, and its ample sources of electric power generated by the hydroelectric dams built by the colonial administration. Most important, perhaps, was the land reform that had been carried out during 1946, in which large holdings were confiscated and redistributed among tenant farmers and small landholders. This provided a basis for rural support and helped legitimize the new state. The state took 25 percent of the harvest as a tax. However, not blessed with good agricultural land and cut off from the rich farmlands of the South, North Korea suffered from chronic food shortages, which would continue to plague the state for decades to come.

Furthermore, the North Korean regime of Kim Il Sung had few of the problems of legitimacy that weakened the South Korean government, since Kim Il Sung, his guerrilla partisans, and the other Communists had untarnished credentials as patriotic, anti-Japanese resistance fighters. Kim Il Sung was not yet the absolute dictator he would later become, but he had the backing of the Soviets and was clearly in overall command of the state. He was aided by a corps of several hundred Soviet-Koreans, who provided administrative and technical expertise, and by the veterans who had fought with the Chinese Communists and thus possessed considerable military experience. Unlike the South, there was no significant internal opposition. The Korean Workers' Party (KWP) was a mass organization of 700,000 members under his control. The Stalinist-model command economy that was constructed under Soviet tutelage was well suited for mobilizing the population for war. A confident North Korean government then sought to unify the country.

ON THE EVE OF THE KOREAN WAR

One of the great controversies in recent history has been the origins of the Korean War. The war has been seen as inevitable by some, a tragic and avoidable mistake by others. The division of Korea into North and South was an unanticipated and unacceptable outcome to almost all Koreans. Leaders in both North Korea and South Korea viewed the establishment of separate regimes as tragic but only temporary. North Korea's 1948 constitution stated Seoul was the capital of the Democratic People's Republic of Korea; Pyongyang was only the temporary capital. In the South, Syngman Rhee also did not regard the division as permanent and issued frequent calls for reunification. Frequent clashes took place along the thirty-eighth parallel.

The volatile situation was only made worse by Korea's entanglement in the Cold War. U.S.-Soviet rivalry already existed in 1945 and intensified over the next several years. The Soviet Union's support of international

Communist movements, and its view of world history as the inevitable struggle between the socialist and capitalist world, with the former eventually victorious, clashed with the American fear of Communism and desire to establish and maintain a peaceful world order with governments amenable to the U.S. and Allied trade and investment. The Cold War came into clear focus with the Truman Doctrine of March 1947 and the American policy of containment. The U.S.-Soviet rivalry focused on Europe, where American and Soviet forces faced each other. The Berlin blockade of 1948–1949 sharpened these tensions; the creation of NATO in April 1949 gave the U.S.-led alliance in Europe an institutional form. While U.S. attention was mainly directed at Europe, Asia was an area of increasing concern for the United States and its allies. The Chinese civil war (1946–1949) ended with the Chinese Communist victory and the proclamation of the People's Republic of China on October 1, 1949. In February 1950, Mao Zedong signed the Sino-Soviet Treaty of Friendship, Alliance and Mutual Assistance, making China and the USSR formal allies. The United States, which had invested considerable military aid in an unsuccessful bid to support the Nationalists under Chiang Kai-shek, now largely wrote him off as he fled to Taiwan. By early 1950, the United States saw the fall of this last stronghold as inevitable. The "loss" of China to the Communists put pressure on the Truman administration to draw the line of containment in Asia, but at the same time, most U.S. policy makers wanted to avoid a land war in Asia, which was less important to them than Europe.

There was consequently a somewhat ambiguous American position on South Korea. The United States supported the state and wanted to prevent Communism from spreading closer to Japan, which all agreed was vital to U.S. interests; however, the American political leaders in the Truman administration and in Congress did not want to invest too much in a land that remained of peripheral concern. When the United States withdrew its troops from Korea it allocated funds for the establishment of a 65,000-man ROK Army and also left behind a 500-member Korean Military Advisory Group (KMAG) to help train this new South Korean force. The United States also provided generous economic aid to Seoul. But this generosity waned; economic aid after 1949 was considerably reduced; and funding for the South Korean Army was limited. Americans were particularly wary of President Rhee's strident nationalism and were concerned over reports of ROK raids along the northern border, as they wanted to avoid the risk of conflict on the peninsula. Only small arms were provided for the ROK forces, and no significant aircraft. Even in small arms, the ROK Army had only a fifteen-day supply in June 1950.[16] The United States was unclear about the extent of its commitment; the most famous example was Secretary of State Dean Acheson's January

1950 press conference in which he excluded South Korea from the U.S. defensive perimeter; it would instead have to rely on the UN.

The Soviet Union, as well, sought to limit its commitment to Korea and was reluctant to see a war start there, but this changed. From the start, the USSR provided an earlier and more extensive buildup of the North Korean armed forces. After the Soviet forces pulled out at the end of 1948, they provided more heavy military equipment including tanks and artillery. Thousands of Koreans were sent to the USSR for training in the use of this equipment. But the key factor in North Korea's military buildup was the determination of its leadership to unify the country by force.

North Korean leaders had hopes that the inevitable armed conflict could be carried out at least in part by Communist guerrillas in the South. There were some active groups in the southern part of the country, particularly in the mountainous areas in the southwest. In addition, the Kangdong Institute under the direction of Pak Hŏn-yŏng trained and sent hundreds of guerrillas to the mountainous areas of the South to provoke a national uprising. However, these guerrilla bands and others drawn from the Yŏsu mutineers were geographically confined to a small area and suffered substantial losses to South Korean counterinsurgency campaigns during 1948–1949 and 1949–1950.[17] Certainly by 1949, if not earlier, Kim was convinced that an invasion by his forces was necessary for unification, although he expected widespread support for such an invasion by disaffected southerners. North Korea's army was large and grew larger, with 150,000 men under arms by June 1950 compared to less than 100,000 in the ROK. It had many more experienced troops than South Korea's military. In late 1946, North Korea began sending recruits to Manchuria to aid the Chinese Communists in that crucial area. Tens of thousands fought in the People's Liberation Army. As the Communists' victory approached, North Korea requested their return and these veterans began streaming back, providing North Korea with experienced troops.[18] With his tanks, artillery, and other arms, and his troops fresh from combat, Kim was convinced any invasion of the South would be easy, a matter of a few days. Seoul was not far from the border and would fall shortly after the invasion, and the ROK would collapse before the Americans could intervene. He was further persuaded by Pak Hŏn-yŏng and his South Korean colleagues, who argued that thousands of South Koreans would rise up in support of an invasion by the North.

On June 35, 1949, the North Koreans created the Democratic Front for the Unification of the Fatherland, a coalition of Communists and the small token non-Communist political groups, whose aim was to unify the Korean peninsula and remove both the "Rhee clique" and the Americans. Meanwhile Kim and Pak made visits to Moscow to persuade Stalin to support an invasion. At first Stalin was reluctant to get involved, but he came to believe that this was a low-risk, sure victory. The Soviets may have also liked the idea of unifying Korea as a strategic buffer state on its border, and of drawing American attention away from Europe. In January 1950 Stalin signaled his support of the plan. Moscow made it clear that it would assist with military planning and training but not with troop support, and it wanted Mao Zedong to commit himself to assist if necessary. Despite some reservations, Mao agreed in April. Moscow sent a team of military experts to assist in drawing up the plans. Kim and his Soviet advisors set the date for late June, just before the onset of the summer rainy season. Some historians have argued that the Korean War had begun before the North Korean invasion on June 25, 1950. Armed clashes involving thousands of troops and hundreds of casualties took place along the border, often initiated by ambitious young officers of the ROK Army. And a North Korean–supported guerrilla insurgency existed in the South. But these were all dwarfed by the immensity of the conflict that began with Pyongyang's invasion.

THE KOREAN WAR

South Koreans often call the Korean War the "June 25th Incident," for it was on June 25, 1950, that this horrendous conflict, perhaps the bloodiest of the Cold War, began. On that day, predawn artillery barrages began on the troublesome Ongjin Peninsula. Within hours, North Korea launched a full-scale offensive along the border. The KPA was initially focused on capturing Seoul. Kim Il Sung's plan was to quickly capture the capital; he apparently believed the rest of the state would then soon crumble. The attack took the United States, the ROK, and most of the world by surprise. Just two days earlier, a UN team of observers had completed an inspection tour of the border without suspecting an imminent invasion. Better equipped with heavy artillery and tanks and better trained with thousands of veterans of the Chinese civil war, the KPA had a clear military superiority over the more poorly equipped and trained South Korean Army. ROK forces defended Seoul for two days and then began to crumble. Seoul quickly fell amid horrendous scenes of thousands of panicked, fleeing civilians. Hundreds were killed as the South Koreans prematurely blew up the Han River Bridge while it was packed with civilians heading southward. The Truman administration reacted almost immediately as soon as the scale of the invasion was confirmed. On June 27, Truman authorized General MacArthur to use U.S. air and naval forces at his disposal to support the ROK Army. Uncertain of support from a Republican-dominated Congress, he went directly to the United Nations and called for a resolution giving the United States authority to intervene.

This passed quickly, as the Soviet Union was boycotting the UN to protest the refusal of the organization to allow the new Communist regime in Beijing to take China's seat, still held by the Nationalist government now headquartered on Taiwan. The UN Security Council resolution called for the withdrawal of forces by the Democratic People's Republic of Korea (DPRK) and called for UN members to assist the ROK. On July 7, the UN Security Council established a unified military command under the United States. Eventually sixteen nations contributed forces. By the spring of 1951, this included 12,000 British, 8,500 Canadian, 5,000 Turkish, and 5,000 Filipino troops.[19] But the U.N. action would mainly be an American operation, with the United States supplying the bulk of the troops, paying the cost, and taking total command.

U.S. troops from occupied Japan, where about 100,000 American forces were stationed, began to arrive in Korea on June 30. America at this time was not well prepared for the conflict. The occupation forces in Japan were largely involved in administrative duties and had little combat readiness. The U.S. armed forces had been downsizing since the end of World War II from 12 million men and women in uniform in 1945 to 1.6 million in June 1950. There were fewer than 600,000 in the army and many of these were in Europe. When the first American troops saw action at Osan, south of Seoul, on July 5, they were forced into retreat along with their accompanying ROK forces.

By this time, the KPA was advancing steadily south. The DPRK's forces captured Taejŏn in early July, then advanced toward Pusan, where the South Korean government had fled. Although the ROK forces were totally outmatched by the KPA and Seoul fell in days, the retreating South Korean troops did not collapse as fast as the North Koreans had expected but often put up stubborn resistance. Nor did large bands of guerrillas appear, although there was some Communist guerrilla activity in the southeastern mountains, remnants of those that had not yet been subdued. Most active leftists in the South had been killed or imprisoned or had fled to the North by June 1950. By and large, the South Korean population fled or acquiesced to the North Koreans but with some minor exceptions did not rise up in arms against their own government. So Kim's expectation that the war would be over in a matter of days was wrong. By early August, the ROK had shrunk to a small area in the southeast corner of the country around Pusan, the so-called Pusan perimeter. But enough U.S. forces had arrived to halt the KPA offensive, and the war temporarily stalemated.

By early August, the Chinese were already becoming concerned, and Mao had decided to send Chinese volunteers to assist Pyongyang if the U.S. forces were to reverse the tide of war. Meanwhile, General Douglas MacArthur, who had been put in command of the UN forces, came up with a daring plan to launch a surprise landing at Inchon (Inch'ŏn), totally outflanking and trapping the KPA. Over the objections of many military officials in Washington, who feared it was too risky, MacArthur brought 80,000 marines and 260 ships to Inchon, negotiating the treacherous tides and sandbars, and landed. Although Soviet and Chinese warnings had been made to Kim Il Sung that the Americans might land on the west coast, he was focusing on the Pusan perimeter and taken completely by surprise. U.S. and ROK forces fought their way back into Seoul, and by the end of September most of the KPA was in nearly total disarray, although some KPA forces managed to retreat intact up the east coast. Had the United States been willing to accept the prewar status quo, the war could have ended soon after. North Korean forces had been defeated at a heavy cost for South Korea. One estimate is that 111,000 South Koreans had been killed, and 57,000 were missing. Over 300,000 homes were destroyed. UN forces lost about 7,000 killed or missing.[20] But the North Korean forces in the South largely disintegrated and were no longer a threat.

Unfortunately, the war did not stop at the end of September. MacArthur, as well as Syngman Rhee, was determined to "roll back" the North Koreans. MacArthur wanted the complete destruction of the DPRK; the South Korean leaders wanted reunification, which now seemed so close. The UN resolution had only authorized that the North Koreans be repelled. Some in the United States and some allies, especially Britain, feared widening the war, for there was the possibility of Chinese or even Soviet intervention. China, which maintained no diplomatic relations with the United States, sent a warning in early October through India's ambassador in Beijing that China would not tolerate a U.S. presence on its border. On September 30, ROK forces crossed the thirty-eighth parallel in pursuit of the KPA troops. Perhaps overconfident after the success of Inchon, Washington now gave MacArthur permission to destroy all KPA forces, and on October 7, the UN passed a vaguely worded resolution that approved the use of UN troops to cross the thirty-eighth parallel for the purpose of establishing a unified government. On October 9, UN forces moved north of the parallel. Throughout October, UN and ROK forces, which were under UN authority, swept across North Korea capturing Pyongyang and other major cities while the DPRK government fled to the mountainous strongholds near the Manchurian border. A concerned Stalin, not yet certain of China's military intention, ordered Kim Il Sung to retreat to Manchuria. On October 20, a triumphant President Rhee visited Pyongyang.

Just as Korea appeared to become reunified under UN forces, the Chinese forces intervened. When the UN forces crossed into North Korea, the Chinese immediately made the decision to begin sending troops. Some members of the Chinese leadership hesitated about intervening, fearing a conflict with the United States, but Mao prevailed. He argued for the need to have a buffer to protect China; he did not want U.S. troops on his border. Mao also hoped to drive the American imperialists out of the Korean peninsula altogether and promote the revolutionary cause in Asia. Moreover, a war would be useful in consolidating the new regime's hold over China and mobilizing the population.[21] The Chinese forces came in as the Chinese People's Volunteers (CPV), not as the regular People's Liberation Army, but they were in fact regular forces led by veteran general Peng Dehuai. On October 19, the Chinese forces under Peng began entering Korea; they did so discreetly, avoiding drawing attention to their large numbers. The UN forces meanwhile fought scattered units of the KPA, guerrillas, and some CPV units, but they did not expect a massive intervention by the Chinese. Chinese warnings to the Americans through diplomatic channels were dismissed, and intelligence analysts disagreed as to the significance of troop buildups along the Manchurian border. On November 24, MacArthur began an offensive to complete the war before Christmas; in response, the Chinese counterattacked in force on November 27. Overextended and overconfident, the UN troops were forced into a full retreat. Chinese forces advanced as swiftly as the UN and ROK forces had done weeks earlier. On December 6, Chinese and North Koreans troops retook Pyongyang; within two weeks, almost all of North Korea was under Communist control. The Chinese advanced south, crossing the thirty-eighth parallel and retaking Seoul on January 4. But by late January their offensive was losing momentum. Driven back to the thirty-seventh parallel, the UN forces regrouped and stopped the Chinese. A new offensive in February was repelled with enormous Chinese losses. The Chinese sought to compensate for their inferior firepower by launching massive assaults, the so-called "human wave" tactic, but the UN forces were able to repulse these and retake Seoul on March 15. The city had changed hands for the fourth time in less than a year.

The Truman administration, having pushed the Communist forces back to roughly around the thirty-eighth parallel, was willing to negotiate a truce. Efforts in this direction, however, were undermined by MacArthur, who stated his position in a public "no substitute for victory" letter that called for widening the war. On April 11, 1951, Truman dismissed MacArthur as commander, replacing him with General Matthew Ridgeway, a competent and more obedient commander. By spring, Mao was ready to accept a stalemate with the peninsula divided approximately where it had been before the outbreak of the conflict. With Stalin's approval, he signaled his willingness to begin armistice talks. In July, formal negotiations began as representatives of the Chinese People's Volunteers, the Korean People's Army, and the United Nations command met. The war, however, would continue for two more years. The initial problems—

the creation of a line of demarcation for the two Koreas, the establishment of a demilitarized zone (DMZ), and the creation of a Military Armistice Commission—were agreed on. It was clear that the boundary line would be roughly similar but not exactly the same as the thirty-eighth parallel, extending a little below it to the west and above it to the east. The main stumbling block was the issue of prisoner exchange. The UN held 95,000 KPA and 20,000 CPV prisoners; the Communists held 16,000 ROK and a small number of UN prisoners. The UN command insisted that the prisoner repatriation be voluntary, while the Chinese and North Koreans insisted on a general exchange. Many North Korean prisoners and some Chinese did not want to return. The small number of North Koreans and Chinese who opted for exchange was unacceptable to the Communists. By early 1952 the talks were at a logjam. Meanwhile, the Chinese People's Volunteers and the Korean People's Army, who had constructed many miles of tunnels and underground fortifications, hunkered down.

The first year of the war had a horrific impact on Korea. When the North Koreans retook Seoul and other parts of the South, they set up people's committees. DPRK officials confiscated the property of the ROK government, its officials, and "monopoly capitalists," and drew up plans to redistribute land in the countryside, completing the partial land reform that had begun under the U.S. occupation. They released political prisoners from the jails, many of whom sought the opportunity to get revenge on the police and others who had persecuted them. Thousands of young men were impressed into the North Korean Army. The Communists committed a number of atrocities. In general, few South Koreans showed much enthusiasm for their liberators, and many fled. Pusan and other southern cites swelled with refugees. Pusan became the wartime capital of the ROK. When the ROK forces occupied the North they in turn carried out ruthless purges of Communists, committing their own share of atrocities. Most people in North Korea showed as little enthusiasm for their liberators as southerners had. As with most civil wars, this was a vicious, unpleasant conflict. For the millions of Koreans caught up in the conflict such as Lee Young Ho, it was a true and confusing nightmare. Lee was a seventeen-year-old high school student in Seoul when the North Koreans occupied the city. His frightened family attempted to stay at home but Lee, venturing on the street, was taken into custody by the occupiers and, without his family knowing his whereabouts, was forced into the North Korean Army, only to desert during the hasty retreat in the fall of 1950. He then wound up fighting in the South Korean Army. He and his family survived, and can therefore be counted as among the fortunate.[22]

The last two years of conventional fighting were largely confined to a narrow strip of land. The allies carried out an extensive bombing of the North. On July 11, 1952, the Americans launched "Operation Pressure

Pump" in which U.S. planes undertook a massive bombing of Pyongyang and thirty other cities. In May 1953 the United States carried out a
bombing campaign directed at dams to destroy the rice crop.[23] Cities in
the DPRK were totally destroyed, as was most of the infrastructure. U.S.
planes, looking for targets, bombed the elaborate irrigation system with
its many reservoirs on which the country's agriculture was dependent.
More Allied bombs were dropped on North Korea than on Germany or
Japan in World War II. With limited air defenses, the North Koreans endured the conflict in underground shelters, somehow surviving.

One of the surprising developments in the war was the survival of the
Kim Il Sung regime. In spite of Kim's disastrous failures he appeared to
have consolidated his power even as operational control over the war effort passed to the Chinese. When the war went against him, he was quick
to put the blame on his rivals in the leadership. His government in the fall
of 1950 retreated to the provincial town of Kanggye, a site protected by
mountainous terrain and near the Manchurian border. There, at a party
meeting in December 1950, he carried out a purge of the party. Mu Chŏng,
the veteran of Yan'an, was dismissed in late 1950 and died shortly after.
The Soviet Korean Hŏ Ka-i (1904–1953) came under attack and committed suicide in the spring of 1953. The Communist leaders from the South
were given special blame for the great guerrilla uprising that had failed to
appear. A show trial convicted the top southern Communists led by Pak
Hŏn-yŏng, and most were eventually executed. The former Communist
leader in the South was arrested, tried, and convicted of treason in August
1953. He was put to death two years later. Half the old Korean Workers'
Party had been lost through death, desertion, or expulsion. Many of these
were expelled for cooperating with the ROK or UN when they reoccupied
much of the North. Kim Il Sung dealt with this by rebuilding the party
during the war, so that by 1953 it had one million members, truly a massive party in a nation of fewer than ten million. Nearly one in four adults
became a party member. The majority of these were uneducated farmers
and workers selected out of their loyalty to the state and party during the
war. Thus it was virtually a new party, a party of common people, not of
the more educated as the old party had been.

The South Korean government carried on as best it could during the
war from its temporary capital of Pusan. All southern cities were swol-
len by hundreds of thousands of refugees. Just keeping people alive
was a major problem. The UN and other aid agencies did heroic work
with the help of Koreans. The war effort in the South brought forth considerable examples of courage and heroism in overcoming incredible
odds. Tent schools were set up, for example, with massive classes so
that the school year could continue, and most children somehow kept
up on their lessons. Unfortunately, the war brought out some horrible

incidents of violence, corruption, and thuggish politics. President Rhee, always of authoritarian nature, used the conflict to try to strengthen his hold on government. To many Koreans, he was a symbol of national resistance. But the reputation of his administration was seriously damaged by scandals. One was the massacre in February 1951 of more than 700 villagers in Koch'ang in South Kyŏngsang Province during anti-guerrilla operations there. Attempts by National Assemblymen to investigate were met with repression. To mobilize all available men for the war effort, Rhee created a National Defense Corps, but this was so riddled with incompetence and corruption it caused a great uproar, and Rhee had its director arrested and executed. More than fifty years later, other atrocities would emerge that were committed by North Korean forces in the South, South Korean forces in the North, by the ROK government against its own people, and by U.S. forces.

North Korean forces executed thousands during their brief occupation of Seoul and other parts of the ROK. They also took thousands of South Koreans with them when they retreated north; most were never heard of again. The ROK also executed many suspected communists. In 1949 Seoul organized 300,000 former or suspected communists into the National Guidance Alliance, designed to keep them under state surveillance. In 1950, as the North invaded, 30,000 were rounded up and 2,993 killed as preventative measure.[24] By some current estimates, up to 100,000 South Koreans were killed by their own government. Nor were the Americans entirely innocent of atrocities. In one highly publicized event that came to light in 1999, U.S. troops in July 1950 deliberately fired into civilians fleeing from the KPA in the central village of No Gun Ri (Nogun-ri), killing a disputed number. And there were the huge civilian casualties from American bombings in North Korea. The United States was accused by the Communist powers of using bacteriological weapons in the North, but this has generally been dismissed as a false charge.

Rhee attempted to appear above political parties, so he associated himself with none. But, worried about the 1952 election, he created his own Liberal Party in December 1951. He then tried to pass a constitutional amendment that would call for a direct popular election for president under the assumption that the National Assembly would not support his reelection. When the National Assembly refused to pass the amendment, he had martial law declared in Pusan and arrested the members. Intimidated, they voted for the amendment and in a direct election with no credible opponent, Rhee was easily elected to another four-year term. Thus, as was the case with Kim Il Sung, Rhee was able to use the wartime conditions to consolidate his power despite setbacks on the battlefield.

The conflict ended in the summer of 1953. The election in November 1952 of President Eisenhower, who had promised to end the conflict, was followed by his visit to Korea. The Soviet Union, however, may not have minded its continuation. The Soviets were careful not to get directly involved in the conflict. They supplied equipment to the North Koreans and Chinese and flew some reconnaissance aircraft but in general did not commit troops. This was in good part because Stalin was not eager to get into a conflict and did not want to take forces away from Europe, which was the area of confrontation with the West that mattered most to the USSR. The war from the Soviet point of view tied the U.S. forces down in the east, lifted pressure from Europe, drained American resources, and cost the Soviets little, since it was fought by the Chinese and North Koreans. However, there was a concern that an Eisenhower administration would place great military pressure to end the war. Mao may have found the cost of the conflict bearable because it was fought with troops from the civil war, there was no shortage of cannon fodder, and the war was useful for rallying support for his new regime. Furthermore, having fought the Americans to a stalemate added to his prestige. Yet as the war dragged on, indications are that Mao was willing to bring it to an end. Stalin's death in March removed an obstacle to peace, as his successors showed little interest in continuing the conflict. North Korea needed a respite from the constant American bombing; its hope of reunifying Korea was clearly dashed, at least for the near future. So in the spring of 1953 all parties were ready to bring the war to an end.

A major exception was Syngman Rhee. The stubborn South Korean leader was both an asset and a liability for the Americans. His personal charisma and oratorical skills were important in rallying the South Korean people for the war effort. However, Rhee quarreled with the Americans over the aims of the conflict. He was unwilling to let go of the hope of reunifying his country and pressured the United States to push the war to complete victory. He was adamantly opposed to a negotiated truce that left the country divided as it had been before. Rhee gave speeches, organized mass rallies, and used every opportunity to call for the continuation of the war until Korea was reunified. He even threatened to continue the war alone if the UN called a truce. So difficult had he become that in 1952 the U.S. government began a secret plan, "Operation Plan Everready," to remove him and replace him with someone thought to be easier for the Americans to deal with. At one point in the spring of 1953 he tried to sabotage the negotiations for prisoner exchange by releasing 25,000 North Korean Communist prisoners being held in the South. Eventually, however, an armistice was agreed to by the UN, North Korea, and China, who signed it on July 27, 1953. It came into force without Rhee's signature.

Historians have debated both the cause and the nature of the Korean War. Could it have been prevented? Who was responsible for it? Given the unacceptability of a divided Korea to most nationalists and Kim Il

Sung's determination to reunify the country, it seemed almost inevitable. In fact, had South Korea's military been stronger, the ROK may have been tempted to invade the North. Some have argued the war could not have occurred without Stalin's approval and Mao's acceptance. Stalin appears to have been initially reluctant to approve an invasion but eventually backed it, perhaps seeing it as a low-risk gamble after having been assured by Kim and Pak Hŏn-yŏng that victory would be swift and certain. The United States has been criticized for not making its willingness to defend South Korea clear. It has often been charged that Secretary of State Dean Acheson's ambiguity about the U.S. commitment to defend South Korea in his famous January 12, 1950, press conference encouraged Kim Il Sung and Stalin to invade, but archival evidence does not suggest this influenced their decision. However, the United States did not provide adequate preparations for the country's defense. Clearly Kim Il Sung is most immediately responsible, as well as Pak Hŏn-yŏng. Hotheads on both sides of the peninsula contributed to the tensions that preceded the war. The United States is to blame for its role in the division of Korea, the USSR for its part in that division and its support of the invasion. China bears some responsibility, and one can even assign responsibility to Japan for creating the situation that led to the Allied occupation of Korea that resulted in the division.

Scholars have also debated whether it should be considered a civil war or an international conflict. It was a civil war that became an international conflict, with both North and South Koreans acting as manipulators as well as victims of the great powers. Historians will, no doubt, long be debating these issues.

THE IMPACT OF THE KOREAN WAR

No one knows for certain the extent of the losses; one estimate places the toll at 750,000 military and 800,000 civilian deaths. Of the military deaths, 300,000 were from the North Korean Army, 227,000 from the ROK Army, and 200,000 from the Chinese People's Volunteers (some estimates place this figure much higher). About 37,000 Americans and 4,000 UN allies were killed. Civilian casualties are hard to estimate. Some estimates place the number of South Koreans who died of all causes including disease, exposure, and starvation at nearly one million. North Korean casualties were extremely severe, with estimates as high as 10 to 15 percent of the country's population of a little under ten million perishing.

The Korean War contributed to the upheaval of Korean society that had begun in the 1930s. In South Korea it expedited the land reform (see chapter 13) and wiped out the wealth of many, acting as a great social leveling process. It also enhanced the power of the South Korean state. The massive U.S. aid that arrived in the wake of the war provided an invaluable economic prop to the Rhee government, since it gave the state access to foreign currency, which it was able to use to reward or discipline businesses and industries, and other potential supporters and opponents. More importantly, the Korean War provided the state a means of legitimizing itself through the use of the ideology of anticommunism. Anticommunism provided a rationale for state power and gave a purpose and raison d'être for the South Korean state. South Korea was on the front line of Communism, a member of the free world that had to be ever vigilant against Communist aggression and subversion. The three-year conflict created a huge military force, which grew from 100,000 troops on the eve of the conflict to 600,000 at the end. After the war, the military forces were kept at this level, well equipped by the United States and increasingly well trained. It was, in fact, one of the ten largest armed forces in the world. The war continued and greatly enhanced the economic and cultural influence of the United States on South Korea. The United States provided $200 million in aid annually for the decade after the war, a figure that accounted for a tenth of the total economy. While most of this economic support was in the form of immediate relief, not industrial investment, it did at least sustain the state until South Korean policy makers were able to work out successful strategies for economic development. The presence of hundreds of thousands of GIs and civilian officials, and the long-term stationing of troops in this historically homogeneous and sometimes xenophobic society, ensured that American culture would flow into the country. It also ensured that South Korea would be linked with the Western world politically, economically, and culturally.

The conflict brought horrific destruction to North Korea. The United States dropped 635,000 tons of bombs in Korea. This was 20 percent more than in the entire Pacific theater of World War II and slightly more than the Americans had dropped on Germany. All this bombing was inflicted upon a small, Pennsylvania-sized country with fewer than ten million people. It does not include the 32,000 tons of napalm that also rained upon the North Koreans.[25] North Korea's cities, even very small ones, were devastated. Official U.S. estimates were that between 50 and 90 percent of eighteen of the twenty-two largest North Korean cities were destroyed, including 75 percent of Pyongyang and 80 and 85 percent of Hamhŭng and Hŭngnam, the two largest industrial cities. This compares with an estimated 43 percent destruction of Japan's largest cities in the Second World War.[26] Yet, despite Kim Il Sung's disastrous failures in launching a war, the conflict had the effect of consolidating rather than weakening his hold on power. Although the Chinese took control of the military operations during the war, they did not interfere with domestic political affairs. In fact, as Andrei Lankov has stated, the war "untied the hands" of Kim Il Sung since it weakened the influence of the Soviet Union. Militarily dependent on China, North Korea achieved a greater measure of political independence from Moscow.[27] Stalin's apparent willingness to abandon North Korea to the UN forces when he ordered Kim to retreat into Manchuria may only have reinforced Kim's need to be militarily self-reliant. Furthermore, Kim Il Sung remained determined to unify the nation. He lost a battle but not the war. As a result, North Korea would remain on a warlike footing, and keep tensions on the peninsula high.

The war that started in order to reunify Korea ended by hardening its division. For all Koreans the division was an unacceptable and temporary condition. The regimes in both Seoul and Pyongyang in 1950 were committed to end this aberration at almost any cost. The tragedy of the Korean War for Koreans was that they suffered so much but failed to achieve the unity they all desired. Instead, the conflict drove the two Koreas bitterly apart and consolidated their separate systems.

KOREA IN GLOBAL PERSPECTIVE: DIVIDED COUNTRIES

Korea was not the only country to be divided in the twentieth century. India, Ireland, and Palestine were all partitioned, but these were along ethnic or sectarian lines. Germany and Vietnam provide better analogies, since they were also divided as a result of Cold War conflicts. The division of Germany into East and West is best known and in some ways most resembles that of Korea, since it was the result of the lines of occupation drawn by the Western powers and the Soviet Union at the close of World War II. After a short occupation—four years versus the three for Korea—two rival regimes were set up, with the Communist East Germany having a smaller population than the non-Communist West Germany. In Germany, too, the two regimes were also partly based on preexisting ideological divisions. But the parallels end there. East Germany was much smaller than West Germany, with only a quarter of the latter's population, versus North Korea, which had half the population of South Korea. Since the North was much more industrialized than the South, the disparities in size and economic potential were less pronounced than between the two Germanys. East Germany was far more the creation and puppet of the Soviet Union and never posed a serious military threat to West Germany. There was no bitter civil war between the two, and in spite of the construction of the Berlin Wall in 1961, East Germany was not hermetically sealed from the West; people from the West did visit relatives in the East, and many Easterners were able to receive West German television. While the desire for reunification remained strong, Germany itself had been created out of various states only seventy-four years before it was divided. The division, while tragic, occurred in a land with stronger regional identities, and a shorter history of unification. Furthermore, the Germans themselves bore some measure of responsibility for their situation, having been a menace to their neighbors.

Vietnam might be a closer analogy. It was divided roughly equally into north and south halves in 1954 following a long war against the French. As in Korea, the division in part reflected ideological divisions inside the independence movement. And like Korea, the division was not acceptable, especially to the North, which waged a long, ultimately successful struggle for reunification. But there were some pronounced differences. Vietnam's divisions reflected a certain historical and geographical logic. Although in each half the overwhelming majority was ethnically Vietnamese, the two population centers in the Hong River Basin in the north and the lower Mekong River Basin in the south were separated by a long, narrow coastal plain and rugged highlands. Lifestyles differed in the two regions, which were in reality separate states for several centuries before reunification in 1802. As tragic and unacceptable as its division was, Vietnam simply did not have a comparable history of unity or the same degree of cultural homogeneity, nor was the division so arbitrarily drawn and imposed. And unlike Korea, North Vietnam and its South Vietnamese Viet Cong supporters prevailed after two decades of fighting.

In short, there is no case truly comparable to the division of Korea, to its suddenness, its arbitrariness, and to the tragedy it resulted in. The border between the two states became the most tense, most sealed, and perhaps most unacceptable of all political boundaries in the second half of the twentieth century.

KOREA IN GLOBAL PERSPECTIVE: THE KOREAN WAR

The Korean War had a considerable impact on not just Korea but on its neighbors and the world. China's historical course was profoundly affected by the Korean War. The Chinese paid a high price for their entry. According to Chinese statistics 152,000 were killed or missing, including Mao's son Mao Anying.[28] Most Western scholars believe the actual figures were far greater. China also paid for the war with the loss of Taiwan. On the eve of the war China was preparing to invade Taiwan, but when the war started Truman sent the Seventh Fleet into the Taiwan Strait, blocking the invasion. Thus the emergence of an effectively independent, prosperous, and democratic Taiwan and the ongoing two-Chinas issue were products of the Korean War. Furthermore, the war had another very significant impact on China. The United States responded to the war by building a defensive wall around the country, with military bases in South Korea, Taiwan, Japan, the Philippines, and Thailand, and with the ships of the Seventh Fleet off the coast. This led to isolation and a siege mentality that contributed to the path of China's development for more than a quarter of a century. Only after 1978 did China break out of this wall and begin to enter extensive intercourse with the West, Japan, and rest of the non-Communist world.

For Japan, the Korean conflict was the turning point in its postwar economic development. During the first five years after its surrender, the Japanese economy languished, and was heavily dependent on American support. Then, the outbreak of the Korean War turned the economic situation around. The U.S. government at the onset of conflict made the decision to take advantage of Japan's proximity, low costs, and recovery needs to use it as a supply base for the war effort. Consequently, the Americans made $2.37 billion worth of special procurements in the four years starting with June 1950, creating a huge demand for ammunition, trucks, uniforms, communications equipment, and other products from Japanese companies.[29] The president of Toyota would later remark, "These orders were Toyota's salvation. I felt a mighty joy for my company and a sense of guilt that I was rejoicing over another country's war."[30] The president of the Bank of Japan, drawing a comparison to the "divine wind" (*kamikaze*) that saved Japan from the Mongols, called the war procurement "divine aid."[31] Yoshida Shigeru, the dominant political figure of the era, agreed, calling the Korean War "a gift of the gods."[32] The war consolidated the power base of the political conservatives and helped to shape Japan's postwar relationship with the United States. It unfortunately had a tragic consequence for the remaining Koreans in the country, who found it difficult to be repatriated to a North Korea hostile to Japan or to a devastated South Korea. They remained a marginalized and mistreated minority.

The Korean War shaped the political alliance system in East Asia for most of the rest of the century. When the war ended, the United States sought to shift some of the effort to contain Communism in Asia to a NATO-like regional collective security alliance including Japan, Taiwan, and South Korea. South Korea became a long-term U.S. client state; the 1954 ROK-U.S. mutual defense treaty formalized this relationship, and 30,000 U.S. troops remained in the country a half century later. The war reinforced the arguments for a continued U.S. presence in Japan that was incorporated into the peace settlement. Already the coming of the Communists in China in 1949 and the February 1950 alliance with the Soviet Union made any friendship between Beijing and Tokyo unlikely, and the U.S. alliance with Japan perhaps inevitable. The war made the arguments for the U.S.-Japan relationship more compelling. A bilateral treaty between Japan and Taiwan in April 1952 and a peace treaty between Japan and South Korea in 1965 completed the American-led alliance system in East Asia. It also led to two decades of hostility and suspicion between the United States and China, with images of China's "human wave" tactics in the conflict contributing to American fear of aggression by fanatic Chinese Communists. The Korean conflict colored perceptions of the need to contain Communism in Asia, and influenced the U.S. involvement in Vietnam.

The Korean War had another less direct or obvious impact on East Asia, with global significance as well. The war created two U.S. client states: South Korea and Taiwan, which, while under the U.S. military umbrella, were also economically linked with the U.S., Japanese, and global markets. Following a decade of massive U.S. aid, they became a favorite place for American, Japanese, and European investment. Partly by emulating Japan's post–World War II developmental state, they flourished and became third-world success stories, providing a model for China after 1978, as well as for other developing nations. Thus, in an indirect way, the Korean War created the political, military, and economic order in East Asia and contributed to the region's rise as a center of the global economy.

Summary of the Instructions of Commanding General Chistiakov at the Meeting of the Five Provinces (November 1, 1945)

To you Koreans. For thirty-six years, the Japanese Imperialists plundered Korean financial resources, limited the freedom of speech, effaced racial independence and national existence, pillaged your language, and in addition dragged you into the war. But now you have been liberated from slavery under the Japanese oppression.

The time for the Korean people to plan their own living has arrived. The Red Army has absolutely no intention to plunder, but rather to restore the independence of Korea. All private properties are under the reliable protection of the Red Army, so there is no cause for fear. We are not going to compel our principles of government on this land. Though we are establishing a democratic form of government here, you have the right to express your own point of view. Every organization must guarantee the freedom of religion. Leaders must settle rapidly all matters concerning mining enterprises. Make a detailed examination of all mining machineries, also of raw materials, and take preparation to train mining technicians as soon as possible. Immediate steps much be taken to convert production of war machineries to production of machineries used in peacetime. All factories must be kept operating. All problems concerning food supply and raw materials must be settled. The Japanese took away most of the food raised by the farmers and made them miserably poor.

In short, this meeting was held to solve the necessary problems for independence and then:

1. Agriculture production and curtailments must be discussed.
2. Problems arising in business must be solved.
3. Financial problems must be solved. Concentrate all individual capital in banks, guarantee monetary payment and capital circulation.
4. There is no central or local administrative organization. You are working temporarily. You must select directors of villages, county and city committees. For discussion, this bill must be divided into four sections.

    a. Agriculture and commerce
    b. Industry
    c. Administration

This meeting must be held again.[33]

NOTES

1. Soo Sung Cho, *Korea in World Politics: 1940–1950* (Berkeley: University of California Press, 1967), 16.

2. Cho, *Korea in World Politics*, 19.

3. Cho, *Korea in World Politics*, 22.

4. Jongsoo Lee, *The Partition of Korea after World War II: A Global History* (New York: Palgrave Macmillan, 2006), 38.

5. Jongsoo Lee, *The Partition of Korea after World War II*, 40–42.

6. Gregory Henderson, *Korea, the Politics of the Vortex* (Cambridge, MA: Harvard University Press, 1968), 114–15.

7. Andrei Lankov, *From Stalin to Kim Il Sung: The Formation of North Korea, 1945–1960* (New Brunswick, NJ: Rutgers University Press, 2002), 2–4.

8. See Jongsoo Lee, *The Partition of Korea after World War II*.

9. Charles K. Armstrong, *The North Korean Revolution, 1945–1950* (Ithaca, NY: Cornell University Press, 2003), 71–74.

10. Andrew C. Nahm, *Korea: Tradition and Transformation* (Elizabeth, NJ: Hollym International, 1988), 353.

11. Cho, *Korea in World Politics*, 220.

12. Bruce Cumings, *Origins of the Korean War*, vol. 1 (Princeton, NJ: Princeton University Press, 1981), 38.

13. Cumings, *Origins of the Korean War*, vol. 1, 506.

14. Hun Joon Kim, *The Massacres at Mt. Halla: Sixty Years of Truth Seeking in South Korea* (Ithaca, NY: Cornell University Press, 2014).

15. George McCune and Arthur L. Grey, *Korea Today* (Cambridge, MA: Harvard University Press, 1950), 243.

16. Adrian Buzo, *The Making of Modern Korea: A History* (London: Routledge, 2002), 77.

17. Wada Haruki, *The Korean War: An International History* (Lanham, MD: Rowman & Littlefield, 2014), 49–50.

18. Zhihua Shen and Danhui Li, *After Leaning to One Side: China and Its Allies in the Cold War* (Stanford: Stanford University Press, 2011), 25.

19. Cumings, *Korea's Place in the Sun*, 265.

20. Cumings, *Korea's Place in the Sun*, 276.

21. Jian Chen, *China's Road to the Korean War: The Making of the Sino-American Confrontation* (New York: Columbia University Press, 1994), 212–15.

22. Richard Peters and Xiaobing Li, *Voices from the Korean War: Personal Stories of American, Korean and Chinese Soldiers* (Lexington: University Press of Kentucky, 2004), 185–98.

23. Bruce Cumings, *The Korean War: A History* (New York: The Modern Library, 2010), 152–154.

24. Jae-Jung Suh, ed., *Truth and Reconciliation in South Korea: Between the Present and Future of the Korean Wars* (London: Routledge, 2013), 6.

25. Cumings, *The Korean War: A History*, 159; Conrad C. Crane, *American Airpower Strategy in Korea, 1950–1953* (Lawrence: University of Kansas Press, 2000), 168–171.

26. Cumings, *The Korean War: A History*, 160.

27. Lankov, *From Stalin to Kim Il Sung*, 62.

28. Shu Guang Zhang, *Mao's Military Romanticism: China and the Korean War, 1950–1953* (Lawrence: University Press of Kansas, 1995), 247.

29. Chalmers Johnson, *MITI and the Japanese Miracle: The Growth of Industrial Policy, 1925–1975* (Stanford, CA: Stanford University Press, 1982), 227.

30. John Dower, *Embracing Defeat: Japan in the Wake of World War II* (New York: W.W. Norton and Company, 1999), 542–43.

31. Roger Dingman, "The Dagger and the Gift: The Impact of the Korean War on Japan," *The Journal of American-East Asian Relations* 2, no. 1 (Spring 1993): 43.

32. John Dower, *Empire and Aftermath: Yoshida Shigeru and the Japanese Experience, 1878–1954* (Cambridge, MA: Harvard University Press, 1979), 316.

33. Armstrong, *The North Korean Revolution*, 252–53.

4

✌

North Korea: Recovery, Transformation, and Decline, 1953 to 1993

THE DIVERGENT PATHS OF THE TWO KOREAS

In the half century after the Korean War, North and South Korea continued on the divergent paths that they had embarked upon in the immediate postwar years. History has no parallel to this development. What had been one of the world's most homogenous cultures, with a long historical tradition, became two radically different societies.

South Korea struggled in the 1950s to recover from the war, relying on massive U.S. foreign aid to ward off hunger and economic collapse. It had an increasingly authoritarian government under President Syngman Rhee that within the bounds permitted by its dependency on the United States attempted to subvert the country's political institutions to maintain power. Rhee was overthrown in a popular uprising in 1960; a short-lived attempt at parliamentary democracy ended in 1961 with a military coup. The military-led regime of Park Chung Hee then embarked upon a government-directed economic development program based on export-led growth, which achieved impressive success. Tied economically to the United States and, to a lesser extent, Japan, South Korea was transformed from a rural to an urban, highly literate society. Park's rule also became increasingly more authoritarian. Assassinated in 1979 amid growing political unrest due to his dictatorial rule, he was succeeded by a new military regime under Chun Doo Hwan. By the 1980s, an expanding and increasingly sophisticated middle class sought direct participation and accountability in government. Spearheaded by student radicals, labor activists, and political dissidents, popular restlessness led to a transition to more democratic government that began in 1987 and resulted in the election of a former political dissident, Kim Young Sam, as president in 1992. Throughout these years South Korea's economy continued to grow, catching up with the more industrialized North by 1970 and surpassing it thereafter. By the 1990s, South Korea was becoming one of the third world's success stories.

North Korea followed a very different trajectory. In contrast to the volatile and dynamic South, the basic institutions in place by 1953 were solidified, and the leadership became more entrenched. Kim Il Sung consolidated power in the 1950s and 1960s, became the absolute leader of the country, and created a personality cult that went beyond that of Stalin or Mao. Kim, seeking in his own way to develop the North into a rich, powerful country and to reverse the outcome of the Korean War, invested his country's resources in heavy industry and in the military. In contrast to South Korea's export market economy, North Korea focused on self-sufficiency. It became one of the world's most isolated states and increasingly an anachronism, adhering to a rigid totalitarianism based partly on the Stalinist model that became discredited in the USSR and China. After an impressive post–Korean War recovery, the concentration on military buildup, the concern with self-sufficiency, and the emphasis on political control over technical expertise led to a stagnating economy, then to a decline into poverty and famine.

Meanwhile, the two Koreas remained suspended in a state of war. No peace followed the Korean War, only an uneasy armed truce that lasted for decades. Tensions between the two led to occasional armed clashes, often sparked by North Korean provocation. These took place between intermittent but short-lived attempts to negotiate some sort of peaceful coexistence.

NORTH KOREA'S RECOVERY

Three years after it launched its invasion of the South, North Korea was in ruins. While the death and destruction in South Korea was enormous, the DPRK suffered disproportionately greater casualties and destruction. Few countries in modern times had ever seen the scale of devastation that characterized North Korea. The destruction inflicted upon the country was horrendous. The bombing leveled virtually every city and sizeable town in North Korea; all of the industry and most of the nation's infrastructure was destroyed. Casualties suffered by North Korea are not known for certain, but it must have been extraordinarily high since the population in 1953 was 15 percent lower than it had been three years earlier. North Korea is likely to have lost a significantly greater proportion of its population than did Germany or Japan in World War II. The death toll was not only a humanitarian tragedy but an economic one since it left the country short of manpower.

Yet North Korea recovered quickly from the physical destruction. The immediate postwar years were focused on rebuilding. A Three-Year Plan, 1954–1956, aimed at economic reconstruction, appears to have been successful, with industrial production in 1957 reaching pre–Korean War levels. Pyongyang was almost completely rebuilt, with its main boulevards and squares suitable for mass rallies and parades; almost nothing of the old city remained. This remarkable feat was accomplished by mass mobilization of the surviving population to clear the destruction and to rebuild houses, schools, factories, and other facilities. Following a pattern that would characterize the DPRK for decades, people were organized military-style in mass campaigns to accomplish state-directed goals. This system was apparently effective for the initial rebuilding efforts after the war.

North Korea had the advantage of possessing 80 percent of Korea's 1945 industry, and 90 percent of its electric power, mostly hydroelectric. Therefore, much of the initial recovery was a matter of rebuilding the existing structures using the Japanese blueprints. Possessing three-quarters of Korea's mines, it had a variety of minerals such as iron, tungsten, silver, uranium, and others it could export to its Communist allies. Still, the recovery was an impressive achievement, and with some new plants under construction it put the country on the road to rapid industrialization. Foreign aid was crucial to the recovery effort. The Soviets and their Eastern European allies supplied technical help and material on a large scale. Some of the prewar infrastructure was rebuilt, such as the chemical fertilizer complex from the colonial period at Hŭngnam.[1] Soviet contributions included the Sup'ing hydroelectric power plant, the largest in Asia; a large steel mill at Sŏngjin (renamed Kim Ch'aek) in the northeast; and the rebuilding of the port of Namp'o. In 1954, aid supplied 33 percent of the state revenues. Soviet aid to North Korea was smaller proportionally than the U.S. aid given to South Korea, which was half of the government budget in the 1950s. It also was distributed over a shorter period of time—South Korea remained heavily reliant on U.S. aid until the mid-1960s, but by 1960 Soviet aid accounted for only 2.6 percent of the DPRK's revenues.[2] Nonetheless, it was crucial for the recovery efforts in the years immediately after the Korean War. Furthermore, the Soviets supplied military aid and important resources such as oil at subsidized prices. Although North Korea had a small number of Japanese-trained technicians, it was greatly assisted in the 1950s by several hundred Soviet Koreans who were able to provide valuable expertise. China also assisted, by use of its troops, who remained in the country until 1958 to provide labor for construction projects.

A key part of the DPRK economic program was the collectivization of agriculture, where farmers were reduced to laborers. Few other changes impacted so many people. While some Communist countries allowed for small-scale markets for private produce, Kim opted for total collectivization. This was part of the pattern of the highly centralized command economy that conformed to the Soviet model. The land reform of 1946 had divided the countryside into small family farms. Tenancy had been ended, but farmers did not have full control over their land—it could be inherited but not alienated. Geography and labor shortage may have contributed to this decision. Food supplies were a problem, since the best agricultural land was in South Korea. Most of North Korea was very mountainous, and the growing season was short. Nor did the DPRK's allies have large food surpluses to give as aid, as the United States was able to give the ROK. Food shortages appeared early. Both in the late 1940s and in 1954 the state had to temporarily ban private trade in foodstuffs and forcibly requisition crops.[3] Furthermore, the Korean War had created a shortage of manpower and of draft animals. Kim and his planners saw the solution in collectivizing and mechanizing agriculture by consolidating the small plots of land into big farms that could be worked by tractors and other machinery.

Farming was collectivized in stages. Compared to the Soviet Union or China under Mao, the process went rather smoothly without upheavals and disasters. In 1954, the state created mutual aid teams called *p'umassiban*. Then rural villages were organized as cooperatives where the majority of farm families lived and worked. At first the declared intention was to move gradually toward collectivization, called "cooperatization" (*hyŏpdonghwa*), but from 1956, perhaps influenced by the speed of Mao's own effort in China, the process was accelerated. At the end of 1957 the nation's family farms had been consolidated into 13,000 state cooperatives. By this time, all private trade in grain was prohibited; all production was sold to the state.

NORTH KOREA'S GREAT LEAP FORWARD

North Korea was now ready to move beyond recovery to launching its Five-Year Plan for 1957–1961. This new plan was intended to emulate the USSR's first five-year plan that had been so successful in transforming the economy in a short period of time. The Five-Year Plan for 1957–1961 sought not recovery but strong positive growth in industry, agriculture, and infrastructure. Kim Il Sung thus followed a path of development similar to and no doubt greatly influenced by that of the Soviet Union under Stalin. It was totally centralized and state directed with no scope for private industry or agriculture. By the late 1950s all private businesses and industries had been eliminated. Basic commodities were collected and redistributed by the state, with no private markets. The few remaining private enterprises were taken over by the state. There was virtually no local or regional autonomy; all decision making down to the basic allocation of food and clothing to each household through the public distribution system was made from the center. In other ways too Kim followed the model of the Soviet Union in its push for rapid growth after 1928. He focused on developing heavy industry that increased the industrial base of the economy and could support a strong military rather than on consumer goods.

In many ways Kim Il Sung's use of mass mobilization, his ambitious targets to transform a poor, agrarian society into an industrial state, and his swift and complete collectivization of agriculture resembled the policies of Mao Zedong, and he was no doubt influenced by Mao. When Mao launched his Great Leap Forward in China in the spring of 1958, in effort to achieve heroic feats of modernization through revolutionary fervor, Kim began accelerating his targets, announcing that the five-year plan would be completed in just three and a half years. And in 1959, he boasted that North Korea would surpass Japan in per capita industrial output in ten years, echoing Mao's boast that China would soon surpass Britain in steel production.[4] Two policies in particular were similar to the Chinese Great Leap Forward: the development of local industries and consolidation of collectives into larger units. Like Mao, Kim Il Sung sought to make each local unit of government self-sufficient in basic necessities, having its own facilities for clothes, footwear, and food processing. This served two purposes: it promoted self-reliance by local communities in case of another war of invasion, and it enabled the central government to focus on heavy industry.

Also appearing to reflect the influence of events in China was the decision to consolidate the newly created agricultural cooperatives into larger units. In October 1958 the state began the amalgamation of agricultural cooperatives into larger units somewhat on the pattern of China's communes. In November it was announced that the nation's 13,309 cooperatives, which averaged 79 households, were to be merged into 3,880 large units of around 300 households each. The move was proclaimed a great "victory" that would increase grain production.[5]

A symbol and a characteristic of this new push for rapid development was the Ch'ŏllima movement, derived from a mythical Korean horse capable of galloping a thousand *li* (several hundred miles) a day. The Ch'ŏllima movement had its reputed origins in December 1956, just before the start of the Five-Year Plan, when Kim Il Sung visited Kangsŏn steel mill to personally direct the work. Inspired by this model, in 1958 he created Ch'ŏllima Workteams, groups of workers who competed to exceed their quotas. The media presented reports of workers accomplishing extraordinary feats of production by working extra hours and putting in near superhuman efforts. Construction projects were completed ahead of schedule and factories exceeded their targets through these efforts.[6] Propaganda organs carried out endless exhortations to increase production, seeking to grind out more output from the people. There was a "Movement to See the Early Morning Stars" to make workers and farmers get up and go to work very early, and a "Movement Not to Have Soup," which originated in textile factories in order to minimize the time lost in bathroom breaks.[7] In 1959, students were sent to construction sites under the slogan "One Stretch After One Thousand Shovels."[8]

The year 1960 was declared a "buffer year," a period of adjustments. Then a new Seven-Year Plan for 1961–1967 was declared; its ambitious targets reflected the optimism of the early years.

Kim continued to seek efforts to overcome bureaucratic inertia, to avoid party officials being cut off from the masses, and to tap the creative energies of the people. To achieve this he developed two new economic policies: Ch'ŏngsan-ri Method in 1960 to spur production on the farm and the Taean Work System in 1961 to increase production at the factory. Like Mao he worried that the new officialdom had become divorced from the people. Based on his on-the-spot guidance system (*hyŏnji chido*), he had high-ranking officials of the Korean Workers' Party visit and work with the farmers. In the Ch'ŏngsan-ri Method, farmers were encouraged to present their grievances and their suggestions for improving production, and to be active participants in the management of the enterprise; and in Taean Work System the management of factories under the control of KWP committees consisted of managers, engineers, plant workers, and party officials. The idea was direct worker participation in the management of plants while preventing arbitrary control of decision making by local managers and bureaucrats. Both, in their effort to seek more worker input, can be seen as attempts to provide a more rational system of economic production and avoid the arbitrary directives issues during the Five-Year Plan that had often proved inefficient. But they did little to change the fundamental features of North Korea's economy—its relentless demands on the workers and farmers with little in the way of material incentives.

From the standpoint of the early 1960s, North Korea's economic development can only be regarded as successful. Industrial production increased three and a half times from 1956 to 1960, admittedly starting from a very low base.[9] The limitation of its methods of modernization by forcing people to constantly toil on focused economic and infrastructural targets was not yet apparent. North Korea's achievements in education more than matched those in economic development. In 1945, nearly half of adults were illiterate, and only one in twenty had a secondary education. The country had a severe shortage of teachers since many were Japanese who had left, and it had no university. The state instituted four-year compulsory schooling. By 1959, with almost all children receiving this basic education, compulsory schooling was extended to seven years. This was again extended after 1967 to nine years. By the 1970s at least ten years of formal schooling was becoming the norm for young people.

THE POLITICAL CONSOLIDATION OF KIM IL SUNG AND IIIS MANCHURIAN GUERRILLA COMRADES

After the Korean War, Kim Il Sung established himself as the unchallenged absolute ruler of North Korea and had narrowed the leadership circle to his fellow Manchurian guerrilla comrades. At the time of its independence in 1948 the leadership in North Korea can be identified as belonging to four main groups: the Soviet-Koreans, the Yanan veterans, the domestic Communists, and Kim Il Sung's ex-Manchurian guerrillas, also referred to as the partisans. Kim Il Sung, while the "leader" of the state, had to contend with these various groups. Gradually he consolidated power and eliminated all but his fellow partisans from important positions. He began this process during the Korean War as he rebuilt the party, but it was only after the conflict ended that the major purges began.

First Kim Il Sung eliminated the domestic Communist leadership—those Communists who had remained in Korea working underground during the colonial period—and their leader Pak Hŏn-yŏng in a major purge in 1953 only a week after the armistice. The leading domestic Communists were put on a public show trial and confessed to being American and South Korean spies. With all important domestic Communists purged, Kim Il Sung turned toward eliminating the Soviet and Yanan groups. This was part of his effort to establish the DPRK's autonomy and protect himself from the de-Stalinization policies of the Soviet Union after 1953. Soviet help was crucial in the beginning but Kim had no desire to be a Russian tributary state. Moscow and its deputies in North Korea held ultimate authority during the years immediately after liberation from Japan. Even after independence in 1948 North Korean leaders, dependent on Soviet aid and military support, consulted with Moscow before making important decisions. This changed with the Chinese intervention in the Korean War. From November 1950 to July 1953 it was the Chinese, not the North Koreans or Moscow, that had operational control over the war. When Beijing took over conduct of the war from the North Korean leadership it also weakened Moscow's political control. After the conflict

the DPRK remained heavily dependent on Soviet aid but the period of tutelage was over. Kim Il Sung was concerned that the Soviets would try to
reestablish control over his country and make it a "satellite" of Moscow.

When the prominent Soviet-Korean Pak Ch'ang-ok and Ch'oe Ch'ang-
ik of the Yanan unsuccessfully attempted to challenge his leadership in
the summer of 1956, Kim turned against their factions. The leaders won
a temporary reprieve when Moscow and Beijing urged Kim to show
restraint. But the following year, in 1957 he launched a major purge
that removed almost all Soviet-Koreans and Yanan group members.
The purge was then enlarged to eliminate all suspected of disloyalty.
More than 100,000 citizens fell victim to arrests during 1957–1959; 2,500
were executed, some publicly. The backgrounds of all citizens were
scrutinized and everyone was placed into three general categories
(*kyech'ŭng*): those deemed "loyal" called *haeksim* or core class, those classified as "wavering" (*t'ongyo*), and those labeled "hostile" (*choktae*). The
loyal or core class members were known as tomatoes—red all the way
through. The "wavering" were apples—red only on the outside—and
the "hostile" were called grapes. This was the beginning of one of the
most distinctive features of North Korean society—its rigid social structure. Each category became what amounted to a hereditary caste whose
status was passed on from parents to children. Accompanying this
purge, the North Korean Cabinet issued Decree No. 149 that prohibited
people belonging to "hostile forces" from living near the border, near
the seacoast, within fifty kilometers of Pyongyang or Kaesŏng, or within
twenty kilometers of any other big city. A last major purge took place
in 1967 when the Kapsan Group, veterans who had provided logistical
support to the guerrillas but were not themselves guerrillas, were eliminated. After that the leadership of North Korea was remarkably stable.
Kim Il Sung's control over the party and its domination by his fellow
ex-guerrillas was near complete.

Kim Il Sung's elimination of all but his fellow Manchurian guerrillas
from the leadership had a profound impact on North Korea's development. The entire society became influenced by the guerrilla culture. Party
propaganda constantly extolled the deeds of the Manchurian fighters,
such as in the canonical four-volume *Memoirs of the Anti-Japanese Guerrillas*.[10] Not only were the Manchurian guerrillas the heroes of stories,
memoirs, fiction, films, and song, they became the only legitimate bearers
of the Korean Communist and national liberation tradition and the model
to be emulated for almost every endeavor. Over the coming years their
role in history only became greater until, as Hoenik Kwon and Byung-ho
Chung have remarked, the anti-colonial armed resistance of Kim Il Sung's
partisans in Manchuria became "the single most important, most sacred,
all-encompassing saga of the nation's modern history."[11]

The purges also had another effect on North Korea's development. Fewer and fewer positions of responsibility were held by people with any exposure to the outside world other than the Manchurian mountain villages near the Korean border. The leadership had become largely constricted to an extremely narrow segment of the Communist and nationalist movements. And they were the least educated. The party's more than a million members, the largest in proportion to the size of its population of any Communist country, were for most part poorly educated, had no foreign experience, and knew of no other leader than Kim Il Sung. Perhaps in no other modern society was power so effectively monopolized by people with so little education and so little experience with the larger world.

Kim Il Sung took measures to insulate his people from foreigners. Restrictions on contact between North Koreans and their allies struck East Europeans as unusually extreme, and they became more extreme in the late 1950s so that it was almost impossible for Soviets or East Europeans to have any kind of social contact with North Koreans. North Koreans who had foreign wives were required to divorce and their spouses were expelled. North Korean students were recalled from the Soviet Union and Eastern Europe so that there were virtually none by 1960. It would be another twenty years before more students were sent.[12]

CREATING A MONOLITHIC STATE

In 1967 a "cultural revolution" was launched not entirely dissimilar from the one Mao was carrying out in China at that time. On May 25 1967, immediately following the last major party purge, Kim Il Sung issued "instructions" calling for the inspection of all books. This led to a nationwide campaign in which all printed material was checked and anything that was not approved was confiscated and burned. This included many of the literary classics and almost anything beyond a narrow range of official DPRK published materials.[13] At the same time, the cult of Kim Il Sung was intensified; party officials began wearing badges bearing his picture. Eventually over the next several years all North Koreans were expected to wear these badges when in public. His instructions were cited at every meeting, his quotes were cited in every article and publication no matter what the topic, and much of the media news was devoted to him.

Kim Il Sung like Mao Zedong was transformed into a peerless thinker. The ideology of the state became based on his *juche* thought (*chuch'e sasang*). *Juche* can be translated as "self-reliance." At its core this was an emphasis on political independence, economic and military self-reliance, and Korean nationalism. North Korean publications explained it as an adaptation of Marxism-Leninism to conditions of the country. In reality it was more vague ultra-nationalism and glorification of the leader than a systematic ideology, and it had little to do with Marxism. The elaboration of *juche* continued throughout the 1970s. According to the 1972 constitution, *juche* was the "guiding principle of politics."[14] North Korean official histories presented an increasingly xenophobic racial-nationalist history depicting the constant struggle of a racially pure, virtuous people against outside invaders. This narrative could be found in South Korean textbooks and in popular culture in the South as well. But North Korea's version of history was more extreme. The acknowledgment of foreign borrowing or assistance was rarely given. For instance, texts dropped all references to even the Soviet Union's role in liberating the country from the Japanese. Full credit was given to the heroic Korean people under the great leader, Kim Il Sung. Those in Korea's past who had sought foreign support were criticized for failing to rely on the Korean people instead. Kim Il Sung used this accusation of being subservient to foreign powers to attack his opponents. In this, the regime was influenced by the rejection by the colonial-era nationalist writers of *sadaejuŭi* (flunkyism), the Korean tradition of serving the great that had made Korea a loyal tributary state of China until the nineteenth century. Koreans in both North and South viewed these former tributary relations as a sign of their past weakness and a national failing. In the South as well, dissidents frequently accused the South Korean regime of being subservient to the United States. The DPRK's emphasis on self-reliance was thus motivated by a fiercely independent strain in twentieth-century nationalism that was strengthened by being thwarted by the Americans from reunifying the country, and by humiliation over its reliance on the Chinese support and Soviet aid for its survival.

Juche thought was the basis of what was called the "Monolithic Ideological System" (*yuilsasangch'egye*), which was summarized in the *Ten Principles for the Monolithic Ideological System*. The principles presented Kim Il Sung as a great revolutionary thinker whose thought must be studied. They stressed the importance of ideological struggle and of following the Great Leader's instructions. Kim Il Sung is not only the supreme and unquestioned leader but the ideological guide whose thought is the basis of society.

In the past, Korea had borrowed beliefs from abroad—Buddhism, originally from India, and Confucianism from China—and then made some adaptations to suit Korean needs or cultural dispositions. But Korean Buddhism and Confucianism, especially the latter, still very much adhered to orthodox forms. In fact, scholars and officials in Chosŏn Korea were very proud to have firmly adhered to the letter of the Confucian classics. Thus, the radical ideological evolution of North Korean Communism was historically unprecedented.

THE CULT OF THE KIM FAMILY

The ideology of *juche* was linked with the cult of Kim Il Sung and his family. The cult of Kim Il Sung went beyond that of Stalin in Russia or even Mao. Kim's propaganda organs began calling him *widaehan suryŏng* (Great Leader) in 1967. Soon his name was preceded by such honorifics as "ever-victorious iron-willed brilliant commander," "the sun of the nation," "the red sun of the oppressed people of the world," "the greatest leader of our time."[15] Kim Il Sung became the infallible leader, and his *juche* thought the infallible truth. So many statues, mosaics, portraits, and shrines to the Great Leader existed that it was almost impossible to be out of sight of one. In every classroom, office, and home his portrait was hung in a prominent place. At the base of these portraits was often a small cloth to clean the glass plate over his picture.[16] Workers and students began their days bowing before his portrait and placed wreaths at his statues on holidays. The holidays themselves centered on his life. The big holidays were April 15, his birthday, and later February 16, his son Kim Jong Il's birthday. His hometown of Mangyŏngdae was a place of pilgrimage. His life and his various heroic activities were the subjects of most of the nation's output of movies, plays, and operas. Kim Il Sung was portrayed as an international figure admired by the oppressed throughout the world. North Koreans were told of tributes to the Great Leader that constantly came in from abroad.

People were taught that under his guidance they were marching "on the road to paradise." Already they had achieved the essential material basics for happiness. Han S. Park wrote in 2002, "Throughout the nation's history, our ancestors thought a paradise to be a society where people enjoy three things: being able to eat white rice, live under a clay-roof, and educate their children. These three 'privileges' were the life-long aspiration for our ancestors. Now we have achieved all three under the wise leadership of the Great Leader. Children were taught to sing, 'we have nothing to envy in the world.'"

Kim Il Sung, worried about his succession, decided to make his son Kim Jong Il his successor, perhaps sometime in the early 1970s. The rise was a slow and cautious one. In 1975, reports began of the "party center," a term that later came to be understood as a reference to Kim Jong Il. In 1980, at the Sixth Congress of the Workers' Party, Kim Jong Il was named to the Presidium of the Politburo, the Secretariat of the Central Committee, and the Military Commission. He ranked fourth in the party hierarchy. By this time it was clear that he was the designated heir. In 1983, he then moved up to rank second in the official leadership hierarchy after his father, and in 1988 he was receiving a level of honorifics in public pronouncements similar to his father. In the late 1960s Kim Jong

Il became involved in the Propaganda and Agitation Department of the party. A man of artistic dispositions, he flourished in this post directing literature, theater, and his great passion, film. Most of his work centered around elaborating on the cult of his father. While continuing to be czar of the arts, Kim Jong Il became the chief ideologist of the party and the definitive interpreter of his father's thought, a position signaled with the publication in 1982 of his treatise, *On the Juche Idea*. It became required reading, a work that received the degree of admiration previously reserved for his father.[17] The "Song of General Kim Il Sung" was played at almost all public events and functioned as a kind of second national anthem. It now became the custom to follow this song with a performance of the "Song of General Kim Jong Il."[18]

With the rise of the son, the entire Kim family was further glorified in all media. This trend toward widening the cult of Kim Il Sung to include his family had already begun, but with the succession being passed on to a new generation, propaganda increasingly emphasized the importance of this unique family in protecting and guiding the nation, as well as embodying the revolution. Texts were rewritten to make the modern history of Korea the history of the Kim family. The official history *Kŭndae Chosŏn yŏksa* (*Modern History of Korea*) claimed that in 1866 Kim Ŭng-u, Kim Il Sung's great grandfather, bravely fought the U.S. imperialists, and as head of the local people he attacked the *General Sherman*. This now became a major incident in Korean history, the beginning of the struggle against American and Western imperialism with the Kim family in the forefront. According to the official histories, Kim Il Sung's father, Kim Hyŏng-jik, led a national liberation movement in the 1910s and 1920s. Kim Jong Il's birth was now fictitiously located on the sacred Paektusan mountain. His mother, Kim Jong Suk (Kim Chŏng-suk, 1917–1949), was elevated to the status of a national hero who had fought the Japanese alongside her husband, becoming known as the "invincible revolutionary."[19] Monuments to her and other members of the Kim family appeared throughout the country.

When Kim Jong Il succeeded his father as leader in 1994 he'd had an extremely long apprenticeship. By the time he had been designated to the inner circle as his father's successor he had already been actively involved in party affairs for a decade. He then continued to acquire key posts over the next twenty years. For thirty years he had been involved in most of the centers of power—party administration, propaganda, the security organizations, the military. Only in two fields was he not known to have been deeply involved: economic development and foreign affairs. For all his odd appearance and his personal eccentricities he had been extremely well prepared to assume power upon his father's death.

KIM IL SUNG'S *JUCHE* SOCIETY

By the 1970s indoctrination in North Korea reached a level of intensity perhaps found nowhere else. Virtually all art, literature, film, and music was directed at glorifying Kim Il Sung, the revolution, and the great leader's philosophy of *juche*. North Koreans learned very little of the prerevolutionary culture, or of art, music, and literature from outside Korea. The cult was accompanied by a severe isolation that prevented the populace having even a minimum of knowledge of the outside world. International news consisted mainly of reports of foreign praises of the Great Leader and meetings of *juche* study clubs in various countries. Foreign visitors to North Korea after 1980 were often amazed by the near total ignorance of the outside world by a generation that had grown up under the regime. Even access to printed materials from the Soviet Union and its allies was extremely restricted.

Despite the egalitarian ideology of Communism, the DPRK developed in ways that mirrored the rigidly hierarchical, hereditary society of premodern Korea. The consolidation of the regime was not accompanied by violent class warfare. Partly this was due to the fact that most of the landlord and business class fled to the South after 1945. There was no war against intellectuals and people with technical skills such as that characterized by Maoist China. In fact, the Korean Workers' Party had for its logo the hammer and sickle plus a writing brush. The latter represented a class the North Koreans called the *samuwŏn*, essentially white-collar professional people such as teachers, government officials, and clerks. But if the creation of North Korean society was not characterized by the violence that had accompanied the creation of the Soviet Union and the PRC, the North Korean revolution nonetheless brought about a profound social upheaval. Those who had served at the bottom of the social scale—peasants and workers—now emerged at the top of society. The social mobility of the early years of the regime was striking. Most of the leadership, like Kim Il Sung, came from rather modest backgrounds. The KWP's membership in the late 1940s was drawn largely from the peasantry, and this was even more so when the party was rebuilt after the Korean War.

However, it was far from a classless society. Rather, a new class system emerged. About 30 percent of the population were part of the privileged core class, 50 percent were identified with the wavering class, and 20 percent with the hostile class.[20] After 1964 these three main categories were subdivided into fifty-one *sŏngbun* (groups) each with its own ranking. There were twelve loyal groups belonging to the loyal or core class (*kyech'ŭng*). These included: workers from working families, former farmhands, former poor peasants, personnel of state organizations, KWP members, family members of deceased revolutionaries, family members of national liberation fighters, revolutionary intelligentsia (those who received education after liberation), family members of civilians killed in the Korean War, families of soldiers who were killed during the Korean War, families of servicemen, and families of war heroes. Nine *sŏngbun* belonged to the wavering class and thirty to the hostile class. The latter included those who had served under the Japanese as officials, former landlords, businessmen, merchants, Christians, active Buddhists, shamans, those who had engaged in pro-Japanese or pro-American activities, or who had family members who had fled to the South. These *sŏngbun* were all based on family background so that each became an inherited status.[21] These were not officially publicized but everyone knew where they belonged. Young people discovered this when they went off to school and were denied permission to attend higher levels of education or join the party. These categories were hereditary and they profoundly mattered. Food rations, access to desired goods, housing, jobs, career advancement, and admittance to higher education were determined by the classification, which was very difficult to change. In many ways North Korea was developing a rigid caste system based on family background. For most people there was little chance of improving upon their inherited social status, although people could be downgraded as a result of improper political behavior. In no other modern society was such a well-defined, inherited system of social status created.

Life for most citizens was based on their assigned place in society. People lived in apartments assigned by rank. The privileged were able to live in Pyongyang. A considerable gap existed between the relatively comfortable life in the capital and the rougher, harder living conditions in provincial cities and in the countryside. Within the top tier of society was a smaller group of the elite who lived in a separate and restricted section of Pyongyang. The uppermost elite enjoyed luxuries unimaginable to ordinary people, such as driving imported cars and drinking imported cognac. An even greater gap existed between the lives of the official elite of higher-ranking KWP members, top bureaucrats, and military officers. This became more pronounced over time. By the 1980s, if not earlier, the very top lived in great luxury, driving expensive German cars, drinking French cognac, and having access to other imported luxuries. The hereditary nature of the ruling elite also became more pronounced over time. By the time of Kim Il Sung's death in 1994, most of the younger high-ranking officials were the sons, nephews, or in-laws of the old guard.

Just as in traditional Korea, the education system reflected the hierarchical nature of society. There were the elite schools, Kim Il Sung University in Pyongyang followed by the technical Kim Ch'aek University. Other schools were of lower rank. Admission was based on family background and ideological purity as much as merit. In pre-modern Korea the civil examinations were used to select high officials but were only opened to members of the *yangban* elite. The DPRK school system functioned in a similar way. Prestige degrees were a means of reaffirming status rather than acquiring it. Youths from twelve to eighteen could try to join the Socialist Youth Organization, later called the Kim Il Sung Youth, an important gateway to better opportunities later in life. But membership in this too appeared to be linked to family status. Thus the egalitarianism and social mobility of the first years was replaced by a rough replication of the rigid, hierarchical structure of society based largely on inheritance that was characteristic of traditional Korea. It also resembled the traditional order in the absence of women from important positions.

Pyongyang was North Korea's showcase city. In contrast to the noise, dirt, and chaos of Seoul, it was a clean, quiet city with some attractive buildings, efficient public transportation, and trees and parks. It had broad streets kept immaculately clean and an impressive subway system. And everywhere were the monuments to the Great Leader, dominating parks, squares, and the skyline. Most visitors reported similar impressions—a clean, orderly, but strangely lifeless city. It was a city devoid of cars, busy markets, or nightlife, striking many foreigners as grimly sterile. The streets were quiet except during the peak hours when people went back and forth to work. At night it was dark. To live in Pyongyang was a privilege and it was difficult for most North Koreans to visit it other than official excursions. However, away from the main streets and squares were muddy streets with crowded, modest housing where most citizens lived.

Art and literature served the state. Writers and artists were under the direction of the Federation of Literature and Art. From 1948 to 1962 this was headed by the novelist and short story writer Han Sŏr-ya (1900–1970?), one of a number of prominent cultural leaders who had voluntarily come to the North after 1945. Han, who had been a successful writer associated with the proletarian literature movement in colonial times, was purged in 1962 as too bourgeois. From the very beginning of the regime, art and literature were seen as vehicles for propaganda. This is an understatement. Artistic expression was so constricted that it was difficult for any creative individual to flourish. A prominent example was Ch'oe Sŭng-hŭi (1911–?), an internationally acclaimed dancer who introduced modern Japanese influences into Korean traditional dance during the colonial period and went to the North in 1946. She adapted Korean and modern dances to revolutionary themes, but she also fell out of favor in the 1960s and disappeared from the public. From the late 1960s restrictions were tightened to the point that much literature was reduced to panegyrics and crude, often violent tales glorifying the deeds of the Great Leader or the heroic struggles of peasants fighting the Japanese or other agents of oppression.

From the 1970s the stage was dominated by collectively composed revolutionary operas such as *P'i Bada* (*Sea of Blood*) first performed in 1971, the story of mass killings under the Japanese with lyrics said to have been composed by Kim Il Sung. Another work, *Kkotp'anŭnch'ŏnyŏ* (*The Flower Girl*), the story of oppressed villagers under the Japanese and a peasant woman-turned-revolutionary, first appeared in 1973 and remained a staple for the next three decades. Most musical output consisted of songs extolling the leadership, such as "Song of General Kim Il Sung," "Long Life and Good Health to the Leader," and "We Sing of His Benevolent Love." One can hardly imagine an artistically more confined or sterile environment. Artists who tried to find any form of creative expression did so within extremely narrow confines. A painter might express the beauty of nature through his or her depiction of falling snow as it fell upon Kim Il Sung in a winter scene from his wartime guerrilla camp.

One of the revolutionary changes the North Korean Communists introduced was the concept of gender equality. Even the sense of womanhood as an identity was an important innovation in the conservative Confucian Korean society. Women enjoyed equality in education and, at least legally, in pay. Women could share equal inheritance, divorce was made easier, taking of concubines was outlawed, and all occupations were in theory open to women.

Women entered the workforce in large numbers. While the ideology of gender equality encouraged this, the prime motivation was a labor shortage. The labor shortage was especially acute after 1953 and remained a problem since so many young men were in the military and because economic growth relied on labor inputs rather than on improving productivity. In 1958, the Cabinet issued a resolution calling for women to join the workforce. Women who did not work were penalized by receiving smaller rations. The effort to free women for labor was accelerated with the 1976 Law on the Nursing and Upbringing of Children. This called for the creation of 60,000 kindergartens and pre-kindergartens that could accommodate three and a half million children virtually all in this age-group.[22] The day care centers also served the function of indoctrinating the young at an early age. They became a great source of pride; a visit to a model day care center was part of the standard tour for foreign visitors.

Another purpose of day care centers was to free women for the workforce. By the 1970s women made up nearly half the labor force, including 70 percent in light industry and 15 percent in heavy industry.[23] But North Koreans were still conservative enough that women were expected to take care of the housework, to cook for their families, and raise children. Married women were often let out of work early to collect children and prepare dinner. According to the 1976 law, women with children under thirteen were to be let out two hours early but paid for eight hours.[24] Most of the jobs filled by women were low-paid, menial ones. Few women enjoyed high-status jobs. It was rare for them to hold jobs as managers. Many were schoolteachers, but by one estimate only 15 percent were university professors. One-fifth of the delegates to the Supreme People's Assembly, the powerless legislature, were women, but there were few women in top positions. The former Soviet intelligence officer Pak Chŏng-ae stood out, until she was purged in the 1960s. Hŏ Chŏng-suk, daughter of prominent leftist intellectual Hŏ Hŏn, served as Minister of Justice for a while, but she too was purged in the early 1960s.[25] Later, Kim Jong Il's sister Kim Kyŏng-hŭi wielded some power, but mainly through her husband Chang Sŏng-t'aek.

Marriages were commonly arranged using the Korean custom of a *chungmae* or matchmaker, much as was done in the South. By the 1980s love matches were becoming more common, again reflecting a pattern of change similar to North Korea's modernizing neighbors.[26] Visitors to North Korea noticed the change, with more young couples appearing together in public. But in many respects it was a puritanical society with premarital sexual relations strongly discouraged. The Law of Equality between the Sexes in 1946 made divorce by mutual consent extremely easy, and for a decade divorce was fairly common. This was a major break from the past. But in the mid-1950s, people were required to go to a People's Court, pay a high fee, and then adhere to a period of reconciliation. As a result divorce once again became uncommon.[27] Family bonds, between husband and wife and especially between parent and child, came under official praise to an extent not found in other Communist states. The 1972 constitution stated, "It is strongly affirmed that families are the cells of society and shall be well taken care of by the State."[28] The nuclear family was idealized and supported.

The birthrate was quite high in the 1940s, 1950s, and 1960s, then fell. Partly this was due to government efforts and partly it was part of the normal demographic transition as the country became more industrialized, urbanized, and better schooled. Early marriages were banned. In 1971 the marriage age was recommended at twenty-eight for women and thirty for men. The long years of military service, small apartments, and the entry of women in the workforce all contributed to a decline in the birth rate. By 1990, the birth rate had fallen to the point that the ban on early marriages was lifted.[29]

EVERYDAY LIFE

In a speech in June 1979 to Labor Administration workers Kim Il Sung declared, "today our people are enjoying a happy life to their hearts' content under the most advanced socialist system. . . . From ancient time, [our]

forefathers desired to build a paradise on earth. This desire has been fulfilled in the era of our Workers Party."[30] Despite this claim, life in North
Korea was something short of paradise.

Living conditions were Spartan at best for most North Koreans. And
sadly there were only marginal improvements in the standard of living
after 1970. From the late 1980s conditions began to deteriorate. The public
distribution system set up at the onset of the regime allocated food, cooking oil, clothes, and other essentials. The standard of living was low. This
was true for both Koreas, but by 1980 most people in the South enjoyed
housing, food, clothing, and recreational opportunities superior to all but
the elite in the North. The gap widened in the 1980s when the North's
economy stagnated while the South continued to boom. Still, there were
marked improvements in the daily lives of most DPRK citizens. Electricity was widely available but not necessarily indoor plumbing; most used
communal toilets and baths. Goods available in the shops were very limited except for those who had access to foreign currency and could shop
at a Rakwŏn (Paradise) store that sold higher quality or imported consumer goods for foreign exchange. Most country homes were extremely
humble and urban dwellers lived in crowded apartment houses or in
wooden shacks. Even in Pyongyang beyond the façade of the modern
public buildings there were unpaved streets and small traditional huts
with communal wells.

North Korea made great progress in improving basic health care. Although medical services were fairly primitive by Western or Japanese
standards, they were adequate enough to raise the life span to about
seventy by 1990. DPRK health statistics have to be viewed with caution;
still, it seemed that North Koreans were by the 1980s healthier and living
longer than their counterparts in most other developing countries. This
progress in health care, however, began to be undercut in the 1990s, if
not earlier, by food shortages leading to under-nutrition and malnutrition. One area where life improved dramatically was education, one of
North Korea's impressive achievements. By the 1960s almost all children
were completing at least elementary school and the great majority of
adults were literate. In the 1970s compulsory education was expanded to
eleven years, although it is not certain when and if this target was actually
met. Higher education expanded more slowly; by the 1980s as many as
one in five secondary school graduates went on to some form of higher
education, mostly technical colleges. A much smaller number entered the
comprehensive universities. Industrial enterprises maintained their own
technical training schools. The regime prided itself on its treatment of
children, with impressive day care centers and recreational facilities for
them. Whatever the quality of the schools and day care centers, children
did not escape the regimented nature of their society.

Daily life for most citizens was tightly organized. In the capital most people went to work early in the morning. Although the eight-hour day had been introduced in the late forties, there were compulsory study meetings and many hours of "voluntary" labor to meet one campaign or another. Young people, especially secondary and college students, often spent much of their time on "voluntary" service such as helping with the planting and harvest, or on public construction projects. Foreign observers sometimes noticed teenagers breaking rocks to build roads, camping out and working around the clock. Dating and romance were initially disapproved of, but this began to change in the mid-1980s, when themes of romantic love reappeared in literature, music, and drama.

North Korea came closer than any modern society to being totalitarian. So much time was taken with official activities that there appeared no room for any private life. In the 1990s famine, corruption, and economic desperation weakened the state's ability to control society somewhat. But in the 1970s and 1980s the DPRK had reached a level of regimentation that is truly remarkable. Kim Il Sung wanted his subjects to possess the will to resist an invasion with a ferocity that was absent in 1950. Therefore he saw that they were continually involved in military drills and exercises. A constant state of alert prevailed, as public rhetoric suggested that an invasion was imminent at any moment. Music, dramas, school lessons, every medium was used to promote a militarily ready society. The vocabulary of public announcements, no matter what subject, was laced with fierce, militant rhetoric. International events were interpreted as either a sign that the United States and its allies were planning an invasion or were used as warnings for the need for preparedness. In the wake of the Cuban missile crisis, Kim argued that the nation must be prepared to expel the "Yankee Imperialist" invaders and their South Korean allies as well as aid revolutionaries in the South. The increased U.S. involvement in Vietnam, the breakdown of talks with the South in 1972–1973, and later the Gulf War of 1990–1991 also were occasions to increase combat readiness. Military training and political indoctrination went together and started from childhood. Children from very young ages were sent to day care centers where their education focused on political indoctrination, even at the kindergarten level. Children were given toy guns to play with and were taught military marches. The dance "My Heavy Little Machine Gun" was standard part of the curriculum for primary schoolchildren. Even math lessons used problems such as how many American wolf-bastards remained after so many had been killed.[31]

Young people practiced carefully choreographed dances and marches for which the country became famous. These were much like massive military drills. Throughout school their free time was taken up by state-sponsored activities. When they reached sixteen the boys went into military service, except for a few who went on to college. Military service lasted until the age of twenty-eight for a total of twelve to thirteen years, later shortened to only eight years; after this was completed they served in the reserves.

Fewer aspects of life so well indicate the extreme indoctrination North Koreans were subjected to than the study sessions they were required to attend. Ordinary citizens spent much of their non-working time attending compulsory meetings. Everyone was assigned a work station—factory, farm, office, shop. There they attended sessions where they read and discussed the newspapers before actually working. There were breaks for calisthenics and frequent after-work political study sessions that could last into the evening. After work they stayed at their worksite to attend meetings or sessions where they reviewed the day's work and discussed future plans and how they would meet the goals assigned in the economic plans. The meetings included self-criticisms and ways to adhere to *juche* principles in their work. Less is known about rural life, where conditions were harder, but we do know that farmers, too, attended discussion centers. It is reported that there were thirty-minute daily sessions in which the newspaper was read and discussed. And on top of this there were the constant mobilization campaigns to meet some special target in which people did "voluntary labor" on weekends and evenings.

Unlike in many Communist societies there were no unofficial organizations of any kind. Religious life was suppressed. By the 1950s there were no functioning churches. Buddhist and Ch'ŏndŏgyo temples were closed except for a few museum temples at historical spots. Any form of religious activity ceased to exist except at the most hidden level. There was an official Korean Christian Association but it was disbanded in 1960. In 1974, it reappeared apparently for propaganda purposes and to function as a means for Pyongyang to obtain contacts with Christian organizations in the South.[32] It served no actual religious role.

As in all totalitarian regimes there was pervasive system of surveillance. North Korea differed from other Communist regimes in that this system only became more elaborate and more pervasive in the first half-century of the regime. This system consisted of overlapping organizations and groupings. Neighbors were supervised by the *inminban*, or neighborhood associations, that kept track of all comings and goings under an *inminbanjang*, usually a middle-aged woman. A popular saying in North Korea was, "An *inminban* head should know how many chopsticks and how many spoons are in every household."[33] Residents of apartment buildings took turns as security guards. All households were subject to the *sukpak kŏmyŏl*, the midnight home check by police and the *inminbanjang*. Security officials would check radios to see that the mechanism that made them fixed to state radio stations hadn't been tampered with, and that there was no unauthorized literature or goods. The Korean Workers' Party also performed a surveillance function, since the one in five adults who were members were under various kinds of supervision and control.

All travel and movement was strictly controlled. People had to register to stay overnight at another home even if it were a relative. Travel of any kind away from one's city or town required a *t'onghaengjŭng* (travel permit). Permission to travel was difficult to obtain for city dwellers. It was even more difficult for farmers. Fearing an exodus of farmers to cities and towns, the state made it extremely difficult for rural people to travel anywhere. Since the collective farm had its own schools, store (or what might better be described as a distribution center), and medical clinic, there was little reason for a resident to leave, making them virtual prisoners on their collectives.

Overseeing all surveillance were the special security police. Notoriously, North Korea ran an extensive chain of prison camps. The North Korean political prison system is often called by outsiders the "gulag" after the system of prison camps of Stalinist Russia. Initially in the late 1940s the country did not have a political prison system and simply sent prisoners to Siberia, but gradually a large and complex system evolved.[34] This underwent organizational changes but eventually developed into four levels of prisons. For minor crimes involving a few weeks' or months' detention there were labor training centers (*nodong tallyŏndae*); for more serious offenses but still under two years there were labor education centers (*nodong kyoyangso*). For serious offenses of more than two years there were labor correction centers (*nodong kyohwaso*). Those charged with political offenses were sent to the *kwalliso*. The *kwalliso*, which can be translated as "place of custody" or "management or administrative center," were divided into the "revolutionization zones" (*hyŏngmyŏnghwa kuyŏk)* and the "total control zones" (*wanjŏn t'ongje kuyŏk*). The former were for prisoners with some chance of rehabilitation. They lived and worked under harsh conditions with a high death toll and spent their "free time" memorizing the works of Kim Il Sung. Those who survived and had showed "correct thought" could be released, although they would have the stigma of being former political prisoners. The total control zones were death camps where conditions were the harshest and there was no attempt at rehabilitation, no hope of release. As in the Soviet gulag, prisoners often were put to work in mines under extreme conditions. Many mined coal. The number of political prisoners grew with the purges of the late 1950s but the number is not clear. Estimates are that by 1980 about 150,000 to 200,000 people were held in the camps, a number that may have remained the same over the next thirty years.

One unusual feature of the prison camps was their size. In the 1980s there were about a dozen political prison camps, but from 1989 that number was gradually reduced until in the 2000s there were only six. The two largest were camp number 15 in Yudŏk and camp number 22 in Hoeryŏng; each held 40,000 to 50,000 inmates. Most of the camps were located in remote, narrow mountain valleys where the steep mountainsides acted as a natural barrier. Rather than fitting a conventional image of a prison, they were more like a string of villages. Perhaps the most unusual feature of North Korean prisons was the *yŏn'goje* connection system, by which whole families could be incarcerated together from grandparents to children. Thus prisoners often lived in huts with their families, children, and even their parents. This meant that the DPRK exercised a collective responsibility system similar to premodern Korea but even harsher and more inclusive. Blood relations were most important. Sometimes a spouse of a political prisoner would be spared, forced to divorce his or her partner and cease any contact.

FOREIGN POLICY

Pyongyang was careful to maintain correct relations with both Moscow and Beijing even as these two powers began a falling-out. From 1956 to 1961 Kim Il Sung made five visits to the Soviet Union, attending three congresses of the Communist Party of the USSR. He visited China in 1958 and 1959.[35] And he visited both in July 1961 shortly before the Fourth KWP Congress concluded negotiations for a Treaty of Friendship, Cooperation and Mutual Assistance with the two powers, signing separate treaties with each just one day apart. Relations with the Soviet Union deteriorated in 1963 as Pyongyang became more critical of its efforts to isolate China. As a result the Soviets reduced aid, which was a blow to North Korea's economy. In 1965, the two sides patched up relations. Then from 1966 to 1970 during China's Cultural Revolution relations with Beijing became tense. But these too were patched up and from then on North Korea skillfully maintained good terms with both its Communist neighbors, using their rivalry as a way to court aid and support from each.

Unification of Korea was a prime objective of North Korea, the center of its foreign policy. The North Korean revolution, with its aim of creating a strong, progressive, independent Korean nation, could only be completed when that happened. From the leadership's point of view the Korean War was only a temporary setback toward the goal of reunification, not a defeat. It is likely that Kim Il Sung never doubted the inevitability of liberating the South, at least not until the last years of his nearly half century in power.

Drawing upon the lessons of the Korean War, the North Korean leadership developed a clearly articulated plan for unification based on promoting the "three revolutionary forces." This was a threefold strategy for achieving unification. First was building North Korea into an economically strong, ideologically pure, militarily powerful base for unification. Second was to foster the revolutionary forces in the South. This, according to Kim was the great failure of 1950. At a meeting of the Central Committee of the KWP on October 3, 1954, he declared, "If we had done a better job of organizing and induced some South Korean people to rise up, call a strike, and engage in a resistance movement, we would certainly have routed the enemy." That remained the goal, to encourage the South Korean people to rise up and overthrow the regime in the south and drive the U.S. imperialists out.[36] A third part of the unification strategy was to promote and unite revolutionary forces throughout the world in order to isolate the South Korean regime and to put pressure on the U.S. imperialists to withdraw from the peninsula.

While the DPRK remained at a state of war with the South in the first decade after the Korean War, priority for scarce resources went to economic development. This changed in late 1962 when the leadership decided to give "equal emphasis" to military buildup and economic development. A new militarization program was announced consisting of four parts or four lines (*sa nosŏn*): arming the entire population, intensifying training for its armed forces, making the entire country into an impregnable fortress, and providing modern equipment for its armed forces. As part of the effort to arm the entire population, the regime created a Worker-Peasant Red Guards (*Nonong chŏgwidae*). This had its origins in early 1959 shortly after the Chinese People's Volunteers withdrew, and now became a large paramilitary force that all able-bodied men between eighteen and forty-five and single women from eighteen to thirty-five were required to join. It soon embraced about a million and a half members who could be called upon for homeland defense. The armed forces were increased in size, gradually reaching parity with and then exceeding those of ROK in numbers despite the fact that DPRK had only half the population of the South. Military service lasted many years, eight or more. By the 1970s North Korea may have had the highest proportion of its population under arms of any nation. As during the Korean War underground factory and military installations were constructed around the country. The elaborate tunnels that hide so much of the country's military activity became permanent characteristics of North Korea, to the dismay of later U.S. intelligence analysts who were heavily reliant on satellite photos. Of no less importance was the fourth policy of developing modern weapons. The production of military hardware, especially from the 1970s, became a central focus of industrialization targets.

To promote the "revolutionary forces" in the South, Pyongyang sent agents there and sponsored a Revolutionary Party for Reunification, whose handful of members were arrested by South Korean authorities in 1968. Meanwhile, the DPRK pursued an opportunistic policy, taking advantage of any seemingly favorable developments in the South or in the international situation. In 1960, for example, when the student-led uprising overthrew the Rhee regime, Kim Il Sung, probing sentiment in the South, proposed a Confederal Republic of Koryo as an intermediate step toward unification. In 1967, North Korea began to take a more provocative stance toward South Korea. In July 1967, the North began training a special Unit 124 to assassinate President Park. On January 16, 1968, the unit infiltrated into the South and three days later thirty-one commandos launched a nighttime attack on the presidential palace, getting within 500 meters before being stopped by security forces. Twenty-seven were killed, one was captured, and three escaped. Between October 30 and November 2, eight infiltration teams each with about fifteen commandos from the same Unit 124 landed on the east coast between Samchŏk and Uljin.[37] Villagers were rounded up and forced to hear speeches about the socialist paradise to the North. Most of the guerrillas were quickly reported and killed or captured, but only after sixty-three southerners were dead.[38] On the sea, 115 southern fishing boats were seized by the North that year.[39] South Korea responded by stepping up patrols of the coastline, tightening security, and offering generous rewards for all reports. These efforts were successful enough to make the infiltrations increasingly difficult.

On the same day commandos stormed the presidential palace in Seoul, DPRK forces seized an American intelligence ship, the U.S.S. *Pueblo*, off the east coast near the port of Wonsan. The attacks on South Korea may have had a purpose of trying to destabilize the country, but it is not clear what purpose the capture of the *Pueblo* served. It was perhaps a fortuitous event. North Korea claimed the ship was in its territorial waters, which the United States denied. The eighty-two-member crew was held captive for eleven months before being released in December. The Americans initially responded with a show of force, sending the aircraft carrier the *Enterprise* into the waters off the east coast. However, rather than leading to military retaliation as Kim Il Sung might have feared, the United States negotiated for the release of the crew, issuing an apology, and the crew signed a confession. In 1999, the *Pueblo* was moved to the site near Pyongyang where the *General Sherman* was destroyed. Anchored next to the Victorious Fatherland Liberation Museum, it was made into a tourist attraction.

The original confession the crew of the *Pueblo* wrote contained puns mocking the DPRK, which the North Koreans did not understand. While this might have provided the Americans with some comfort, the North Koreans learned a valuable lesson—the United States did not want a military confrontation. Later North Korea would engage in provocative acts and then seek to negotiate with the Americans, frequently both winning concessions and demonstrating its military prowess to its people. In fact, the following year, in April 1969, North Korea shot down a U.S. EC-121 spy plane, again with no serious retaliation from the Americans. However, the aggressive attacks of the late 1960s failed to provoke popular support or destabilize the South and were never repeated on the same scale.

Perhaps sensing that the thaw in relations between the United States and China that was dramatized by President Nixon's visit to China in February 1972 offered the possibility of a U.S. withdrawal from the peninsula, Kim Il Sung began a more conciliatory policy toward South Korea. After secret talks, North and South Korea issued a joint communiqué on July 4, 1972, stating three fundamental principles on unification. First that unification must be carried out independently, without outside interference. Second, it must be achieved peacefully. Third, it must be implemented as a great national unity based on the homogeneous people first, and the differences in ideas, ideologies, and systems would be worked out later. The two governments created a South-North Coordinating Committee to work on steps toward achieving reunification based on these principles.[40]

Several meetings were held but little progress was made. The talks petered out because Kim Il Sung lost interest when he realized that a withdrawal of U.S. troops was not imminent, and, in fact, would not be on the table for serious consideration. The 1972–1973 negotiations began a pattern that would be repeated for the next four decades. North Korea would initiate or respond to offers for talks. There would be some diplomatic or even cultural and economic exchanges. Optimism would rise over the prospect of a thaw in relations. Pyongyang would then set conditions that were difficult or unrealistic or that it knew that the South would find unacceptable. Seoul would offer small confidence-building measures that would eventually be rejected with the DPRK insisting that major issues be discussed. Talks would break down and Pyongyang would ratchet up the tension with its rival again.

North Korea continued to carry out provocations in the South from time to time. On December 11, 1969, North Korean agents hijacked a YS-11 civilian airplane with fifty-one passengers, and on June 22, 1970, they set off a bomb at South Korea's national cemetery in an attempted assassination of Park.[41] On January 23, 1971, they attempted to hijack a Korean Air Lines plane; on February 4, 1972, they kidnapped five fishing boats and wrecked one. There was the kidnapping of a fishing boat on August 30, 1976.[42] Among the most menacing activities was its construction of tunnels under the demilitarized zone (DMZ). The DPRK constructed tunnels under the border capable of providing passage for substantial numbers of troops. The first was discovered in November 1974. It was 3.5 kilometers long, ran 1.2 kilometers under ROK territory, contained a narrow-gauge railroad, and was capable of transporting a regiment an hour. Three more were found in 1975, 1978, and in 1990. The second was even wider, capable of being driven through by small vehicles and transporting a division in an hour.[43] A particularly dramatic provocation occurred on August 15, 1974, celebrated as liberation (from Japan) day in South Korea. An agent of a North Korean front organization in Japan made an attempt on President Park as he was making a televised speech. The assassin missed Park but fatally wounded his wife. In August 1976, North Korean soldiers attacked and killed two American officers who were trimming a tree in the area. In 1981, Pyongyang carried out an assassination plot against the visiting President Chun Du Hwan in Canada, and on October 9, 1983, it killed seventeen top-ranking ROK officials in another attempt on Chun's life during his visit to Burma. North Korean agents blew up a Korean Air flight in 1987, killing all aboard. These provocative acts seemed irrational and reckless, creating in the minds of many outsiders an image of a dangerously unpredictable and relentlessly hostile regime. They were not intended to immediately foment a pro-North rebellion, since even Kim Il Sung must have understood how limited his support was in the South, but were attempts to destabilize the South. Kim Il Sung held the firm conviction that he represented the will and the progressive forces of the Korean revolution and of Korean nationalism. Eventually the people of the South would rise up, eventually the Americans would withdraw, and eventually the situation would be ripe for reunification. The terrorist attacks were intended to speed this process along. And continuing tensions with the South served a domestic purpose, to maintain a state of military alert and preparedness.

In the 1960s Kim Il Sung became active in establishing close relations with the third world. This was part of the three-revolutionary-forces strategy. North Korea sought to create an international environment that would isolate South Korea, pressure the United States to withdraw its troops, and win the support of the progressive nations to its cause of national reunification. This also served to move the DPRK beyond the shadow of its two patrons, the Soviet Union and China, and announce its presence as an independent state. Additionally, being a major world leader may have added to Kim's prestige at home as well as appealing to his vanity. This became even truer in the 1970s when Kim Il Sung began portraying the DPRK to his people as a shining example of progressive socialism admired around the world. Above all it was another front in his rivalry with the South. He wanted to demonstrate that the DPRK was the true representative of the Korean people and to isolate South Korea. As a result a competition began between the two Koreas as each sought to receive more diplomatic recognitions than the other.

North Korea initially had some success in gaining third-world support for its demand for the withdrawal of all foreign troops from Korea. In

1975, it became a full member of the Non-Alignment Movement (NAM), a group of neutral, mostly postcolonial states. A committee of the General Assembly in 1975 passed a pro–North Korean resolution on the Korean Question that year. By the 1980s Pyongyang established relations with 110 countries around the world. It had more missions abroad than its rival South Korea and its voice was heard louder in third-world forums. A constant stream of leaders from Africa and other third-world countries visited Pyongyang, where no matter how small or how little actual strategic or economic importance they might have had, they were sure to receive an enthusiastic welcome from the thousands of North Koreans who dutifully turned out on the streets to greet them. These visits were highlighted as acknowledgment of the global recognition of the great leader and his achievements. In an outreach effort, North Korea sent performance troupes and exhibitions around the world.

These often expensive efforts produced little in the way of practical benefits, and the goodwill and influence they developed was often undermined by the clumsy and ill-informed behavior of North Koreans. Much of this problem was based on the ignorance of North Koreans of the outside world as well as the general lack of experienced diplomats. NAM representatives soon tired of having North Korea use its meetings as forums for pushing its agendas. The crude use of bribery and bluster to try to get their way offended many governments. Many were becoming wary of the growing cult of Kim Il Sung, and some were also concerned over the country's acts of terrorism against its southern neighbor. Its terrorist activities, especially the 1983 Burma bombing, also undermined its status. Nor did Pyongyang generate much of a popular following outside its borders. North Korea sponsored 200 organizations in 50 countries, but these never generated much local support and remained depended on DPRK funds.[44] In the 1980s third-world countries became more drawn to South Korea, where that country's economic success and growing prosperity proved more attractive than the DPRK version of Korea. Thus, this part of the three-revolutionary-forces strategy proved as unsuccessful as the other two: his effort to build up the DPRK as an economically powerful and unchallenged superior Korea, and to promote the revolutionary forces in the South.

ECONOMIC PROBLEMS

After an impressive decade of recovery and growth, the North Korean economy began to slow down. Under a Seven-Year Plan from 1961 to 1967, rapid industrialization continued but the shift to military building after 1962 and the cut in Soviet aid in the mid-1960s delayed its completion until 1970. It was followed by a Six-Year Plan (1971–1976). Although declared a success, it too was extended one year, suggesting that the state was having trouble meeting its economic targets.

To promote economic production Kim attempted to kindle revolutionary zeal and launched military-style campaigns. Attempts were made to meet economic targets by applying as much labor as possible. Office workers, students, and soldiers all were sent on construction projects to help with the spring planting or autumn harvests. In 1974, the regime launched the Three-Revolutions Teams movement. Inspired, at least in part, by the Red Guards in China's Cultural Revolution, teams of young revolutionaries went into mines, factories, and other production centers to increase output by stimulating the revolutionary enthusiasm of the workers. They attacked "bureaucratism" and called on workers to develop innovative solutions to problems. Speed battles were launched in which workers and farmers were urged to labor tirelessly for days on end to spur production. After 1978, China abandoned this approach for a more market-oriented economic development. North Korea, however, persisted in it.

By the early 1970s, the North Korean leadership had come to realize how dated its technology was. Most of the country's power plants and steel mills were from the colonial period. Kim Il Sung may have also become concerned over South Korea's rapid industrialization under Park. In 1972, he began a buying spree of Western plants and machinery. Petrochemical, textile, concrete, steel, pulp, and paper manufacturing plants were purchased, but the equipment was too sophisticated, the country lacked parts or money to buy them, and the electricity supply was often unreliable, rendering many of these purchases of limited use. Furthermore, North Korea was unable to earn the foreign exchange to repay the loans and eventually defaulted on them. The country was starved of foreign currency to buy needed materials for industry as well as luxury items for the elite. Remittances from Koreans living in Japan provided some hard currency, but in the 1970s the DPRK began to engage in counterfeiting, drug smuggling, and other illicit activities, many carried out through an Office 39 tasked with the purpose of acquiring badly needed foreign exchange.

In the 1980s Pyongyang launched large-scale, poorly conceived, showy development plans that were largely failures, such the West Sea Lock Gate, a massive reclamation project that drained a coastal area, producing only land too salty for any agricultural use. Huge sums were squandered on display projects, such as a virtually unused express highway between Pyongyang and Kaesong that existed only to impress visitors, or the world's tallest hotel that was never completed due to structural problems. Among the most severe problems were energy and food shortages that only became worse in the 1980s, seriously hampering the economy. Up to the 1970s, North Korea maintained an impressive level of economic development. However, by the 1980s its economic stagnation became a sharp contrast with the booming South Korean economy.

There were some hints that the DPRK would follow the reforms being carried out in China under Deng Xiaoping. Under the encouragement of China the DPRK issued a Joint Venture Law of September 1984 that appeared to welcome foreign trade and investment and give more emphasis to light industries. What may have been a hesitant move toward following China's path in carrying out economic reform was quickly aborted when relations with the Soviet Union improved. The Soviet Union appeared to court North Korea as a way of countering its strategically weakening position in East Asia, where the United States and Japan were strengthening ties with China. Following Kim Il Sung's six-week visit to the Soviet Union in the spring of 1984, Moscow began offering an increase in trade on favorable terms. This enabled Kim to resume the pattern of economic development he was comfortable with. Buoyed by Soviet aid, he launched the Third Seven-Year Plan, 1987–1993, which adhered to the highly centralized economic development model with its focus on military-related production. The increased Soviet support was short-lived, however, as the Soviet Union under Gorbachev became interested in improving relations with the West, reforming its own economy, and reducing military commitments. As a result of this change in policies, the Soviet Union established economic ties with South Korea. The USSR's trade with the ROK increased after 1988, while its trade with the DPRK sharply declined. By 1989, the Soviet Union had stopped major weapons shipments and ended its joint military exercises. Facing the decline in Soviet aid and pressure from China to open itself up to Western trade and investment, North Korea in 1991 created the Free Trade and Economic Zone in the Rajin-Sŏnbong area. The very remoteness of this site in the extreme northeast perhaps reflected the regime's ambivalence about the project. At any rate, this, like the 1984 initiative, was not followed up, and there was no significant economic reform.

Instead of opening up to foreign trade and investment or experimenting with private markets, North Korea continued to adhere to its highly centralized command economy. Much of the country's resources went toward supporting its vast military forces. By the 1990s the number of troops in the armed forces was enormous. Pyongyang claimed to have only 400,000, but most outside observers calculated their forces at 1.2 million troops including a 50,000-person navy, making North Korea's armed forces by then one of the largest in the world. Perhaps 5 percent of the total population or 8 percent of the adult population was on active duty in 1990, a percentage unmatched elsewhere in the world. In addition, 7.5 million were in the reserves. Kim Il Sung continued to view the economy through narrow military lenses, surrounding himself with ex-guerrilla fighters and becoming, as Japanese scholar Wada Haruki has called the DPRK, a "guerrilla state."

Before 1980, North Korean achievements in modernizing the country initially appeared to be a success story. In the early 1970s, a handful of journalists from non-Communist countries were permitted to visit, going on carefully managed tours and sometimes being granted an interview with Kim Il Sung. They were often impressed with what they saw. Allan Bouc from the French newspaper *Le Monde*, visiting in 1971, commented favorably on the level of industrialization, noting that all the vehicles he saw from bicycles to trucks were locally manufactured. He described the countryside as characterized by "beautiful, well-irrigated rice paddies, worked on by tractor." The cities and towns were neat with central squares that had well-cared-for flower beds. He saw "no idlers, street peddlers or useless occupations."[45] Another foreign journalist on a twenty-day tour that year noted, "Three things impress the visitor: The well-cared-for children, the adoration of Premier Kim Il Sung, and massive construction."[46] Harrison Salisbury, the first prominent American journalist to enter North Korea since the Korean War, reported of his 1972 visit that the country had made a "tremendous technical and industrial achievement." Visiting the Hamhŭng-Hŭngnam area on the east coast, he saw "endless vistas of industrial smokestacks."[47] Another visitor that year, John H. Lee, observed "a well-organized, highly industrialized socialist economy, largely self-sufficient with a disciplined and productive labor force." He noted, "although consumer goods are sparse and factory equipment is sometimes outmoded, the overall industrial plant compare favorably to anything in Asia outside Japan." He noted that unlike in most developing countries, modernization seemed evenly developed without the usual disparity between the cities and the countryside.[48] Several years later another Western journalist contrasted the orderly industrial society of North Korea with South Korea, noting the lack of slums, prostitution, or children selling gum that could be seen in Seoul.[49]

However, the economy largely stagnated after 1980; by the end of that decade it began contracting and standards of living entered a sharp decline.

KOREA IN GLOBAL PERSPECTIVE: NORTH KOREA AS A COMMUNIST COUNTRY

How can we characterize North Korea? Some observers, such as Adrian Buzo and Paul French, have labeled North Korea a Stalinist state. In fact, this is a most common characterization of the DPRK. It is argued that Kim Il Sung took Stalinist Russia as his model, with its highly centralized command economy, its emphasis on autarkic development rather than international trade, the priority given to heavy industry to support a large military, the complete collectivization and mechanization of agriculture, and the use of both propaganda and state terror to promote production. Even Kim Il Sung's cult of personality resembled Stalin's. This is not surprising since almost every Communist regime established in the years after 1945 was influenced by the Soviet example. Besides, Kim Il Sung lived in the Soviet Union during World War II, was put in power by the Soviets, and depended on them for aid.

However, Kim Il Sung's regime also resembled Maoist China. Like Mao, he was enamored of the potential of mass mobilization to achieve development targets, used self-criticism campaigns to instill correct thinking, and made use of the "mass-line" methods in which cadres both taught and learned from the people. His cult of personality, in which his "thought" was viewed as among the highest ideological achievements of humanity, can also be seen as Maoist. It is clear that the DPRK borrowed from and was influenced by some aspects of Maoism—the Three-Revolutions campaign of the mid-1970s is an example. However, much of the Maoist-type features of North Korea appear to have been independent developments, perhaps not so unusual considering the similar cultural backgrounds of the two societies. North Korea deviated in many ways from Maoism. There were no campaigns against intellectualists, although, of course, independent thinkers were not tolerated. There was less suspicion of technocrats, no backyard steel mills, and no Cultural Revolution. Nor were there any attacks on the family. In contrast to the radical swings in policy that characterized the PRC after 1949, the DPRK adhered rigidly to the same methods and policies from the 1950s to the 1990s. In this way, North Korea resembled Albania under the four decades of Enver Hoxha's Communist dictatorship more than it did China.

Some aspects of North Korean Communism appear to be sui generis. There was the Korean belief in the transformative power of education, a tradition derived from Confucianism as practiced in that country, which is evident in the constant "learning sessions" and other propaganda lessons. Familial language was used to an extent not found in other Communist regimes and was a contrast to Mao's own war on the family. In fact, the Confucian way in which the leadership was portrayed as benevolent rulers and society was described as an extended family bound together by reciprocal love was distinctive. So was the degree to which the regime was openly nationalist. Only North Vietnam was similar in being so nationalistic, but Hanoi's nationalism never displaced Marxism-Leninism to the degree it did in the DPRK. Other Communist regimes sought to isolate themselves from the world economy; none ideologically isolated themselves to such a degree by evolving such a self-referential, all-encompassing system of thought as *juche*.

North Korea differed from most other Communist states in other ways as well. The rivalry between Moscow and Beijing enabled North Korea to achieve a degree of political autonomy to pursue its own path, which was absent in Mongolia or the Eastern European states. It could be argued that none went through such a bitter colonial experience. Certainly none suffered from anything on the scale of the self-inflicted humiliation and destruction that resulted from the Korean War. North Korea was much more industrialized and urbanized than China or Vietnam. As late as the 1970s nearly four out of five Chinese lived in the countryside compared to only one in three in North Korea. It was also a small state, with a sense of its vulnerability that was locked in competition with a larger claimant to the mantle of heir to national unity. And although the leaders of the DPRK had more impressive anti-imperialist, independence-fighter credentials, the ROK had two-thirds of the population and the traditional capital. The DPRK without Seoul was like a claimant to being the real France without having Paris.

North Korea continued to call itself socialist and maintained many features reminiscent of Stalinist Russia. However, with its elaborate hierarchical structure based on family background, its Kim-family cult, its extreme ultranationalism, and its *juche* ideology that eventually ceased to be Marxist in any meaningful way, it had evolved along its own path.

Kim Il Sung, from "Report on the Work of the Central Committee to the Fourth Congress of the Workers' Party of Korea," September 11, 1961

Author Note: With the successful carrying out of the anti-imperialist, antifeudal democratic revolution in the northern part of the country after the Liberation, North Korea gradually embarked on the path of transition to socialism; socialist transformation began at that time.

Before the war, however, because the necessary social, economic, and material conditions were not yet fully mature, socialist transformation was only partial, the main work being to prepare for it. In the post-war years, socialist transformations of agriculture, handicrafts, capitalist trade, and industry were undertaken on a full scale and in 1958 it was completed in all these fields almost simultaneously.

The Chollima Movement

The splendid achievements in socialist reconstruction of our country have been scored in the midst of the great upsurge of socialist construction and in the course of the Chollima movement.

The Chollima movement is a manifestation of the tremendous creative power of our people who have firmly rallied around the Party. It is a nation-wide popular movement for the utmost acceleration of our social construction.

Our country had inherited a backward economy and culture from the old society and, in addition, went through a fierce war of three long years. We are building socialism in the conditions of north-south division of the country, standing face to face with the U.S. imperialists, and at the same time we are struggling for peaceful unification. In such a situation our struggle was bound to be exceedingly intense. Quickly to get rid of the backwardness left us by history, to accelerate the unification of the country, which is our supreme national task, we had to march ahead much faster than other people.

In view of this requirement of the development of our revolution, our Party mapped out a plan for definitely speeding up socialist construction in the North, and, on this basis, organized and mobilized the entire working people in the heroic struggle for socialist construction.

The working people of our country, educated and trained by the Party, were fully aware of the urgent requirement of the development of our revolution and of the historic mission they were entrusted with, and gave unanimous support to the Party's line of speeding up socialist construction.

In active response to the appeal of the Party, "Dash forward at the speed of Chollima!" our working people dashed ahead through thick and thin to carry out the task put forward by the Party. They rushed on and on, emulating each other, overcoming all obstacles and difficulties.

Thus, innovations were made and world-shaking miracles wrought almost every day on all fronts of socialist construction.

Our heroic working class built 300,000- to 400,000-ton-capacity blast furnaces, each in less than a year, laid a standard-gauge railway more than 80 kilometers in length in 75 days, and set up a huge, up-to-date vynalon factory on a spot which had been only a waste land in a little over one year. Our working people turned out more than 13,000 extra machine tools over and above the state plan within a year by initiating the machine tool multiplying movement. Within a period of three to four months they erected over a thousand factories for local industry by utilizing idle material and manpower in local areas.[50]

Kim Il Sung, from "Socialist Construction in the Democratic People's Republic of Korea and the South Korean Revolution." Lecture at the Ali Archam Academy of Social Sciences of Indonesia, April 14, 1965

The South Korean Revolution

Being a revolution for liberating one half of our country's territory and two-thirds of its population still held in bondage by foreign imperialists, the revolution in South Korea is an important component part of the Korean revolution as a whole. For the unification of our fatherland and the victory of the Korean revolution, it is necessary to strengthen the revolutionary forces in South Korea while promoting socialist construction in the North.

Since the first days of their occupation of South Korea, the U.S. imperialists have pursued the policies of military aggression and colonial enslavement. As a result, South Korea has been turned entirely into a colony, a military base of U.S. imperialism.

The South Korean "government" is a puppet regime set up with the armed support of the U.S. imperialists; it is nothing but a tool faithfully executing the instructions of its U.S. overlords.

Through this puppet regime and the use of so-called "aid" as a bait, the U.S. imperialists have placed all the political, economic, cultural and military affairs of South Korea under their control.

U.S. imperialism has thus set up a system of colonial rule following its occupation of South Korea, and, on this basis, has been enforcing an unprecedented military dictatorship over the South Korean people.

Today the national economy of South Korea is totally bankrupt and its industrial output stands at no more than 85 per cent at the time of Liberation.

Today there are roughly seven million unemployed and semi-employed in South Korea. And each year more than one million peasant households suffer from lack of food during the lean spring months.

The people are entirely denied political rights and are exposed to terrorism and tyranny.

Therefore, to attain freedom and liberation, the South Korean people must drive out the U.S. imperialist forces of aggression and overthrow the landlords, comprador capitalists and reactionary bureaucrats who are in league with them. U.S. imperialism is target No. 1 of the struggle for the South Korean people.

There can be neither freedom and liberation for the people in South Korea, nor progress in South Korean society, nor the unification of our fatherland, unless the U.S. imperialist aggressive troops are driven out and colonial rule is abolished.

Thus the revolution in the South is a national liberation revolution against the foreign imperialist forces of aggression, and a democratic revolution against feudal forces.

The motive force of this revolution in South Korea is the working class and its most reliable ally—the peasantry—together with the students, intellectuals and petty bourgeois who are opposed to the imperialist and feudal forces. The national capitalists, too, may have a share in the anti-imperialist, anti-feudal struggle.[51]

Popular North Korean Children's Songs

Nothing to Envy in the World
We Have Nothing to Envy in the World
Skies are blue and my heart is happy.
Play the Accordion.
Wonderful is my fatherland
Where the people live harmoniously
Our father is marshal Kim Il Sung,
Our abode is the bosom of the party,
We are brothers and sisters,
We have nothing to envy in the world.[52]

The Song of Paradise
Let us all sing of our socialist nation
Of the Paradise on earth free from oppression.
[the song ends with the following lines:]
We are free from exploitation, even from any tax or levy
Free from worries about food or clothing entirely,
Oh, how blessed we are all in the grateful embrace
That treasure man more than anything else.
Oh, ours is a socialist nation, best in the world
The great leader has built [it].[53]

NOTES

1. Stephen Kotlin and Charles K. Armstrong, "A Socialist Regional Order in Northeast Asia after World War II," in *Korea at the Center: Dynamics of Regionalism in Northeast Asia*, Charles K. Armstrong, K. Gilbert Rozman, Samuel S. Kim, and Stephen Kotlin, eds. (Armonk, NY: M.E. Sharpe, 2006), 110–25.

2. Kotlin and Armstrong, "A Socialist Regional Order in Northeast Asia after World War II," 121.

3. Stephan Haggard and Marcus Noland, *Famine in North Korea: Markets, Aid, and Reform* (New York: Columbia University Press, 2007).

4. Robert Scalapino, "Korea: The Politics of Change," *Asian Survey*, 3. 1 (January 1963): 31–40, 63.

5. Chin O. Chung, *Pyongyang Between Peking and Moscow: North Korea's Involvement in the Sino-Soviet Dispute, 1958–1975* (Tuscaloosa, AL: The University of Alabama Press, 1978), 33, n. 42, 170.

6. Dae-Sook Suh, *Kim Il Sung: The North Korean Leader* (New York: Columbia University Press, 1988), 165.

7. Ilpyong J. Kim, *Historical Dictionary of North Korea* (Lanham, MD: The Scarecrow Press, 2003), 24.

8. Bon-Hak Koo, "Political Economy of Self-Reliance: Juche and Economic Development," in *North Korea, 1961–1990* (Seoul: Research Center for Peace and Unification of Korea, 1992), 85.

9. Lim Jae-Cheon, *Kim Jong Il's Leadership of North Korea* (London: Routledge, 2009), 91.

10. Andre Lankov, *From Stalin to Kim Il Sung: the Formation of North Korea, 1945–1960* (New Brunswick, NJ: Rutgers University Press, 2002), 205.

11. Heonik Kwon and Byung-ho Chung, *North Korea: Beyond Charismatic Politics* (Lanham, MD: Rowman & Littlefield, 2012), 16.

12. Andrei Lankov, *The Real North Korea: Life and Politics in the Failed Stalinist Utopia* (Oxford: Oxford University Press, 2013), 18.

13. Lim, *Kim Jong Il's Leadership of North Korea*, 42.

14. Charles Armstrong, "A Socialism of Our Type: North Korean Communism in a Post-Communist Era," in Samuel S. Kim (ed.), *North Korean Foreign Relations in the Post–Cold War Era* (Oxford: Oxford University Press, 1998), 32–55, 33.

15. Suh, *Kim Il Sung: The North Korean Leader*, 322.

16. Helen-Louise Hunter, *Kim Il-song's North Korea* (Westport, CT: Greenwood, 1999), 16.

17. Adrian Buzo, *The Guerilla Dynasty: Politics and Leadership in the DPRK 1945–1994* (Sydney: Allen & Unwin, 1999), 105.

18. Andrei Lankov, *North of the DMZ: Essays on Daily Life in North Korea* (Jefferson, NC: McFarland & Company, 2007), 38.

19. Lim, *Kim Jong Il's Leadership of North Korea*, 89.

20. Ralph Hassig and Kongdan Oh, *The Hidden People of North Korea: Everyday Life in the Hermit Kingdom* (Lanham, MD: Rowman & Littlefield, 2009), 298.

21. Lankov, *North of the DMZ*, 68–69.

22. Jin Woong Kang, "The Patriarchal State and Women's Status in Socialist North Korea," *Graduate Journal of Asia-Pacific Studies* 6.2 (2008): 55–70.

23. Kang, "The Patriarchal State and Women's Status in Socialist North Korea," 66.

24. Kyung Ae Park, "Women and Revolution in North Korea," *Pacific Affairs* 65, no. 4 (Winter 1992–93): 527–545.

25. Lankov, *North of the DMZ*, 75.

26. Lankov, *North of the DMZ*, 131.

27. Lee Mun Woong, *Rural North Korea Under Communism: A Study of Sociological Change* (Houston, Texas: Rice University Press, 1976), 71–72.

28. Jin Woong Kang, "The 'Domestic Revolution' Policy and Traditional Confucianism in North Korean State Formation: A Socio-cultural Perspective," *Harvard Asia Quarterly*, 2006, 34–45.

29. Lankov, *North of the DMZ*, 133.

30. Young C. Kim, "North Korea 1979: National Unification and Economic Development," *Asian Survey* 20.1 (January 1980): 53–62.

31. Lankov, *North of the DMZ*, 47.

32. Lankov, *North of the DMZ*, 207–208.

33. Lankov, *The Real North Korea*, 39.

34. Lankov, *The Real North Korea*, 49.

35. Suh, *Kim Il Sung: The North Korean Leader*, 178.

36. Byung Chul Koh, *The Foreign Policy Systems of North and South Korea* (Berkeley, CA: University of California Press, 1984), 269.

37. Narushige Michishita, "Calculated Adventurism: North Korea's Military-diplomatic Campaigns," *Korea Journal of Defense Analysis* 16 no. 2 (Fall 2004): 188–197.

38. Mitchell Lerner, Mitchell, *"Mostly Propaganda in Nature," Kim Il Sung, the Juche Ideology and the Second Korean War* (Washington, D.C.: Woodrow Wilson International Center for Scholars, 2011); Suh, *Kim Il Sung: The North Korean Leader*, 232; Lankov, *The Real North Korea*, 30.

39. Soon Sung Cho, "North and South Korea: Stepped-Up Aggression and the Search for New Security" *Asian Survey* 9, no. 1 (January 1969): 29–32.

40. Buzo, *The Guerilla Dynasty*, 95.

41. Michishita, "Calculated Adventurism: North Korea's Military-diplomatic Campaigns," 188–197.

42. Yongho Kim, *North Korean Foreign Policy: Security Dilemma and Succession* (Lanham, MD: Lexington Books, 2011), 102.

43. Byung Chul Koh, *The Foreign Policy Systems of North and South Korea*, 288.

44. Suh, *Kim Il Sung: The North Korean Leader*, 267.

45. Allan Bouc, "A Visit to North Korea," *New York Times*, June 14, 1971.

46. Benedict S. David, "Visitor to North Korea Describes Vast Building Drive," *New York Times*, August 10, 1971.

47. Harrison Salisbury, *To Peking and Beyond: A Report on the New Asia* (New York: Quadrangle Books, 1973), 200.

48. John H. Lee, "By Any Standards Industry Is Powerful," *New York Times*, June 4, 1972.

49. Selig S. Harrison, *Korean Endgame: A Strategy for Reunification and U.S. Disengagement* (Princeton, NJ: Princeton University Press, 2002), 27.

50. Kim Il Sung, *Revolution and Socialist Construction in Korea: Selected Writings* (New York: International Publishers, 1971), 30, 42–44.

51. Kim Il Sung, *Revolution and Socialist Construction in Korea*, 99–103.

52. C. I. Eugene Kim, "Introduction: A Long Journey," in C. I. Eugene Kim and B. C. Koh, eds., *Journey to North Korea: Personal Perceptions* (Berkeley: University of California Press, 1983): 1–23.

53. Kim, "Introduction: A Long Journey," 1–23.

5

South Korea: From Poverty to Prosperity, 1953 to 1997

In March 1961, the *New York Times* reporter A. M. Rosenthal did a series on South Korea. It concluded with an article entitled "Outlook Dreary for South Korea." "South Korea," the report starts, "the poorer half of one of the poorest countries in the world, is trying to exist as a nation with too many people and too few resources." No one knows the answers to the country's economic woes, the author reported, except for "a Korea dependent for the foreseeable future, perhaps for decades, upon the self-interest and charity of . . . the United States."[1] This was not an unusually pessimistic assessment; for most outside observers, South Korea's prospects for the future looked grim. Overcrowded, possessing modest resources, artificially severed in half and cut off from the more industrial and developed North, riddled with official corruption and political instability, few countries must have seemed a less promising candidate for an economic takeoff. So how was it possible that South Korea could have become an economic powerhouse in just several decades? How could it have become one of the few postcolonial states to enter the ranks of developed countries? How could it have become not only one of the most prosperous, but also most democratic societies in Asia?

THE SYNGMAN RHEE YEARS, 1953–1960

Certainly there was little in the first years after the Korean War to hint at South Korea's dramatic economic transformation. In 1953, it was a nation shattered by three years of war. Seoul was in ruins, and a great deal of infrastructure had been destroyed. Thousands of families were returning from refugee camps to ruined homes; many were separated from relatives in the North with whom they had no contact. Almost every family had a member or close relative killed or missing. Economically the southern provinces of Korea that made up the Republic of Korea were poorer than they had been before World War II. The country was dependent on massive economic assistance from the United States and also the spending of the large number of American forces in the country.

It was also a changed society. South Korea was still a mostly rural, agricultural country where traditional values were strong and loyalties were still primarily focused on family, clan, and locality. But the land reform that took place during the Korean War (see below) created a countryside of small family farms no longer dominated by the *yangban* class. And the Korean War had accelerated the growth of the urban population, as many refugees fled to the city during the conflict and stayed there. Although less than one in four people lived in urban centers, this was still a significant increase. The urban population, mostly poor, was more open to new ideas, influenced by democratic concepts, and concerned with opportunities for economic and social advancement. In short, the countryside was still conservative, but it was no longer dominated by the old aristocratic landholding families; and the cities were filled with a restless, volatile population.

Politically South Korea was dominated by the seventy-eight-year-old President Syngman Rhee. Still intellectually bright, energetic, and politically shrewd for his advanced age, he was unfortunately too rigid, authoritarian, stubborn, and concerned with maintaining his power to be the effective leader that South Korea needed to create a stable political system and pull itself out of poverty. His Liberal Party had no real ideology other than perpetuating Rhee's rule and using his administration to personally advance the political and economic fortunes of its members. Rhee and his Liberal Party supporters did not refrain from using bribery, intimidation, manipulation, and thuggery to maintain themselves in power. In the May 1954 elections, the Liberal Party received 114 seats, a modest majority. The conservative opposition Democratic Party won only 15 seats, with independents filling most of the other seats. The Liberal Party then pushed for a constitutional amendment that would enable Rhee to run for a third term. In November 1954, the proposed amendment received 135 votes, one short of the two-thirds needed. Then, under pressure, the presiding officer at the Assembly ruled that since technically 135.3 were needed for a two-thirds majority, this could be rounded off, and the amendment passed.

Rhee then went on to win a third term in 1956. However, his corrupt regime was gradually losing its hold. A long-time nationalist hero, his support among the urban population was declining. The aging president was also facing a more effective opposition. In September 1955, the Korean Democratic Party merged with various anti-Rhee groups to form the Democratic Party. This began the dominant pattern of South Korean politics for the next half century: a basic two-party system, with the two parties marked less by clear ideological difference than by different coalitions of factions, most of the factions centered on an individual leader. In the 1956 elections, huge political rallies were held in support of the Democratic candidate, another aging political veteran, Sin Ik-hŭi (1894–1956). Sin died weeks before the election; still, Rhee received only 56 percent of the votes, compared to 72 percent in 1952. In rural areas the Liberal Party was able to maintain its support, often by playing on the naivety of voters, in many cases pressuring schoolteachers, respected figures in villages, to instruct their students' parents to vote for Rhee. Many urban voters cast their ballots for a third-party candidate, Cho Pong-am (1898–1959), a socialist and principal architect of the land reform. Cho received 30 percent of the votes and carried a number of southern cities including Taegu, the third largest and the scene of leftist violence in 1946. Rhee later had Cho arrested on charges of treason and executed him in 1959. The Liberal Party candidate for vice president, Yi Ki-bung (1896–1960), lost to the Democratic candidate, Chang Myŏn (1899–1966), by 41.7 to 39.6 percent. Significantly, Chang won overwhelmingly in urban areas.

A growing urban population, the increasing disgust with corruption, and the disappointments over the slow pace of economic recovery and growth made Rhee's hold on power increasingly tenuous. Social changes were taking place that were working against the regime. The urban population doubled from 15 percent in 1945 to 30 percent in 1960. The growth of an increasingly literate class is indicated by newspaper circulation that had grown five times in the fifteen years after liberation to more than two million by 1960.[2] In May 1958 the Liberals received only 38.7 percent of the vote against 29.5 percent for the Democrats, despite use of voter manipulation and vote fraud. To counter these trends, the Liberal Party pushed through a new National Security Law in December 1958 that made it easier for the government to crack down on critics under the name of endangering national security. In 1960 Rhee ran for a fourth term and the Democrats nominated Cho Pyŏng-ok (1894–1960) as their candidate. But he too died just before the election. Attention then shifted to the vice presidential race, where Chang Myŏn faced the Liberal party challenger, Yi Ki-bung. Yi had become Rhee's designated successor; Rhee had even adopted his son to seal a family connection. Since Rhee was eighty-five and thought not likely to live much longer, the general feeling was that the vice president would most likely end up being the next president. With no opposition, Rhee received 88.7 percent in the official count, while Yi Ki-bung, who was widely unpopular and who had lost in 1956, was officially announced the winner by an absurdly large landslide. The blatant vote rigging led to riots in the southern city of Masan. The demonstrations protesting the elections spread to Seoul, where thugs from the Anticommunist Youth Corps attacked students from Korea University. It was a common tactic of Rhee to use thugs to break up demonstrations, much as King Kojong had done before him. The next day, April 19, some 30,000 university and high school students marched toward the presidential mansion, where police fired on them, killing 139 and wounding hundreds of others. This event later became an annual day of commemoration, "Student Revolution Day." When demonstrations continued in the following days and the students were joined by their professors, the military commander in Seoul, General Song Yo-ch'an (1918–1980), refused to obey orders to fire on them. Under intense U.S. pressure and with public support clearly lost, Rhee resigned on April 26 and left for exile to Hawaii, dying there five years later. Yi Ki-bung, his elder son who had been adopted by Rhee, his younger son, and his wife killed themselves. Chang Myŏn had earlier resigned, so as the highest-ranking official, Foreign Minister Hŏ Chŏng (1896–1988) formed an interim government that drew up a new constitution.

The legacy of the Rhee regime is mixed. It is easy to dismiss it as corrupt, authoritarian, and inept. Decades later, however, some South Koreans have a more charitable view of Rhee as an effective and patriotic leader. Many of the problems his administration faced were enormously daunting. His government did secure vast amounts of U.S. aid, valuable in recovering from the devastation of the Korean War. His refusal to reestablish ties with Japan was counterproductive economically, but this stemmed from a real fear of reestablishing the country's dependency on and its domination by the former colonial ruler. His virulent anticommunism made any kind of reconciliation with North Korea impossible. Yet it is unlikely that any reconciliation was possible in any case, in light of the deep differences between the two states and North Korea's determination to reunify the country on its own terms. His regime saw the rapid expansion of education that was so crucial to the country's transformation, although it is debated how much credit his administration deserved for this development. Whatever his achievements, his use of thugs, intimidation, and vote rigging to maintain himself in office, and his abuse of power to eliminate opponents, left an unfortunate political legacy.

THE DEMOCRATIC EXPERIMENT, 1960–1961

South Korea then had a brief experiment with a more democratic government. On June 15, 1960, a new constitution was drawn up that created a parliamentary, cabinet form of government, which the Democratic Party had been calling for. There was a bicameral National Assembly. The president was chosen by the National Assembly, not by popular election, and his power was greatly reduced, with much of it going to the new post of prime minister. National Assembly elections were then held on July 29, with the Democratic Party receiving 175 of the 233 seats in the lower house. The Democratic Party consisted of two major factions: the New and the Old Faction. Chang Myŏn of the New Faction was selected as prime minister, Yun Po-sŏn (1897–1990) of the Old Faction as president. This power sharing did not prevent a party split, with Yun's Old Faction forming the New Democratic Party in September. Thus Chang Myŏn headed the cabinet without a majority of the seats in the Assembly. His weakened government was constantly seeking allies, reshuffling the cabinet, and changing ministers.

The Chang Myŏn administration labored under many disadvantages. Besides lacking a solid working majority, it worked within a constitution that had created a weak executive and a strong legislature, a reaction to Rhee's abuse of executive powers. But there was little party discipline among the legislators, making it difficult to carry out programs for reform. Nor was there a desire to carry out sweeping changes, since conservatives dominated the government. The new government of the Second Republic, as it was called, was largely made up of members of the elite. It was out of touch with the more radical calls for social justice advocated by labor, student, and other dissident groups. It did respond to the public calls for the investigation and removal of members of the bureaucracy and the police who had abused their power under Rhee. The government was initially reluctant to carry out a major purge, but bowing to public pressure, it dismissed 17,000 police officers. Unfortunately, this had the effect of weakening the effectiveness of the police, needed to control the disorder in Seoul. The crime rate soared.

A series of strikes plagued the country as labor leaders, teachers, and others called for the removal of all members of the old regime and the enactment of laws addressing their grievances for better pay, improved working conditions, more freedom to organize, for immediate national unification, and direct negotiations with Pyongyang. The demands for higher wages became more strident as workers faced galloping inflation. The decision by the Chang government to devalue the *hwan* (South Korea's currency, later renamed the *won* [*wŏn*]), from 650 to 1,300 to the U.S. dollar, resulted in inflationary pressures, adding to the distress of wage earners as well as making the business community uneasy. Support from the business community further eroded when the Assembly moved to pass legislation punishing corrupt businessmen with ties to the Rhee regime, although the final bill was fairly innocuous.[3]

An illegal teachers' union sprang up that carried out in-school hunger strikes calling for better pay, recognition of their union, dismissal of unpopular principals, and other reforms. Students who had spearheaded the overthrow of the Rhee administration were emboldened to pressure the government for more reforms. In South Korea's Confucian society there was a long tradition of remonstrance—public expressions of moral outrage by students and young scholars over official conduct. This tradition was reinforced by the successful student-led uprising against Rhee. Yet student demonstrations, many calling for radical and unrealistic measures, added to the sense of turmoil and ineffectiveness of the democratic government. With demonstrations in Seoul an almost daily event, there was an impression that the government was unable to establish order. This was particularly true after militant students broke into the Assembly to pressure the members to act on their demands. Already plagued by instability, inflation, and a sense that the country was edging toward chaos, the government faced a new challenge when student leaders and other radicals decided to meet with North Korean representatives. Early in 1961, several small radical parties were formed calling for the withdrawal of all foreign troops from Korea, a demand supported by student radicals. In May of 1961, students called for a meeting with their fellow students from the North at P'anmunjŏm. The call for dialogue with the North made conservatives nervous. They distrusted Pyongyang and saw any attempt to open a dialogue with them as playing into the DPRK's hands. The instability was also seen as a possible invitation to the North to invade again. Not only was the democratic government struggling to cope with the volatile situation, it is not clear how committed most South Koreans were to democracy. The Democratic Party leaders themselves often acted in an undemocratic manner, reissuing the National Security Law that Rhee had used to silence political opponents.

THE MILITARY COUP

At the same time, the military was becoming restless. South Korea had vast armed forces numbering 600,000. Trained and equipped by the United States, its military was in many ways the most modern, effective institution in the country. Under Rhee the military had little political influence. Rhee skillfully played the factions in the army against each other, especially the northeast and northwest factions consisting of Japanese-trained officers from these two regions of the country. Underneath the higher-ranking generals were more youthful officers trained in the Korean Military Academy during the late 1940s; some also had military training under the Japanese. Mostly they were young, under forty years of age. Their promotion and advancement in the ranks was blocked, since their superiors monopolized the higher ranks. The most important group of dissident officers came from the eighth class of the Korean Military Academy, who graduated in 1949 just before the Korean War. This class of officers had seen much action in the war and had formed a strong bond. Their leader was Kim Jong Pil (Kim Chong-p'il) (1926–), a former member of the ROK Army Counterintelligence Corps. One of the few college-educated military officers with important rank, the thirty-five-year-old had begun recruiting and planning for the coup before the April 1960 student revolution.[4] Kim was married to a niece of General Park Chung Hee (Pak Chŏng-hŭi), a major general respected and trusted by the junior officers. He and his junior officers were concerned about more than the reform of the military and the removal of senior corrupt or incompetent officers. They also were concerned about the growing strength of the leftist movement among labor, students, and teachers; about the corruption of businessmen; about the venality and ineffectiveness of the civilian politicians; and about the country's weakness in the face of the North Korean threat. In the spring of 1961, Kim and his coconspirators plotted to overthrow the state under the leadership of General Park Chung Hee.

In the predawn hours of May 16, 1961, some 1,600 troops occupied key positions in Seoul. The military conspirators then took over the major government buildings. Chang Myŏn fled to a Catholic convent, while the plotters announced over Radio Seoul that the country was under military rule. Martial law was declared and a strict curfew was imposed. A Military Revolutionary Committee was then organized. Chang came out of hiding to serve on the committee, hoping to avoid bloodshed and not wishing to create an incident that would encourage a North Korean attack. President Yun also agreed to support the committee. Chang soon resigned, and the Military Revolutionary Committee, which was firmly in military hands, took over. The Second Republic had ended and a period of military rule had begun that was to last three decades.

The new military rulers created the Supreme Council for National Reconstruction (SCNR). In June they issued a Law for National Reconstruction that gave the SCNR control over the government, and the National Assembly was dissolved. The military detained Chang Myŏn and most of his colleagues and carried out a purge and dismissal of more than 40,000 members of the bureaucracy.[5] Political activity was banned and 4,000 politicians were prohibited from political activity for six years. The military rulers established a Revolutionary Tribunal that tried thousands of offenders for corruption or for activities favorable to the enemy (North Korea).

The key figure in the new government was Park Chung Hee. Park was from a humble background and rose through intelligence and a remarkable self-discipline. Born in 1917, the youngest of seven children in a poor peasant family, he excelled as a young pupil and gained entry to the elite Taegu Normal School in 1932. After graduating, he taught school for three years, and there remained in Park's personal style something of the stern schoolmaster lecturing to his students. He later enrolled in the Manchukuo Military Academy, and in 1944 was commissioned as a second lieutenant in the Imperial Japanese Army, returning to Korea in 1946 as a captain. Park was never involved in nationalist politics but appeared to be a loyal Japanese subject. However, he had a brother involved in leftist politics after the war and was himself implicated in the Yŏsu military rebellion in 1948, when he was sentenced to life imprisonment. He was pardoned but dismissed from the army and then reinstated at the start of the Korean War. Park finished the war as a brigadier-general.[6]

In the army he did not join any fraternal organizations and was not associated with any faction, remaining aloof with an unblemished reputation for honesty. Small in stature, Park was not charismatic but was respected for his intelligence and discipline. The new military leader did not plot to seize power but was selected by the coup plotters as their leader. Once in power, he assumed the role of leadership with efficiency and skill. Park proved a pragmatist; he wanted to create an orderly and strong ROK but was open to advice from experts. Under this leadership the military government ran the country with an efficiency and purpose not previously seen.

The SCNR imposed law and order, arresting members of criminal gangs and parading them down the streets. Even "corrupt businessmen," including many of the leading business figures, were arrested, publicly humiliated, and released after they paid fines. With puritanical zeal they cleaned up red light districts and closed dance halls, bars, and coffee shops. Many newspapers and other publications were shut down. Anyone suspected of being a Communist was arrested.

To consolidate power, coup leaders purged the military, forcing many senior officers to retire and placing members of the eighth military academy class in key positions. One of the most important actions at the time was the creation of the Korean Central Intelligence Agency (KCIA) by Kim Jong Pil, whose own background was in the Army Counterintelligence Corps. This was developed into a sophisticated organization for domestic and international intelligence. It eventually grew into a vast apparatus with tens of thousands of agents. The KCIA was financed by a variety of funds, ranging from government kickbacks to money from rightists in Japan to its own business operations, including Walker Hill, a gambling resort for foreigners used to gain access to foreign exchange. Its tentacles reached into almost every school, business, and political or social organization. It even extended overseas, where the KCIA kidnapped dissident Koreans to bring them back home for punishment and bribed foreign officials to shape policies favorable to the ROK.

ECONOMIC TRANSFORMATION

South Korea's economic takeoff, its spurt of rapid industrialization and economic growth, began in the early 1960s under the direction of the military government. It was under the nearly three decades of military-led governments that the economic transformation that pulled the country out of poverty occurred. This economic transformation is sometimes referred to as the South Korean "economic miracle" or the "miracle on the Han," the latter referring to the Han River that flows through Seoul. The years before 1961, by contrast, are dismissed as a time of stagnation, inflation, corruption, and dependence on foreign aid. However, there was some real economic growth under the Rhee regime, much of it due to U.S. aid. In the 1950s, South Korea was one of the largest recipients of American assistance; Washington financed most of the ROK operating budget, paying the entire cost of its large military. With such aid, South Korea's basic infrastructure was largely rebuilt by the late 1950s, bringing the country back up to its prewar level. Still, real economic growth was only 4 percent a year, less than 2 percent per capita when the high birthrate is factored in. This real but modest rate of growth meant that in 1960 the country was still extremely poor.

Rhee followed an import substitution industrialization policy typical of many postcolonial states after World War II. The United States encouraged Seoul to establish trade relations with Japan, whose own economy was undergoing a strong recovery in the 1950s. But Rhee would not sign a peace treaty or establish diplomatic relations with the former enemy. His anti-Japanese sentiments, while shared by most Koreans, went to extremes. ROK patrol boats frequently clashed with Japanese fishing vessels that were violating the country's territorial waters. These minor disputes were played up in the media and dramatized with government-sponsored anti-Japanese rallies, giving the impression at the time that the ROK was in a two-front conflict with North Korea to the north and Japan to the south. Rhee's policies, nonetheless, reflected genuine fears that their country would become an economic colony of Japan. For this reason, his administration resisted the advice of American advisors who encouraged the production of agricultural products such as rice and seaweed for the Japanese market. If he had followed this advice it would have largely re-created the economic structure of the colonial period.

Reasonable as his refusal to be a supplier of raw materials to Japan was, Rhee did not have a truly constructive alternative. Instead, he largely relied on U.S. aid and an overvalued currency to keep the country economically afloat and himself in power. American aid was essential. The massive amounts accounted for nearly 80 percent of all government revenues and a substantial portion of South Korea's entire GNP. Much of this went to the economic recovery efforts, including rebuilding infrastructure destroyed in the war. Foreign aid, along with the inflated exchange rate, was also used to support crony capitalism. The government gave out import licenses to favored businessmen to buy commodities. Since the official exchange rate of the *hwan* did not reflect any market reality, this meant that import licenses were highly profitable. Part of the profits would go to Rhee's Liberal Party. Among the goods imported were items such as sugar and flour supplied at bargain prices through a U.S. food aid program known as P.L. 480. Yi Pyŏng-ch'ŏl, who later founded Samsung, exemplifies how this system worked. He purchased imported sugar at low prices for his Cheil Sugar, using his government-issued foreign exchange license to become the country's largest refiner while also becoming an important financial contributor to the pro-government Liberal Party. In this manner, the small capitalist class became dependent on the regime. Meanwhile, the country exported little. In 1956, exports amounted to $25 million and imports $389 million, the huge deficit made up for by the infusion of U.S. aid funds. The slow pace of economic recovery in South Korea despite massive aid was worrisome to the Americans, who by 1956 had become aware of the much faster recovery in North Korea.[7] In 1957, they began cutting aid and insisting on a program that involved limiting the budget deficit to curb inflation, and they pressured Rhee to devalue the currency. These measures weakened the regime in the later 1950s but did not result in any economic improvements.

Nonetheless, some of the basic foundations were being established for the country's later economic growth. As riddled with self-serving, corrupt officials as it was, the Rhee administration also had many able and talented people in the areas of economics, education, and finance. To these were added a steady stream of South Koreans who were going to the United States to study science, engineering, economics, education, and a variety of other fields. They often were employed as young technocrats by the government. In 1958, the administration created the Economic Development Council, a body of these technocrats that began to draw up plans for long-term economic development. Although the Rhee administration collapsed in 1960, before they could be implemented, these plans formed a basis for those of the Park Chung Hee regime after 1961.

In addition, two fundamental changes took place in South Korean society before 1961 that contributed enormously to the country's economic takeoff. One was the rapid expansion of education (see below). The other was land reform. As John Lie and others have pointed out, land reform was a crucial element in South Korea's economic as well as social modernization. The powerful popular demand for land reform was only partially satisfied by the U.S. occupation authorities when they redistributed Japanese holdings. Rhee's conservative supporters were largely from the landlord class and were less than enthusiastic about a more comprehensive redistribution of land. Worried by the effect of North Korean propaganda on restless peasants and pressured by the United States, the National Assembly passed a land reform act in 1949, but it was only during the Korean War that this was carried out. Under the land reform, property holdings were limited to 7.5 acres; farmers receiving redistributed acreage had to pay 150 percent of the annual value of the land received over a ten-year period. The result was dramatic. In 1944, 3 percent of landowners owned 64 percent, but in 1956 the top 6 percent owned only 18 percent; tenancy had virtually disappeared.[8] The land reform not only ended peasant unrest, it changed rural society. Land reform in South Korea delivered a major blow to the old order, perhaps not as completely and as suddenly as in North Korea, but it was still revolutionary. The domination of the countryside by the landowning elite had finally come to an end.

But whereas land reform in the North was followed by collectivization, in which the state replaced the *yangban* as landlords and much of the old landed class fled south or disappeared, the results were different in South Korea. Traditional peasants became small entrepreneurial farmers. The conservative landlords, rather than disappearing completely, now directed their capital and energy toward business or education.[9] Since the 1910s some members of the landed aristocracy had been entering business; the land reform accelerated this trend. Many others established private schools, universities, and private educational foundations. In this way, land reform contributed to the foundations of a prosperous society. It brought stability to the countryside and redirected much of the capital and entrepreneurial energy of the old landlord class toward commerce, industry, and education.

ECONOMIC GROWTH UNDER PARK CHUNG HEE

The military government that came to power in 1961 inherited a poor nation with only a modest rate of economic growth that was embarrassingly dependent on the United States for aid. It faced a rapidly industrializing North Korea and an economically expanding Japan that threatened to absorb the country as part of an East Asian economic sphere. The slow pace of growth was not just frustrating to the Americans but to many Koreans. It was clear that the country was falling behind North Korea. It was also frustrating to see the nation mired in poverty while Japan boomed, and to see the contrast between its impoverished citizens and the well-fed American troops.[10] South Korea possessed a military that was strong in manpower but, like the economy in general, was totally dependent on U.S. equipment and aid. Freeing the nation from its "mendicant" status and lifting it out of poverty became the military government's highest priority. Park himself seemed to understand the importance of making South Korea economically strong. In a sense, his vision was not too different from that of the military leaders that ruled Japan during the Meiji period with the slogan "rich country, strong military." Indeed he modeled himself in part on the Meiji leaders and on other strong leaders who modernized and developed their countries, such as Pasha Kemal (Ataturk).[11] South Korea's small and fragile industrial base compared unfavorably with the more industrial North and its strong recovery. The ROK's economic dependence on U.S. aid was not only a sign of its weakness and a national humiliation, but also a limitation on its sovereignty. The desire to free the nation from its economic dependence on the United States was reflected in the motto of the First Five-Year Plan, *charipkyŏngje* ("self-reliant economy"), proclaimed from public billboards and on numerous placards.[12] In this respect Park resembled Kim Il Sung as well. Both were at heart economic nationalists who sought a Korea economically strong enough to be capable of supporting a large military and to be free from dependence on outside powers. Park later questioned whether South Korea could preserve its "self-respect as a sovereign nation, independent, free and democratic," being so dependent on the Americans. Park was troubled that the United States had "a 52 percent majority vote with regard to Korea."[13] This referred to the fact that the American aid accounted for over half the government's budget. The similarity in the way leaders of both Koreas saw economic development linked with military strength and self-reliance is seen in a slogan Park used in his industrialization effort: "construction on the one hand, national defense on the other" (*ilmyŏnkŏnsŏl, ilmyŏnkukpang*), which echoed Kim Il Sung's contemporary call for "arms in the one hand, hammer and sickle in the other."[14]

Park admired the Japanese state-directed economic development he witnessed as a young man. Thus the influence of the North, with its ambitious economic plans for rapid industrialization, the influence of prewar Japan, and his own experience in a disciplined modern army led him to support a state-directed, planned program of economic development. Yet, initially, the coup leaders appeared not to have had clear ideas about what to do about the economy. At first they issued decrees regarding rural debt relief and price support for rice to alleviate the plight of farmers. Disgusted with the corrupt relationship between businessmen and the government, they detained and fined fifty-one of the leading business-figures, including the country's richest, Yi Pyŏng-ch'ŏl. But this quickly changed as the military leaders soon realized that they needed the skills of the entrepreneurs to promote economic growth. They released the businessmen after each signed an agreement stating, "I will donate all my property to the government if it requires it for national reconstruction."[15] Park then appointed thirteen of them to the Promotional Committee for Economic Reconstruction, with Yi Pyŏng-ch'ŏl as chair.[16] Thus began the military government's partnership with the country's entrepreneurial elite that continued for a generation. It was a partnership in which the state in the early years was firmly dominant.

Then the SCNR issued a Five-Year Economic Development Plan. The need for long-range economic planning had become apparent to many government bureaucrats. The SCNR's Five-Year Plan was largely based on the one that the Chang Myŏn administration had outlined the previous year, which in turn was based on the one being drawn up in the waning days of the Rhee administration. So in this sense, it was not a radical break but part of a general move by the technocrats for comprehensive government-directed planning. Several steps were taken to direct the state toward economic growth, perhaps the most crucial being the nationalization of all commercial banks and the reorganization of the banking system to give the state control over credit.[17] Money could now be lent out to businesses according to the needs of the economic plan. To direct the overall economic development the government established an Economic Planning Board (EPB) staffed by young talented technocrats to work out the details of the plan. To ensure that the economic plan would be under technocrat supervision, Park made the EPB head a deputy prime minister, outranking all other cabinet members. The plan called for a 7.1 percent economic growth rate for 1962–1966 by encouraging the development of light industries for export. This target would have been a large improvement over the 4 percent growth of the previous few years. Although many foreign advisors were skeptical about reaching this goal, the state exceeded it. After expanding only a modest 4.1 percent in 1962 the economy grew 9.3 percent in 1963, and boomed each of the next three years. The final result was that under the First Five-Year Plan economic growth averaged 8.9 percent, launching South Korea on its path to rapid industrialization. Exports grew 29 percent a year, manufacturing 15 percent a year.[18] It was followed by a Second Five-Year Plan, 1967–1971, which placed greater emphasis on improving the basic infrastructure, including transportation and electric power.[19]

In addition to directing low-interest loans to businesses fulfilling the plan, the government also created a number of centers to promote research and the dissemination of technical knowledge to business enterprises. One of the first, established in 1966, was the Korean Institute of

Science and Technology. It also promoted technical education, building a number of new vocational middle and high schools and two-year technical colleges. Students were encouraged to study abroad, although many of these did not return. Another factor was the greater professionalization of the state bureaucracy under Park. Promotion was based on clear guidelines for merit, and recruitment was through a highly competitive examination system. Good pay and benefits, job security, and enhanced prestige attracted many of the most talented to the civil service, including a steady stream of those trained at the best universities overseas. As a result, a highly competent, respected set of officials were able to help guide and promote economic and social development.[20]

Since Park's economic development policies were driven by economic nationalism and the desire to achieve autonomy for his country, he was concerned about avoiding foreign economic control. Consequently, he initially limited direct foreign investment into the country. But then, on the advice of his economists, he began easing up on these restrictions. The Foreign Capital Inducement Act exempted foreign investors from income, corporate, and property taxes for five years. And he was still heavily reliant on the United States, which held considerable economic and political leverage. This was highlighted when the United States forced Park to restore civilian rule in 1963. He then ran for and was elected president, and was reelected in 1967. From 1963 to 1971 he ruled in a semi-authoritarian fashion, with his official party, the Democratic Republican Party, maintaining a majority in the National Assembly. Park managed to keep just enough semblance of democratic government to please the Americans, while remaining effectively in control of the country. Gradually, as the economy grew, the United States began to scale back aid, but in the 1960s and 1970s, U.S. aid and technical assistance were still absolutely indispensable to South Korea's economic development. Moreover, throughout the 1960s, 1970s, and 1980s, the United States absorbed the majority of the country's exports.

Park may have resented Washington's interference in the country's internal affairs, but he also was able to use political and military relations with the Americans for economic development purposes. A significant example was the ROK participation in the Vietnam War. Park made an agreement with the Johnson administration in 1965 to provide troops for Vietnam in return for considerable concessions. These were formally worked out in the 1966 Brown Memorandum, named after the U.S. ambassador to the ROK. A bill authorizing the sending of troops was passed in 1965 when the opposition was boycotting the National Assembly because of Park's efforts to normalize relations with Japan. Park committed the country to supplying 20,000 troops to support the U.S. military effort, a number that increased over the next several years. Eventually

300,000 ROK troops did tours of duty there between 1965 and 1973. In the 1966 Brown Memorandum, the United States formally agreed that South Korean firms were to be given lucrative contracts to supply goods and services to the South Vietnamese, American, and Allied military forces. South Korean firms constructed many military installations, helping to establish a new overseas industry for South Korea that proved useful for earning foreign exchange. South Korean firms such as Hyundai gained valuable experience in completing construction and transportation projects for the United States in Vietnam. Later Hyundai and other Korean construction companies applied their experience in building to meet short timetables to win contracts in the Middle East and elsewhere. In addition to these contracts, the United States further agreed to modernize the ROK armed forces and provide military and other aid.

Economic development was greatly facilitated by normalizing relations with Japan. By 1964, Japan was emerging as a great economic power, showcased by the Olympics it hosted that year. Japan had a booming economy, rising labor costs, and capital for foreign investment. Korea, next door, in the same time zone, with historical ties, with many in its business community fluent in Japanese, was a natural place for investment. Korean cheap labor and Japanese capital and technology were a good match. Yet there was bitterness in Korea toward Japan, a fear that close economic partnerships with its former colonial ruler would replicate the preliberation dependent status and would lead to an economic recolonization. For this reason, Syngman Rhee was not the only South Korean to reject the resumption of trade and economic ties with Japan. Normalization, therefore, was a sensitive issue. Koreans demanded reparations from Japan, and safeguards, as well as Japanese admissions of injustices done in the past. The Park administration saw how clearly advantageous, even necessary, normalization would be to economic development. Opponents of the regime, and there were many who resented the rule by military or ex-military men, found this a useful issue, since Park's and many of his supporters' past links with Japan made his administration vulnerable to charges of pro-Japanese sentiment. Attempts to begin normalization in 1964 led to massive student demonstrations. In June, Park had to declare martial law and sent two combat divisions into the streets to restore order. The National Assembly approved normalization on August 14, 1965, only after the opposition walked out in protest and troops had cleared the streets of protesters. The treaty went into effect in December 1965. Japan agreed to pay $800 million in aid. The fishing dispute was settled by both sides agreeing to twelve-mile (twenty-kilometer) economic zones; Koreans living in Japan were guaranteed residency rights and equal rights to public education or welfare, although some social welfare benefits were not granted in practice for another two decades.[21]

With this agreement the reparations issue was closed. Far more important than Japanese reparations money, which was modest, was the flow of investments that contributed to the already strong growth of the ROK economy. In the years after the treaty, Japan was a major foreign investor in South Korea, second only to the United States. In a decade after the treaty, trade between the two countries expanded more than ten times; Japan supplied nearly 60 percent of the foreign technology between 1962 and 1979.[22] Without the U.S. market and Japan's investments and technology transfers, it's difficult to imagine how South Korea's economic transformation could have been accomplished.

There was a shift in economic policies in the early 1970s associated with the more authoritarian turn in the Park regime. After declaring martial law and writing a new constitution in 1972 that gave him nearly dictatorial powers, Park pushed the country more ruthlessly in the direction of heavy industrial development. His new Third Five-Year Economic Plan for 1972–1976, unlike the two earlier plans, called for investment to be channeled into heavy and chemical industries. This is often referred to as the HCI (heavy and chemical industry) phase of South Korea's economic development. In place of textiles and footwear, the ROK would focus on developing steel, shipbuilding, petrochemical, and automotive industries. In 1973, six industries were targeted: steel, chemical, metal, machine building, shipbuilding, and electronics. This stage of industrial development was concentrated in five small provincial cities, four of them in Park's home Kyŏngsang area in the southeast part of the country: Yŏsu-Yŏchŏn for petrochemicals, Ch'angwŏn for machine-building, P'ohang for steel, Okp'o for shipbuilding, and the Kumi complex for electronics.[23] To oversee this new stage of economic development he created a Corps for Planning and Management of Heavy and Chemical Industries, headed, significantly, not by a technocrat but by a political appointee. The shift to these heavy and chemical industries required the government to play an even greater role in aiding and guiding industrial development. Favored companies expanded, some into industrial giants.

Park ignored many of his technocrats as well as foreign experts, who felt that Korea was not ready or large enough for these types of industries. He did not want to stay with an expanded textile industry. While light industries such as manufacturing of textiles and wigs were important for economic growth, they could not provide the basis to support a militarily and economically strong state that would be less dependent on the Americans. A desire to be able to eventually supply most of its own military equipment and to be economically autonomous was a major incentive for this push. In some ways, in its emphasis on heavy industry, South Korea resembled its northern rival. This is not surprising, since the desire for heavy industry was also part of the South's desire to match developments in North Korea. How could South Korea continue to pursue the manufacture of apparel, shoes, and wigs when the North was producing steel? There was also a sense of competing with Japan. The HCI program was another manifestation of economic nationalism and South Korea's need to compete with its neighbors, which drove so much of its economic development.[24]

South Korea again did better than most foreign observers expected. The economy grew by double digits despite a less favorable international situation in the 1970s. In the decade from 1972 to 1982 steel production increased fourteen times. Some industrial sectors, such as the petrochemical, did not become that competitive; however, others did. Pohang Iron and Steel Company (POSCO), a state-owned corporation, opened the world's largest steel-making complex. Under its capable manager, Pak T'ae-jun, it proved to be an efficient operation that successfully competed in the world steel markets. Similarly, South Korea emerged in the 1980s as the world's second-largest shipbuilder, with a reputation for being able to complete orders for new ships quickly and on time. Still there were many problems. The timing was unfortunate, since these energy-intensive industries were launched at the time of sharp increases in petroleum prices. The 1973–1974 oil shock, when the price of crude oil quadrupled, hit the South Korean economy hard, since it had to import all its energy. Inflation soared to 40 percent in 1974. However, the flow of foreign exchange to pay for more costly imported oil was soon compensated for in part by the flow of the earnings from Korean construction companies and their workers in the Middle East. Thus South Korea weathered the economic crisis quite well. A more serious problem was the mounting foreign debt, as the country was a major borrower to finance not just new investments but huge infrastructure projects such as expanded power generation, telecommunications, port facilities, and roads. An example of the last was the new express highway linking Seoul with Pusan. Foreign debt rose from $2.2 billion in 1970 to $27.1 billion in 1980.[25]

CHAEBŎLS

The policies of the 1970s contributed to one of the distinctive features of South Korea's development, the concentration of so much of the economy into huge family-owned conglomerates known as *chaebŏls*. The term itself is the Korean pronunciation of the Chinese characters used to write *zaibatsu*, the prewar 1945 Japanese conglomerates that in many ways they resembled. The growth of *chaebŏls* was due to more than just the entrepreneurial skill of a handful of talented businessmen; it was also the product of government policy. Banks, all state-owned after 1961, poured credit into a few companies to develop industries targeted for development. The state gave the *chaebŏls* exemptions from import duties on capital goods and offered special rates for utilities and the state-owned rail system. Smaller firms and those engaged in enterprises not favored by the development plans found it difficult to gain access to credit, nor could they receive all these special discounts and exemptions. Each *chaebŏl* leader found it necessary to work closely with the government and contribute generously to government political campaign coffers and to pet projects favored by the Park and later Chun regimes. However, a key to understanding the South Korean system is that the *chaebŏl* had to be efficient. It was not political connections but their ability to produce results, that is, to efficiently meet economic targets and compete in the domestic and foreign marketplaces, that brought about government support. The government did not allow any *chaebŏl* to achieve a monopoly but rather encouraged competition among several in each industrial sector to keep them efficient.

In the 1970s, when the state pushed for heavy industry, the *chaebŏls* grew at the fastest rate. The top ten conglomerates grew at 27 percent a year, three and a half times the GDP growth rate.[26] As they grew, they tended to expand horizontally, branching out into a highly diversified range of activities often far removed from their original core businesses. Samsung branched out from food processing to enter electronics, heavy equipment, and automobiles; Hyundai from construction to shipbuilding and automobiles. The *chaebŏl* founders were an extraordinary group of talented entrepreneurs driven by nearly limitless ambition and often possessing considerable personal charisma. Although it is possible to see them as the product of government economic policies, it is hard to imagine South Korea's economic takeoff without them. This was in sharp contrast with Taiwan, or later with China, where small and medium-size industries dominated the export economy.

One of the most dynamic of these entrepreneurs was Chung Ju Yung (Chŏng Chu-yŏng). Born of humble rural background in Kangwŏn Province in what later became North Korea, Chung attended a traditional village Confucian school. He came to Seoul in his teens, worked on the docks, and then started an auto repair business in 1940 that grew during the war to about seventy employees. After 1945, he established a construction company that worked for the U.S. Army and the Korean government. A hardworking, efficient entrepreneur, he prospered with state support in the 1960s. Chung became one of the favored entrepreneurs of the Park regime for his ability to complete tasks ahead of schedule, such as a bridge over the Han River. After 1965, Hyundai Construction received many contracts to build in Southeast Asia during the Vietnam War, and in the 1970s in the Middle East. Chung established Hyundai

Motors in 1967 to build the first South Korean car, which became known as the Pony. He established Hyundai Shipbuilding and Heavy Industries in 1973 in response to the HCI initiative. Later in the early 1980s Hyundai entered the electronics industry. By then, the Hyundai Group was the largest *chaebŏl* in Korea.

Lee Byung-chul (Yi Pyŏng-ch'ŏl), unlike Chung, came from a wealthy landowner family. In 1938, after a brief unsuccessful attempt to run a rice mill, he founded a small trading company in Seoul. He used his entrepreneurial experience to establish the Cheil Sugar Refinery in 1953. He also established the Cheil Textile Company. Closely associated with the Rhee regime, he received profitable import licenses in return for contributions to Rhee's Liberal Party, becoming the country's wealthiest entrepreneur and controlling several commercial banks and insurance companies. As Korea's richest businessman and closely associated with Rhee, Lee became a prime target of Park's anticorruption campaign. After paying a fine in 1961 and having his bank holdings expropriated, he was enlisted by Park Chung Hee to help encourage other businessmen to cooperate with the military government's plans for industrial development. In fact, Lee is often given credit for helping to convince Park and the other members of the junta of the need for a cooperative relationship between the business community and the military government. Lee's Samsung (Three Stars) group acquired a reputation for being efficient and well managed. Involved in many areas, in the late 1960s Lee made electronics his prime focus. By the early 1980s Samsung was one of the world's largest manufacturers of TV sets. In the mid-1980s it moved into the semiconductor business being promoted by the government.

Kim Woo Jung (Kim U-jung) (1936–) was born near Taegu in 1936, and thus was a generation younger than most of the *chaebŏl* founders. He established the Daewoo trading company in 1967 when he was barely in his thirties. Exporting fabric and other materials, he attracted the attention of Park, who was looking for aggressive entrepreneurs for his HCI push. In 1975, with government financial assistance, Kim established the Daewoo group. He acquired Shinjin, an unsuccessful automotive company, and began building cars for General Motors, then acquired the failing Okp'o shipyard and become a major shipbuilder. Kim's relative youth and his education made him an attractive symbol of the go-getting Korean entrepreneur. He was famous for working 100-hour weeks and never taking off a day except for one morning of truancy for his daughter's wedding. His autobiography was a best seller.

Koo In-hwoi (Ku In-hoe) (1907–1969) was one of the oldest of the *chaebŏl* founders. He founded Lucky Chemical Company in 1947, said to be named after the popular American cigarette Lucky Strike.[27] It became the country's major toothpaste manufacturer. In the 1960s he went into the electronics business under the Goldstar label. In 1995, the Lucky-Goldstar company changed its name to LG, eventually becoming one of the world's largest consumer electronics firms.

Ssangyong (Twin Dragons) was founded by Kim Sung Kon (Kim Sŏng-gŏn). It began as a textile company in 1939. In the 1950s Kim prospered in the cement business, obtaining like his fellow entrepreneur, Lee Byung-chul, import licenses from the Rhee government. The Park regime found him an efficient, resourceful entrepreneur, and Ssangyong branched out into many industries, including trading, construction, and automobiles, becoming one of the six largest *chaebŏls* in the 1970s and 1980s.

The *chaebŏls* at their core were essentially family-run businesses. The top managerial positions were held, in roughly hierarchical order, by family members, followed by high school and college classmates, and people from the same hometowns. The immediate family members were most important. Chung Chu Yung had eight sons, the so-called "eight princes" who constituted the upper management of the various Hyundai companies.[28] Modest inheritance taxes and strategic marriages kept much of the ownership in family control. Most were products of the post-liberation period. Of the fifty largest *chaebŏls* in 1983, ten predated 1945, and nineteen were established in the 1950s.[29] A few new conglomerates appeared in later years; most, however, were well established by 1980.

TRANSFORMATION OF THE COUNTRYSIDE

The industrialization of South Korea was accompanied by a transformation of the countryside. At first, rural areas lagged behind in development. Then, in part to shore up his rural base of support, Park launched the New Village (Saemaŭl) Movement in the winter of 1971–1972. The rural population had not enjoyed the economic boom of 1961–1971; most still lived in poverty. The Saemaŭl Movement was an attempt to mobilize the rural communities for the purpose of carrying out modernization efforts. Local governments were enlisted in programs to educate farmers to modernize their farms and their homes. To symbolize this change, all rural households had to replace their thatched roofs with tiles, which were more fireproof and considered more modern, although the poor often had to settle for corrugated metal roofs painted blue or orange to look like tiles. The movement encouraged self-help and the adoption of new progressive values in ways similar to the government-sponsored rural movements of the 1930s. In its rush to promote modernization, many traditional customs that the Park administration regarded as wasteful or backward were discouraged. This has led critics to accuse the Saemaŭl Movement of undermining traditional rural culture. Certainly some of the policies were heavy-handed, such as forcing farmers to grow new high-yield varieties of rice even though consumers preferred more traditional rice. But the program brought many benefits to farmers. Village committees were established to formulate and carry out their own improvement schemes. This proved a path for social mobility for the elected men and women who served as Saemaŭl leaders. And many of the leaders were women, some drawn from the 1960s rural birth-control movement (see below).[30] Most important was the price support given to farm crops, especially rice. It meant higher food prices for urban workers, who often struggled on low wages, but it produced higher income for farmers and eventually reduced rural poverty. By the mid-1970s the Saemaŭl Movement was a model for other similar movements—factory *saemaŭls*, school *saemaŭls*, *saemaŭls* in offices—but these were not very effective. And even the original Saemaŭl began to lose its momentum.

General economic growth might have been as important or more important in transforming the countryside as specific programs targeting farmers. The construction of roads, the completion of rural electrification, the introduction of telephones and of televisions all ended rural isolation and also contributed to the greater information about and access to markets. Chemical fertilizers, mechanized equipment, and the demand for agriculture products in the urban centers made farming more lucrative. Meanwhile, industry produced a far greater percentage of the economy. Expanding industry and services provided many opportunities. As a result, millions of Koreans left their rural homes to find work in the cities. Parents sent their kids to the cities to get a better education, and their children seldom returned. In 1960, farmers made up 61 percent of the population. This fell dramatically to 51 percent in 1970 and to 38 percent in 1980. By the end of the Park era, South Korea caught up to the North in the percentage of nonfarming population. In both Koreas a little more than a third of the people worked the fields by 1980, but in South Korea a high percentage of this population was elderly as young people were moving to the cities. For the first time in its history, Korea was primarily an urban, nonagricultural land.

Families became smaller. The International Planned Parenthood Federation introduced family planning to Korea, forming the Planned Parenthood Federation of Korea in 1961. The Park administration made family planning part of its Five-Year Plans. South Korea's technocrats accepted the argument by Western advisors that cutting the birthrate was essential for fast economic growth and modernization. Working with the Planned Parenthood Federation of Korea, the state sent family planning staff to local clinics. Especially effective was a program to recruit women in rural communities to receive training and spread knowledge of birth control to their neighbors. These efforts were accelerated in 1966, which the government, promoting IUDs and vasectomies, declared the Great Year of Family Planning. In 1968, the Ministry of Health and Social Welfare created Mother's Clubs for Family Planning and introduced oral contraceptives.[31] The family planning movement was incorporated into the Saemaŭl Movement in the 1970s. Again, in 1974, the state launched a renewed campaign for birth control, declaring it another Family Planning Year, and began a female sterilization campaign in the 1980s. But by the late 1980s the birthrate had fallen so sharply that family planning was no longer a worry. It is not clear how much these efforts to promote birth control contributed to economic development. With increased women's literacy and urbanization, the birthrate would have fallen in any case. Furthermore, some economists in recent years have questioned the importance of birth control in assisting economic growth. What is clear is that South Korea made the demographic transition with the same speed that it made its economic transition into a modern industrial state.

ECONOMIC DEVELOPMENT IN THE 1980S

In 1980, South Korea faced a serious economic crisis. The second oil shock of 1979 contributed to an already double-digit inflation rate. Inflation reached an alarming 44 percent in 1980, threatening the competitiveness of the country's exports. Then there was the turmoil and uncertainty that followed Park's assassination in October 1979. A poor rice harvest due to unfavorable weather compounded problems. The nation's GNP, which had been growing in excess of 8 to 10 percent annually, contracted to 6 percent in 1980. The country's economic woes appeared to be more than just a temporary problem. Foreign debt was mounting. The HCI policy resulted in huge loans, since Park relied heavily on foreign borrowing to finance the necessary expenditures on infrastructure that accompanied it. Corporate debt was also rising as the *chaebŏls* borrowed to finance expansion. It also appeared that the highly centralized command structure of the economy, in which businessmen were directed by a few high-placed officials in the EPB, the Ministry of Finance, and the Ministry of Industry and Commerce, was showing its limitations. South Korea's economy was becoming more complex, the business groups larger and stronger, and its exports more diverse. To some foreign observers, South Korea seemed to have reached a plateau, as far as it could go with its export economy based on cheap labor and foreign investment.

As they had been earlier, these foreign observers proved unduly pessimistic. The South Korean economy recovered in 1981 and resumed its impressive growth rates. Some reforms were carried out to make the economy slightly less centralized and more flexible. The government forced a number of mergers and closures in some deeply indebted sectors such as heavy industry and shipping to make them more efficient. The country began moving into more high-tech industrial areas such as consumer electronics, computers, and semiconductors. A surge in the U.S. economy beginning in 1982 helped exports, oil prices dropped, and foreign investments continued. In 1983, the first Hyundai cars were exported. By 1986–1988 the growth rate reached its peak, when with an average of 12 percent, it was the highest in the world.

Problems remained. Throughout the 1980s the country suffered from huge trade deficits with Japan. Korean firms bought capital equipment and industrial parts from their former colonial occupier. These were essential to the manufacturing of the export goods they sold to the United States. The results were trade surpluses with America that were negated by deficits with Japan, and the country seemed stuck at the intermediate technology phase. Lingering anti-Japanese sentiment made this reliance on Japanese technology humiliating. South Korea, however, maintained its ability to work out technology transfer arrangements so that this dependency on imported technology lessened. Government-funded research centers, meanwhile, made impressive strides in promoting technological and scientific expertise.

EXPLAINING SOUTH KOREA'S ECONOMIC MIRACLE

South Koreans often attribute their nation's economic growth to traditional values loosely associated with Confucianism. By this they mean hard work, discipline, respect for learning, frugality, and the importance of family. In the past, Western scholars associated traditional Confucian values with conservatism, hierarchy versus equality, and conformity to group versus individualism, and they held it responsible for the economic backwardness of Korea and China. Then in the 1980s, some writers started to refer to a "Confucian ethos" that contributed to the economic success of South Korea, Singapore, Hong Kong, and Taiwan. South Koreans also came to attribute much of their success to these traditional values. It is possible to make an argument linking traditional values to hard work, the emphasis on education, the high esteem in which civil servants were held that attracted talented technocrats to serve the state, and even to the willingness to delay gratification that resulted in the high savings rate that characterized the period of rapid economic growth. Yet South Koreans possessed this "Confucian" heritage before 1961, as did North Koreans. It is therefore necessary to look at specific development policies and historical contingencies for explanations of the economic transformation.

U.S. aid is often cited as a source for South Korea's economic miracle. Vast amounts of aid were poured into the country. From 1946 to 1976 the United States provided $12.6 billion in economic assistance; only Israel and South Vietnam received more on a per-capita basis. To put this into comparative perspective: $6.85 billion was given in this period to all of Africa, and $14.89 billion for all Latin America.[32] Much of the assistance to Korea was relief, not development aid. The greatest amounts of aid came in the decade that followed the Korean War, for reconstruction, food aid, and supplies of building materials. Aid also provided much of the fiscal support for the ROK government, especially under Rhee. Besides the aid money, South Koreans received technical training from the United States. This ranged from a program to train statisticians to the many economists and engineers who received a U.S. education. While this was only a small proportion of the aid programs, it provided the country with a large core of well-educated and trained bureaucrats, educators, and other skilled, professional people.

Perhaps more important than aid was the stability offered by the U.S. troops stationed in that country, which made it less risky for foreign investors, and the openness of the American market to South Korean exports. These two factors were important after 1961, when the country began promoting foreign investment and export-oriented industries. In other words, it was not only direct American aid but also the favorable conditions created by the United States that South Korea was able to take advantage of during the crucial years of economic growth from the early 1960s through the 1980s. South Korea's position on the front line of the Cold War also helped, such as the participation in the Vietnam War that provided aid and construction contracts. The ROK vigorously sought every useful support it could get from the United States by having an effective embassy and active lobbying interests in Washington. Korean immigrants sometimes were helpful; they provided a link to the American wig business, to name one industry.[33] U.S. advice was not always helpful. Americans were often skeptical of South Korean plans for economic development. For example, the Korean government was forced to reject advice that the First Five-Year Plan focus on the export of rice, pork, laver (edible seaweed), tungsten, iron, and graphite.[34] This type of commodity-exporting economy was exactly what Korean economic planners sought to avoid. One can only imagine what would have happened if South Koreans had decided to emphasize rice exports to Japan in the 1950s. In the 1970s, the United States through the World Bank pressured the country to temporarily drop its plans for a steel industry. South Koreans learned a lot from their U.S. counterparts, but it was often when they ignored U.S. advice and forged their own path that they were most successful.

Japan has often been given a great deal of credit for South Korea's economic development. Some observers of the country's economic development have attributed much of it to the colonial legacy, which, they argue, left some fine infrastructure such as the rail network, a number of skilled workers, experienced bankers and entrepreneurs, and high standards of education and bureaucratic efficiency. Certainly many features of South Korea's industrialization bore a major imprint of the Japanese colonial model: the close government-business relations, the role of the state in directing the economy to achieve national goals, and the concentration of capital into big *chaebŏls*, which closely resembled the pre-1945 Japanese *zaibatsu*. However, one has to be cautious in attributing too much of the country's economic development to Japanese rule, which was harsh, exploitative, and left the country still primarily agricultural and impoverished, with an economy directed toward and dependent on Japan. Furthermore, most of the top skilled jobs were done by Japanese who left, and the education system they established fell far short of the nation's needs or the public's demand. Nonetheless, South Korea did benefit from its proximity to a booming Japan that was looking for overseas investments. South Korea was nearby and shared many cultural similarities; furthermore, there were Japanese entrepreneurs with experience doing business in Korea in prewar times. Japanese investment, joint ventures, and crucial technology transfers were important, but total Japanese investment in Korea was smaller than U.S. investment. Perhaps as important as investment was the example of Japan as a successful model. The desire to emulate Japan's success was both an incentive as well as a practical example to follow. Japan, like North Korea, was also a competitor that spurred South Korean leaders to push for economic development by linking it to national security.

A popular explanation for South Korea's economic success was the fact that it had a strong state capable of overriding vested interests.[35] The general interpretation is that South Korea inherited a powerful centralized bureaucracy and national police from the Japanese colonial administration, and that the security-minded American military occupation and the Syngman Rhee regime that followed made use of these instruments to suppress leftist dissent and maintain internal security. After 1961, the military rulers further centralized authority and directed the state toward economic development. The state then was able to achieve autonomy and impose its will on society. This argument appears most valid for the 1960s and 1970s when the military government was able to exercise discipline over the business class and suppress labor movements. It was less true after 1980 when the *chaebŏls* became powerful interests, when labor became more restless, and when the middle class became more insistent in its demand for greater say in policy making. Even under Park, the state never had complete autonomy; it had to make concessions to public opinion to maintain support, and it was never free from corruption.[36] Bribery, kickbacks, secret political funds, and bank accounts by officials and businessmen under false names were very much a part of the South Korean system. The state still had the ability to favor or undermine *chaebŏls*. This was demonstrated in 1985 when the Pusan-based Kukje group, the seventh largest, ran afoul of Chun Du Hwan, who succeeded Park Chung Hee. When the group's head refused to provide the requested financial contributions to the regime, Chun decided to punish him by pressuring banks to demand repayment of loans, forcing the firm to liquidate. The collapse of Kukje was a disturbing reminder of the close political links between corporations and state. But this incident was an exception. By the 1980s the *chaebŏls* were becoming too big to fail, since a collapse of a major group could bring down the entire economy with it.

South Korea's economic transformation was also made possible by the social transformation that was occurring in the country. Old social classes and social barriers were breaking down; the society was opening up to talent, becoming both highly competitive and more literate. While economic development contributed to and accelerated this process of social transformation, many fundamental changes preceded it. The upheavals that resulted from the colonial period, the Second World War, the partition, and the Korean War had created a more fluid and unsettled society, a society open to change. It was a society in which millions had left home to work in the northern regions before 1945 or in Manchuria, China, and Japan. These millions of people had been exposed to a world beyond the village and were restless and open to new opportunities. There was also a sense of optimism, a belief in the possibility of a better life, noted by foreign observers and often regarded by them as unrealistic.

EDUCATION

Another important factor in explaining the economic miracle was the creation of a highly literate population. The optimism and belief in the possibility for individuals and families to improve their status and condition in life was reflected in the desire for education. Immediately after liberation in 1945, new schools mushroomed and enrollments exploded. There was clearly a pent-up demand for education, since the expansion of schooling under the Japanese had proceeded so slowly. In response, the framers of the 1948 constitution made primary education a right. The Rhee administration in 1949 adopted an educational system patterned after the U.S. system and on the one the American occupation had established in Japan. Six years of elementary school were followed by three years of middle school, three years of high school, and four years of college. Secondary schools were divided into academic and vocational, but graduates from both were eligible to enter university. Unlike the more restrictive elitist education of colonial times, South Koreans opted for an open-ended system to maximize access to higher levels of schooling.

The country faced enormous problems. Half the teachers had been Japanese who returned home, there were few textbooks in Korean, and many school buildings were destroyed in the Korean War. Also, there were only limited funds to support a comprehensive educational system. Nonetheless, enrollments expanded spectacularly. Between 1945 and 1960 primary school enrollment grew by three times, secondary schooling eight times, and higher education ten times. Class sizes were enormous, with as many as 100 students in a class, and with two and even three shifts a day. During and after the Korean War, classes often were conducted in tents. By 1960, primary schooling was nearly universal and the dropout rate was minimal. To finance the schools the government simply transferred the burden to children and their families by charging various fees. Since the state concentrated on primary education, half the high schools and three-quarters of the colleges and universities were established by private foundations. Many foundations were supported by former landowners seeking new opportunities now that they had lost their agricultural estates. After 1961, the state shifted its attention to secondary education. In 1960, 29 percent of those of secondary school age were enrolled in middle and high schools; by the late 1980s that figure was over 90 percent. Particularly notable was the fact that girls by 1960 were completing primary school at nearly the same rate as boys, although women continued to lag behind men at the secondary school level. Extensive in-service training programs kept the level of professionalism high. So successful was the ROK's educational development that by the 1990s other nations began to see the system as a model of excellence.

As with the case of the "economic miracle," South Korea's education "miracle" needs some explaining. The state provided some help with its teacher-training programs. It contributed to educational expansion with its open-ended educational system and its emphasis on trying to maintain fairly uniform standards throughout the country, even in remote rural areas. The main engine of educational expansion, however, was a nearly universal popular demand for schooling. The state could never build schools fast enough to meet this demand. Parents were willing to make enormous sacrifices to obtain schooling for their children. A farmer who sold his only ox to pay school fees became a stereotype based on the reality of the sacrifice the majority of Koreans unhesitatingly made. Families often sent sons and daughters to live with relatives where schools were better.

This social demand for schooling created considerable problems. Great pressure was placed on students to pass the middle school entrance exam and then the university exam. The former was eliminated in the late 1960s, but this only increased the focus on the all-important college entrance exam. Middle-class families spent considerable sums on after-school lessons at cram schools, and on private tuition. These private lessons, combined with the numerous fees and parent-teacher association contributions, made the education system quite costly. While the South Korean government spent a smaller percentage of its annual budget on education than many developing countries, the average family spent a higher percentage of its income on schooling than almost anywhere else. The education itself was focused on rote memorization and examination preparation, much to the disapproval of American educational advisors. Efforts by the state to limit the number of university students and to promote vocational education met with public resistance and were consequently only modestly successful.

Despite these problems, the transformation of South Korea into a highly literate, well-schooled nation was a key component of its economic and social development. Educational development did not just keep pace with economic development, it preceded and outpaced it. While it is difficult to establish a direct correlation between education and economic development, South Korea in the 1960s, 1970s, and 1980s was able to offer a labor force that was literate, numerate, and used to learning while still low wage. As the country developed, the high levels of schooling made it better prepared to enter the information age. Furthermore, the sequential nature of educational development—the emphasis on first pushing for universal primary education, then middle, then high school, and then finally making higher education broadly available—differed from most developing countries, which often establish fine universities while leaving many children with inadequate or no available basic schooling. This did much to ensure a balanced, broad-based social and economic modernization without leaving pockets of underdevelopment. It also meant a well-informed population. By the 1990s newspaper readership was among the highest in the world. South Korea's educational transformation by providing a well-educated citizenry not only contributed to its economic growth but also probably facilitated the transition to democracy.

KOREA IN GLOBAL PERSPECTIVE: EDUCATIONAL DEVELOPMENT

After World War II there was a worldwide expansion of education; historically it was a revolution of sorts. Between 1950 and 1990, for the first time, most of the world's people became literate and education was almost universally accepted as a norm for all children. South Korea's educational development can be seen as part of this revolution in literacy. Few nations, if any, however, saw such a dramatic rise in education. In 1945 the majority of the adult population was illiterate, a little over half were enrolled in primary school, and only 5 percent had a secondary education. By 1960, the ROK had an extremely high rate of school enrollment of children in elementary school for a poor developing country. The nation continued to improve educational standards at a rate outpacing its economic performance. At every stage from 1950 to 2000, South Korea had the highest rate of educational attainment of any country within comparable GDP per-capita range. As a result, South Korea began its industrial takeoff with a better-educated population than most other nations, including China, Vietnam, Thailand, and India. Educational development, in general, correlates well with economic development, but in few other places does this correlation seem so dramatic.

Other aspects of South Korean education were distinctive as well. The dropout rate in schools after 1945 was extremely low, in fact, the lowest of any developing country with reliable statistics. Compared to most developing nations, the school system was fairly open, with relatively little tracking. Teacher-training standards were unusually high. Perhaps the most distinctive features of South Korean education were the sequential nature of educational development, the uniformity of educational standards, and the extent that the cost was shifted from the state to the families of students. Only a relatively small number of countries, such as Japan in the late nineteenth and early twentieth centuries and later Taiwan, so focused on developing schooling in stages—providing universal primary education, then secondary school, and finally higher education. There was less regional disparity in schooling than in most other developing countries. Statistics in the 1960s through 1980s showed a much narrower gap between urban and rural levels of schooling than in most developing countries or than in many developed nations. The vigorous pursuit of uniformity of standards may not have served the more gifted students well, but at least it brought the population up to comparatively high overall standards of literacy and numeracy. In this respect, the ROK's educational development was similar to Japan's but differed from that of most other nations. Overall state expenditures on education were about average for a developing country. Much of the expense was borne privately, especially at the higher levels. Charging school fees is a common practice in poor countries; what was unusual was how universally families somehow managed to pay them. There was little resistance to sending children, including girls, to school; even poor farmer parents seemed willing to make whatever sacrifices were necessary.

KOREA IN GLOBAL PERSPECTIVE: ECONOMIC DEVELOPMENT

South Korea's economic takeoff was one of the most dramatic in modern history. Foreigners after 1945 pointed to the country's lack of resources and its dense population as great obstacles. But history has shown there is little correlation between natural resources and development. In fact, reliance on commodities such as mineral and agricultural products has often proved to be an ineffective path to development, since commodity prices are subject to sharp swings, resulting in a boom-bust cycle, and they do not necessarily lead to the development of important technical skills. The path to development the ROK followed—export-led growth focusing on manufacturing—has been the most successful in achieving long-term sustained economic growth. South Korea's growth rates were not unique. Japan's growth rates before World War I and after the Korean War were also impressive. Indeed, Japanese growth rates from 1950 to 1970 were similar to South Korea's from 1965 to 1995. Taiwan and Singapore grew at comparable rates. None of these societies, however, was as poverty-stricken or had such dismal prospects as did the ROK in 1960. China might be more comparable, but its growth, due to its vast size, has been more regional, with large segments of the country and its people left behind.

It is difficult to compare South Korea's economic development with other nations. The country has been labeled one of the "Little Tigers" along with Taiwan, Hong Kong, and Singapore. Yet, each was quite different. Hong Kong and Singapore were cities without large numbers of rural peasants, and were already international trading centers before their industrial booms. Taiwan, with half of South Korea's population, is more comparable, but it too differed. It had a large professional class that fled from the mainland of China in 1949, often with some capital, an advantage South Korea did not have. It followed a somewhat different development trajectory, focusing on small family firms, not large business concentrations, and there were more state enterprises. Thailand and Malaysia have also been considered later members of the Pacific Rim boom-economies. The economic growth of these countries, however, was based on commodities—rice for Thailand; oil, tin, and rubber for Malaysia—as well as on manufacturing, and their economic rise was less dramatic. In short, there were a number of factors that were distinctive to South Korea's success: the intense rivalry with North Korea; its strategic value to the United States, which poured in so much aid, opened its markets, and provided enough security to attract investors; its proximity to Japan at a time when the Japanese were looking for places to invest; the existence of Japan as a model; the openness of Korean society to change; and the universally held zeal for education as a means of advancing social status.

Park Chung Hee, from *The Country, the Revolution and I*

Why were we obliged to carry out the revolution [the military coup of May 16, 1961]? Why did the people support the revolution? . . .

The April 19 Student Uprising and the May 16 Military Revolution signify the most decisive political disruption during the 16 years following the Liberation. These two revolutions, by students and by the Army, were successful because the courage, passion and strength necessary to save the nation and people could not be found anywhere but in these two special communities. Communities which ordinarily must remain detached from politics. For what reason did students put their studies aside? For what reason did soldiers leave their primary duty to defend the country to take part in this march of revolution?

At this point, two years after the event, there is no need to emphasize afresh that without the revolution the country would have fallen! National morality would, at this moment, have completely disappeared! It was too late, by far.

It was too late, by far, to expect the miracle of national salvation from boastful politicians. Too, it would have been foolish to expect this from civilians. What was the situation which, at that moment was so pressing, so desperate?

I will recall fragments of the past—a past which I felt to the depth of my bones at the time of the revolution, and await your candid and honest judgment.

In human life, economics precedes politics or culture.

In this light, the economic situation of Korea is most urgent.

The national economy was completely devastated by internal poverty throughout the Yi Dynasty and the cruel colonial extortion under Japanese rule. More recently it was the result of the unbalance of natural resources, due to the division of the nation, after the Liberation and the Korean War in the 1950s. The treasures of the country were on the point of exhaustion.

Just as an individual, without ability to help himself financially, has to depend on others, so the hope for the wholeness of a nation without its economic independence is literally to look for fish in a forest. What was our economic situation? Statistics show the following.

Every year countless numbers of people had to fight hunger. The ideas that a man has the right to eat and live is no luxury, no excessive ambition. It is a minimum right that should be guaranteed absolutely. Even that this idea has to be brought into question, signifies that we have other aims than merely to extend our barest existence. . . .

The key industries of the nation were in a pitiful state. Farming villages were impoverished and miserable beyond description. The crowd of unemployed intellectuals in the cities was a heart-breaking sight. . . .

We say the country was poor. How poor? Here is a living proof! It is none other than the Supplementary Budget of the Democratic Party government in 1961; the year of the revolution!

The total size of the budget was 608,800 million hwan, of which the United States counterpart funds supplied 316,900 million hwan, including 13,000 million hwan in the proceeds of $10 million worth of surplus farm products, to finance national construction development projects. This represents 52% of the total budget when compared with the 291,900 million hwan in domestic resources.

Thus, more than half of the national budget, the basic housekeeping of national management, depended upon the United States.

Though nominally independent, the real worth of the Republic of Korea, from the national statistical point of view, was only 48%. In other words, the U.S. had a 52% majority vote in regard to Korea, and we were dependent to that extent. . . .

We have to accomplish, as quickly as possible, the goal of an independent economy. We must manage our own affairs as our own responsibility. Before May 1961 this was the primary objective which made me undertake the revolution. Independence! There is no other net to catch this elusive goal except economic independence.

—from *The Country, the Revolution and I*[37]

NOTES

1. A. M. Rosenthal, "Outlook Dreary for South Korea: Crowded Nation Has Few Resources—Long Reliance on U.S. Held Inevitable," *New York Times*, March 21, 1961.

2. Joungwon Alexander Kim, *Divided Korea: The Politics of Development, 1945–1972* (Cambridge, MA: Harvard University Press, 1975), 157.

3. Han Sung-joo, *The Failure of Democracy in South Korea* (Berkeley: University of California Press, 1974), 169.

4. Joungwon Kim, *Divided Korea*, 229.

5. Joungwon Kim, *Divided Korea*, 233.

6. Chung-shik Lee, *Park Chung-Hee: From Poverty to Power* (Palos Verdes, CA: KHU Press, 2012), 6–17.

7. Gregg Brazinsky, *Nation Building in South Korea: Koreans, Americans, and the Making of Democracy* (Chapel Hill: University of North Carolina Press, 2007), 103–4.

8. Cho Jae Hong, "Post-1945 Land Reforms and Their Consequences in South Korea," PhD dissertation, Indiana University, 1964.

9. John Lie, *Han Unbound: The Political Economy of South Korea* (Stanford, CA: Stanford University Press, 1998), 9–18.

10. Laura C. Nelson, *Measured Excess: Status, Gender, and Consumer Nationalism in South Korea* (New York: Columbia University Press, 2000), 11.

11. Park Chung Hee, *The Country, The Revolution and I* (Seoul: Hollym Corporation, 1970), 17–120.

12. Eun Mee Kim, *Big Business, Strong State: Collusion and Conflict in South Korean Development, 1960–1990* (Albany: State University of New York Press, 1997), 103.

13. Park, *The Country, The Revolution and I*, 28.

14. Hyung-A Kim, *Korea's Development under Park Chung Hee: Rapid Industrialization, 1961–79* (London: Routledge Curzon, 2004), 111.

15. Hyung-A Kim, *Korea's Development under Park Chung Hee*, 81–87.

16. Hyung-A Kim, *Korea's Development under Park Chung Hee*, 87.

17. Jung-en Woo, *Race to the Swift: State and Finance in the Industrialization of Korea* (New York: Columbia University Press, 1991), 84.

18. Eun Mee Kim, *Big Business, Strong State*, 105.

19. Lie, *Han Unbound*, 73.

20. Byung-Kook Kim, "The Leviathan: Economic Bureaucracy under Park," in Byung-Kook Kim, Ezra Vogel, and Jorge I. Dominguez, eds., *The Park Chung Hee Era: The Transformation of South Korea* (Cambridge, MA: Harvard University Press, 2011): 200–232.

21. Stewart Lone and Gavan McCormack, *Korea Since 1850* (New York: St. Martin's Press, 1993), 147.

22. Lone and McCormack, *Korea Since 1850*, 148.

23. Woo, *Race to the Swift*, 132.

24. Linsu Kim, *Imitation to Innovation: The Dynamics of Korea's Technological Learning* (Boston: Harvard Business School Press, 1997), 48.

25. Linsu Kim, *Imitation to Innovation*, 32.

26. Woo, *Race to the Swift*, 128–29; Eun Mee Kim, *Big Business, Strong State*, 51.

27. Chan Sup Chang and Nahm Joo Chang, *The Korean Managerial System* (Westport, CT: Quorum Books, 1994), 40.

28. Chang and Chang, *The Korean Managerial System*, 40.

29. Eun Mee Kim, *Big Business, Strong State*, 114.

30. Lone and McCormack, *Korea Since 1850*, 150.

31. Seungsook Moon, *Militarized Modernity and Gendering Citizenship in South Korea* (Durham, NC: Duke University Press, 2005), 84–85.

32. Woo, *Race to the Swift*, 45.

33. Lie, *Han Unbound*, 66–67.

34. Lie, *Han Unbound*, 56.

35. See Alice Amsden, *Asia's Next Giant: South Korea and Late Industrialization* (London: Oxford University Press, 1989); Stephan Haggard and Chung-in Moon, "Institutions and Economic Policy: Theory and a Korean Case Study," *World Politics* 17, no. 2 (January 1990): 210–37; Chalmers Johnson, "Political Institutions and Economic Performance: The Government-Business Relationship in Japan, South Korea, and Taiwan," in *The Political Economy of the New Asian Industrialism*, ed. Frederic C. Deyo (Ithaca, NY: Cornell University Press, 1987), 136–64; Edward S. Mason et al., *The Economic Social Modernization of the Republic of Korea* (Cambridge, MA: Harvard University Press, 1980).

36. Michael J. Seth, "Strong State or Strong Society?" *Korean Studies* 21 (1997).

37. Park, *The Country, the Revolution and I*, 25–29.

6

South Korea: Creating a Democratic Society, 1953 to 1997

There was no more radical way in which South Korea evolved differently from the North than its transformation from an authoritarian state to a democracy. And this transformation was just as unpredicted as its economic "miracle." The early years of the Republic of Korea did not offer much promise for the emergence of flourishing democratic institutions. Although it had the outer appearance of a multiparty democracy, the Rhee administration was authoritarian, and its Liberal Party used bribery and intimidation to remain in power. South Korean prisons held thousands of political opponents, and the elections of 1960 were blatantly rigged. Following a student-led uprising in 1960, the one-year experiment in a parliamentary democracy produced a somewhat chaotic, weak, and ineffective government followed by a military coup and nearly three decades of military-dominated government. Yet despite this saga of political instability, authoritarianism, and military coups that was so characteristic of developing nations, South Korea developed a stable, democratic political order.

MILITARY AUTHORITARIANISM

The military coup in 1961 had been welcomed by much of the public. After the corruption of the Rhee administration and the perceived incompetence of the short-lived government of Chang Myŏn, 1960–1961, most South Koreans were hopeful that the military could bring some improvement. Many South Koreans were skeptical of democracy. In a poll conducted in 1963 among students who had participated in the revolt against Syngman Rhee, 86 percent thought that Western-style democracy was not suitable for Korea.[1]

Yet from the beginning the United States exerted pressure on the military rulers to return the government to civilians. In August 1961, Park announced plans to restore civilian rule by May 1963. In December 1962, the military leaders drew up a new constitution that restored the strong executive presidency that existed under Rhee and the unicameral legislature. That month, Park announced he was retiring from the military in order to run for president. In January he lifted the ban on political activity. In February 1963, he created the Democratic Republican Party (DRP). Park, reluctant to give up power, decided in March to extend military rule for four more years. This brought a sharp reaction from the United States, on whom his government was heavily dependent, making Park's room for action very limited. At that time, U.S. aid still accounted for 50 percent of the national budget and 72 percent of the defense budget.[2] Bowing to American pressure, Park agreed to go ahead as planned with the elections, which inaugurated what was known as the Third Republic.

The elections in 1963 were reasonably fair, although funding from the Korean Central Intelligence Agency (KCIA) and government support gave the pro-government DRP an advantage. The opposition was also disadvantaged because the October 15 date for the presidential election was not announced until a few weeks earlier, giving the opposition less time to organize. Park ran as the DRP candidate and Yun Po-sŏn, the former president, ran as the opposition candidate. Park received about 47 percent of the vote to Yun's 45 percent. In November, elections were held for the National Assembly. It is interesting that for all its advantages, the DRP won only a third of the vote, but because the opposition was divided it was the largest share of the vote. Under the complicated election rules, the party that won the largest share of votes received two-thirds of the at-large seats. This ended up giving the DRP 110 of the 175 seats. While there was considerable freedom of the press and free scope for political activities, Park maintained control of the army, the bureaucracy, and the powerful KCIA to effectively carry out policy.

With real evidence of economic development Park was able to win a second four-year term as president in 1967, again defeating Yun Po-sŏn, this time 51 percent to 41 percent. In 1969, Park decided to seek a third term. As in 1954, the ruling party sought a constitutional amendment, and as in 1954, this was strongly resisted by the political opposition. Students and others demonstrated, and finally the amendment was passed by the dubious method of the DRP meeting secretly in an annex to the National Assembly and passing it without the presence of the opposition members. A referendum was then held approving the third term. Nonetheless, Park's position was not entirely secure. As under Rhee, a clear difference was seen between the urban and rural populations. Most farmers were poor, but due to the land reform most owned their farms; therefore, they were more accepting of the status quo. They also maintained the traditional respect for authority and held firm anticommunist attitudes. With the movement of young people to the cities, rural communities were older and more conservative. This was the political base of the Park regime, much as it had been for Rhee. And like Rhee and his Liberal Party, Park and the DRP did not do well in the cities. In 1971, the opposition united under a young, charismatic politician from South Chŏlla Province, Kim Dae Jung (Kim Tae-jung) (1925–2009). Kim represented part of a new leadership among politicians. The older generation was drawn from the conservative elite, who were wealthy and often foreign educated. Kim, like Park, was from a humble background and was a self-made man. In 1971, he ran an effective campaign. Park won 51 percent to 44 percent but again did poorly in the cities, a bad sign in a country that was rapidly urbanizing. Shortly after the election in December 1971 Park issued a state of emergency.

THE YUSHIN ERA, 1971–1979

A number of developments in 1971 appeared to make the world a bit more precarious for the ROK. President Nixon announced in the previous year his intention to withdraw two combat divisions, about 20,000 troops, from Korea. In 1971, the U.S. rapprochement with China began, and it was clear that the United States intended to eventually withdraw from Vietnam. All this suggested that the U.S. commitment to South Korea might not be as secure as the ROK had thought. American decline was also suggested by Nixon's decision to take the United States off the gold standard, creating economic uncertainty. And then there was America's protectionist pressure on South Korea to limit textile exports. Textiles were Korea's biggest export, and the United States was its biggest market, so this was a serious blow. These factors, plus the new energy shown by the opposition, may have contributed to Park's decision to suspend the constitution and declare a state of emergency. On October 17, 1972, he proclaimed martial law, suspended the constitution, dissolved the National Assembly and the political parties, and prohibited all political activities. All this came as a shock to much of the public. Park placed restrictions on free speech and other civil liberties. The Third Republic was at an end. The eight years in which a semi-authoritarian military regime operated under the veneer of a democratic multiparty system was replaced by a more thoroughly authoritarian state. Park's government was now a dictatorship with only the thinnest veneer of an open society. Even before this, Park had made use of the KCIA and the National Security Law to threaten and arrest dissidents. In one notorious case, more than 200 Koreans living in Europe in 1967 were kidnapped and sent to Korea for trial in what became known as the East Berlin Spy Incident. From 1972 on, he became less restrained in the pursuit of perceived threats to his power or to national security.

The new government he created was called Yushin, the name of a series of "revitalizing" (*yusin* in Korean) reforms that created a new Yushin Constitution. The term itself, interestingly, was the same given by Japan (pronounced *Isshin* in Japanese) for the reforms carried out in the late nineteenth century. The new constitution gave the president almost total powers. He was not elected directly by the voters but by a National Council for Unification. Since this was a body created by the president, who headed it, this meant the president, in practice, elected himself. The National Assembly had little power to check the president, who appointed one-third of its members. Important matters could be carried out through national plebiscites. A public referendum in November 1972 approved the constitution and the so-called Fourth Republic was launched. Park also strengthened his authority by issuing a number of emergency decrees. Most notorious of these was Emergency Measure No. 9 in May 1975, which prohibited criticism of the president. With the aid of the KCIA, Park ruthlessly went after enemies, arresting and torturing them, and forcing confessions. Even Koreans overseas were sometimes kidnapped or murdered by his agents. The most notorious case was the kidnapping of Kim Dae Jung, who had gone into exile in the United States and then in Japan. He was abducted from his hotel room in Tokyo, placed on a boat, and tied with weights as if to be thrown overboard. At the last minute, an American official who had gotten word of his abduction issued a warning to Park, and Kim's life was spared.

Park was able to justify his political repression as part of the need for national security. In this he was aided by North Korea. There were the DPRK's aggressive incidents along the DMZ in 1967; the 1968 commando attack on the Blue House, the presidential mansion; and later that year the landing of commandos along the northeast coast. Some promising exchanges took place between the two powers in 1972, but when these broke down in 1973 the government could point to the insincerity of the enemy. The discovery of the tunnel built by the North Koreans under the DMZ that had been constructed during the talks reinforced this argument. Indeed, the tension with the DPRK made for a dangerous situation and may have helped people tolerate a higher level of political restrictions in the name of national security. The Park regime also sought legitimacy through economic performance. And this too was creditable, since economic growth was improving the standards of living for most citizens and creating a large middle class able to enjoy a degree of material comfort previously confined to the privileged elite. Much of the business community was supportive of the regime. Park himself was personally honest, hardworking, much respected, and dedicated to lifting the country out of poverty. The assassination of his wife at a public event in 1974 added a measure of personal sympathy for him. The assassin, probably working with North Korea, had been aiming at Park.

Park also navigated international relations competently, which was important, as South Korea was highly dependent on the United States militarily and economically. Park sought to achieve as much political autonomy from Washington as possible while at the same time maintaining America's commitment to defend the ROK, to keep its markets open to Korean goods, and to provide technical assistance and loans. He skillfully aligned South Korea with the United States when President Johnson needed support in the Vietnam War, gaining, as we have seen, considerable benefit in return. Conditions soured a bit under the Nixon administration, with its measures to protect textiles, its plans to reduce its troop commitments in Korea, and its opening with China. They were especially tense under the Carter administration, which announced plans for troop reductions and made a point of promoting human rights. On balance, Park managed to weather rough spots in relations with the Americans reasonably well. Relations with Japan following the normalization of relations in 1965 mainly focused on economic issues, with Tokyo being an important source of foreign investments and loans. The Korean public remained, however, resentful of Japan, a resentment encouraged by South Korean history textbooks that highlighted the victimization of Korea by its neighbor. The Japanese government's reluctance to accept responsibility for its colonial rule, as well as Tokyo's approval of history textbooks that whitewashed Japan's imperialist past, provided fuel for lingering anti-Japanese sentiments. Meanwhile, South Korea gradually expanded its diplomatic relations with nations around the world, but until the 1980s the country was very much in the shadow of the United States and focused on its rivalry with the North.

Even though the threat of North Korea, economic growth, the support of the business community, and its general competency in managing both economic and foreign affairs worked to the Park regime's advantage, and despite the often ruthless persecution of its opponents, a vigorous dissident movement emerged. This movement consisted of students, intellectuals, labor activists, Christian groups, and people from the southwestern part of the country who felt left behind in development projects that favored Seoul and Park's home region in the southeast. The students were carrying on a long Confucian tradition of being upholders of moral righteousness. Taking advantage of the years of relative freedom from family and work responsibilities, they often devoted time to political and social issues. Participating in a political movement eventually became almost a rite of passage for young Koreans before graduating and entering business, government, and the professions. There was also the legacy of the April Student Revolution that had toppled Syngman Rhee in 1960. Major student protests erupted during the 1964–1965 normalization treaty controversy and in 1969 over the attempt to amend the constitution to allow Park a third term. The more oppressive rule of the Yushin government drove the student movement underground but did not smash it. Violent student protests erupted from time to time, followed by harsh suppression. By 1979, the student movement was becoming more violent and more openly opposed to Park's continual rule. Students were not the only ones to protest. In December 1973 opponents of the regime launched a One Million Signatures Campaign for Constitutional Change that called for the end of the Yushin system, freeing of political prisoners, press freedom, and an independent judiciary.[3] Nothing came of it, but this showed that there was still a significant opposition.

The increasingly better-educated South Korean society produced not only more students but also more intellectuals and artists. Kim Chi-ha (1941–), a poet, became the most famous of these dissident artist-intellectuals. His poems "Groundless Rumors" and "Cry of the People" became generally known and were a highly effective way of pointing out the social inequities of society for a poetry-loving people. He attacked the Park regime's political abuses and the economic growth at the expense of the poor laborers and others left behind. His most famous long poem, "Five Thieves" (1970), summarized the frustrations and anger of many South Koreans over the political-industrial system Park had created. His five thieves were: military generals, the bureaucrats, rich industrialists, cabinet ministers, and national assemblymen.

South Korea had a small but politically active labor movement after 1945 but this had largely died out in the 1960s. After 1970, labor became more politically active again. A key incident was the self-immolation on November 13, 1970, of Chŏn T'ae-il, a poor garment worker in Seoul. His shocking act of protest over labor conditions drew attention to the plight of the country's growing labor force. Union members grew in numbers and assertiveness in the 1970s. Two Christian groups, the Young Catholic Organization and the Protestant-sponsored Urban Industrial Mission, were important in supporting labor. A number of dissidents were drawn from the North and South Chŏlla provinces. The general development of Korea under Park was focused on the Seoul area and on the southeastern North and South Kyŏngsang provinces. This was part of the natural Seoul-Pusan axis, which linked the capital with its most important port and the traditional gateway to Japan, South Korea's second-largest trading partner. But the focus of development on this area was also due to the fact that Park and much of the key leadership came from the southeast and favored their home area. The agriculturally rich Chŏlla region, once the most important rice basket in Korea, was relatively neglected. Regional resentments became strong. Contributing to this resentment was the fact that Kim Dae Jung, the country's best-known dissident, was from the area. Together these groups formed a growing dissident movement.

Park himself seemed to have become more isolated by the late 1970s, even from his supporters. In 1975, he removed Kim Jong Pil as his premier and replaced him with a professional bureaucrat of no political ambition, Choi Kyu Hah (Ch'oe Kyu-ha) (1919–2006). Personal access to him was controlled by his head of the Presidential Security Force, Ch'a Ch'i-ch'ŏl. Meanwhile, relations with the United States had soured, in part because of the "Koreagate" scandal in spring of 1975. A Korean businessman, Tongsun Park, had been involved in bribing U.S. congressmen. This led to an investigation by Congress of the activities of the KCIA in the United States, including the kidnapping and harassment of Korean-Americans and ROK nationals in America. Korea was also hit by the second oil shock of 1979. This blow to the economy coincided with an increase in political unrest including a more vigorous political opposition by a faction of the New Democratic Party led by Kim Young Sam (Kim Yŏng-sam) (1927–2015). In August 1979, the brutal treatment of 200 female textile workers of Y. H. Trading Company who were holding a demonstration in the opposition party's headquarters triggered a new round of militant activity of students, labor, and opposition politicians. In early October, Kim Young Sam gained control of the NDP. When he called Park a dictator in a *New York Times* interview, the DRP reacted by expelling him from the Assembly. This led to a walkout by the opposition and a new round of demonstrations by students, workers, and others calling for his reinstatement. The demonstrations spread to the Masan-Pusan area, the home of Kim Young Sam and a major industrial area with many restless workers. Martial law was declared there. Kim Chae-kyu, head of the KCIA, is said to have urged Park to work out a compromise with the opposition, while Park appears to have leaned toward using the military to put demonstrations down. On October 26, Kim Chae-kyu shot and killed Park and his bodyguard Ch'a Ch'i-ch'ŏl as they were dining in a KCIA compound near the Blue House. Choi Kyu Hah then became acting president.

SEOUL SPRING, 1979–1980

The assassination of Park led to a brief period of political openness sometimes called "Seoul Spring." Initially shocked by the sudden death of the man who had governed the country for eighteen years, most of the politically active population was eager to bring the repressive Yushin era to an end and move to a more representative government and freer atmosphere. Choi Kyu Hah was elected under the Yushin constitution by the National Council for Unification on December 6. He was considered by most a caretaker until the transition to a new government could take place. Choi moved quickly to free hundreds of political prisoners, including Kim Dae Jung, who had been under house arrest; abolished Emergency Measure No. 9; and promised that a referendum would be held on a new constitution within a year. In February, full civil rights were restored to Kim Dae Jung and hundreds of other political figures.

The new atmosphere led to political jockeying for power among the factions of the Democratic Justice Party and the New Democratic Party. In the DRP, Kim Jong Pil, who had long been thought a successor to Park Chung Hee, fought for leadership with Lee Hu Rak, who had also served as head of the KCIA. And Kim Young Sam and Lee Cheul Seung contested for leadership in the New Democratic Party, a contest joined by Kim Dae Jung when he was released from house arrest. Meanwhile, a small clique of generals began consolidating power within the army. The leader was Chun Doo Hwan (Chŏn Tu-hwan) (1931–), a two-star general who headed the Defense Security Command. His principal allies were General Roh Tae Woo (No T'ae-u) (1932–) and Chŏng Ho-yong. All three were major generals of the eleventh class of the Korean Military Academy who had graduated in 1955. They were from the Taegu-Kyŏngsang Province region, the same region as Park Chung Hee, hence they became known as the "T-K faction." In South Korea, school and regional ties were extremely important, and this group shared both. The generals seized control of the army in a coup on the night of December 12–13 that became known as the 12-12 Incident. Chun, in charge of Army Security Command, ordered the arrest of Chŏng Sŭng-hwa, army chief of staff and head of the Martial Law Command, for alleged complicity in the assassination. The Capital Garrison Commander and Commander of the Special Forces were also arrested as a regiment from Roh's Ninth Division moved into Seoul. In contrast to the bloodless coup of Park Chung Hee in May 1961, this was a violent incident involving exchanges of fire at the ROK Army Headquarters and Ministry of Defense in central Seoul. Some high-ranking commanders fled for their lives to the nearby U.S. military base in Seoul. Having taken command of the army, Chun and his group took control of the KCIA in the spring, while gradually assuming control of the government that was still nominally under the civilian leadership of Choi Kyu Hah.

In March, the universities reopened. Students began demanding greater campus autonomy and the purging of administrators and professors associated with the Park regime. They also protested the continuation of martial law and the Yushin constitution, and demanded the immediate implementation of democratic government. Students also wanted to address issues of economic and social inequality. When in April 1980 Chun illegally assumed control of the KCIA, student demonstrations began to spill into the streets; by May massive demonstrations in Seoul were presenting an atmosphere of instability, just as they had in 1960 and the spring of 1961. In mid-May, Chun moved troops and armored vehicles into the streets to protect government buildings as up to 100,000 students carried out boisterous demonstrations calling for his resignation and that of Prime Minister Sin Hyŏn-hwak, the lifting of martial law, and more rapid abolition of the Yushin system. With the encouragement of Kim Young Sam and Kim Dae Jung, the students called off further demonstrations on May 16. The next day, May 17, Chun proclaimed Martial Law Decree No. 10, extending martial law throughout the country, closing universities, and banning labor strikes. All political activity was prohibited, and twenty-six opposition leaders including Kim Dae Jung were arrested.

Anti-Chun feeling was especially strong in Kwangju. Kwangju was the largest city in South Chŏlla, the center of government opposition and resentment at the domination of government by the military from the southeast and the consequent economic neglect of their region. On May 18, Chŏnnam National University students in Kwangju demanded the release of Kim Dae Jung, who was a local hero from the nearby port of Mokp'o. Offices of the government-controlled broadcaster were burned. Special Forces commander Chŏng Ho-yong sent paratroopers who brutally attacked protesters. The alienated citizenry supported the students in a full-scale insurrection, seizing weapons, forcing the paratroopers to withdraw, and taking over the city. A Council of Citizens then attempted to negotiate with the armed forces; appeals to the United States for mediation were ignored. On May 27, Chun sent in regular troops of the Twentieth Division to retake the city in a bloody campaign with heavy civilian casualties. The official number killed was 200. The actual number killed is not known for sure, but is most likely much higher, with the figure of 2,000 often cited. The Kwangju Incident remained as an important legacy and left a stain on the Chun regime that it never quite recovered from. The official pronouncement that it was a Communist rebellion that had been crushed was believed by very few and only damaged the credibility of the regime. Kwangju became a symbol of civilian resistance to military rule and helped to radicalize the student and dissident movement and alienate much of the middle-class population from the government. It also led to anti-U.S. sentiment. A 1978 agreement creating the U.S.-ROK Combined Forces Command gave control of selected units of the ROK regular army to the commander of American forces in Korea. Many South Koreans came to believe that the American military commander and therefore the

U.S. government must have given at least tacit approval to the movement of troops to quell the rebellion. However, this was not the case, since the dispatched paratroopers were outside the control of the commander.

Chun then took the final steps in consolidating his power. In late May he organized a Special Committee for National Security Measures with Choi as nominal head. It contained both civilian and military officials, but Chun and his clique were clearly in charge. In August, Choi resigned and the National Council for Unification elected Chun. Chun then revised the constitution, creating what became known as the Fifth Republic. The revised constitution gave a bit more authority to the National Assembly but was not radically different from the Yushin constitution. This constitution was then approved by plebiscite in October, and in February 1981 a new National Assembly was elected. The Democratic Justice Party, as Chun's party was called, received 35 percent of the vote, but due to the proportional voting system it won a solid majority of seats.

THE FIFTH REPUBLIC

Chun, like Park, was born in rural poverty, the sixth of nine children in a peasant family. Also like Park, he was from Kyŏngsang Province and had chosen a military career as a way to advance out of his poor, rural background. He graduated from the Korean Military Academy, where he married the commandant's daughter. Rising up through the ranks, he proved to be an able military man, distinguishing himself in Vietnam. In many ways he was similar to Park. He was pragmatic, more interested in practical results than ideology, with the same vision of an economically strong ROK. His administration continued Park's developmental policies, which gave priority to economic development. However, Chun never commanded the respect that Park Chung Hee did. Partly this was a product of his personality; he had little charm and did not display the intellectual acuteness of his predecessor. Moreover, unlike Park, he was surrounded by scandal. His wife and family members were constantly rumored to be involved in shady financial deals (which later proved true), and in general he seemed less able to control corruption in his administration. Unlike Park's wife and daughter, who were widely admired, Chun's wife and family were treated with derision and contempt for their influence peddling. Perhaps his greatest liability was the messy way he seized power, from the heavy-handed coup of December 12, 1979, to the bloody Kwangju Incident.

The discontent with the new administration was due to more than Chun's unpopularity and lack of charisma. South Korean society had changed in the two decades between Park's military coup and Chun's consolidation of power. It was now more educated and affluent; there was a large middle class and a general feeling that while Korea was making great economic progress it was still politically backward. Most middle-class Koreans wanted a say in how their country was run. The quick resumption of military rule in 1980 came to many as a disappointment, much more so than in 1961, when the military seizure of power was actually welcomed as a relief from chaos and corruption. Many South Koreans were tired of military rule. While many Koreans accepted the argument that the dangerous security problem with North Korea called for order, stability, and a strong military, they did not interpret this to mean military rule. There was also a feeling that if South Korea wanted to join the ranks of advanced countries such as Japan, the United States, and Western Europe, it had to move beyond the politics of military coups and strongmen to more representational government, more political freedom, and orderly process.

Chun, despite his unpopularity, received some credit for the economic recovery that began in 1981. While much of this recovery was due to the drop in oil prices and strong economic growth in the key export markets of the United States and Japan, his administration did manage the economy competently. The decision in 1981 by the Olympic Committee to award the 1988 games to Seoul gave another boost to the regime. Chun also attempted to give a veneer of liberalism to his rule. The midnight-to-four curfew that had been in place for decades as a security measure in all but the inland province of North Ch'ungch'ŏng was lifted in January 1982. Other measures included easing travel restrictions and ending the requirement that schoolchildren wear militaristic-style uniforms and keep their hair short. People on the street no longer had to stand at attention when the national anthem was played at 5 p.m. But in reality South Korea remained an authoritarian state. Arrests and closed trials of dissidents were common; the press was censored; editors, reporters, and broadcasters were given official "guidance"; and the judiciary was subservient to the administration. The ruling Democratic Justice Party held a solid majority in the National Assembly due to the use of proportional seating. The party benefited from a steady flow of financial donations from business interests. Deprived of its leadership, the opposition was rather tame.

1987: A POLITICAL TURNING POINT

The major turning point in South Korea's political evolution took place in 1987 when power began to shift away from the military-dominated regime and a genuine transition to democracy began. The events of that year caught some observers by surprise; however, they were preceded by developments that gradually weakened the Chun government, which in the early 1980s had seemed securely in power. In May of 1982 a financial scandal broke out that implicated some of Chun's in-laws, the first of a series that would undermine his credibility. The opposition became more active, assertive, and willing to work together to resist the government. Kim Young Sam, under house arrest, held a hunger strike, and Kim Dae Jung, who was allowed to go to the United States "for medical treatment" as a result of U.S. pressure, began to issue statements from exile critical of the government. In 1984 Kim Dae Jung, while still in exile, and Kim Young Sam formed an umbrella group of opponents of the regime, the Consultative Committee for the Promotion of Democracy, to bring about democratization. In January 1985, members of this group formed a new united opposition party, the New Korea Democratic Party (NKDP). This party was able to capture 102 of the 299 seats in the National Assembly elections of February 1985. Early in 1985 Kim Dae Jung returned to Korea and was immediately placed under house arrest, but his return intensified the opposition to the regime.

The Chun administration was also increasingly plagued by labor and student unrest. The anti-Americanism of student protesters, who blamed the United States for what they believed was its complicity in the Kwangju massacre, was also troubling. In 1984, Chun ended the heavy-handed police surveillance on college campuses and released many students who had been arrested. About 1,000 expelled students were reinstated. As with his loosening of restrictions on political activity, the ending of the late-night curfew, and other modest moves toward liberalization, these measures were not effective in reducing the hostility of the opponents of the regime. Despite more conciliatory measures, student demonstrations only grew in frequency.

Meanwhile, Chun stuck to his pledge to limit himself to a single seven-year term. With a growing opposition and concern about a smooth transition to his heir, Roh Tae Woo, his government began negotiations with the New Korea Democratic Party in 1986 on a new constitution. The main issue was whether to adopt a cabinet-style government with a titular head of state. The NKDP wanted a direct election of an executive presidency. The government wanted a strong National Assembly, which it felt it could control through its well-funded and well-disciplined party, the Democratic Justice Party (DJP). The opposition fragmented into competing factions; despite the current coalition, it had less chance of controlling the Assembly. Therefore the opposition favored a strong presidency, which it felt it could win if united behind a single candidate. The deadlock, which seemed to jeopardize the smooth transition to the end of military rule, resulted in a split when NKDP leader Lee Min-woo decided to seek a compromise with the administration. Kim Dae Jung and Kim Young Sam then left the party and formed their own, the Reunification Democratic Party, with Kim Young Sam as the party leader and Kim Dae Jung still officially banned from political activity as the unofficial coleader. With the opposition taking a hard line against the government, Chun decided to end the negotiations over the new constitution. Meanwhile, the death in January 1987 of Pak Chong-chŏl, a Seoul National University student, while being questioned by police, led to a new round of student demonstrations and public disgust with the administration's handling of them. In addition, international events had already added to internal tensions in 1986 when the People Power uprising overthrew the Marcos dictatorship in the Philippines, an event the Korean public followed with great interest.

On April 13, 1987, Chun announced that a new president would be decided by the National Council for Unification. In other words, he would, in effect, keep the presidential system with the strong executive presidency and handpick his successor, which everyone knew would be Roh Tae Woo. The April 13 announcement set in motion a period of political turbulence as students and political activists held increasingly larger and more massive protests. Much of the middle class, dismayed at not being able to select the next president, sympathized with the demonstrations. Every sign was that most citizens wanted some meaningful participation in the political process. The student demonstrations continued to grow in number and size, further inflamed by incidents of police brutality. On June 10, the DJP nominated Roh as their candidate, a fact that made his ascension to power a matter of course. Thousands of office workers and sympathetic citizens from various walks of life now joined the street demonstrations. They grew so disruptive that only military intervention could restore order. It was clear to many in the government that much of the public supported the demonstrators and that a crackdown could have dangerous consequences. To add to the government's concerns, the International Olympic Committee threatened to relocate the games if there was further unrest. Not only Chun but especially Roh, who chaired the ROK Olympic committee and had staked much of his prestige on successfully hosting the games as a way of displaying South Korea's economic development and maturity as a nation, could not afford to risk losing the games. American and other international opinion was sympathetic to the democratic movement, and a crackdown would be an enormous loss of face. Nor was there full assurance that the government could count on the conscript army to take extreme measures if necessary to end the protests. Yet further demonstrations could threaten stability and embolden North Korea into a rash action. Chun offered to compromise with the opposition on June 22, but this had little effect. On June

26, more than 100,000 ordinary Koreans joined a peaceful protest march in Seoul. Three days later, on June 29, Roh with Chun's approval issued a declaration that the DJP would accept a new constitution with provisions for direct presidential elections. The government also announced it was ending censorship, releasing political prisoners, and removing all obstacles to political activities.

TRANSITION TO DEMOCRACY

The events of 1987 launched a transition toward democracy. The presidential elections were freely contested, but the rivalry between Kim Young Sam and Kim Dae Jung split the opposition. In addition, Kim Jong Pil, one of the former leaders of the 1961 military coup, also ran, so Roh Tae Woo faced the "three Kims" in the December presidential election. Roh, carrying the rural areas and receiving the support of many conservative working- and middle-class voters concerned about stability, won with 37 percent of the ballots cast. Kim Young Sam, carrying his home Pusan area and receiving much of the white-collar vote, received 28 percent. Kim Dae Jung carried his home Chŏlla region, where he obtained 90 percent of the vote in Kwangju, and captured support from labor and the left for a total of 27 percent. Kim Jong Pil received 8 percent of the votes, much of it in his home area in Ch'ungch'ŏng in the central part of the country. Under the new constitutional amendments the president was elected for a single five-year term.

Roh's five-year administration, which began in 1988, was a transitional period. A member of Chun's military clique and probably the second most important person in the Fifth Republic after Chun, Roh accepted the restrictions on his authority imposed by a more democratic political order. He avoided the aloof style of his predecessors, carrying his own briefcase to work, posing as the *"pot'ong saram"* (ordinary person). His power was further restricted when the opposition parties gained control of the National Assembly in the April 1988 legislative elections. The DJP pulled just 25 percent of the vote, obtaining only 125 of the 299 seats; the remainder were held by major opposition parties. With opposition parties holding a majority for the first time in history, the National Assembly began to play a more assertive role in governance, carrying out investigative and oversight functions. The judiciary, too, began to assert itself. In June 1988, 300 judges demanded that the judicial independence lost under Park Chung Hee be restored.[4] A new chief justice was appointed who was not tied to government officials. All this suggested that South Korea was becoming a representative democracy with independent branches of government. However, much of the governing structure, including the close ties between the ruling party, the bureaucracy, and the major *chaebŏls*, remained. One product of this link was a hostile attitude toward organized labor; the government showed little reluctance to use force to put down strikes. The Roh government also continued to make use of the National Security Law, intended to deal with North Korean subversion and to clamp down on leftist dissidents. Nor was the military completely free from interference in domestic matters. In 1990, for example, it was revealed that the Army Counterintelligence Corps was engaged in illegal surveillance of civilians.

The first year of the Roh administration saw one of the major turning points for South Korea: the successful hosting of the 1988 Summer Olympics in September. After the Western boycott of the Moscow games in 1980 and the Soviet boycott of the Los Angeles games in 1984, these were the first Olympics in twelve years attended by almost all nations. For Koreans it was a way of showcasing the country's rise from the rubble of the Korean War to a modern, industrial state. As a public relations event, it was highly effective. Most visitors were surprised at how modern and prosperous Seoul was, including its newly completed, clean subway system. The games provided an opportunity to broaden South Korea's relations with other nations, most importantly the Soviet Union and China. After the Olympics, the government further lifted travel restrictions, and South Koreans began to travel overseas in great numbers. The country was emerging as a presence in the world, and its people were becoming more cosmopolitan. The economy was also booming at double-digit rates at this time, benefiting from what Koreans called the "three lows"—the low price of oil, reducing the country's energy bill; the low interest rates abroad, which reduced the costs of borrowing; and the low Japanese yen, that is, the strong yen that made Korean products more competitive.

But from 1989, things became more difficult for the Roh administration. It faced an upsurge in radical student activity. The most dramatic incident was a student disturbance at Dongeui University in Pusan that left seven riot policemen dead. Violent student activities brought on a government crackdown that threatened to derail the democratization process. Labor activity also challenged the administration. The sharp rise in labor strikes that accompanied the events of 1987 continued into 1988 and 1989. Labor union membership grew quickly. In June 1987, only 22 percent of the workforce was unionized and of these 82 percent belonged to the government-approved and politically tame Federation of Korean Trade Unions. Only 3 percent belonged to the illegal and radical labor federation known as the Chŏnnohyŏp, which often led violent strikes. After 1987 union membership and strike activity grew at an explosive rate. Labor strikes were often violent and threatened to hamper the country's economic growth. Overall wages rose sharply in the late 1980s and early

1990s, in part due to the greater power of labor unions, increasing about 15 percent a year. This contributed to inflation, leading to the appreciation of the *won* and to the subsequent loss of competitiveness for South Korea's products overseas. Massive trade imbalances with the United States, the biggest overseas market, led to American pressure on the ROK to force it to adopt a code of voluntary restraints on exports. A boom in real estate and a soaring stock market proved unsustainable. Land prices had begun to reach absurd levels. In 1990, the total value of land was equal to 70 percent of that of the United States, which had ninety times the area of the ROK.[5] Land prices were more than twice as high as those in famously expensive Japan. Stock prices surged. This not only brought up fears of an economic bubble but also threatened to undermine the trend toward greater economic equality. The public grew concerned over conspicuous consumption. The government launched a campaign of avoiding "excessive consumption" to allay these concerns and to prevent a flood of consumer imports that would weaken the balance of payments. Stock prices began to fall in 1990, and as the real estate market cooled, so did the economy.

South Korea's foreign policy under Roh was aimed at developing closer ties with the Communist nations. Roh called his policy *Nordpolitik*, and it was modeled in part after the West German policy of *Ostpolitik*, which had similar aims. The policy was well timed, since under Gorbachev the Soviet Union was eager to develop economic ties with booming South Korea. The two countries exchanged trade offices in 1989 and full diplomatic relations in September 1990. China moved more cautiously, but it too was attracted to the prospects of trade and investment with South Korea. Despite the ideological differences, the two countries shared cultural ties and geographical proximity. For the ROK, China presented great opportunity for investment and trade. In the autumn of 1990 the two countries opened trade offices; in August 1992 they established full diplomatic relations.

The principal aim of *Nordpolitik* was to isolate the DPRK, removing any objections for North Korea's allies to establish closer ties. In a much stronger position, and with North Korea's economy entering a crisis, Seoul hoped to work toward closer ties with its nemesis. From July 1990 to December 1991 the two Koreas engaged in talks at a fairly high administrative level. This led to the Agreement Concerning the Reconciliation, Nonaggression, Exchanges and Cooperation in December 1991. But little came of this, and the talks stalemated as North Korea resumed its customary confrontational public statements. However, the new relations with the Soviet Union, China, and Eastern Europe were psychologically important to South Korea. For decades the country had been perceived as a client state of the United States. South Korea was now developing its own foreign policy and being respected as an important economic power and political player in the international arena.

The political calm of 1988 ended after the Olympics, when the opposition-controlled National Assembly began investigating corruption under the Chun regime. Many of Chun's aides and in-laws were indicted, and Chun himself was forced to apologize on television for the corruption and the abuse of power under his administration. Then he retreated to a remote Buddhist monastery. In January 1990, Kim Young Sam worked out a deal merging his party with the DJP and the smaller party led by Kim Jong Pil to form the Democratic Liberal Party (DLP). The new party now had a solid majority in the Assembly. The DLP, however, was weakened by internal rivalries, so it was not an effective vehicle for Roh to push through his agenda. In the March 1992 Assembly elections the DLP lost a number of seats to the political party of Kim Dae Jung. As part of the deal, Kim Young Sam was to be the DLP candidate in the 1992 presidential election. Roh became a lame duck.

In December 1992, the DLP ran Kim Young Sam as its candidate against his old-time rival Kim Dae Jung. A third candidate entered the race, the seventy-six-year-old Hyundai founder, Chung Ju Yong. Chung, angry with the government over disputes with his company, used his vast personal wealth to finance his campaign, but he never had a serious chance of winning. He received 16 percent of the vote. Kim Dae Jung, with a loyal following in his home of Chŏlla and among many in the moderate left, received 37 percent. Kim Young Sam won with 42 percent of the vote, gaining the support of conservatives and liberals, benefiting from the considerable resources of the government machine that endorsed him, and winning overwhelmingly in his home province, South Kyŏngsang. Regional affiliation was the greatest factor in voting, not ideology. Kim Dae Jung, for example, received 88 percent of the vote in Chŏlla and an extraordinary 95 percent of the vote in Kwangju. Kim Young Sam was inaugurated president in February 1993. It is interesting to note that there was no military man or ex-military man running for the office. The integrity of the voting process was largely accepted by all parties; the idea of military intervention in the political process was becoming unthinkable. The transfer of power to a former political dissident was smooth, orderly, and already seemed normal. Without the drama of 1987, voters were more complacent or less excited, with only 77 percent casting ballots compared to 87 percent five years earlier.

Democratization was a process that was far from complete by the 1990s. Government institutions were still not as transparent as in most Western democracies. The National Security Law was still in effect and the internal security organs were still powerful, though reined in a bit. Surveys done from the late 1980s through the mid-1990s by Doh C. Shin and Geir

Helgesen suggest that traditional values were still strong. While most Koreans had become committed to the ideals of democracy and political equality, Koreans still placed greater importance on the judgments of morally upright leaders than on democratic process and attached greater importance to social harmony than to political and social pluralism.[6] Nonetheless, South Korea had moved a long way toward developing an orderly democratic system.

UNDERSTANDING THE DEMOCRATIC TURN

The events of June 1987 were a turning point in the history of South Korea. The country now began a clear, if sometimes rocky, transition to democracy. Thus South Korea had a democratic transformation to match its economic one. This political shift away from an authoritarian regime to a more open political system had many causes. The experience of 1960–1961 when democracy was associated with social disorder had faded, and there was a widespread desire to end nearly three decades of military-dominated government. A culture that had traditionally disdained the military with the old Chinese adage "the best iron is not used to make nails and the best men are not used to make soldiers" underwent major changes. The Korean War created a huge army and the need for all men to serve in it. A military conscription was enacted in 1949, but it was in full effect only after the Korean War. All men were required to serve three years, then another eight years in the Homeland Reserve Force with annual military training. Later the period of active service was reduced to between twenty-six and thirty months, according to type of service. Universal conscription promoted a sense of national solidarity and eroded class barriers to some extent. It did not, however, fully overcome Korean traditional attitudes toward the military. Park, Chun, and their generals-turned-cabinet-ministers donned civilian clothes to gain respect and acceptability, but the public was never completely comfortable with rule by military or ex-military men. By the 1980s, most were eager to see a return to civilian rule.

Another factor that helped foster the end of military rule was the strengthening of big business. The *chaebŏls* had a close relationship with the ruling parties. But as the economy grew, the leaders of big business felt confident enough to compete in the international markets without the close supervision of the state. They came to view a civilian government as being more conducive to their pursuit of profit without excessive bureaucratic restraint. Furthermore, many in the business community shared the public perception that democratic government was a necessary development for the country's continued progress.

The democratization was also brought about by major cultural and social changes in South Korean society. This included two dramatic breaks with the Korean past important for understanding the evolution of democracy in the ROK: the spread of egalitarian ideals and the increase in social mobility. The upheavals of Japanese colonialism, especially during World War II when millions were mobilized for the war effort; the dislocations following the collapse of the Japanese empire and the partition of the country; the land reform; and the destruction caused by the Korean War all had a social and economic leveling effect. The old rigid hereditary-based hierarchical society dominated by the *yangban* class and its descendants had come to a final end. At the same time, the democratic ideals promoted by both leftists and by conservatives who proclaimed their adherence to American-style liberal democratic ideals took deep root. This can be seen in education where the public clamored for open access to all levels of education, where even the humblest families sacrificed for the chance that their son or daughter might achieve a higher level of schooling and move up the social ladder. A popular belief that by industriousness and talent people could rise to wealth and power was an important factor in the country's development. People worked hard and made personal sacrifices in the belief in a better future for themselves or their children. As Laura Nelson has observed, "the carrot of a better, more equitable, wealthier, democratic (and unified) Korea was dangled before the population."[7] Egalitarian ideals were reflected in the education system, where government policies promoted equal opportunity in education and uniformity of school standards.

There were also countertrends to the establishment of an egalitarian society. Industrialization led to the rise of an extremely wealthy entrepreneurial class. It was a class enriched in part by access to low-interest credit denied to small businesses or private individuals, and reinforced by low inheritance taxes. Many married within that class, with CEO sons marrying the daughters of CEOs, threatening to create a new hereditary elite. Real estate prices also posed a threat to equality. While wages rose sharply in the 1970s and 1980s, real estate prices rose even faster. Added to the similar rise in the cost of education, the entry into a middle-class lifestyle was often frustratingly difficult.[8] Nonetheless, the overall trend, especially in the 1980s and early 1990s, was toward greater income equality. In fact, during this period South Korea had one of the most equitable distributions of wealth of any developing country.

This more egalitarian society was becoming increasingly middle class in its identification and values. The economic boom and the expansion of education had expanded the ranks of well-informed, urban middle-class voters who were often embarrassed about the status of their country as a military-style authoritarian state. Most Koreans by the 1980s identified themselves as middle class even if in many cases this was as much an aspiration as a reality. They were literate and widely read; newspaper circulation had risen to among the highest in the world, and Korean newspapers gave excellent international news coverage. By the mid-1980s almost every household had a TV and most watched the well-produced nine o'clock news on the major networks. South Koreans were curious about the world. They were also a rank-conscious culture, concerned about how they stood in the world. They knew which countries were at the top: the United States, Japan, and the nations of Western Europe. South Koreans wanted their nation to measure up to that group. The Park administration had boasted in its last days that South Korea would be a fully industrialized first-world nation before the end of the century. Although regarded by outsiders and some Koreans as unrealistic, there was no doubt for most Koreans that it would be possible. But being a "first world" nation to most Koreans meant not just economic development but reaching political maturity.

Most of South Korea's middle class accepted an open, democratic society as part of what it meant to be a "successful" first-world nation. Thus, the goal of being a rich and strong nation that Park Chung Hee and almost every Korean nationalist aspired to had become linked in the minds of the public with being a democratic society. South Korean textbooks discussed democracy and identified the country with the Western democracies, and democratic ideals of representational government, popular sovereignty, and human rights had won wide acceptance as important, desired values. They were all perceived as the traits of a modern society. When it came time to vote, many were quite conservative, but they did want to vote, and in a meaningful way.

U.S. influence also contributed to the democratization in South Korea. As Gregg Brazinsky has pointed out, to a considerable extent the political evolution of the country was shaped by the way American nation-building efforts interacted with Korean internal developments.[9] American culture deeply penetrated South Korea. Much of this was in the form of pop culture—movies, music, and fashions—but it also included education and ideas about society and politics. Korean textbooks taught U.S.-inspired principles of human rights and democracy, often with American examples as models. The thousands of Koreans who studied in America generally came back with favorable impressions of American values and culture, even if they were sometimes critical of specific U.S. policies. The ROK's client status with the United States in some ways resembled Korea's pre-1876 relations with China. While determinedly independent, South Koreans looked to the United States as a big brother—the major buyer of its exports; its military guarantor; and the source of the most advanced learning, technology, and culture.

American political influence came in many ways. Koreans went to the United States for higher education, not only in science and engineering but also for degrees in social sciences, humanities, and education. The United States sponsored in-service training programs for bureaucrats. Washington funded publications such as *Sasanggye,* an influential journal of political and social thought. A U.S. Leader Program inaugurated after the Korean War brought government officials and political figures to the United States for three months to observe America's economic and political system. Among the important figures that came out of that program were political opposition leaders and later presidents Kim Young Sam and Kim Dae Jung.[10] The United States had a major role in educational development, too; U.S.-trained officials dominated the Ministry of Education and often inserted American political values and ideas into the curriculum and teacher-training programs. American influence and the American model contributed to the acceptance of ideas of human rights, individual freedom, and democratic accountability of political leaders.

The rise of Christianity in South Korea also added to the pluralism of society and provided an institutional basis for political opposition. Christian missions were an important vehicle for the spread of new ideas, and Christians were disproportionately active in the pre 1945 nationalist movement. Yet in 1945, Christians made up only a small percent of the population, with the greatest concentration in the north, especially in the Pyongyang area. After 1945, millions of South Koreans converted. According to a 1983 survey, there were 1.6 million Catholics and 5.3 million Protestants.[11] Other estimates are higher, and the numbers grew until leveling off in the early 1990s, by which time a quarter to one-third of the population described themselves as Christians (the estimates vary). Crosses lit up the skylines of major cities at night. Many were small storefront churches, but there were some mega-churches, most notably the Yŏŭido Full Gospel Church in Seoul. With 800,000 members, it was the world's largest. Converts to Christianity cut across social classes, with many of the middle class as well as the working-class poor joining churches.

Most churches were not centers of social and political activism; more often they preached the gospel of material success. But some Christian ministers contributed to the rise of the labor movement and led human rights campaigns, and Myongdong Cathedral in downtown Seoul became a center used by political protesters. Both Catholic and Protestant groups had been active in organized labor. Cardinal Stephen Kim (Kim Su-hwan) (1922–2009), the Catholic archbishop of Seoul, was an important moderate voice in the opposition to government oppression and to the social injustices caused by the country's rapid industrialization. Another sanctuary was provided by the Presbyterian minister and ecumenical movement pioneer Kang Wŏn-yong (1917–2006). His Christian Academy, a seminar house, was a safe meeting ground for intellectuals and political activists. The fact that churches had international links provided considerable protection to political dissidents and social activists, as they had to a lesser extent during colonial rule. A roughly equal number of Koreans called themselves Buddhist and there was a rise in smaller religious groups as well. Most non-Christians were less involved in politics, but a few Buddhist groups also became active in human rights movements.

STUDENT ACTIVISM

While the democratization of South Korea was primarily the product of an emerging pluralistic, middle-class society culturally linked with the West, the events of 1987 were spearheaded by the student movement. South Koreans were often tolerant of student activism, accepting that students had a right to point out injustices and the moral shortcomings of those in public life. Student remonstrance against government misconduct was a Korean tradition with premodern roots, reinforced by the contributions of student demonstrators in colonial times. The repressive nature of the Yushin government in the 1970s, by not allowing students to air their grievances, had the effect of radicalizing them, creating an underground movement that felt increasingly alienated from the political and economic system. This radicalization and the formation of strong underground organizations intensified under the Fifth Republic. There were several strands to the ideology among the students as well as other dissidents. One was nationalism. The early nationalist intellectuals of the late Chosŏn had criticized the Yi dynastic government for what was called *sadaejuŭi*, or flunkyism, in the face of China; and in the colonial period radical nationalists saw the moderates and conservatives guilty of being Japanese flunkies and collaborators. Many saw Park's normalization treaty with Japan in 1965 in this light, as toadying to Tokyo. Some radical Koreans after 1980 accused the Chun administration and its supporters in the current military-political-economic establishment of being U.S. flunkies. A deep anti-Americanism developed among student radicals in part due to the belief in U.S. support for or involvement in the Kwangju Incident. This impression was reinforced when in early 1981 the newly inaugurated President Reagan honored Chun as the first foreign head of state to be invited to the White House. Remarks by the man Reagan appointed as his ambassador, Richard Walker, who criticized the opponents of the regime and called the students "spoiled brats," also contributed to the growing hostility toward the United States by young people. The anticommunist rhetoric of the Reagan administration, although directed at the Soviet Union, seemed to echo that of the military rulers who had used the threat of Communism to strengthen their rule. In part, this anti-Americanism was the product of a young generation born after the Korean War, less concerned with the threat of North Korea, with none of the images of the Americans as liberators from the Japanese or the North Korean invaders. Instead they saw the United States as an imperialist bully that had divided their country and propped up oppressive military regimes that were economically and militarily dependent on Washington. Student radicals launched attacks on American targets, most notably on the U.S. information office and library in Pusan, which they burned in March 1982. Every American facility, even libraries, took on the appearance of armed fortresses.

Another element in student radicalism was neo-Marxism. Western critics of international capitalism were being translated and read. These included thinkers such as the South American dependency theorists, who saw the world economy as structured in such a way as to keep the poor nations of Asia, Africa, and Latin America dependent on the rich nations; American Immanuel Wallerstein, whose world-systems theories argued along similar lines; and the Italian Marxist Antonio Gramsci, with his ideas of hegemony. The fact that this radical literature was sometimes banned only added to its appeal. In sum, many radicals saw South Korea's capitalist system as benefiting only the rich, based on exploitation of the poor, and linking the ROK to the international capitalist system that was led by the United States and Japan. Thus, criticism of capitalism and the economic inequalities it created was connected to the nationalist criticism of a government subservient to foreign interests. This sometimes led to a more sympathetic view of North Korea and its *juche* philosophy. It also led to student involvement in the labor movement.

A key concept in radical ideology that was emerging in the 1970s and 1980s was *minjung*. The word can be translated as "the masses," or simply as "the people." The term was used in several ways. It was seen as defining the non-elite of society, the ordinary people within whom the national spirit was embodied in its purest form. *Minjung* thinkers saw Korean history as the struggle of the common people, ordinary men and women, against political repression, economic exploitation, and social injustice. It was thus linked to the concept of the nation as understood by the old radical nationalists. For some Christians, *minjung* became associated with the social justice movement within some churches, especially Catholic liberation theology. For others it was a way to capture the essence of what it was to be Korean. It led to a renewed interest in Korean folk culture and traditions. Student protestors would often dance to traditional folk instruments as if calling upon the spirit of nationalism before charging out into the street to make battle with the riot police. *Minjung* thought, neo-Marxism, nationalism, antiforeignism, and even Christian social activism often became fused into the struggle against not just the military regime but the entire political, social, and economic system. Although few outside student, intellectual, and radical political circles shared this basic critique of society, the highly motivated students were able to act as the vanguard of political dissent. In 1985, student radicals organized the Sammint'u (Struggle Committee for Minjung Democratization), which demanded the withdrawal of the U.S. military presence from South Korea, the destruction of the military-capitalist regime, and the unification of Korea. In 1986, this organization split into the Minmint'u, which focused on anti-imperialism and antifascism, and the more radical Chamint'u, which focused on organizing a domestic revolution. The latter organization was less interested in organizing students than in organizing the "masses."[12] These organizations effectively operated to organize protests despite police crackdowns. Although student radicals were a small minority, a much greater number of university students participated in their protests. In 1984, it was estimated that 10 percent of all college students were involved in political protests, and this percentage grew over the next three years. It was, however, only in 1987, when middle-class Koreans joined or actively encouraged them, that student demonstrations posed a major threat to the government.

ORGANIZED LABOR

The rise of labor also contributed to the ending of the authoritarian political system. Democratization took place in a society that was undergoing rapid social change. In the decades after the Korean War, millions left the countryside to move into the city, and industrialization and universal education created a large literate industrial working class. Out of the working class came the labor activists, who formed another element in the dissident movement that helped bring an end to the military regime. While organized labor appeared to have suddenly emerged in the late 1980s as a major force in the country's economic and political life, South Korea's labor movement had roots back in the colonial period. Labor unions were active in the 1920s, including a major labor strike in the port of Wonsan in 1929. Because of government repression in the 1930s, the labor groups survived only covertly and were affiliated with the Communist movement. Organized labor reemerged immediately after liberation as a major force. The chief organization was the leftist-dominated National Council of Korean Trade Unions (Chŏnp'yŏng). Established soon after the Japanese surrender, from August 1945 to March 1947 it carried out 2,500 labor demonstrations involving 600,000 participants.[13]

Labor unrest reached a peak in the fall of 1946 when a quarter of a million workers were on strike at one time. The American occupation authorities and their conservative Korean allies organized the Korean Federation of Trade Unions (Noch'ong or KFTU) in 1946 to counter its influence. The Chŏnp'yŏng was eventually outlawed, and the KFTU served for the next four decades as the only legally recognized labor organization. The latter was largely controlled by centralized government with little grass-roots support. The pent-up demand for a truly effective and representative labor organization became clear when the National Council of Trade Unions (No Hyŏp) was organized in 1960, following the fall of President Rhee. It quickly developed a large and militant membership that carried out a number of strikes and demonstrations until banned by the military government in 1961.

The labor force grew rapidly in the 1960s under Park's drive for industrial development, but the workers were kept under tight restrictions. South Korea had a system of company unions that were easy for large employers to control. All these company unions also belonged to the KFTU. Efforts to organize strikes were brutally repressed by the police. Conditions for labor reached their nadir when Park in December 1971 decreed the Law Concerning Special Measures Safeguarding National Security, which suspended the right of collective bargaining and collective action.[14] While the government used manipulation of the official labor union and police intervention to control labor, Korean industrialists used Confucian terminology of paternalism, loyalty, and harmony to try to create a sense that the company was a big family where the management was concerned for its workers who in turn should be loyal. In theory, the two, labor and management, worked in harmony. In practice, corporate heads were quick to call upon riot police to break up demonstrations. They also employed thugs called *kusadae* (save our company group) to beat labor organizers, a practice that became common in the 1980s.[15]

Working conditions were often appalling, with scant regard for safety and long hours. Korean workers had what was probably the longest workweek in the world. In the 1970s the average South Korean worker put in 53.1 hours, compared with 51 hours for those in Taiwan and 39.7 hours and 38.8 hours per week for American and Japanese workers, respectively. The workweek peaked at 54.5 hours in 1986.[16] Twelve-hour shifts six days a week were common at many companies. Some workers received only every other Sunday off. Long hours and minimal concern for safety resulted in an appalling accident rate that was fifteen times that of Japan in 1976.[17] The willingness of South Koreans to work long hours and the relative lack of labor unrest as a result of government control was one of the attractions to foreign investors. The American Chamber of Commerce and *Forbes* magazine, among others, advertised

South Korea as a good place for investment, where Korean workers "cheerfully" worked sixty hours a week for low pay.[18]

Industrial workers not only had to deal with government oppression and the ruthless business practices of a country hell-bent to increase industrial output at all costs, but also traditional Korean prejudices against manual labor. Industrial workers were referred to by the pejorative terms *kongsuni* (factory girl) and *kongdori* (factory boy).[19] Such sentiments meant that, whenever possible, Korean workers sought to pass themselves off as members of the middle class and pushed their children to achieve white-collar status through schooling.

Despite the tame company unions and government measures to repress worker activism, labor unrest periodically resurfaced. The most dramatic incident took place in 1970, when Chŏn Tae-il, a worker in the P'yŏnghwa Market—a block-long four-story complex of small garment factories and clothing shops employing some 20,000 workers—burned himself alive out of protest of the treatment of laborers. But there were many other less-publicized acts of violent protest. Christian groups became important in organizing labor starting in the 1960s, especially the Urban Industrial Mission (UIM). Originally this group, drawn from Presbyterian and Methodist churches, formed to proselytize among factory workers, but the pastors became increasingly concerned about the working conditions of their converts.[20] As small groups gathered for Bible readings, they discussed their hardships. This proved an effective vehicle for labor organization, since the UIM had international links, including foreign pastors, making open suppression by the South Korean government difficult. There was also a Catholic group, the Young Christian Workers, established in 1958, that also became involved in labor activities. With its international links, it enjoyed a similar advantage.[21]

An interesting feature of the South Korean labor movement was the major contribution of women. About one-third of industrial workers in the 1970s and 1980s were women, most young and single. About 90 percent were of rural or provincial background.[22] They often lived in company dormitories, nicknamed "beehives" for their tiny, cramped rooms. Women workers were disproportionately represented in the huge, labor-intensive garment industry. They played an important role in fanning the flames of labor unrest, carrying out high-profile strikes at the Dongil Textile Company in 1972 and at the Y.H. Trading Company in Pusan in 1979.

The pent-up frustration of laborers was seen in the outburst of some 400 strikes and demonstrations during the "Seoul Spring" of 1980. This was followed by another wave of repression with the consolidation of the Chun Du Hwan regime that year. But labor unrest grew in the 1980s. It was abetted by a modest lessening of political control in the mid-1980s, because the regime sought to achieve legitimacy and deflect international criticism as it prepared to host the Asian Games in 1986 and the Olympics in 1988. Two hundred independent labor unions were organizing in 1984, and the number of strikes increased. A turning point was the strike in Kuro, the industrial section of Seoul, in which workers from many industries participated. It started among apparel workers but was joined by many others in that busy manufacturing zone.[23] Many of these strikes were spontaneous outbursts of protests, but they were also organized by college students and other political dissidents, and by increasingly effective labor organizers. During this time, student radicals began joining labor unions after graduating or by leaving school, and they helped to spread the antigovernment ideology. In 1986, the number of strikes more than doubled from the previous years. An especially violent protest over labor conditions occurred in Inch'ŏn that year when student radicals joined with labor activists. The biggest outburst in labor unrest came in 1987. In that year there were 3,749 labor strikes compared to 276 the previous year.[24] The sharp upswing in labor unrest in 1987 became part of the political upheavals of that year.

SOCIAL AND CULTURAL TRANSITION

The democratization of South Korea was part of a broad social and cultural change that included the rise of the middle class, of an industrial working class, and of Christianity, and the spread of egalitarian ideals. Another important component of the social and cultural change was the movement for greater legal and social equality for women. At first, attitudes about the role of women in society and the nature of the family changed slowly. After liberation, many South Korean officials and intellectuals were more concerned about preserving or restoring what they sometimes called "laudable customs and conduct" (*mip'ung yangsok*).[25] This concern was reflected in what was known as the Family Law, the parts of the civil law code that governed family relations. The Family Law, compiled in the 1950s and finished in 1958, was in many ways very conservative: it preserved the patriarchal family structure with the husband as head of the household; favored the eldest son in inheritance; and in divorce, which was uncommon, men generally received custody of children. The maintaining of these practices was important, it was argued, to preserve the essential nature of Korea's cultural traditions.

In the 1950s and 1960s women organized to challenge these traditions and the laws that protected them in the name of women's equality. A Federation of Korean Women's Groups (Taehan yŏsŏng tanch'e hyŏphŭihoe) led by Lee Tai-young (Yi T'ae-yŏng) (1914–1995) fought during the 1950s and 1960s for legal reforms establishing the equality of men and women in marriage, divorce, child custody, and inheritance. Lee, the daughter of a miner, worked as a seamstress before becoming South Korea's first woman lawyer in 1952. She founded the Korea Legal Aid Center for Family Relations, a nonprofit that provided assistance to poor, uneducated women and was a champion of equal justice and rights for women. Early women's rights advocates were up against entrenched patriarchal attitudes. With the expansion of women's education, however, and the gradual acceptance of the ideas of equality, attitudes toward these matters began to change. Even under the very conservative Yushin period in the 1970s, a Pan-Women's Group for Revision of the Family Law succeeded in revising the law in 1977 to give greater rights to women in these four areas: marriage, divorce, inheritance, and child custody.[26]

More significant changes took place when women's rights became part of the great upsurge in political and social activism of 1987. In that year, female activists created the Korean Women's Association (Han'guk Yŏsŏng Tanch'e Yŏnhap).[27] In 1989, the Family Law, in part due to the pressure from this and other groups, was again revised, with most of the old patriarchal provisions eliminated or modified. Up to that time the eldest son was still expected to succeed as the head of the house, receive extra property in inheritance, and take care of his parents in old age. Under new legal revisions, complicated by court rulings, this was no longer automatically the case. Other changes were slowly taking place. The emphasis on universal education meant literacy rates among women were as high as for men, and there was no significant difference in the percentage of women completing secondary education. But in higher education women tended to be confined to nonprofessional programs, studying home economics, English, and fine arts. South Korea lagged far behind most industrial nations in the early 1990s in the percentage of women represented in law, medicine, and the other professions. Few served in government, and they were still expected to resign from work when they married.

Intellectual and cultural life in South Korea reflected the turbulent social and political transformation of society. Among the best-known political dissidents was the poet Kim Chi-ha. The South Korean government promoted officially favored artists in much the way that the North did, building large theaters such as the huge Sejong Cultural Center in downtown Seoul in the 1970s. Most artists and writers operated outside this official sphere and were often alienated from the state until the transition to democracy. Few could escape the political and social upheavals of their time, which often informed their work. An example was Yi Chung-sŏp (1916–1956), a Japanese-trained artist who died in poverty. Some of his paintings were officially disapproved of as too erotic, but he came to be recognized as an important modern artist, especially for his paintings of the ox representing Korean fortitude and hardship.²⁸ Pak Su-gŭn (1914–1965), a self-taught oil painter, also struggled with poverty most of his life but won public acclaim in his last years for his works that depicted ordinary people in everyday Korean life. Painter Whanki Kim (Kim Hwan-gi) (1913–1974), architects Kim Chung-ŏp (1922–1988) and Kim Su-gŭn (1931–1986), and video artist Nam June Paik (Paek Nam-jun) (1932–2006) received international recognition.

Writers struggled with the country's rapidly changing society and turbulent history. Ch'oe In-hun (1936–), novelist and playwright, wrote *The Plaza* (*Kwangjang*) (1964), the story of a captured soldier disillusioned by both North and South Korean political and social systems. He was the first prominent writer to criticize both Koreas. Another writer was Yi Mun-yŏl (1948–) whose father defected to the North in 1950. Consequently, his family was socially stigmatized, watched by the police, and forced into poverty. He gained acceptance to the prestigious Seoul National University but dropped out and began his career in the 1970s as a writer of short stories and novels that attempted to come to an understanding of Korea's recent history. In his novel *Son of Man* (*Saram ŭi Adŭl*) (1979) he questioned the uncritical acceptance of Christian dogma by many Koreans. Yi Mun-gu (1941–2003), through his series of novels *Our Town* (*Uri Tongnae*) (1977–1981), dealt with the modernization penetrating rural life in his home Ch'ungch'ŏng region, while generating an appreciation for its dialect. Pak Wan-sŏ (1931–2011), known for her novel *Naked Tree* (*Namok*) (1970) set during the Korean War, later wrote *Lean Years of the City* (*Tosi-e Hyungnyŏn*) (1979) about the urban middle class dealing with modernization. Cho Se-hŭi (1942–) wrote a series of novels, *A Dwarf Launches a Little Ball* (*Nanjangi ka Ssoa Ollin Chagŭn Kong*) (1976–1978), about slum dwellers who were victimized rather than uplifted by the rush for industrialization. Pak Ki-p'yŏng (1957–), a labor activist better known by his pen name Pak No-hae, was called the "faceless labor poet" for his underground poems dealing with the hardships and injustices experienced by workers. He was arrested under the National Security Law and spent eight years in prison. Another poet, Ko Ŭn (1933–), became an active participant in the democracy movement, was arrested four times, and suffered serious injuries from a police beating. He emerged as one of the country's leading poets and has been translated into many languages.

Government censorship of literature and the arts was lessened starting in 1988. On the eve of the summer Olympics the Roh Tae Woo administration lifted the ban on thousands of works of art, music, and literature. Previously underground works by dissident South Koreans were now openly published, displayed, and performed. North Korean writers such as Han Sŏr-ya were published, and works of artists like Yi K'wae-dae (1913–?) who had gone to the North were exhibited in Seoul in the early 1990s. Chŏng Chi-yong (1902–1950), an apolitical poet whose works had been banned simply because he had been taken captive by the North Koreans during the Korean War, were now published. Chŏng's poem "Nostalgia" (1939) became included in school textbooks. Shortly afterward the bans were also lifted on the works of the European-based artist Yi Ungno (1905–1989) and the composer Yun Yi-sang (1917–1995), who were involved in the East Berlin Spy Incident. South Korea still had a ways to go to honestly deal with its past, but by the 1990s it enjoyed more political and cultural freedom than Koreans had known since the late Chosŏn.

KOREA IN GLOBAL PERSPECTIVE: DEMOCRATIZATION

South Korea's political development in many ways followed a pattern typical of postcolonial states after World War II. Constitutions were written and ignored, authoritarian regimes followed each other, leaders established cults of personality, and the military intervened. As with most developing nations, governments faced the problem of political legitimacy. But in South Korea the problem of political legitimacy was especially difficult since it faced a rivalry for the mantle of Korean nationalism with the North, whose leaders possessed more impressive anticolonial credentials. Just as North Korea sought to win legitimacy by presenting itself as part of a universal, progressive system that offered great promise for the future, South Korean leaders linked their state to the West, to the "free world," and its promise of progress and prosperity. Yet, the governments of the ROK could never feel entirely comfortable with the liberal democratic system of government promoted by the United States. Furthermore, unlike North Korea's *juche*, South Korean leaders had no uniquely Korean ideology. Rhee relied principally on anticommunism as a means to rally support for the state. Park continued the anticommunist tradition but also made use of economic nationalism and economic performance. After 1961, governments sought to gain support by achieving economic growth and prosperity in much the same way as the contemporary government of Taiwan also did and Beijing has done since the 1980s.

South Korean administrations also used the external threats to justify political repression, much as many developing countries and as North

Korea's government did. The fact that the threat of renewed conflict was real and necessitated an elaborate security apparatus made it especially easy to justify political repression. The monthly air-raid drills and late-night curfews were constant reminders of a state under siege. In the name of national security, ROK governments jailed opponents, kidnapped some abroad, and carried out judicial murders. The KCIA, which Chun renamed the National Security Bureau, provided a vast system of internal espionage. Indeed, South Korea had many of the elements of a thorough police state. But unlike North Korea it could not isolate its people, since it was committed to the international marketplace and its alliance with the United States compromised the ability to tighten control over all dissent. Each regime had to make some concessions to representative government and to an open society.

South Korea's democratic transition has been linked with the so-called "third wave" of democracy. According to this interpretation of world history put forward by Samuel Huntington, the spread of democratic governments has occurred in waves when certain international conditions seem favorable. A wave of democracy took place after World War I; another started in the mid-1970s with Portugal and Spain and continued in the 1980s as democracy was restored in some Latin American countries such as Brazil and Argentina. Then a third wave occurred in Eastern Europe with the fall of Communist regimes in 1989. South Korea and Taiwan were part of this "wave." However, it is not clear how much these external events influenced the ROK's democratic transition. While the People Power movement in the Philippines may have provided some encouragement to protesters in South Korea, its transition to democracy was due to its own internal developments. In this it most resembled Taiwan. Both states had identified with the Western democracies but were in reality ruled by authoritarian regimes suffering from a problem of legitimacy in the face of a Communist rival. Governments of both sought to gain support through economic development. Both countries were highly influenced by the United States, had increasingly well-educated populations, avoided the enormous disparities in income and education characteristic of most developing nations, and had by the 1980s become predominantly middle class societies. As was the case in Taiwan, Korea's authoritarian traditions seemed unpromising soil for the flourishing of a truly pluralistic, democratic society; yet in retrospect, it appears that by the late twentieth century the social and cultural changes that had taken place in the country had prepared it well for a successful transition to democracy.

Kim Chi-ha

"Five Thieves"

And there lived five thieves
In downtown Seoul.
Their den at Tongbingo-dong is located high upon the bank of the Han
　River.
It is built at the foot of a naked mountain,
Bare as a plucked chicken-butt.
To the south it commands
A good view of the river,
Where dung floats on the putrid water,
And to the north it boasts its magnificence
Towards Sungbook-dong and Suyou-dong.
And, in between, a row of crowded shacks,
Small as hermit-crab shells and dirty as boogers.
The five thieves built splendid flowery palaces
With high gates on Changchung-dong and Yaksoo-dong.
There, where the kisaeng music never stops
And the sounds of cooking never cease,
Is the very den of the notorious "Five Thieves,"
That sonuvabitch Plutocrat, sonuvabitch Aristocrat, sonuvabich
　Technocrat, sonuvabich Autocrat,
And sonuvabith Bureaucrat,
Their conceited heads as big as Nam Mountain
And their necks as tough as Dongzhuo's navel.
. . .

[*Author Note:* The poem goes on to describe each of the five thieves; the last
is the Bureaucrat.]

The last contestant appears,
That sonuvabitch thief named Bureaucrat.
Having waxy eyes suffering from cataracts,
His dirty face is beyond comparison,
But he looks around with glaring eyes,
While he controls the army
With his golf club in his left hand.

When he caresses his mistress' breasts
And writes slowly on them
"More produce, more exports, and more construction," she responds by
　saying
"Ah! Oh! It tickles."
"Are you saying national affairs are
Ticklesome, you ignorant bitch?"

Export more goods, even if we die of hunger.
Produce more goods, even if they don't sell.
Let's build a bridge over the Straits of Korea
With the bones of the people who starved to death
And have an audience with the Japanese gods.

—from *Heart's Agony: Selected Poems*[29]

NOTES

1. Hyung Gu Lynn, *Bipolar Orders: The Two Koreas Since 1989* (Halifax, NS: Fenwood, 2007), 29.

2. Joungwon Alexander Kim, *Divided Korea: The Politics of Development, 1945–1972* (Cambridge, MA: Harvard University Press, 1975), 233.

3. Sunhyuk Kim, *The Politics of Democratization in Korea: The Role of Civil Society* (Pittsburgh: University of Pittsburgh Press, 2000), 59.

4. Adrian Buzo, *The Making of Modern Korea* (New York: Routledge, 2007), 162.

5. Hong Yung Lee, "South Korea in 1991: Unprecedented Challenge, Increasing Opportunity," *Asian Survey* 32, no. 1: 64–73.

6. Doh C. Shin, *Mass Politics and Culture in Democratizing Korea* (New York: Cambridge University Press, 1999); Geir Helgesen, *Democracy and Authority in Korea: The Cultural Dimension in Korean Politics* (New York: St. Martin's Press, 1998).

7. Laura C. Nelson, *Measured Excess: Status, Gender, and Consumer Nationalism in South Korea* (New York: Columbia University Press, 2000), 20.

8. Nelson, *Measured Excess*, 15.

9. Gregg Brazinsky, *Nation Building in South Korea: Koreans, Americans, and the Making of Democracy* (Chapel Hill: University of North Carolina Press, 2007).

10. Brazinsky, *Nation Building in South Korea*, 59–62.

11. Chae-Jin Lee, "South Korea in 1983: Crisis Management and Political Legitimacy," *Asian Survey* 24, no. 1: 112–21.

12. Stewart Lone and Gavan McCormack, *Korea Since 1850* (New York: St. Martin's Press, 1993), 161.

13. Hagen Koo, *Korean Workers: The Culture and Pattern of Class Formation* (Ithaca, NY: Cornell University Press, 2001), 26.

14. Koo, *Korean Workers*, 29.

15. George E. Ogle, *South Korea: Dissent within the Economic Miracle* (London: Zed Books, 1990), 62.

16. Koo, *Korean Workers*, 48–49.

17. Koo, *Korean Workers*, 55.

18. Ogle, *South Korea: Dissent within the Economic Miracle*, 23.

19. Koo, *Korean Workers*, 15.

20. Koo, *Korean Workers*, 71–73.

21. Ogle, *South Korea: Dissent within the Economic Miracle*, 88.

22. Ruth Barraclough, *Factory Girl Literature: Sexuality, Violence, and Representation in Industrializing Korea* (Berkeley, CA: University of California Press, 2012), 64.

23. Ogle, *South Korea: Dissent within the Economic Miracle*, 88.

24. Koo, *Korean Workers*, 159.

25. Ki-young Shin, "The Politics of the Family Law Reform Movement in Contemporary Korea: A Contentious Space for Gender and the Nation," *The Journal of Korean Studies* 11 (Fall 2006): 93–126.

26. Shin, "The Politics of the Family Law Reform Movement," 104.

27. John Lie, *Han Unbound: The Political Economy of South Korea* (Stanford, CA: Stanford University Press, 1998), 161.

28. Keith Pratt, *Everlasting Flower: A History of Korea* (London: Reaktion Books, 2006), 258.

29. Chiha Kim, *Heart's Agony: Selected Poems*, Won-Chung Kim and James Han, translators (Fredonia, NY: White Pine Press, 1998), 103–4.

7

Contemporary North Korea, 1993 to 2015

In the 1990s, the two Koreas experienced major changes that both reflected and highlighted the contrasts in their separate, divergent paths. In North Korea, Kim Il Sung died in 1994 and was succeeded by his son Kim Jong Il. The country maintained its militant, isolationist, totalitarian system, while the economy went into a decline. The economic decline became a crisis when the population was devastated by a massive famine in 1995–1997, and the country had to seek foreign aid to prevent collapse. This was in contrast to South Korea, where the transition to democracy proceeded with the orderly elections of Kim Young Sam in 1992 and another opposition leader, Kim Dae Jung, in 1997, and where economic growth continued if at a slower rate.

IN DECLINE: A PERIOD OF CRISIS

Toward the end of the 1980s the DRPK became increasingly isolated. Its economic woes and diplomatic failures were in contrast to South Korea's booming economy and growing stature in the world. The contrast between a struggling North Korea and a dynamic South Korea was highlighted when Seoul was awarded the 1988 Olympics. After bids to cohost it failed, Pyongyang attempted to discourage countries from participating. However, only four countries—Cuba, Madagascar, Albania, and Seychelles—joined its call for a boycott while China participated, and the games were a success. The early 1990s were a period of steep economic decline. The most severe blow to North Korea's economy was the fall of the Soviet Union in 1991 and the loss of its principal economic patron. With the new Russian government more interested in trade and investment with South Korea than in propping up the North, the DPRK economy began to contract. Severe energy shortages, along with aging equipment, led to a decline in industrial output. Pyongyang did not have the foreign exchange to pay for imported oil, and it was no longer receiving cheap, below-market-value oil from Russia. China provided some, but not enough. These problems only added to an agriculture threatened by flooding from deforestation; the unproductive, ill-conceived projects; and the burden of a vast defense system. In 1993, the regime was no longer hiding the fact that its latest Seven-Year Plan had not been successful in meeting its targets. In January 1994, Kim Il Sung admitted to his own people that there were economic problems. Previously such an admission would have been unthinkable.

As the DPRK's position grew more unfavorable, it became more reliant on the development of weapons of mass destruction, primarily on nuclear warheads and a missile delivery system, to compensate for its economic weakness. The missiles also provided a source for foreign revenue, being one of the country's few marketable products. North Korean technicians increased the capacity of the nuclear research reactor at Yŏngbyŏn and constructed a new one. In 1977, Pyongyang had allowed the International Atomic Energy Agency (IAEA) to inspect its first reactor, but in the 1980s it began a secret project to build a facility for reprocessing fuel into weapons-grade material; it also began testing chemical high explosives. After the United States became aware of this, North Korea agreed to join the Nuclear Non-Proliferation Treaty. In 1990, satellite photos revealed a new structure that appeared to be capable of separating plutonium from nuclear fuel rods. The United States was becoming increasingly worried that the DPRK was developing nuclear weapons. This along with a DPRK program to develop missiles was making Washington, as well as Tokyo and Seoul, nervous. Under international pressure, North Korea signed safeguards with the IAEA in 1992. But in January 1993, inspectors were prevented from going to two previously unreported facilities. The Clinton administration announced that if North Korea reprocessed plutonium, it would be crossing a "red line" that could result in military action. And indeed, the administration was so concerned that it seriously considered a military strike on the main reprocessing facility. The arrival of former president Jimmy Carter in Pyongyang in the summer of 1994 led to a defusing of the crisis, as the two sides began working out an agreement satisfactory to both nations.

North Korea was not the only state on the peninsula to have a nuclear and missile program. Park Chung Hee in the mid-1970s began secretive programs to acquire advanced weaponry, including nuclear weapons.

In 1975, he worked out an agreement to have France build South Korea a nuclear processing facility, but Washington pressured France to cancel the deal. A second nuclear deal between South Korea and France in 1978 was also blocked by the United States. The South Korean government then continued a clandestine project to develop its own nuclear weapons, but this too was eventually terminated, as the Americans found out about it. The Park government managed, however, to develop a guided missile, which it tested in 1978 to the surprise and anger of the United States. South Korea in the 1980s began the construction of nuclear energy plants, which by the end of the century generated much of its electricity, but its dependency on the United States for military protection, as well as public opinion after 1987, inhibited the development of weapons of mass destruction. South Korea, instead, sought to keep the peninsula free of nuclear weapons.

No sooner had the 1994 nuclear crisis passed when the DPRK faced another crisis, the death of Kim Il Sung from a heart attack on July 8. His death, which came only two weeks after Carter's visit, was a shock. Kim Il Sung, although eighty-two, seemed in vigorous health. He was, as he had so carefully planned, succeeded by his son Kim Jong Il.

UNDER KIM JONG IL

Following the death of his father on July 8, 1994, Kim Jong Il assumed power in what appeared to be a smooth transition. He had been groomed as his father's successor for more than two decades and by the early 1990s shared power with him. Those who had expressed the slightest reservations about this unusual father-to-son transfer of power had been removed years earlier. This is suggested by the fact that no purges or changes in leadership accompanied the son's ascension.

In 1997, following the end of a customary Korean three-year period of mourning, Kim Jong Il assumed the position of General Secretary of the Korean Workers Party. His assumption of power was accompanied by a more prominent role for the military. The key positions in the state were increasingly held by military men. When the Tenth Supreme People's Assembly met in September 1998, it amended the 1972 state constitution and made the chair of the National Defense Council, a position held by Kim Jong Il, the head of state. Political power appeared to be shifting away from the Korean Workers Party and toward the military. In 1998, Kim Jong Il began to espouse the "Military First" (*sŏn'gun*) policy, which made it clear that military needs would have priority. While this policy was not a break with North Korea's military-centered society, the structural change in government was new. By establishing his power base in the military and keeping his generals happy, Kim Jong Il was probably securing his own position. The other major change in the formal structure of government was the elimination of the presidency. This was done by declaring that the late Kim Il Sung held the position eternally.

Contrary to the predictions of many foreign observers, Kim Jong Il appeared to be firmly in power. Lacking the revolutionary credentials or physical stature of his father, he seemed an unlikely candidate for supreme leader. His heavy drinking and fondness for women and luxurious living, his artistic temperament, his elevated shoes and bouffant hairstyle compensating for his short height, and his sometimes bizarre behavior made him the subject of ridicule and contempt abroad. Yet he had a shrewd intelligence and had learned well how to firmly grasp and maintain his hold on power.

IDEOLOGY

While still vaguely calling itself socialist, North Korea became a nationalist-militarist state with little connection to Communism. No Communist state, for example, had ever made the military the highest governing organ. With the collapse of Communism, the regime all but abandoned any pretense of being a Marxist-Leninist state. By the early 1990s, almost all references to Marxism-Leninism ceased. Instead, references were made to "our way of socialism (*urisik sahoejuŭi*)." *Juche* continued as the "guiding principle." A new *juche* calendar was adopted in 1997, with the year of Kim Il Sung's birth, 1912, the year one. *Juche* was defined in more explicitly nationalist terms. In 1997, Kim Jong Il declared that *juche* "clarified that the country and nation are the basic unit for shaping the destiny of the masses."[1] Citizens were not only to study and follow *juche* but also to have *juche*. And having *juche* meant they must "submerge their separate identity into the collective identity of the Korean nation."[2] The centrality of ethnic-racial nationalism as the basis for both the state and for national unity was made clear in a speech the following year when Kim Jong Il declared that "the Korean nation is a homogeneous nation that has inherited the same blood and lived in the same territory speaking the same language for thousands of years." The people of both North and South share the "same blood and soul of the Korean nation," and are "linked inseparably with the same national interests and a common historical psychology and sentiment." Therefore "the reunion of our nation that has been divided by foreign forces is an inevitable trend of our nation's history and the law of national development."[3] The family cult had continued unabated, Kim Jong Il, the former Dear Leader, becoming the Great Leader but with a different Korean term (*Widaehan Ryŏngdoja*) to distinguish him from his father (*Widaehan Suryŏngnim*), also translated in English as Great Leader. While extravagant praise was heaped on Kim Jong Il, there was no diminishing of the veneration of his father, Kim Il Sung, the founder, builder, and towering figure of the Democratic People's Republic of Korea. Kim Il Sung remained the "eternal president."

An extreme manifestation of nationalism and the family cult was the revival of interest in Tan'gun, the mythical founder of the first Korean state, who, according to tradition, was born in 2333 BCE. In South Korea, October 3 is a national holiday celebrating Tan'gun's birth, and his name is conjured up from time to time by politicians and editorial writers as a symbol of the uniqueness and antiquity of the Korean nation. Most textbooks and professional historians, however, treat him as a myth. In the DPRK, Tan'gun, regarded by North Korea's Marxist historians as a feudal myth, was ignored. It therefore came as a surprise when North Korea announced on the eve of National Foundation Day 1993 that its archaeologists had excavated remains believed to be those of Tan'gun from a site near Pyongyang. According to a North Korean radio broadcast, eighty-six bones had been dug out of the ancient royal tomb together with a gilded bronze crown and some ornaments, and these were believed to belong to Tan'gun and his wife. The bones were further stated to be 5,011 years old; Tan'gun was estimated to have been about 170 centimeters tall. Few scholars outside North Korea took these claims seriously. South Korean archaeologists, for example, voiced suspicions about the authenticity of the claim, agreeing among themselves that the finding probably had been fabricated. The existence of bronze ornaments found in the tomb shed doubt on the dates, since no bronze work more than 3,000 years old had previously been found on the peninsula.[4] Furthermore, these findings by North Korea were also linked to the reported discoveries of early human remains, *Pithecanthropus*, suggesting that Tan'gun and the Korean nation had descended from a distinct line of humans. The DPRK announced, "Scientific evidence therefore supports the claim that there is a distinctive Korean race and that the foundation of the first state of the Korean nation by Tan'gun was a historic event, which laid the groundwork for the formation of the Korean nation."[5] By 1998, the DPRK became more emphatic in this claim. "Tan'gun is now a historical figure who founded the first Korean state about 3000 BCE, which centered on Pyongyang." The basin of the river Taedong, they declared, was "the cradle of mankind," since the remains of *Pithecanthropus* were found dating back to one million years ago.[6]

North Korea has long claimed that Kim Jong Il was born in Paektusan on the China–North Korea border, a sacred spot and considered the birthplace of Tan'gun. Thus, in a very indirect way, the Kim dynasty was linked to the ancient progenitor of the Korean people. Now this connection was made more explicit. Sixty years after the establishment of the Democratic People's Republic of Korea its ideology amounted at its core to little more than glorifying the leader and the nation and demanding absolute loyalty to both. The nation was defined in ethnic-racial terms. Kim Il Sung and Kim Jong Il were viewed as the great protectors of the Korean race, a race that throughout its history had been subject to invasion and violation from outsiders, such as the Japanese in colonial times and the United States in more recent years.[7] The unity of the Korean race meant the division of the country was unnatural, its reunification a necessity and inevitable once the South Koreans were free from their enslavement by the Americans.

FAMINE

Soon after becoming the sole ruler, Kim Jong Il faced a horrific food crisis. The immediate cause was the widespread flooding in August 1995 that destroyed much of the nation's rice crop. North Korea possessed limited farmland and a short growing season. To overcome this handicap the regime spent large efforts on elaborate irrigation systems, expanding the arable acreage by filling in the shallow seas along the west coast and by clearing forested mountainsides. Some modest progress was made in creating new farmland from the sea, but at a great expenditure of resources. Geographic limitations were made worse by years of economic mismanagement. The irrigation systems often required pumps that needed imported fuel oil, which created problems when the supply of cheap Soviet oil ended. Other unsound agricultural practices only made things worse. Seeds were closely planted, making the crops vulnerable to pests and exhausting the soil. To compensate, intensive use was made of pesticides and chemical fertilizers, the latter also falling victim to petroleum shortages. Mechanized agriculture meant that tractors became idle for lack of oil. Shortfalls of food grew worse during Kim Il Sung's last years, when the country may have produced only 60 percent of its needs.[8] In the late 1980s rice rations were cut 10 percent, the government announcing the cut as "patriotic rice" donations to the military. The idea of getting by with less reached a grim point in 1991 with the "Let's eat two meals a day" slogan.[9] China supplied some food, but due to rising agricultural prices Beijing cut food supplies in the mid-1990s. The greatest problem was deforestation. The forested hillsides of this mountainous country were cleared to plant crops, even in areas too steep to be suitable for farming. One aid official in 1997 observed entire hillsides torn away by erosion due to these shortsighted policies.[10] The state also encouraged livestock raising, especially poultry and pigs, but these required feed. In a measure to deal with the scarcity of meat, Kim Il Sung launched a campaign to encourage goat raising, although the country has limited grazing land and goats further contributed to erosion.[11] Deforestation and erosion resulted in the disastrous floods that were the immediate cause of the severe famine of the 1990s. Particularly hard hit was the northeastern part of the country.

North Korea responded to the famine in an unprecedented manner—by publicly reporting the floods. It then openly sought foreign aid, perhaps a sign of desperation. A number of foreign relief agencies came in, such as the UN-related World Food Program, the Food and Agricultural Organization (FAO), the United Nations International Children's Emergency Fund (UNICEF), and the World Health Organization. Some European countries also offered aid. By 2000, these international agencies were providing 40 percent of North Korea's food needs. International aid workers confronted a historically unprecedented situation. There was massive starvation, but unlike the usual chaotic conditions that accompany famine, they found a tightly controlled police state determined to limit the interactions between relief workers and the people they were helping. DPRK officials insisted on managing the distribution of food. Aid workers complained about lack of access to victims and were frustrated over their inability to determine just where the food was going.[12] Rumors circulating among donors, often proved correct, were that food aid was being diverted to the military, whose needs were the highest priority for the regime. This led to a controversy over whether food aid was being used to feed the army and party at the expense of others in more dire need, especially children; but the extent to which this was true could not be verified.[13] There were also some disturbing reports that rice being supplied by Japan and South Korea was being resold abroad to earn foreign exchange.

Malnutrition was already becoming a problem; the sudden food shortage only made things worse. By the end of 1995, many thousands of people, mostly the elderly, the ill, and young children, had died of starvation. In that year it was estimated that half the country's crop was lost. The situation only worsened in 1996, when perhaps a much larger number died of causes related to food shortages; more perished in 1997–1998, although the food shortage was becoming less severe. Estimates of the number of people who died run as high as 2 million, although a more probable figure is that there were between 600,000 and 1 million excess deaths due to the famine out of the total population of 20 million people.[14] This was, nonetheless, a truly appalling number. It should be pointed out that these numbers are just estimates, since no statistics have been published. All agree that the famine was horrific. A survey in 1998 by United Nations experts estimated that 63 percent of all North Korean children exhibited signs of long-term undernourishment, including lassitude, susceptibility to minor illness and infection, increased mortality, impaired cognitive functions, and stunted growth.[15] Foreign aid workers commented that children often appeared several years younger than their real age. Just how bad conditions in the northeast were could not be verified, since international relief staff were not permitted into the area.

After 1998, conditions improved and starvation was more rare, but chronic undernourishment remained a problem, especially for children. Meanwhile, many aid organizations, exasperated by the restrictions placed on their activities, the insistence that they use only non-Korean-speaking personnel, and the lack of information over where food was being distributed, began to pull out. Other groups, by accepting these limitations and by carefully steering away from politics, remained in the country.

CRISIS AND SUMMITRY

Meanwhile, tensions between North Korea and its neighbors continued over the problem of nuclear weapons. During Kim Il Sung's last days, war had narrowly been averted as the Clinton administration considered taking military action against North Korea. After Kim's death, negotiations continued, and in October 1994 what became known as the Agreed Framework or the Geneva Framework Agreement was signed. Under this, the first bilateral agreement signed between the United States and North Korea, Pyongyang agreed to suspend its nuclear program and permit its nuclear plant at Yŏngbyŏn to be opened to inspection by the International Atomic Energy Commission. Since the DPRK claimed the program was needed for nuclear energy, the United States agreed in exchange to supply North Korea with heavy fuel oil. An international consortium consisting of the United States, South Korea, and Japan would build two light-water nuclear reactors that could not be used to make weapons-grade material. Japan would chip in, paying for part of the cost of the fuel and the nuclear reactors. This left unanswered the question of how much weapons-grade plutonium North Korea had already extracted before it shut down the plant. Most experts believed it was enough to build one or two nuclear bombs.

Another issue was the DPRK's missile program. North Korea already possessed short-range missiles and was developing a medium-range one. In August 1998 it test-fired a medium-range Taepo-dong 1 ballistic missile that flew over Japan and crashed into the Pacific Ocean 1,500 kilometers away. U.S. intelligence believed it was a failed attempt to launch a satellite, but the military implication was clear. Short-range missiles threatened South Korea, and this medium-range missile was capable of targeting Japan's major cities. The provocative testing led to government and public outrage in Japan, where North Korea was perceived as its most serious security threat. Japan responded by suspending its 20 percent contribution to the nuclear reactor program. In September 1999, the United States, in what was called the Perry Report, offered food aid, economic relations, and full diplomatic recognition if the DPRK would agree to discontinue its development of weapons of mass destruction.

While tensions were again easing between the United States and North Korea, the new South Korean president, Kim Dae Jung, inaugurated what he called the "Sunshine" policy toward North Korea in 1998. It was an attempt at peaceful engagement that aimed to expand trade and economic and cultural links between the two countries and to gradually coax the DPRK toward reform, thus reducing tensions and easing the transition to the day when the two Koreas could unite. In April 1998, the two Koreas began talks in Beijing. Pyongyang wanted Seoul to supply it with fertilizer. The ROK insisted that any food-related aid would have to be accompanied by the exchange of home visits by divided families. The DPRK refused. Instead it criticized South Korea for not sending a condolence mission to Kim Il Sung's funeral, for politicizing rice deliveries during the famine, and for obstructing its effort to improve relations with the United States and Japan. Relations deteriorated further when on June 15, 1999, a North Korean torpedo boat was sunk and five other vessels damaged in a naval clash off South Korea's west coast.

Nonetheless, South Korean president Kim Dae Jung was determined to improve relations with North Korea. In March 2000 he gave his "Berlin Declaration," in which he offered North Korea security guarantees, economic assistance, and help in supporting the DPRK internationally. He then secretly arranged an aid package to encourage a summit conference. On April 10, the surprise announcement came that the leaders would meet for the first summit conference between the two Koreas. In June, Kim Dae Jung traveled to Pyongyang with an entourage of South Korean reporters and concluded a five-point agreement on peace; reunion visits for separated families; and for the expediting of economic, social, and cultural exchanges. For the first time, the two sides accepted that creating one system of government for all of Korea was a task for a future generation, agreeing only to work for a federation. It was, on the surface, an acceptance that the division of Korea into two very different states was a long-term reality. An exchange of family reunions occurred in August and September, and the North and South Korean Olympic teams marched together at the games in Sydney in the fall of 2000. Meanwhile, Kim Dae Jung's visit was followed by visits from Russian president Vladimir Putin in July, American secretary of state Madeleine Albright in October, and officials from China and the European Union. It appeared North Korea was breaking out of its long isolation.

The unprecedented visit of Kim Dae Jung to the DPRK caused great excitement in South Korea. But the high expectations that followed the summit were not met. When a groundbreaking ceremony took place in September 2000 for the construction of a rail link between the two countries, no DPRK officials showed up. Nor was there a follow-up visit by Kim Jong Il to South Korea as promised. Instead the DPRK placed more missiles near the border, apparently in an attempt to extract more economic aid from South Korea.[16] Relations became more strained in late 2001. Planned family reunions did not take place, and there was no significant progress in dialogue between the two Koreas. Partly this was due to the hard line the new George W. Bush administration took toward North Korea. The new administration was critical of the Sunshine policy, which they thought rewarded bad behavior. With the new focus on anti-terrorism after September 11, 2001, this policy only hardened.[17]

TENTATIVE REFORMS

In the wake of the economic crisis, major changes took place in North Korean society. Famine conditions in the mid- and late 1990s resulted in a partial breakdown in the carefully controlled public distribution system by which food and goods of various sorts were allocated. People were forced to look for food where they could find it. Small private plots appeared, and an informal market for agricultural products emerged. Even the movement of people, once strictly controlled, broke down as individuals wandered to wherever they could find food or work. Thousands of North Koreans illegally crossed into China, where they took whatever work they could find and smuggled money and goods back into North Korea. Many of these refugees in China lived under appalling conditions, but they often managed to earn money to bring back with them as they returned home. This contributed to a flourishing black market in food and smuggled goods. Authorities tended to ignore these developments. Still, those who crossed into China were subjected to extortion, intimidation, and arrest.

At first it did not appear that the famine would generate any basic reforms. Rather, the government's response to economic decline was to launch a new Ch'ŏllima campaign in 1998. This changed four years later with the currency reform. Partly to regain their tight grip over the economy and to obtain revenue by taxing this private market, the DPRK announced a series of radical economic measures on July 1, 2002. The reforms sought to bring the artificially low prices in line with real market values. Citizens were billed for items such as housing, food, and fuel that had previously been provided by the state at virtually no cost. Wages increased twenty times to compensate for these changes. The reforms placed North Korea on a more money-based economy and introduced economic incentives and accountability for managers. It appeared that the types of economic reforms that were introduced in China over the span of a decade were implemented here all at once.[18] The price reforms of 2002 were designed to end the distortion in the relative prices of goods, to eliminate the gap between state and market prices so that farmers would sell their products to the state instead of only in private markets, and to encourage the production of goods that could be sold abroad for hard currency. They may have also been intended to alleviate the drain on state finances caused by heavy subsidies on certain staples such as rice.[19] It also enabled the state to gain some control over the growing black market and to be able to tax it. The price reforms resulted in severe inflation. Wages could not keep up with items such as rice that increased fifty times in cost over the next year. This reform was followed by the creation of a Sinŭiju Special Economic District near the Chinese border, but this proved to be an aborted effort.

The change in direction was suggested by the elections in August 2003 for the new Supreme People's Assembly, which saw the emergence of more reform-minded technocrats. Pak Pong-ju (1939–), a former minister from the chemical industry, for example, replaced the older, less economically experienced Hong Song Nam (1929–2009) as premier. Pak had visited Seoul in the fall of 2002 for a tour of South Korean industries and was regarded as representing a younger, more pragmatic, and technically knowledgeable generation.[20] Instead of the highly centralized system of previous years, some economic decision making was transferred from the central government to local production units. Workers were evaluated on their productivity and the profit of their factories, and factory managers were now able to directly export products.[21] Already the state had permitted the sale of farm products, but by 2003 it was allowing the sale of consumer and industrial products. A mini-consumer boom appeared, at least in Pyongyang, where the ownership of bicycles and electronics increased. Even a few privately owned automobiles were sold, although traffic in the capital was still extremely light. There was even an underground market for videos from South Korea, as well as a black market for used players to watch them on. The food situation improved somewhat, as the economy experienced modest growth. Private markets were not limited to farmers selling their goods but state organizations and even the military engaged in market activity to raise revenue.

By 2005, the DPRK was asking the World Food Program to switch from relief assistance to development aid. Nonetheless, North Korea was still dependent on food aid. In 2006 this food aid still made up a substantial portion of its basic needs. Trade with the South increased, growing sixfold from 2000 to 2005. One thousand South Koreans crossed the border per day in 2005, and 3,000 were working in the North.[22] The year 2004 saw the opening of the Kaesŏng Industrial Complex, where a number of South Korean companies were opening plants that promised thousands of jobs for North Koreans. By 2011 there were 48,000 North Koreans at Kaesŏng working for 120 South Korean companies, although in that year troubles with the North Korean government and lack of profitability caused doubt about the long-term prospects for the industrial zone. The number of South Korean tourists coming to the North was expanding also, mostly to the Kŭmgang (Diamond) Mountain area near the west coast. Direct flights from Seoul to Pyongyang were inaugurated by the DPRK's state airline, Air Koryo.

There were, however, also signs that the DPRK was still less than fully committed to fundamental market reforms. In 2005, there was a partial revival of the state distribution system. The government tried to limit the private markets by prohibiting women under fifty and men from participating in them. Furthermore, in 2006, more floods, always a great threat due to the deforestation of the country, resulted in hundreds of reported deaths. The South Korean–based Buddhist NGO Good Friends, however, suggested the real death toll was 50,000.[23] Meanwhile, South Korea suspended tourism to Kŭmgang Mountain after a South Korean woman visitor was shot and killed by North Koreans in 2008 for straying beyond the area open to tourism, closing a lucrative source of foreign exchange for the DRPK.

North Korean society itself seemed to be changing. The division of the population into three classes: loyal or core, wavering, and hostile, and the *sŏngbun* system had begun to break down in the 1990s. By the early 2000s, it was gradually being replaced by more informal status categories based not on party membership and family background but on access to hard currency; connections with friends and family across the border; access to private markets and to private kitchen gardens; and money earned by women peddling greens, homemade food, and private livestock. Those with relatives in Japan that could send money or gifts also had an advantage. Thus many people of formerly low status were able to advance economically if not socially.[24] But not everyone benefited. Most remained very poor and malnutrition and the threat of famine were prevalent. Corruption became widespread with many officials and military involved in illegal trade or making profits by demanding bribes from those who were.

Especially tragic was the plight of North Korean refugees. The border between North Korea and China was never hermetically sealed. During Mao Zedong's disastrous Great Leap Forward, which brought about mass hunger in China, some ethnically Korean residents in Manchuria crossed into North Korea in search of food. With the famine in the late 1990s, thousands of North Koreans began crossing into China, walking across the frozen Tumen and Yalu rivers, bribing border guards and risking arrest to look for food and work in China. Many returned or made multiple trips, so the population was not stable, but at any one time there were as many as 200,000 North Koreans living in China, mostly near the border. They faced arrest when returning; many were sent to prison camps. The remainder became caught in an uncertain limbo, fearing punishment if they went back but living miserable and dangerous lives as illegal aliens in China. Many of the women entering China became victims of human traffickers, working in brothels, or becoming unwilling brides of Chinese suffering from a shortage of women.[25] Beijing refused to acknowledge them as political refugees or grant them asylum. China also denied NGOs seeking to offer assistance access to the North Korean community.

CONFRONTATIONS AND THE POLICY OF SURVIVAL

While North Korea was carrying out its peculiar economic reforms, tensions with the United States increased. Conditions for improved relations with Washington seemed less likely with the Bush administration, which was critical of South Korea's Sunshine policy of seeking accommodation with Pyongyang. President Bush labeled North Korea as one of the "axis of evil" in a January 2002 speech, and he told a reporter, "I loathe Kim Jong Il." Trouble with Tokyo also emerged. In September 2002, the prime minister of Japan, Koizumi, made a historic visit to Pyongyang, where the two sides signed the DPRK-Japan Pyongyang Declaration, in which North Korea accepted that Japan "keenly reflected" upon its past and "apologized from the heart" for the damage and pain inflicted by colonial rule.[26] In an ill-calculated gesture of goodwill, Kim Jong Il admitted that the DPRK had kidnapped thirteen Japanese citizens; eight had died and the remaining five could return to Japan. Japanese public opinion reacted strongly to this admission of what had long been suspected—that North Korean agents had come to Japan and abducted its citizens. This led to a deterioration in relations as Japanese public opinion became outraged over the DPRK's reluctance to repatriate the remains or allow children of abductees to visit Japan. As a result, Tokyo found it publicly difficult to provide any significant aid concessions.

The following month, a new crisis arose with the visit of the U.S. envoy James Kelly. Before the signing of the Agreed Framework, North Korea had clandestinely extracted about twenty-four kilograms of plutonium, enough for two or three twenty-kiloton bombs. Many foreign observers suspected that Pyongyang already possessed a couple of weapons. From 1994 to 2002 spent fuel was kept in storage ponds, and as late as July 5, 2002, the U.S. national security advisor, Condoleezza Rice, stated that her country was keeping to the 1994 agreement, although it was delaying the full implementation of the Agreed Framework until all parts of the agreement could be certified by IAEA inspectors. In November 2001, however, American analysts completed a report asserting that North Korea had begun construction of an enriched uranium plant. Kelly presented the North Korean authorities with the evidence that American intelligence had found of a program to produce highly enriched uranium. When the North Koreans appeared to admit (accounts of this are confusing) that they had been secretly working on a second path to developing nuclear materials, the United States reacted strongly and suspended the Agreed Framework.

One of the first casualties of this new crisis was the construction of the light-water nuclear reactors in North Korea. In 1995, the United States, South Korea, and Japan had created the Korean Peninsula Energy Development Organization (KEDO) to construct light-water nuclear reactors with a planned completion date of 2003. The countries ran into problems arranging the financing of the corporations, so construction did not get under way until 2000, a delay that angered North Korea and raised doubts about the sincerity of Washington, Seoul, and Tokyo. By 2002, several hundred South Korean workers were on the site pouring concrete, but soon after, work halted due to the crisis of 2003.

North Korea announced its decision to lift its freeze on nuclear facilities in Yŏngbyŏn and told IAEA inspectors to leave by the end of the year. On January 10, 2003, Pyongyang declared it was withdrawing from the Non-Proliferation Treaty of Nuclear Weapons (NPT), the second time since 1993. Perhaps nervous after the U.S. invasion of Iraq in March 2003 that removed the regime there, North Korea attempted to use the crisis as an opportunity to establish bilateral talks with the United States. In what it termed its "bold bid," it offered to eliminate its nuclear program in exchange for economic assistance, security guarantees, and diplomatic normalization. Bush's response was to state, "See, they are back to blackmail."[27] Meanwhile, the United States pushed for the Proliferation Security Initiative designed to impede the illicit trade of weapons of mass destruction (WMDs). Although the United States refused to meet in bilateral talks, seeing this as a reward for bad behavior, it did engage in a series of six-nation talks starting in August 2003. These involved China, South Korea, Russia, and Japan. All of North Korea's neighbors sought to cool the crisis. Over the next several years there were several rounds of six-party talks, but little progress was made. North Korea sought diplomatic recognition from the United States and an agreement not to use military force against it, while the Americans insisted on nuclear dismantlement first before any agreements were made. Meanwhile, the U.S. Congress passed the North Korean Human Rights Act of 2004, committing the United States to aid and protect North Korean refugees.

On July 4, 2006, North Korea test-fired a series of missiles including, unsuccessfully, a long-range missile potentially capable of reaching parts of the United States. In the fall of that year it detonated a small nuclear bomb. These actions were probably intended to increase Pyongyang's leverage in talks, as well as to draw U.S. attention to the need to negotiate with the DPRK. Both China and South Korea reacted angrily to the nuclear test, which created fears of a Northeast Asian nuclear arms race, since South Korea and Japan might feel pressured to develop their own nuclear forces. Yet there were no real reprisals. China, concerned that too much pressure on North Korea might lead to its collapse, followed by chaos on its border and huge numbers of refugees, was reluctant to place too much pressure. Consequently, it continued to provide some cheap oil and some economic support. Seoul shared the same fears, hoping that its trade and investment in the North would bring about a gradual transformation in that society, ease tensions, and make a future reunification less costly. Consequently, the South Koreans maintained their Sunshine policy, although they did make some cuts in aid. When the six-party talks resumed in 2007, the United States showed more willingness to meet bilaterally with North Korean officials.

In February 2007 North Korea agreed to shut down the nuclear reactor at Yŏngbyŏn and to permit IAEA inspectors to return. Pyongyang also agreed to "disable" all nuclear facilities and give a full accounting of all their nuclear programs. This was hailed by the United States and other countries as a great breakthrough. Washington agreed to return frozen assets held by the Banco Delta Asia in Macao; to supply heavy fuel oil; and, along with Japan, to move toward normalization. The United States also held out the carrot of taking the DPRK off the list of state sponsors of terrorism. There was concern among many nations that the DPRK might sell its nuclear technology abroad. This concern was reinforced by a nuclear facility the North Koreans were helping Syria to construct until it was destroyed by an Israeli air strike in September 2007. In a further agreement in the fall of 2007, the DPRK promised not to transfer nuclear materials, weapons, or weapons-making knowledge, suggesting the country was moving toward greater cooperation with the United States and other nations. IAEA inspectors returned, and in 2008 the main nuclear cooling tower at Yŏngbyŏn was destroyed. Still there was some skepticism within the United States, South Korea, and Japan over whether Pyongyang would ever give up its nuclear weapons or even cease production of more.

Relations with South Korea appeared to move in a generally positive direction, with exchanges between the two continuing. The increased trade and contact that followed the summit conference in 2000 between

ROK president Kim Dae Jung and Kim Jong Il in Pyongyang continued. In 2007 the two Koreas reached an agreement on a joint fishing area off the west coast of the peninsula and on developing the port of Haeju south of Pyongyang. The election of Lee Myung-bak (1941–) as president of the ROK in December 2007, however, changed the tone of the relationship. The new president was critical of the large but poorly monitored aid it was supplying and the DPRK's lack of significant political or substantial economic and social reform. Lee insisted on linking aid to reform, and as this was not forthcoming the ROK ceased supplying food and fertilizer. The shooting of a South Korean tourist in the summer of 2008 by a North Korean guard angered the South Korean public, contributing to doubts about how much the North really sought better relations. Tensions were again raised as Pyongyang launched a multistage rocket on April 5, 2009, in a trajectory that sent it over Japan. North Korea officially described it as a successful effort to put a satellite into orbit, but foreign intelligence services reported no evidence of a satellite, nor did the missile, potentially capable of reaching Alaska, travel as far as intended. But it sent a signal to the new Obama administration in Washington of North Korea's capacity to stir up trouble if ignored. On May 25, 2009, North Korea tested a second and larger nuclear bomb. The sinking of a South Korean naval vessel, the ROKS *Cheonan*, in March 2010 only added to Pyongyang's international isolation. On November 23 of that year North Korean artillery shelled the South Korean island of Yeonpyeong (Yŏnpyŏng), killing four people, including civilians, and injuring nineteen others. This act, the first such cross-border bombardment since the Korean War, outraged the South Korean public.

What seemed apparent was that the North Korean leadership had no clear plan except to survive. Their foreign policy had degenerated into little more than blackmail. Attempts were made to extract as much aid from South Korea and the United States and other countries as possible, creating crises and then moderating their behavior when concessions of food, fuel, and financial aid were offered. Meanwhile, North Korea's modest reform efforts begun in 2002 also seemed to be slowing down. Driven by fear of losing control of society, the government banned private trading in grain in 2005. Other attempts were made to limit the extent of the marketization of the economy, and restrictions were placed on the ability of workers to leave failing state-owned enterprises to seek work elsewhere.[28]

The DPRK still remained one of the most repressive societies in the world, possibly the most repressive. The elaborate system of state security developed under Kim Il Sung continued to keep watch over the population. A Ministry of Public Security administrated the police and watched over citizens. Those found guilty of political offenses were turned over to the State Security Agency, whose task was to monitor political behavior and thoughts and to oversee the prison system for political prisoners. The prisoner system was divided into reeducation camps for ordinary criminals and others for political prisoners. Life in the former was brutal, often involving forced labor in logging, mining, and tending crops. Prisoners reeducated themselves by such means as attending political sessions and memorizing the speeches of Kim Jong Il. Hunger, malnutrition, and starvation were common in prison camps, although they were also common among the general population. A separate system of camps for political prisoners existed that was estimated to hold 200,000 people, although some estimates were lower. These were even harsher, with prisoners unable to wash and wearing clothes until they were rags. Entire families were imprisoned, including children. Reports by refugees suggested these political prisons amounted to virtual death camps. According to the testimony of one survivor, most of the 6,000 persons that were in her prison in 1987 had perished by the time she was released in 1992.[29] Public execution of prisoners was common, especially in the late 1990s.The practice was reportedly renewed in 2007, after becoming less common after 2000. According to unconfirmed accounts, entire stadiums were filled with spectators required to watch them.

The government was also becoming increasingly corrupt. Members of the elite, the military, and the police were involved in black-market and smuggling activities or taking bribes from those who were. Informal transportation systems, using military or civilian government vehicles or the railway, distributed food and black-market goods. The market had become so lucrative for the country's elite that it was difficult for the state to control it. Various regulations to restrict market hours and limit the goods that could be sold proved to be difficult to enforce. Men were forbidden to engage in market activities, but an earlier ban to limit markets to women over fifty was modified to women over forty, and even this was not regularly enforced. By some accounts, private markets accounted for nearly half of all the food families received, much of it food aid stolen by officials. Other estimates are that more than half the household income of families came from private markets. However, the regime, apparently uncomfortable with the idea of flourishing private markets, made another attempt to control them. In late 2009 the government suddenly announced currency reform. The old notes were devalued by 99 percent, and people were allowed to exchange only forty dollars' worth of old notes for the new, the rest becoming worthless—an attempt to wipe out capital accumulation. This announcement was reported to have been greeted by rare displays of public anger. The government also banned the possession of foreign currencies.

At the same time, after having been told for years that they were the envy of their southern cousins, the North Korean people began acquiring knowledge of the outside world via those who had traveled to China, through pirated videos, through South Korean stations that could be heard on imported radios smuggled into the country, and through cell phones. This along with the pervasive corruption by civilian and military authorities threatened to undermine whatever public support there was for the regime. The scale of public cynicism was suggested by a series of interviews of refugees in China published in early 2008. The interviewers found that there was a widespread belief among the refugees that officials regularly stole or otherwise denied food aid to those in need.[30]

NORTH KOREA UNDER KIM JONG UN

From 2008 to 2011 politics revolved around the question of succession. In August 2008, Kim Jong Il suffered a stroke. When he reemerged in public his gaunt pallor and loss of weight indicated poor health. That the media showed him looking so unhealthy also suggested that the public was being prepared for a day when he would not be around. An urgent task was to prepare for that day. It seemed almost a necessity that the succession would remain in the Kim family. The entire ideology of the state was so centered on the Kim Il Sung family that it was difficult to conceive of how anyone outside the family could comfortably serve as the legitimate leader. Kim Jong Il designated his youngest son, Kim Jong Un (Kim Chŏng-ŭn), as his successor. Kim Jong Un was born January 8, either 1983 or 1984, the second son of Kim Jong Il's third wife, the Japanese-born dancer Ko Young-hee, and the youngest of Kim Jong Il's three sons. He entered an English-language International School at Bern, where he attended for several years but left in 1998. Back in North Korea he attended Kim Il Sung University, where he received a degree in physics and also received a degree at the Kim Il Sung Military Academy. Little was known about him until 2009 when rumors began that he had been chosen by his father as the successor. He looked strikingly like his grandfather, Kim Il Sung. His hair was cut in a similar style, and some South Koreans rumored that he'd had plastic surgery in order to enhance this resemblance. He made his first public appearance at the Third Party Conference, where he was appointed vice chairman of the KWP's Central Military Commission. On December 17, 2011, Kim Jong Il died, and on December 28, 2011, Kim Jong Un was declared Supreme Leader. Surrounding Kim Jong Un was an inner core of leaders thought to serve as the young son's mentors or regents. These included Kim Jong Il's sister, Kim Kyŏng-hŭi, and her husband Chang Sŏng-t'aek (sometimes written Jang Song Thaek). Kim Kyŏng-hŭi had long been close to her brother, and her husband at times had even been rumored as a possible successor.

Not long after taking power Kim Jong Un began to purge the military. During his first two years in power, about half of all the top-ranking generals were removed from their positions, including Ri Yong-ho, seen as one of the most powerful men in the regime. The most dramatic development was the purge of Chang Sŏng-t'aek from power. On December 8, 2013, he was shown on television being unceremoniously dragged from a Central Committee meeting. He was publicly charged with plotting to overthrow the government and shot four days later. This was unprecedented in several ways. It was the first known execution of a top leader in decades, it was the first time a top official was publicly arrested or tried since the purges of the 1950s, and it was the first time someone so closely related to the ruling family was known to have been executed. Speculation arose as to whether this meant Kim Jong Un was uncertain of his power, since his father rarely purged top officials while he was in power, or whether it represented a ruthlessness or even recklessness on the part of the young leader. Unconfirmed reports suggested that the animosity between Kim and Chang had arisen over conflicts over access to foreign exchange between rival patronage groups, and that Chang had developed his own independent power base that was a threat to Kim's absolute authority.[31]

Meanwhile, efforts were made to emphasize Kim Jong Un's place in the "Paektu Bloodline." In the spring of 2014 the ninety-two-year-old Kim Young Ju (Kim Yŏng-ju), the younger brother of Kim Il Sung and once a possible successor to Kim Il Sung, was named honorary vice-chairman of the Supreme People's Assembly. A powerless post, it nonetheless served to underline the continuity of the Kim family. Meanwhile, the Ten Principles were amended to include loyalty to Kim Jong Un. More special days were added to the calendar including December 27, Kim Jong Il's death day, and December 26, the birthday of Kim Chong-suk, Kim Jong Il's mother.

Despite the purges, in some ways the new transition in leadership resembled the previous one in 1994. No radical changes took place in policy and many familiar figures still populated the leadership ranks.

On February 29, 2012, in a "leap year agreement," North Korea would halt its nuclear program, open its nuclear facilities to international inspections, refrain from new missile tests, and agree to return to the six-party talks. In return the United States would supply 240,000 tons of nutritionally enriched foodstuffs such as biscuits. These special foods would alleviate the food shortage and would avoid the problem of monitoring where the food aid went, since there was little market value for these foods and they would not be coveted by the elite, as rice would be. The agreement was a verbal commitment, subject to somewhat different interpretations by the two sides, yet regarded as an important breakthrough. Almost immediately North Korea violated it when it announced plans for a missile test during the centennial celebration of Kim Il Sung's birth. In an unprecedented move, foreign observers were invited, but like the two previous attempts to launch a satellite from a multistage rocket, this failed. In December 2012 North Korea successfully launched a satellite. On February 12, 2013, the DRK tested another nuclear device.

In the spring of 2013 North Korea began manufacturing another crisis. Using regularly scheduled joint military exercises between the U.S. and ROK forces, it began to accuse Washington and Seoul of planning aggression against the DPRK. There was nothing new in these charges, but the rhetoric was more heated than usual. On March 7, Pyongyang threatened to launch a preemptive nuclear strike against the United States, calling it the "sworn enemy of the Korean people." The following day it announced that it was cancelling its non-aggression pacts with South Korea, closing the border crossing, and disconnecting the hotline. On March 13, it announced that it was unilaterally ending the 1953 Armistice. At the end of the month it actually cut the hotline, declaring on March 30 that it was in "a state of war" with South Korea. The DPRK declared that it "exercises the right to launch a preemptive nuclear strike in order to destroy strongholds of the aggressors."[32] Propaganda videos showed missiles destroying U.S. cities, and one that showed Obama in flames became an Internet hit. Significantly, North Korea withdrew the 53,000 workers at the Kaesong Industrial Complex, even though this was an important source of foreign exchange. On May 18 and 19 it fired four short-range guided missiles into the waters off the coast. The level of violent rhetoric went beyond that of the past. Yet despite the talk of war, observers in Pyongyang saw little evidence of the country being on a war footing. Soldiers seen in the capital in April were mainly busy planting flowers and sprucing up the city for Kim Il Sung's birthday. And in early June, the rhetorical attacks abated, and Pyongyang announced it was willing to open the first dialogue in years with the South. The Kaesong Industrial Complex was reopened in September 2013. Yet the regime maintained a constant state of tension with the South and the United States as it continued the practice of forging internal unity by creating a sense of being under siege by outside forces.

Kim Jong Un pursued what he called his "new strategic line," a policy of simultaneously increasing the country's military capabilities while pursuing economic growth. Of course, there was nothing new about this policy, which largely echoed the "equal emphasis" policy inaugurated in 1962. The poverty-stricken country was not able to maintain a credible balance to the South in conventional forces. Its military equipment was antiquated, short of fuel, and its soldiers often undernourished. It therefore looked for unconventional means. Besides nuclear weapons the DPRK invested in cyber warfare, creating a Unit 121. Despite that fact that North Korea was the only nation on earth not significantly connected to the World Wide Web, access being limited to a tiny group of trusted officials, it made some headway in this field. Its capabilities came as a surprise when it apparently hacked into SONY Pictures, an American affiliate of the Japanese corporation, in late 2014. This cyber attack came in response to the movie *The Interview,* a comedy about two Americans who assassinate Kim Jong Un. North Korea denied carrying out the hacks, but had warned the studio of the consequences of releasing the film. Following more threats, most theaters were afraid to show the movie and it was distributed on a limited basis. This Internet attack and blackmail raised the specter of a disturbing new form of terrorism. North Korea has also attacked South Korean Internet sites and attempted, with only limited success, to hack into the country's nuclear power stations.

The economic sanctions have increased North Korea's reliance on China since there are few other channels for trade or investment. Much of the trade with China is done through the neighboring provincial governments of Liaodong and Jilin.[33] A combination of geography and the growing demand in China for mineral resources encouraged investment in North Korea. The Chinese were particularly interested in the DPRK's considerable mineral resources. For a small country, North Korea is well endowed with minerals. It has globally significant deposits of iron ore, coal, limestone, magnesite, copper, lead, graphite, tungsten, zinc, molybdenum, and some gold. It may also have significant deposits of rare earths. A number of small and medium Chinese firms became involved in mineral exports. Beijing had begun to see North Korea as useful for its plans to develop the relatively poor northeast region. The largely forlorn Rasŏn Special Economic Zone in the extreme northeast corner of the country began to have greater attraction as an outlet to the sea since the port of Rajin was only fifty kilometers from the border. To encourage commerce in Jilin and to link it with North Korea, the Chinese government in 2009 launched a Changchun-Jilin-Tumen Regional Economic Pilot Zone, or Changjitu, with a goal of tripling income in the region by 2020.[34] As they invested in infrastructure they saw the port of Rajin as a key component. In the summer of 2012 Chinese tourists arrived in enough numbers that hotels were overbooked on the weekends.[35] But doing business in North Korea was not easy. As other investors had found, there was little rule of law, corruption was rampant, and regulations were subject to sudden and arbitrary change. However, China's economic ties with North Korea had a character different from those with other states. North Korea's proximity, its historical ties to China, and the special geopolitics of the region all led to concerns that it was becoming what the South Korean press called "the fourth Northeast province" (the other three being the Manchurian provinces of Liaoning, Jilin, and Heilongjiang; the first two form the border with the DPRK).

There were signs that the regime was making some cautious moves toward economic reform. North Korean officials were sent to China to look at economic reforms. There was also interest in looking at Vietnam as a model for reform. China carried out economic reforms after 1978 by giving greater economic independence to private producers—farmers, manufacturers, and local managers. But Vietnam's economic reforms carried out from 1986 were led and directed by party cadres, or at least to a greater extent than in China. In 2013 the state began implementing the June 28 Policy that reduced production units to household size and allowed farmers to keep up to 30 percent of their crop. In 2014 it issued the "May 30 Measures" to be implemented in 2015 reissues that would give farmers up to 60 percent of the crop. In reality, production was shifting to families. Furthermore, they increased the size of private family plots to 3,300 square meters, up from the tiny kitchen plots of only 100 square meters. Under a "director responsibility system," factory managers were given far more freedom to buy and sell materials. They were also given to power to hire and fire workers and determine pay scales. The reform measures had the potential to transform agriculture but it was not certain how effectively they would be implemented. The country desperately needed foreign capital, which, considering the international sanctions and the general wariness of doing business in the country, seemed unlikely.

Life remained grim for most North Koreans. Rations were still too meager to support most families. Rice could be purchased on the market, but one kilo in 2012 cost about what an average worker made in a month—that is, if he actually received his wages, which often was not the case. Talk of reform was only leading to climbing prices as many were hoarding food in the hopes of making greater profits. Food shortages were severe in much of the country, with the major exception being the privileged capital of Pyongyang. A United Nations report in May 2012 gave a grim account of malnutrition. It found nearly a third of children under five years of age suffered from stunting and asked for $198 million in food aid. The UN also found unheated hospitals lacking all medicines other than those they had received from relief administrations. DPRK officials made more open reference to the food shortages to their people than they had done in years. However, state media blamed foreigners for manipulating the prices of food and urged citizens to be self-reliant rather than look to outside powers for assistance. "Dry bread at home is better than roast meat abroad," a Korean Central News Agency editorial proclaimed.[36] In 2015, reports of some improvements as a result of agricultural reforms appeared to have been undermined by the severe drought that summer. The harshness of everyday life was suggested by the new requirement that students bring firewood to school to heat the classroom stove. Previously this was supplied by local government.[37]

Meanwhile, the prospects for unification seem to become ever less promising. Attitudes toward North Korea among the younger generation in South Korea had changed from a fashionable admiration by many college students and younger intellectuals to a disdain for what they regarded as backward and brainwashed cousins. By the early 2010s there were 20,000 North Korean refugees living in the South. They were smaller in statue, less healthy, less well educated, and suffered from discrimination. South Koreans associated them with laziness, irresponsibility, drunkenness, criminal activity, and seeking government handouts. Between 1990 and 1994 there were only 86 defectors, from 1994 to 2000 100 a year, and then more than 1,000 a year in 2002. The number began to taper off after 2011.[38] South Korean culture penetrated north. In 2010 the two biggest hit TV dramas in South Korea were reportedly both known and popular in the North. Girls Generation, a K-pop all-girls group, was also popular.[39] North Korea even tried to create its own tamer version of K-pop with a girls' band, Moranbong Band. The Kim Jong Un regime attempted to tighten control over the borders and crack down on South Korean videos, CDs, and DVDs. But with cell phones becoming more popular and corruption still rife it was becoming increasing difficult for the regime to insulate its people from the outside world.

Since the early 1990s outsiders had been predicting the collapse of North Korea. Yet, the state survived the death of its founder and that of his son and successor. It survived a catastrophic economic decline following the fall of its chief benefactor the Soviet Union, and an even more catastrophic famine. In the mid-2010s, the political purges and inexperience of its young leader, the continued economic failures, and the difficulty of keeping its population in ignorance of the outside world again called into question the long-term viability of the North Korean system unless it underwent radical change.

KOREA IN GLOBAL PERSPECTIVE: NORTH KOREA'S FAMINE

It is difficult to get a good idea of the scale of North Korea's 1995–1998 famine. Estimates of deaths vary from 200,000 to an unlikely 4 million and every point in between, although the careful estimates made by Marcus Noland place the number between 600,000 and 1 million. The lack of official statistics and the limited access granted to foreigners make for much guesswork. Still, the world was horrified at the sheer scale of starvation at a time when the state continued its nuclear weapons and missile program and extravagantly celebrated the birthdays of Kim Jong Il and Kim Il Sung and other special events glorifying the regime. The callousness of the regime to the suffering of its own people shocked outsiders.

Mass famines resulting from failed policies happened in other Communist regimes. The number who died from the collectivization of agriculture during the First Five-Year Plan in Russia 1928–1932 was appalling. Estimates vary, but from 6 to 8 million peasants perished. At least 1 million out of a population of 6 million died in Cambodia under Pol Pot in 1970–1975, most from starvation. The Great Leap Forward in China in 1958–1962 resulted in the greatest famine of modern times—20 million may have died from starvation in rural China; some calculations are even as high as 30 million or more. Proportionately, the scale of North Korea's famine may be no greater than that of Russia or China, and less than Cambodia. And unlike China, which never publicly admitted its famine, the DPRK eventually called for help from the international community. The nature of North Korea's famine also differed. While these other famines took place in the midst of upheavals caused by sudden implementation of radical new economic policies, North Korea's transition to socialist agriculture went fairly smoothly. It was only after several decades of accumulated failed economic policies that the country plunged into catastrophe. Furthermore, North Korea's famine, unlike the other cases, was partly caused by external developments, primarily the Soviet aid cutoff. It was also preceded and followed by a long period of chronic hunger. The greatest tragedy may be the long-term consequences of years of chronic undernourishment among the nation's youth.

KOREA IN GLOBAL PERSPECTIVE: NORTH KOREA AS A FAILED STATE

North Korea has often been described as a failed state whose demise was frequently predicted. With the collapse of the Communist regimes in Eastern Europe and the Soviet Union in 1989–1991, some in the West expected the DPRK of Kim Il Sung to go the way of the Romania of Nicolae Ceausescu, overthrown in a violent upheaval. The economic meltdown that followed the loss of Soviet aid in 1991 was also seen as a sign of a pending collapse. Yet the regime survived. Partly this was due to the ideological autonomy of North Korea, its *juche* thought increasingly stressing the uniqueness of the state, insulating it from the fall of Communism elsewhere. And North Korea was never part of the Soviet Warsaw Pact alliance. Like the People's Republic of China, and the Communist regimes in Vietnam and Cuba, it was able to survive. China's assistance greatly helped, and South Korea emerged as an economic prop, supplying generous aid. North Korea also made attempts at reforms. It appeared to experiment with a number of things: fenced-off tourist resorts for South Koreans to spend hard currency; the industrial zones for South Korean firms, also carefully fenced off; currency reforms; limited private markets; and some educational exchanges. Ideology was not an obstacle, since it had deviated so far from orthodox Marxism that almost any change of policy could be justified.

Yet if the DPRK did not collapse like the USSR, neither did it carry out sweeping economic reforms, as did China in the 1980s or Vietnam in the 1990s. There are a number of reasons for this. The country was too small to experiment with special economic zones that could be placed far from the capital and insulated from most of the country, as China was able to do. But more fundamentally, reforming the economy of North Korea would have been a much more difficult task than it had been in China or Vietnam. Both of those countries remained predominantly rural at the start of their reform process, with over 70 percent of the population still peasants, and their industrial infrastructure was relatively small. The DPRK, by contrast, was a highly urbanized, industrial society with only 30 percent living in the countryside and with a huge industrial labor force. Transitioning from state enterprises to the private market would have been more complicated. Furthermore, the country was to some extent trapped by its confrontational stance toward the major sources of foreign investment and trade: the United States, Japan, and South Korea. Nor did North Korea have a Deng Xiaoping who had been a victim of the erratic and disastrous policies of the previous leader. Kim Jong Il and his leadership were all products of the Kim Il Sung regime, had benefited by it, and were less likely to undermine a system that had personally served them well. Nor was there any great upheaval in North Korea, only an economic decline.

Another reason there were no major changes was that unlike the other Communist regimes, North Korea was locked in a rivalry with South Korea over claims to be the true Korea. The economic disparity in wealth between the two countries—estimates in 2015 suggested the per capita income of the South was as much as twenty times that of the North—threatened the survival of the regime. It was unlikely that the DPRK could compete for the loyalty of its citizens with the dynamic consumer economy and popular culture of South Korea, the latter being immensely popular throughout much of Asia. Then there was the fate of East Germany, which collapsed within days of letting its people travel to West Germany. In other words, the risks of opening the country were just too great for the leadership. The result was a survival strategy, using small concessions and nuclear blackmail as a way of coaxing maximum aid from South Korea and the United States.

North Korea is a failed state in terms of its inability to provide a decent living standard for its people or to adjust to the global economy. But the ruling elite maintain a firm grip on power. In this respect it most resembles Myanmar (Burma) prior to 2011, with its secretive, isolationist, and repressive rulers firmly in control of an economically failed state. Its inexperience in dealing with the outside world led to clumsy miscalculations, and it has shown a callous disregard for the welfare of its citizens. Its leadership, however, seems adept at survival. Its foreign policy is characterized by confrontation, but it shows no desire for a real conflict, in which the DPRK's antiquated armed forces would suffer disastrous defeat. The sheer scale of repression makes any kind of open opposition impossible. The general population does not have the organizational means or the access to knowledge to form a large-scale resistance and is too preoccupied with survival. Eventually the regime might collapse or undergo internal reform, but in the summer of 2015 neither was obviously on the immediate horizon.

"Publishing Comrade Kim Jong Il's *Brief History*," foreword to *Biography of Kim Jong Il: The Democratic People's Republic of Korea Official Biography*

Comrade Kim Jong Il, General Secretary of the Workers' Party of Korea, is the most faithful successor to the revolutionary cause of Juche, the Supreme Commander of the revolutionary armed forces of Korea and the great leader of the Workers' Party of Korea and the Korean people. In the first days of his revolutionary activities he set it as his lifetime task to complete the cause of Comrade Kim Il Sung, the great leader of the Korean people, and has scored immortal exploits [of] the Party and the revolution, for the country and the people.

The historical course of his leadership over the Workers' Party of Korea has covered the arduous and trying period in which the internal and external situation of the revolution was very complex and the Party and the revolution were faced with tasks more difficult and enormous than ever before. In the arduous days when the fierce class struggle between socialism and capitalism was waged amid the protracted confrontation with the allied forces of imperialism of the world, Comrade Kim Jong Il, as the closest comrade and most faithful assistant of Comrade Kim Il Sung, has always held fast to the banner of socialism, the banner of the revolution, and turned misfortunes into blessings and adversities into favorable conditions, thus leading the Korean revolution to continuous upsurge and brilliant victory.

Through energetic ideological and theoretical activities he systematized Comrade Kim Il Sung's revolutionary ideology into the ideology, theory and methodology of Juche, developing it to be the immortal revolutionary banner of the era of independence. He also worked out powerful ideological and theoretical weapon[s] for the Korean revolution by giving scientific and theoretical answers to the urgent problems arising in the revolution and construction.

He advanced the idea that the working-class party must become the party of the leader and put the idea into practice. In this way he brought about a fundamental change in the building, activities and work of the Party, strengthened the Workers' Party of Korea founded by Comrade Kim Il Sung to be a revolutionary party of the Juche type and improved its militant efficiency and leadership.

In command of the overall revolutionary armed forces he developed the Korean People's Army to be the genuine armed forces of the Party and the leader and to be the invincible revolutionary armed forces that staunchly safeguard the Party and the cause of socialism by force of arms and turned the country into an impregnable fortress in which the entire population are under arms.

He put forward a fresh line to imbue the whole society with the Juche idea and stepped up the three revolutions—ideological, technological and cultural—strengthening the single-hearted unity of the revolutionary ranks to be invincible. He ushered in a new economic and cultural construction.

Sharing joy and sorrow with the people at all times and through genuine popular politics, he has made the whole country a large revolutionary family in which all people are united around the Party and the leader. He has also shown deep concern [for] providing the Korean people with worthwhile and happy lives.

Through tireless revolutionary activities spanning over 30 years he ushered in a new era of prosperity for Kim Il Sung's nation of Korea.

The editorial board publishes Comrade Kim Jong Il's *Brief History* to help those who want to know the history of Comrade Kim Jong Il's activities.[40]

An Account of the Famine

By about 1996, the numbers of beggars thronging the markets had burgeoned. Tired, ragged children wandered through the city. People gave these beggar gangs the name *chebi*—"swallows"—because this bird, which leaves in the autumn and comes back in the spring, is constantly in search of warmth and food. First of all there were the *kotchebi*: the very young street children. They were called this because *kot* means "the bud of a flower." And Kim Il Sung, as I have said before, had announced that children were the "flower-buds of the nation." Then there were the adolescents, called *chongchebi* (*chong* means "youth"). Finally, the old people who begged for their food were called *nochebi* (*no* means "old"). The ones called *kotchebi* were children abandoned by parents who could no longer feed them, or who wandered the streets because there was nothing left to eat at home. Unless they had deliberately left the family home, tired of seeing their parents tearing each other apart in constant arguments over the shortage of food. Since it is traditional in Korea for a husband to expect his wife to cook for him, he would accuse her of mismanaging the household budget, of being lazy . . . and the argument would follow on from that. Famine-related rows were very common.

The famine encouraged the most selfish kinds of behavior. My grandmother sold soya dishes and soups, a little trade that helped her to survive. She worked not at the market but in her own home, and customers came to see her there. I remember one father who regularly came to my grandmother's house in secret to eat his fill far from the eyes of his family. He paid her with sacks of coal that he went and collected in the mines that had been spared from flooding, and urged my grandmother not to mention his visits to anyone. My grandmother preferred to be paid in money, but since this rather special customer had the same surname as us, she treated him sympathetically.

The customers who dropped in at the house sometimes spoke of the prostitution that had spread as a result of the famine, and the presence of wealthy Chinese traders. In many of the towns in the north—the border town of Namyang, but also Chongjin, Wonsan, Hamyung—girls of fourteen or fifteen were selling themselves for practically nothing. Prostitutes risked being sent to a penal labor colony, and recidivists could be sent to prison. Nonetheless, many of them continued to ply their trade, especially with army officers and Party cadres. Most of the cadres also had mistresses, usually widows, whose husbands had died of hunger. Everyone knew this, but no one spoke of it; particularly not the legitimate wives of the cadres, who feared that kind of opprobrium more than anything.

Apart from the market, the station was also a hideout for *kotchebi*. In normal times there was a daily train for Chongjin, but the shortage of petrol and electricity had reduced the rail service to one departure every two weeks. The Onsong-Pyongyang line sometimes took a month to reach the capital—as opposed to five hours under normal conditions. So the station was filled with people waiting for trains that never came. It had turned into a big dormitory, where destitute crowds slept night and day on plastic sheets that they had found who knows where. Skeletal children wandered through the waiting room, all of whom suffered from skin complaints. Some of them were very young: I remember kids of one or two who couldn't even stand upright. They walked on all fours on the filthy floor, picking up whatever they could with their black fingers. They put anything they found into their mouths to see if it was edible. There were so many of them that people no longer paid them any attention. At night some of these children, left to their own devices, slept in the station, and others took refuge in houses deserted by their occupants, who had either died of hunger or left in search of food. But in winter, the station was the favored spot for these desperate souls. Even if the building was not heated, at least the walls were a shelter against the freezing north wind.

—from *This Is Paradise! My North Korean Childhood*[41]

NOTES

1. Hyung Gu Lynn, *Bipolar Orders: The Two Koreas Since 1989* (Halifax, NS: Fenwood, 2007), 108.

2. Charles Armstrong, "A Socialism of Our Type: North Korean Communism in a Post-Communist Era," in *North Korean Foreign Relations in the Post–Cold War Era*, ed. Samuel S. Kim (Oxford: Oxford University Press, 1998), 32–55, 36.

3. Gi-Wook Shin, *Ethnic Nationalism in Korea: Genealogy, Politics, and Legacy* (Stanford, CA: Stanford University Press, 2006), 93.

4. "Tan'gun Remains Reportedly Found," *Korea Newsreview*, October 16, 1993, 30–31.

5. "Pyongyang—Capital of the Korean Nation," *Korea Today*, no. 2 (1995), 43–45.

6. Korean Central News Agency, broadcast March 13, 1998, *BBC Worldwide Monitoring*, March 14, 1998.

7. Brian Myers, *The Cleanest Race: How North Koreans See Themselves—and Why It Matters* (Brooklyn, NY: Melville House, 2010).

8. Adrian Buzo, *The Making of Modern Korea* (New York: Routledge, 2007), 175.

9. Kongdan Oh and Ralph C. Hassig, *North Korea: Through the Looking Glass* (Washington, DC: Brookings Institution Press, 2000), 52.

10. Andrew S. Natsios, *The Great North Korean Famine* (Washington, DC: United States Institute of Peace Press, 2001), 12.

11. Han S. Park, *North Korea: The Politics of Unconventional Wisdom* (Boulder, CO: Lynne Rienner, 2002), 93.

12. See L. Gordon Flake and Scott Snyder, eds., *Paved with Good Intentions: The NGO Experience in North Korea* (Westport, CT: Praeger, 2004).

13. John Feffer, "North Korea and the International Politics of Famine," *Japan Focus* (October 2006).

14. Marcus Noland, "Famine and Reforms in North Korea," Institute for International Economics, WP 03-5, July 2003).

15. Buzo, *The Making of Modern Korea*, 176.

16. Samuel S. Kim, "North Korea in 2000: Surviving through High Hopes of Summit Diplomacy, *Asia Survey* 41, no. 1 (January/February, 2001): 12–29.

17. Yinchay Ahn, "North Korea in 2001: At a Crossroads," *Asia Survey* 42, no. 1 (January/February, 2002): 46–55.

18. Yinchay Ahn, "North Korea in 2002: A Survival Game," *Asia Survey* 43, no. 1 (January/February, 2003): 49–63.

19. Ruediger Frank, "Economic Reforms in North Korea (1998–2004): Systematic Restrictions, Quantitative Analysis, Ideological Background," *Journal of the Asia Pacific Economy* 10, no. 3 (August 2005): 278–311.

20. Kyung-ae Park, "North Korea in 2003: Pendulum Swing between Crisis and Diplomacy," *Asia Survey* 44, no. 1 (January/February, 2004): 139–46.

21. Meredith Jung-en Woo, "North Korea in 2005: Maximizing Profit to Save Socialism," *Asia Survey* 46, no. 1 (January/February, 2006): 49–55.

22. Jung-en Woo, "North Korea in 2005," 52.

23. Feffer, "North Korea and the International Politics of Famine."

24. Feffer, "North Korea and the International Politics of Famine."

25. Kathleen Davis, "Brides, Bruises and the Border: The Trafficking of North Korean Women into China," *SAIS Review* 26, no. 1 (Winter-Spring 2006): 13–41.

26. Ahn, "North Korea in 2002," 49–63, 55.

27. Park, "North Korea in 2003," 139–46.

28. Stephan Haggard and Marcus Noland, "North Korea 2007: Shuffling in from the Cold," *Asia Survey* 48, no. 1 (January/February 2008): 107–15.

29. U.S. Department of State, *Country Reports on Human Rights Practices: Democratic Republic of Korea* (Washington, DC: U.S. Department of State, February 25), 205; see also Kang Chol-Hwan, and Pierre Rigoulot, *The Aquariums of Pyongyang: Ten Years in the North Korean Gulag*, Yair Reiner, trans. (New York: Basic Books, 2001).

30. Yoonok Chang, Stephan M. Haggard, and Marcus Noland, "Exit Polls: Refugee Assessments of North Korea's Transition" (Working Paper No. 08-1, Peterson Institute for International Economics, Washington, DC, January 2008).

31. Choe Sang-hun, "North Korea's Leader Is Said to Oust Uncle in Power Play," *New York Times*, December 13, 2013.

32. Martin Facker, Choe Sang-hun, Su-hyun Lee, "As North Korea Blusters, South Flirts with Talk of Nuclear Arms," *New York Times*, March 11, 2013.

33. James Reilly, "The Curious Case of China's Economic Aid to North Korea," *Asia Survey* 54.6 (November–December 2014): 158–183.

34. Drew Thompson, *Silent Partners, Chinese Joint Ventures in North Korea*, U.S. Korea Institute at SAIS, February 2011; http://uskoreainstitute.org/research/special-reports/silent-partners-chinese-joint-ventures-in-north-korea.

35. Andray Abrahamian, "A Convergence of Interests: Prospects for Rason Special Economic Zone," Washington, D.C. Korean Economic Institute, February 24, 2012, 69–80; http://www.keia.org/sites/default/files/publications/rason_sez_paper.pdf.

36. Jean H. Lee, "North Korean Hunger: Millions of Children Deprived of Food, Medicine, Health Care," Huffington Post, June 12, 2012.

37. Lee Sang Yong, "Residents in NK Devise Own Methods to Survive Harsh Winters," *Daily NK*, December 1, 2014.

38. International Crisis Group, *Strangers at Home: North Koreans in the South*, Report No. 208 (Brussels: International Crisis Group, 2011), 14–15.

39. Woo Young Lee and Jungmin Seo, "Cultural Pollution' from the South?" in *North Korea in Transition: Politics, Economy and Society*, Kyung-Ae Park and Scott Snyder, eds. (Lanham, MD: Rowman & Littlefield, 2013).

40. Democratic People's Republic of Korea, *Biography of Kim Jong Il* (Pyongyang: Foreign Languages Publishing House, 1998).

41. Hyok Kang with Philippe Grangereau and Shaun Whiteside (translator), *This Is Paradise! My North Korean Childhood* (London: Little, Brown, 2007), 121–25.

8

Contemporary South Korea, 1997 to 2015

By the early 1990s South Korea was entering the ranks of the developed countries and successfully negotiating the transition to a democratic society. But this did not mark an end to the society's rapid evolution. Many of the social and cultural changes that had been taking place in previous decades began to accelerate, creating a society that in many ways was a profound departure from its past.

RETURN TO CIVILIAN GOVERNMENT

The transition to democratization continued under the Kim Young Sam administration. In February 1993, Kim Young Sam was inaugurated president of the Republic of Korea, an important step in the country's democratization. Long one of the country's leading dissidents, he was now the first democratically elected civilian president in more than three decades. Kim was elected on the ticket of the Democratic Liberal Party, a coalition of the old supporters of the Fifth Republic, including those associated with Chun Doo Hwan and Roh Tae Woo, as well as a variety of other conservatives and moderate reformers. Kim Young Sam, an experienced and able politician, soon proved to be no puppet of the former military rulers. Using a corruption probe into the military, he forced many high-ranking officers to resign. In particular, he removed from key posts those associated with the secret and powerful Hanahoe society within the military, whose members included Chun Du Hwan and Roh Tae Woo. Kim reformed the Agency for National Security Planning, as the KCIA had been renamed

under Chun, curbing its domestic surveillance. As part of his reform image, he publicly disclosed his financial assets and had the members of the
cabinet and other high-ranking officers reveal theirs. This resulted in the
resignation of many holdovers from the Roh administration, including
the head of the National Police.[1] Kim Young Sam's main reform program
was aimed at the pervasive corruption in business and government that
not only offended the moral sensibilities of the public but was also seen as
a hindrance to the nation's transition into a modern first-world state. His
own reputation for personal honesty was his most important asset in this
campaign. In the summer of 1993, he passed the "Real Name" reform that
ended the practice of opening up financial accounts under false names.
This practice had been used to provide a channel for tax evasion, money
laundering, and bribery. All sorts of illicit financial activities by private
and public officials were carried out secretly through these accounts. The
reform was a step toward making South Korean business more transparent. These measures proved popular; his approval ratings soared to 90
percent in the first months of his administration.

After his first year in office, there was a lull in reforms; in fact, there
was relatively little fundamental reform under Kim Young Sam. This
was especially true in the economic structure. Some red tape was cut,
and some state-owned companies were privatized, most importantly
the Korean Electric Power Company. But the reforms were limited.
No major restructuring of industry or the banking world took place,
despite the fact that many businesses had become overextended financially. There were some halfhearted efforts to deal with this. A Chaebŏl
Specialization Reform was incorporated into the current Five-Year Plan,
and in line with this, in January 1994 the top thirty *chaebŏls* had to list
core industries that would be their focus. But this effort to prevent
overexpansion and needless duplication of investments was not implemented. The number of subsidiaries owned by the major *chaebŏls* actually increased 10 percent between 1993 and 1996.[2] Most significantly,
the same alliance of big business supported by loans from the state-
owned banks, the bureaucracy, and the ruling government persisted.
Labor continued to be restive, with some violent labor strikes by the
militant unions. Wages rose much faster than productivity, threatening
the competitiveness of Korean exports. One change was brought about
by international forces—South Korea was receiving increasing pressure
from the United States and the signatories of the Uruguay Round of
the General Agreement on Trade and Tariffs to open its markets. However, there was strong opposition from farmers and their sympathizers
against lifting the restrictions on the importation of many agricultural
products, especially rice. Kim Young Sam's administration also faced

student protests against government corruption or against what they perceived as the administration's anti–North Korean positions.

The limited nature of the reforms was highlighted by the fact that Kim Young Sam did not repeal the National Security Law. Like his predecessors, he found the broad powers it gave him and the vague definitions of antistate activity useful. And Kim was not afraid to use the police against protestors, including organized labor. To many observers the Kim Young Sam administration was looking more like the previous one. His popularity began to wane. Contributing to his declining approval ratings was infighting among members of his own party, which weakened his administration, and an economy that continued to grow but not at as fast a rate as in the past.

In one democratic reform, a local autonomy law was passed in 1994 that made mayors and county and provincial administrator officials elective and gave local government greater powers to collect revenue independently of the central government. This was a historical reversal for the highly centralized government of Korea. In the local elections in June 1995 that followed this reform, Kim Young Sam's DLP did poorly.

Perhaps to shore up his sagging support, in the summer of 1995 Kim began bringing charges against former presidents Chun and Roh, accusing them of corruption, of military insubordination, and of treason. The bitterness over Kwangju remained, and much of the public wanted those involved to be punished. Disgust at the former presidents was fueled by revelations that they had been guilty of stashing away vast sums of money. Roh, who was not as personally disliked as Chun, was found to have squirreled away $650 million in a so-called "governing fund" (*t'ongch'i chagŭm*). Investigations also revealed the close connections between the former presidents and the major *chaebŏls*. All nine of the leading *chaebŏls* had contributed funds, illustrating the depth of crony capitalism. Kim Woo Jung, the head of Daewoo, and Lee Kun Hee (Yi Kŭn-hŭi) (1942–), the head of Samsung, were indicted.[3] Chun was sentenced to death and Roh to life imprisonment, although both were later released.

The move buoyed support for Kim Young Sam's administration, and his party did well in the April 1996 National Assembly elections. His popularity soared in the opinion polls, but then, largely hurt by scandal, declined again. The president tried to reform business by introducing tougher campaign finance laws and requirements for high-ranking bureaucrats to register assets, but he was undermined by the Hanbo scandal that broke in early 1997. A number of his close associates were involved in accepting payments from the Hanbo Iron and Steel Company, which was seeking their help in keeping the heavily indebted, troubled company from liquidation. The taint of corruption was made worse by the conviction of Kim Young

Sam's second son for influence peddling. Meanwhile, labor unrest grew in 1996–1997, accompanied by a revival of student radicalism. In August 1996, 3,500 members of a radical student group that adhered to the North Korean position on unification and inter-Korean relations were arrested. Of these, 280 were charged under the National Security Law.[4]

Still, for all the problems, the economy was doing well. South Korea's GNP grew 7 percent in 1996, and that year marked its membership in the Organization of Economic Cooperation and Development (OECD), a thirty-member group of developed nations. Symbolically, South Korea had graduated from a developing country to the ranks of the wealthy developed nations. But the following year, events suggested that its graduation might have been too soon. The Hanbo affairs turned out to be indicative of deep financial trouble in many South Korean companies. Many had overexpanded, supported by low-interest loans from the state-controlled banks. The size of corporate debt by 1997 reached frightening proportions, just as the national foreign debt had in the 1970s and early 1980s. At the same time, South Korea was dealing with rising labor costs and competition from China. Several large companies, including Sammi and the distiller Jinro, were facing bankruptcy in 1997. In the summer of that year, Thailand underwent a financial meltdown, as its currency collapsed and the stock market plummeted. This set off a domino effect, as worried foreign investors in Asia's fast-growing developing economies began to take their money out. In October, the Hong Kong stock market collapsed. Stock prices fell sharply in Seoul, and then there was a run on the won, which as a result lost nearly two-thirds of its value. Suddenly running out of foreign currency, the ROK government in November was forced to call upon the International Monetary Fund (IMF) for help. An emergency package of $57 billion in loans and backup was quickly put together, the largest such measure ever created up to that time.

In the midst of this financial crisis, Kim Dae Jung was elected president on December 18, 1997, defeating the conservative candidate Lee Hoi Chang (Yi Hoe-ch'ang) (1935–) by only one-half of a percentage point. The election marked the first true peaceful and orderly transition of power from one political party to another. It was an important step in the process of democratization. The very fact that a politician so hated by the former military regime could be elected and inaugurated in an orderly manner, and that it was all taken routinely, was a sign of how far the country had moved in the past decade. In fact, the election was largely devoid of excitement. Kim Dae Jung was now in his seventies, making his fourth try at the presidency. He had his strong supporters in the south-western Chŏlla region but was viewed with less enthusiasm elsewhere. Enough voters, however, wanted a change that they were willing to vote for him rather than a member of Kim Young Sam's party.

ECONOMIC CRISIS AND RECOVERY

Kim Dae Jung had to deal with one of the country's worst economic crises. He began negotiating with international financial officials and working out a recovery plan before his inauguration. He then navigated the "IMF crisis," as South Koreans called it, with considerable skill. Kim was aided by the gravity of the financial crisis, which engendered a national consensus that the economic structure of the nation needed major reform. Under the "Korea Inc." system, economic growth had centered on the government-*chaebŏl* axis. This axis had to be broken. A number of measures were recommended by both Korean and foreign experts: leaner *chaebŏls* focused on core businesses with less diversification, more transparency in banking practices, and more flexible labor. Each of the big companies, Daewoo, LG, Samsung, Hyundai, and Ssangyong (SK), had expanded their tentacles into so many different businesses that they over-invested in plants, resulting in wasteful and unnecessary competition. Previous attempts at reform had proved difficult since the big *chaebŏls* regarded themselves as too big to fail, and they could usually rely on politicians who were concerned about protecting constituents' jobs and investments to intervene on their behalf. No matter how indebted the big conglomerates became, the banks could be counted on to lend them more money, since neither the banks nor the government felt they could afford to have the huge companies go bankrupt, thus their debts kept mounting. But restructuring businesses was difficult, since firms "doctored" their financial statements so much that it was difficult for banks to distinguish between good and bad loans.

Initially, the Kim Dae Jung administration made some real progress at economic reform. A number of banks were forced to close or merge, and there was some business restructuring. In the past, administrations had boasted of South Korea's negligible unemployment rate, and they were reluctant to see employees let go or companies go under. But this changed by necessity. President Kim Dae Jung worked out an agreement with the labor unions to accept cuts and layoffs. A tripartite presidential panel for labor, capital, and government reached agreement on reducing working hours from forty-four to forty hours starting in 2001. In a major concession to foreign pressure, the country's stock market and its real estate markets were opened to foreign investment. Foreign companies were allowed to take over Korean companies, including hostile takeovers. In a society that had long feared foreign economic domination, this was a radical break with the past.

The reforms were painful. Unemployment rose from 2 to 8 percent in a country with little in the way of a social safety net, where most households had a single breadwinner. Perhaps the personal embarrassment at losing a job was most difficult. The suicide rate went up 50 percent. A phenomenon known as *nosukja* appeared. These were unemployed men who slept in subway stations rather than go home jobless. Women seeking income turned to prostitution full- or part-time, until they numbered an estimated one million, and layoffs were sometimes accompanied by violence.[5] The won settled at a rate that was worth only half of what it had been, making the imports and overseas travel that Koreans so loved very costly. The economy contracted 5.8 percent in 1998; only once since the Korean War, in 1980, had this happened.

Yet, assisted by the low won, which made exports more competitive, the economy recovered. South Korea soon surprised the international community by paying off the emergency loans quickly. The GDP rose 10 percent in 1999 and 9 percent in 2000. The privatization of the huge Pohang Iron and Steel Company was completed, and a start was made at privatizing the electric power company, KEPCO. Both were important, since the reduction of the public company workforce was regarded as a necessary reform. The government attempted to improve the social safety net by expanding industrial compensation insurance to all types of workplaces, increasing the number of public pension recipients, and separating the prescription and dispensing of drugs to control costs. In August 2000, the IMF declared Korea's graduation from its emergency loan program. Unfortunately, the economic reforms ended too soon. After the initial emergency reforms, the banking and industrial sector did not undergo further substantive changes. Furthermore, before 1998 was over, the labor unions began resisting any further layoffs. And there remained a deep uncertainty about the future. A second round of financial restructuring in early 2000 was not completed. It was clear that the government was losing momentum in corporate reform. Other drags on the economy were the protracted sale of Daewoo Motors, which General Motors eventually bought; a decline of semiconductor prices; and oil price hikes. Efforts at economic reform also ran into problems over issues such as regulations on ceilings on investments and on the debt-capital ratio. Both business and opposition politicians opposed these proposed measures designed to contain corporate debt.[6]

Despite the incomplete economic reforms, and the tough competition South Korea faced from Chinese manufacturers, the economy in the early twentieth century continued to grow, if at a slower rate than in previous decades. By 2006, Koreans achieved what they called the *imanbul sidae* ($20,000 per-capita income era) regarded as a benchmark, meaning it had a level of economic development close to the OECD average. The government began a campaign to become the ninth member of the group of eight major world economies (G-8). It did succeed in becoming part of a G-20 of the major world economies during the economic summit in late

2008. Its exports in the 2000s surged, and it began accumulating a large foreign reserve. By 2008, it had become one of the world's major holders of U.S. debt, an impressive achievement for a country that had been itself in serious debt a decade earlier. South Korean products, especially consumer electronics, telecommunications equipment, and automobiles, had begun to acquire a reputation for quality. Indeed, the country was becoming a technical innovator that could compete with its Japanese and Western rivals in quality, design, and innovation. Yet the country had suffered from unemployment rates that, although modest by European standards, were historically high; its rate of investment was low enough to cause worry about future competitiveness; and it was still a manufacturing-based economy that was slow in making a structural shift toward a service economy. There was also a concern that the move to a more flexible labor policy and the neoliberal economic policies that the government had pursued, even if only partly carried out, were creating greater income inequality. This in fact became the case after 1998, along with less job security for workers who were no longer given virtually guaranteed lifetime employments. Future growth was also clouded by the fact that the "crony capitalism" that saw big business and government working in collusion had not yet disappeared.

DOMESTIC POLITICS

Kim Dae Jung's swift response to the economic crisis earned him respect among domestic and foreign observers. Long labeled a dangerous radical by his opponents, he proved to be cautious and moderate. He sought to reform the economic structure but not to change it. Ironically, for someone who had strong support among labor, Kim was forced to impose some sacrifices on labor by getting unions to accept layoffs and asking them to refrain from strikes. To the disappointment of some, he retained the National Security Law that had been used in the past as a means of jailing dissidents under its broad authority and vague definition of national security.

His party, the Millennium Democratic Party, or MDP, formed a coalition with the United Liberal Democratic Party of his former opponent, Kim Jong Pil. This very coalition with one of the stalwarts of the Park Chung Hee regime suggested the non-radical nature of his administration. In the April 2000 National Assembly elections, the two parties combined fell short of a majority, while the main opposition Grand National Party (GNP) also failed to get a working majority, so Kim Dae Jung's government ruled without control of the Assembly. After the elections, the heads of the two major parties, Kim's MDP and the GNP, met and agreed to the "politics of mutual survival." Nonetheless, the parties quarreled, and the result was that Kim Dae Jung's ability to govern was somewhat weakened. The need for the president to work with many different parties meant that Kim Dae Jung could not exercise the same degree of power as some of his predecessors, although the president still had enormous authority. The low voter turnout—only 57 percent voted in the 2000 Assembly elections—indicated both complacency and apathy. This was partly because the stakes seemed less momentous than in the past, but there was also a cynicism about the ability of politicians to make important changes. Another feature that was apparent was the strong hold of regionalism. The GNP won sixty-four of sixty-five seats in Kyŏngsang, the traditional southeast stronghold of the establishment, and the MDP twenty-five of twenty-nine seats in Chŏlla, the southwest support base of Kim Dae Jung and the region that had long been a bastion of political opposition. South Korean politics thus was based less on ideological divides than on emotional appeals to ties of home region and personal loyalty to individual politicians. A more promising sign was the active role of civic groups in discrediting candidates they saw as unfit to hold office and in rewriting election laws and monitoring the election process; especially active was the Civic Alliance for the 2000 General Elections.

The summit with North Korea and the awarding of the Nobel Peace Prize in the fall of 2000 momentarily boosted his popularity, but soon Kim Dae Jung's support began to decline. A number of problems, including the usual scandals, began to mar his administration. Close confidants were involved in insider trading, embezzlement, and stock-manipulation scandals. All three of his sons were involved in financial irregularities; one was sentenced to four years' imprisonment. His investigation of tax evasion by twenty-three newspapers in 2001, announced at a televised town hall meeting, drew charges of attempting to intimidate a mostly conservative and critical press.[7] A new medical prescription program was passed to assist with the country's modest and inadequate social safety net, but this ran into problems, as it quickly became apparent that there were not adequate funds for the program. Labor became restless and labor stoppages increased. And there was a general disappointment over the failure to follow up on the initial reforms of the country's business and banking structure. His administration also suffered from disappointment over the failure to see marked improvement in relations with North Korea following his summit and the opposition's continual criticism of his Sunshine policy. A particular blow was the resignation of the unification minister, who was thought of as the chief architect of the Sunshine policy, following the visit of some legislators to Mangyŏngdae, Kim Il Sung's birthplace.

In 2002, the ruling party held an American-style primary to select its presidential candidate. To the surprise of many, the winner was Roh Moo-hyun (No Mu-hyŏn) (1946–2009), a fifty-six-year-old human rights lawyer who won over Rhee In-je (Yi In-je) (1948–), the favorite of most of the party. Roh (pronounced No) was popular among what became known as the 386 generation: people in their thirties who had entered college in the 1980s and had been born in the 1960s. This generation was tired of the old-style politicians, many of whom had been active for a generation or more, and they were attracted to Roh, a political outsider, born in poverty, largely self-educated, with only modest experience in national politics but with a long and distinguished record as a fighter for social justice. His mostly young supporters formed the *No* (*Roh*) *sa mo* (gathering of those people loving Roh), an Internet fan club to generate interest in their candidate and as a vehicle to express their political views. Large numbers of young people campaigned for him bearing piggy banks, representing the small collections of money from ordinary people with which they sought to finance his campaign. Roh's nomination was challenged by Chung Mong-jun (Chŏng Mong-jun) (1951–), youngest son of Hyundai founder Chung Ju-young. Chung Mong-jun, handsome and charismatic, had served as cochair of the Organizing Committee for the 2002 World (Soccer) Cup that was held jointly in South Korea and Japan. South Korea did surprisingly well, coming in fourth place, and the games went smoothly. Chung was given much credit and was able to bask in the glory. The two agreed to a television debate in which the viewers would then decide who won, Roh agreeing to step down if he lost. The results were that viewers, by 46.8 to 42.2 percent, thought Roh won, so Chung withdrew. Chung then, at the last moment, withdrew his support for Roh.

Roh faced Lee Hoi-chang of the GNP, a sixty-seven-year-old former Supreme Court judge and veteran politician who had narrowly lost to Kim Dae Jung. Lee had strong support from older and more conservative voters but suffered from a series of embarrassing revelations. To the old problems of his two sons avoiding military conscription for dubious reasons were added new reports of his luxurious lifestyle. Also damaging was the revelation that his daughter went to Hawaii to give birth in order for his grandchild to acquire U.S. citizenship.[8] Roh had many liabilities as well. In a country that respected education Roh had never gone to college, although he had passed the bar exam. He held many unconventional views, made anti-American remarks, had a politically radical past, and had little administrative experience. He had a father-in-law who died in prison without ever renouncing Communism. Nor did he seem to have much knowledge of the world; he had never been outside of Korea. Nevertheless, the "Roh wind," as his enthusiastic support was called, was

strong enough, and Lee Hoi-chang was damaged enough, to give him a
very narrow win: 48.91 to 46.59 percent.

Roh Moo-hyun, an establishment outsider, created an administration of
outsiders. He filled his administration with people who had long records
in activism—many had gone to prison—but with little or no political experience. Many of his personnel came from the Lawyers for a Democratic
Society (*Minbyŏn*), an organization of young progressive lawyers. Among
his appointees drawn from this organization were his minister of justice,
a forty-year-old woman, and the director of the National Security Agency.
He also appointed professors from provincial universities and members
of various political watch groups to his administration. As did every
president, Roh created his own political party, the Uri (Our Open Party),
out of former members of the MDP and others.

Unfortunately the inexperience of Roh and his staff quickly became
apparent when he made many embarrassing remarks and political
blunders. Members of his administration also got involved in scandals,
including illegal political contributions from LG and Hyundai. He also
faced a rise in labor unrest. Farmers protested his efforts to establish
a free trade agreement with Chile as a prelude to further agreements,
including with the United States. Korean farmers with small farms depended on generous state price supports for their crops and feared their
livelihoods would be threatened by cheap imported foodstuffs. They
carried out dramatic protests, both at home and abroad. Although the
farmers and their families made up less than a tenth of the population
in this now overwhelmingly urban society, as in Japan and Taiwan, they
formed a powerful political lobby. Roh continued with Kim Dae Jung's
Sunshine policy, but his efforts were undermined by the revelation that
in his eagerness to arrange the summit in 2000 with Kim Jong Il the
former president had the Hyundai Group secretly offer North Korea
$500 million in economic development projects. Slumping in the opinion
polls, Roh announced that he would hold a referendum on December
15, 2003, on his performance and would step down if the voters disapproved of it. Opinion polls suggested he would win, since the voters did
not want to go through selecting another president so soon after the last
election, and also suggested that they did not want the referendum; neither did the opposition, and it was cancelled.[9] An effort to impeach the
president by the GNP backfired when public opinion strongly opposed
it and contributed to a strong showing by the Uri Party in the April 2004
National Assembly election, when it received a bare majority of 152 out
of 299 seats. With allied parties, Roh now had a comfortable majority.
Following this election, the constitutional court reinstated Roh, who had
had to temporarily step down during the impeachment proceedings.
But in 2005, the opposition GNP won almost all the by-elections, and

Roh's standing in public opinion fell to new lows; by 2006 he began to be viewed as a weak, ineffectual lame duck president.

Roh's party had carried out what has been described as an "ongoing cultural war in the South over policy toward the North."[10] The culture refers to the generation gap. Older voters looked at North Korea with great suspicion. Memories of the June 25, 1950, invasion and the terrorist acts committed since shaped much of their perception, while younger voters had much less hostility. The latter viewed the North Koreans as their poor cousins needing assistance. But although there were some nominal attempts to rehabilitate former radical patriots and other symbolic acts, the Roh administration marked no sharp change in South Korea's domestic or foreign direction. He sent troops to Iraq, supporting the alliance with the United States despite his history of anti-American rhetoric, and did not abolish or radically modify the notorious National Security Law. He even showed symptoms of the authoritarian tendency, seeking to intimidate the predominantly conservative major newspapers by threatening to pass laws that would limit their market share and make it easier for the government to sue them.[11]

There were some positive signs of a maturing democracy. Previously buried topics from the past were examined. The government established a Truth and Reconciliation Committee to deal with mass murders during the Korean War. The commission uncovered more than 1,000 executions, including 200 committed by U.S. troops (see below).[12] An investigation into the 1973 kidnapping of Kim Dae Jung revealed that Park Chung Hee approved it. However, some of the Roh administration's attempts to right the wrongs of the past were politically motivated; in particular, the examination of Korean collaborators in colonial times was directed at the new opposition leader Park Geun Hye (Pak Kŭn-hye) (1952–), daughter of Park Chung Hee, reminding the public that her father had served as a military officer in the Japanese Army.

In April 2007, the administration worked out a free trade agreement with the Americans, but this ran into opposition in the United States, where there was growing sentiment against open-ended free trade agreements, and in the ROK with strong opposition among farmers and various citizen groups. Meanwhile, 2007 saw a major scandal involving Samsung, now the nation's largest *chaebŏl*. Samsung was the symbol of a sophisticated, competitive, innovative, high-tech Korea. Yet the scandal, which involved the bribing of government officials for favors on a considerable scale, showed that crony capitalism was still alive and well.

In the December 2007 presidential election, Lee Myung-bak (Yi Myŏng-bak), the Grand National Party candidate, easily defeated the ruling party candidate, Chung Dong-young (Chŏng Tong-yŏng) (1953–), who was handicapped by President Roh's unpopularity. A former Hyundai executive and popular mayor of Seoul, Lee Myung-bak had been nicknamed "the bulldozer" for his assertive, energetic, can-do attitude. Lee promised to accelerate economic growth and to close the economic gap between South Korea and the richest countries. His pledge to put the nation back into the fast track of economic development appealed to many voters, as, despite the 5 percent growth rate, the public was worried about the economy. Lee won in a landslide election and then saw his public approval plunge in the first several months in office. He announced his "747 plan" to achieve 7 percent growth, to reach $40,000 per capita income in 2012, and to be by then the world's seventh largest economy. This was to be achieved in part by combining pro-business policy, lessening regulations on big business, streamlining the bureaucracies, selling off state enterprises, and pushing for a number of major infrastructure projects, including the Four Rivers Project, an inland canal system. His policies failed; his economic targets were derailed by the Great Recession of 2008, and by resistance from a public often infuriated by the heavy-handed authoritarian manner in which he attempted to implement these policies. In April 2008, when he unilaterally ended the ban on imported U.S. beef, the anger spilled out into massive public protests. In addition, the high fuel, food, and commodities prices that the resource-poor nation was facing meant that rather than entering another boom, the ROK was looking to face slower growth, if not recession. The demonstrations, mostly peaceful candlelit affairs, were still disruptive, and the efforts by some organizers to use mass mobilization to bring down a newly elected president disturbed some observers who saw them as a sign of South Korean democracy's lack of maturity. However, there was no serious likelihood that the verdict of the polls would be overturned, and Lee's unpopularity was largely the product of his style of governing, which reminded the public of its authoritarian past.

He was succeeded by his GNP revival Park Geun-hye (Pak Kŭn-hye) (1952–), daughter of Park Chung Hee. In December 2012 she defeated the opposition candidate Moon Jae-in, Roh Moo-hyun's former chief of staff, in a close election that divided along generational lines. She won overwhelmingly among over-fifty-year-old Koreans, many now viewing her father's rule with nostalgia, and lost heavily among younger voters. She promised a moderate administration, expanding the social safety net and reining in the powerful *chaebŏls* while fostering economic growth. In 2013 Park began to promote "the creative economy," preparing the country for the post-industrial age. Her administration, however, suffered from lackluster economic growth and from what the public perceived as an inept government response to the April 16, 2014, Sewol ferry disaster in which 304 died, mostly high-school students on an excursion. Nor was there much progress toward reining in the power of the *chaebŏls*.

An interesting development in South Korean politics was the growth of NGOs, which had become a major force in South Korea. Exploding in number in the 1980s, NGOs were instrumental in shaping national debates and policies on key issues. Some were quite large and powerful. The Citizen's Coalition for Economic Justice, formed in the summer of 1989, campaigned for a more equitable distribution of income and against corruption in government. The Korean Women's Association, formed in 1987, became an effective champion of women's equality. The Korean Federation of Environment Movements, organized in 1993, conducted several successful antipollution campaigns and forced Taiwan to cancel a nuclear waste deal with North Korea.[13] Beginning in 1992, the Citizens Coalition for Fair Elections kept close track of future elections, investigating the dubious connections and qualifications of candidates. In 1999, a group organized the Citizens' Groups' Solidarity Roundtable for Judicial Reforms, and later a number of small groups coalesced to form the Citizens Solidarity for the General Election, which created lists of politicians not to be nominated or elected because they had been involved in corruption, bribery, or human rights abuse activities. After 2000 there was a marked growth of NGOs based outside of Seoul. Very few South Korean NGOs had foreign links; they were locally organized, for the most part led by moderate middle- and working-class Koreans, and played an important role in consolidating democracy within the country.[14]

FOREIGN POLICY

South Korea's foreign policy in the early twenty-first century faced two major issues: how to deal with North Korea, and how to adjust itself to the realities of a rising China. While no longer a mere client state, South Korea's relationships with the United States were still fundamentally important, as were those with Japan, and the country sought to play a larger role in the global community. Kim Dae Jung's major initiative in foreign policy, his so-called Sunshine policy, resulted in the summit conference with Kim Jong Il in Pyongyang in June 2000 and earned Kim Dae Jung the Nobel Peace Prize that fall. The aftermath of the summit resulted in a lively debate in the South. Conservatives were skeptical of any real change in the North, viewing this as only one in the long series of tactical moves that had led to many false starts in improved relations, such as in 1972, 1984–1985, and 1990–1991. The government countered by arguing that there was no reasonable alternative but to try to gradually open the North to international trade and investment. The Sunshine policy was a truly radical shift in foreign policy, a break with the nearly half century of hostility South Korea had maintained toward the North. It was in part a product of growing confidence in the ROK, as well as a concern for the possibility that the DPRK could collapse and bring chaos to the peninsula. Initially, there was great excitement; among some, especially the young, there was even a short-lived enthusiasm for Kim Jong Il. From 2001, however, the Sunshine policy was bringing a disappointing return, and it became clear that the summit that had excited the South Korean public would not be a turning point. It was, however, not an entirely false start, and trade and investment between the two countries grew, haltingly but significantly.

Besides his North Korean policy, Kim Dae Jung initially maintained good relations with China, Japan, and the United States. However, with the inauguration of George W. Bush in 2001, relations with the United States became more strained. The Bush administration was scornful of the Sunshine policy, which it regarded as rewarding bad behavior, and sought to take a hard line against North Korea. After September 11, 2001, the U.S. focus on terrorism and its labeling of North Korea as a terrorist state and a member of the "axis of evil" provided a less comfortable international environment for the Kim Dae Jung administration's foreign policy. To some extent, the ROK worked at cross-purposes with the United States after 2002. South Korean presidents Kim Dae Jung and Roh Moo-hyun held to the idea that the best way to deal with North Korea was to open the country up into trade and development. They encouraged South Korean investment in the North and provided generous foreign aid, while the United States sought to isolate the regime. Under president Roh, aid and investments in the North continued to grow, despite mixed results in improving relations. He rejected conservative critics in his own country that this had to be linked to demonstrative progress on the part of the DPRK in improving its human rights record, reducing its military buildup along the border, working toward denuclearization, carrying out substantial economic reforms, and allowing more family reunifications. The last was still a sensitive issue, especially for the older generation. Many South Koreans, perhaps as many as three-quarters of a million, had relatives in the North.[15]

While there was little progress in these areas, Roh went ahead with a second summit meeting in Pyongyang in October 2007. Roh Moo-hyun and Kim Jong Il agreed on the construction of two shipyards in the North; on improvements in North Korea's railway system, which would make future rail links between South Korea and China easier; and to work toward more joint representations at international events. Tensions increased in 2008 with the inauguration of President Lee Myung-bak, a critic of the Sunshine policy. Lee made public comments critical of the North's human rights record, its failures at reform, and its military-first policies. This in turn resulted in angry and threatening responses from Pyongyang. Relations with the North worsened in 2010 with the sinking of the destroyer *Cheonan (Ch'ŏnan)* in March and the shelling of the South Korean island of Yeonpyeong (Yŏnp'yŏng) by DPRK artillery in November. The latter incident in particular caused public outrage. Brief hopes of a more liberal turn under Kim Jong Un were quickly dashed by the third nuclear detonation in February 2013 and the barrage of exceptionally bellicose anti-Seoul rhetoric in the spring of that year. Pyongyang cut the hotline between the two capitals and closed the Kaesŏng Industrial complex for several months. Relations improved marginally later in the year but a generally wariness in dealing with the North characterized the mood in the South.

Several other issues made for difficulties in foreign relations. Seoul had to deal with the issue of the tens of thousands of North Korean refugees in China. Many of them made spectacular and dangerous attempts to make it into the ROK's Beijing embassy in an effort to seek asylum in the South. The refugee problem was a touchy issue. The Chinese were strongly opposed to granting asylum, and Seoul did not want to anger China or jeopardize improved relations with the DPRK, so at first it ignored the plight of these desperate people fleeing poverty and repression. The ROK, however, was forced to accept refugees in light of international publicity about their plight. South Koreans remained ambivalent about these new arrivals to their country, fearing their settlement might encourage even more to come.

A newer challenge for South Korean foreign policy was the rise of China. While most Koreans initially greeted its economic rise as a positive development, frictions arose. One dealt with history. In China, the work produced by the Northeast History Project, a government-funded program that supported archaeological and historical research in Manchuria, led to Chinese claims that the ancient kingdom of Koguryŏ was a Chinese state. This angered many Koreans, not only extreme nationalists who used the boundaries of Koguryŏ as a basis for claiming that most of Manchuria was once Korean territory, but all Koreans, for it implied that northern Korea itself was once Chinese. The issue aroused passions in Korea. By 2004, it had become a thorn in the relations between the two countries and a cause of concern among Koreans over their increasingly powerful neighbor.[16] The Roh, Lee, and Park administrations all maintained cordial relations with China while remaining wary of its military rise. The latter became particularly concerned in 2013 when Chinese leader Xi Jinping pursued a more assertive policy overseas. In the fall of 2013, Beijing declared an air defense identification zone that required all planes flying over a large area of sea south of the country to identify themselves, a move that was in violation of international law and was ignored by Seoul. Despite South Korean anger over this assertion of power, Xi Jinping visited Seoul in July 2014, the first time a Chinese leader had visited the South before visiting the North. Both Park and Xi reaffirmed their support for a nuclear-free Korean Peninsula and for the expansion of trade agreements.

The growing importance of China was most striking in its economic relations. Trade with China grew dramatically in the 2000s. In 2004, exports to China, led by the country's demand for steel, were up 48 percent in that year alone; China by then had displaced the United States as South Korea's largest trading partner. By 2012 bilateral trade reached $215 billion. South Korean firms were moving much of their manufacturing to China, taking advantage of lower labor costs and geographical proximity. In June 2015, Beijing and Seoul signed a free trade agreement that promised to greatly expand trade between the two countries. Tourism flourished in the 2010s as millions of Chinese began to pour into the country to sightsee and shop. Yet there was no consensus over exactly what direction the country's foreign policy should be regarding its huge neighbor, with some Koreans worried about possible Chinese attempts to establish hegemony over the region, including a possible takeover or absorption of the North.

South Korea's relations with the United States were complex. Most of the older generation remained pro-U.S., distrustful of the DPRK, and cautious about relations with China. But anti-Americanism was in the early 2000s strong among the younger generation. Yet when the United States announced in 2003 and 2004 its plans to reduce troops in Korea by a third, opinion polls showed that most Koreans accepted the need for a U.S. alliance and were not enthusiastic about the withdrawals. Economic ties with the United States were still important, with American firms by far the top investors in the country. The South Korean government, even under the left-of-center president Roh Moo Hyun, supported the Global War on Terror, including $45 million during 2002–2004 for reconstruction in Afghanistan. In February 2004, the National Assembly voted 155 to 50 to dispatch 3,600 troops to Iraq, the third-largest contingent, despite strong public opposition to the war. The enormous unpopularity of President Bush contributed to troubled relations. Under Barack Obama the United States sought to maintain good relations with Seoul to help balance the rise of China, and most Korean policy makers understood the usefulness of having an actively engaged Washington in their part of the world. The United States was now seen less as a big brother (and sometimes bully) than as a useful partner with which South Korea shared a broad range of security as well as political, cultural, and economic interests.

South Korea's foreign policy had always been closely aligned with U.S. foreign policy. There was also a belief that geopolitics in Asia were shifting, with an emerging Chinese superpower likely to play the dominant regional role in the near future. Rather than rely on the U.S.-Japanese alliance, some South Koreans felt that they should seek to create a more independent military force and that the country's foreign policy should accommodate or at least recognize China's needs and interests more. Nonetheless, ties between the two countries remained strong. Anti-Americanism seemed to be waning. Bilateral trade flourished, and a free trade agreement was signed in 2012 after years of negotiations. The United States remained the favorite destination for students in the 2010s, and many families had relatives in America.

South Korea maintained strong economic ties with Japan but the relationship continued to be haunted its troubled past. In April 2001, a new Japanese-government-approved history textbook angered Koreans, who claimed it presented distortions about the past. In the view of most Koreans, this was part of the failure of Japan to fully acknowledge the injustices it had perpetrated against Korea in the past. This was reinforced by occasional visits by Japanese prime ministers to the Yasukuni Shrine, where a number of World War II military leaders were buried. The dispute over the island of Tokto in the Sea of Japan, which the Japanese called Takeshima and held a territorial claim to, was another irritant. In 2013 the new prime minister, Abe Shinzo, pursued a more nationalistic interpretation of history that outraged most South Koreans and plagued the relations between the two countries. These tensions hindered efforts by the United States to develop strong trilateral military and political cooperation between Seoul, Tokyo, and Washington as a counterweight to China.

South Korea, both its leaders and the public, sought to play a larger role in world affairs as a contributor to international peace, security, and progress. The country became an active member of many international organizations. It contributed peacekeepers to Lebanon, South Sudan, and Haiti. It became a major donor nation providing assistance to poorer nations. An example was World Friends of Korea, South Korea's equivalent to the U.S. Peace Corps. It was inaugurated in 1990, and in 2013 it had 3,000 volunteers serving on aid projects in scores of poor countries in Africa, Asia, and Latin America.[17]

RETHINKING REUNIFICATION

A significant change in South Korea was the attitude toward reunification. The public was no longer as enthusiastic about reunification as it had been in the past. In the years after 1953 nearly every South Korean dreamed of uniting the two states. They began to reconsider this after the reunification of Germany in 1990, when the problems and costs of unification became apparent. The growing disparity in income and the widening gap in culture and lifestyles between the two societies made the process and costs of absorbing the North and its 24 million people even more daunting. Whereas East Germans had a per-capita income of over one-third of West Germans at the time of reunification, it was estimated that North Korea had only one-fifteenth to one twentieth the GDP per capita of the South in 2015. The differences in the two economies can be seen in the volume of international trade. In 2014, the total foreign trade, exports and imports, of North Korea was about US$10 billion compared to South Korea's more than US$1.1 trillion. The total power generation of North Korea was only 1 percent of that of the ROK. This shocking disparity would be enormously costly to overcome. By some estimates, reunification would cost at least US$1 trillion. What South Koreans now sought was reform in the DPRK and a gradual integration of the economies of the two Koreas. But indications were that cultural integration would be difficult as well. In 2015, there were already more than 20,000 North Korean refugees living in the South, where they were handicapped by the lack of appropriate job skills and work habits and suffered discrimination from their South Korean neighbors.

A SOCIETY UNDERGOING RAPID CHANGE

South Korea in the first decade of the twenty-first century was a society still undergoing rapid change. As was the case with its economic development, a social transition that took decades in most other countries occurred over a relatively few years. One of the most dramatic changes was demographic. The once high birthrate fell sharply in the 1960s with a government-sponsored birth-control program. By 1983, it was only slightly above the replacement level, with women having an average of about 2.1 children. Other changes also contributed to the creation of a two-child norm by the end of the 1980s. The urbanization of the population, now crammed into small apartments and townhouses; the enormous expense of education; and the high literacy rate of women were important. Cultural norms changed as well in what was still a rather conformist society. Increasingly, a small family with a son and a daughter had become the ideal. However, by the late 1990s the birthrate continued to fall, dropping below the natural replacement rate. The sharpest drop was in the five-year period 1997–2002, blamed on the economic crisis of the late 1990s. But the return of good economic conditions did not reverse this trend. In 2004, the birthrate had fallen to 1.08, one of the lowest in the world, even lower than Japan's 1.3 rate, which was the cause of so much concern there. Although this rose a bit by 2014 to 1.2, it was the third lowest among sovereign countries—only Taiwan and Singapore were lower—and alarmingly below the replacement rate.[18] As a result, South Korea's population, which stood at 51 million in 2015, was expected to decline to 40 million by 2056 and 20 million in 2100. A 2014 parliamentary study went even further, predicting Koreans would become extinct in 2750.[19]

This led to a related problem of an aging society. South Koreans were living longer; life expectancy had reached about seventy-five for men and eighty-two for women in 2008 and was still rising, but the birthrate was dropping. As a result, South Korea was rapidly becoming an "aging society" with 14 percent of its population over sixty-five in 2015, and the number was expect to rise to 25 percent by 2030 and 38 percent by 2050, which would be one of the highest, if not the highest, in the world. At that time there would be only 1.4 adults of working age for every senior citizen. The workforce was expected to shrink after 2016.[20] Becoming the world's fastest-aging society was becoming the nation's greatest challenge. The government responded by passing a law in 2013 making sixty the minimum retirement age, and it began providing financial subsidies for parents with multiple children. Local governments came up with many incentives, offering bonuses for a second and third child, and offering free babysitting services. The government discouraged abortions. It also called for lowering housing costs, work/childcare balance, and reducing the costs of weddings. At the same time there was concern over the rising poverty levels among those over sixty-five, reported in 2015 to be three times the national average.[21]

A major factor contributing to the low birthrate was the cost of education. The zeal for education, what Koreans called their "education fever," was a factor in the country's remarkable economic and social transformation, and it remained in the early twenty-first century one of its greatest assets. In 2012, 98 percent of all twenty-five- to thirty-four-year-olds had completed upper-secondary education, the highest percentage of the thirty members of the Organization for Economic Co-operation and Development (OECD) representing the developed, industrialized nations. Sixty-three percent of this age-group had completed some form of tertiary education, also the highest of any OECD country. Educational levels, in terms of percentage of students completing secondary school and going on to tertiary education, were among the highest in the world.[22] The quality of education improved as well with South Korean primary and secondary students consistently scoring near the top in international comparative tests of math, science, and reading skills. In fact, South Korea's educational system received international praise, from U.S. President Obama to Pearson, a British-based educational service organization that in 2013 ranked it the best in the world.[23] As impressive as these achievements were, they had many problems. Education remained strongest at the lower levels, but at the tertiary level research facilities had not reached the standards of the world's best universities. Importantly, this educational achievement came at enormous costs. The financial burden of education on families was heavy. In addition to private tutoring and after-class cram schools, many middle-class parents began sending students abroad to attend high school with families in the United States or other English-speaking countries so that they could master English, an important skill. Numerous surveys found that South Korean families spent a higher proportion of their income on schooling than any other people in the world. The costs threatened to undermine efforts at promoting equal opportunity in a society concerned not to replicate its long history of hereditary inequality.

But these were not the only costs of education. The preoccupation with education placed enormous stress on young people, who studied from early morning to late at night, causing some experts to wonder if South Korean students were being robbed of childhood. Furthermore, it was a major contributing factor in the low birthrates. Most studies suggested that the high cost of educating children resulted in Koreans putting off marriage until fairly late and deciding to have only one child. Since the mother's role in supervising education became almost a full-time job, this also inhibited women from entering the job market and the professions. Much of the preoccupation with education focused on obtaining prestige degrees. The national obsession for academic credentials is common in many societies but it seemed to have reached an extreme in South Korea. The problem was highlighted in 2007 in what was called the "Shingate scandal." A thirty-five-year-old art professor, Shin Jeong Ah (Sin Chŏng-a), who had risen to prominence in the Korean art world in large part due to the influence of her lover, a presidential advisor, was found to have a fake degree from Yale.[24] This led to revelations of many prominent people who had falsified their degrees. In many cases they possessed genuine credentials that seemed quite acceptable, but in a society that rewarded "brand" diplomas, these otherwise qualified people found it worth the risk of faking more prestigious degrees.

The rising costs of education contributed to a disturbing trend toward greater income inequality. One of South Korea's proud achievements after the Korean War was a burgeoning middle-class society with a more even distribution of wealth than was found in most countries. The 1997 economic crisis reversed this trend. More frequent layoffs, the greater use of temporary workers who received less pay and fewer benefits than permanent employees, and the move toward a more knowledge-based society all contributed to a shrinking middle class, greater poverty, and an ever-wealthier upper-middle class. One measure of income equality was the Gini coefficient, based on disposable income. In this measurement, the lower the number, the more equitable the income distribution. The number had lowered steadily since the 1970s, and in 1997 at .283 it was low by international standards but rose to .311 in 2011, lower than the United States or Japan but higher than the EU average.[25] The middle class may have been shrinking. As early as the 1980s, most of the public called themselves middle class in surveys. By the mid-1990s between 70 and 75 percent of adults considered themselves as such. A myth emerged that all South Koreans were becoming part of a single, large middle class, with economic and social class lines disappearing. However, the number of those who regarded themselves as middle class fell to 55 percent in 2015.[26]

There were various signs that reality was moving away from the dream of a single middle-class society. People from well-to-do families tended to marry others from wealthy families. In a country where a prestige degree still offered so many advantages, the accelerating cost of tutoring placed children with less wealthy parents at a growing disadvantage. While disparities in South Korea were still less than in many other countries, including the United States, Koreans were fearful of replicating the inherited privileged status groups that had characterized so much of their past. It was not an unreasonable fear, since the economic elite tended to intermarry, and an enormous amount of wealth was controlled by a relatively small number of these families. By one measure, thirty leading *chaebŏl* families controlled 40 percent of the economy in the 2000s. Meanwhile, as was common with many developed nations, South Korea's move into the knowledge economy was threatening to create a huge gap between highly skilled professionals and less educated industrial and clerical workers. Industries were moving production offshore, to China, Vietnam, and elsewhere, while trying to be lean and efficient at home by reducing payrolls and hiring more temporary workers. A great gap was emerging between regular workers on long-term contracts with full benefits and relative security and irregular, part-time, temporary or short-contract employees who made much less with minimum benefits. The latter grew from about a quarter to more than a third of the workforce between 2000 and 2012. Meanwhile, the upper-middle class, a large group but smaller than the older concept of middle class, enjoyed a new cosmopolitan lifestyle, which included sending their children overseas to learn English, buying imported brand-name products, joining health clubs, and taking frequent vacations abroad.

This problem of inequality was compounded by an undeveloped social safety net. Unemployment in 2014 was only a modest 3.9 percent, but most experts believed the real figure was much higher. And it did not include senior workers forced to work part-time or take "honorary" retirements. This problem was related to the practice by South Korean firms of promoting employees according to seniority. As older workers were expensive, they were forced to retire early to reduce costs. Many who were unable to support themselves on retirement savings became part-time workers. Many young people also found themselves in temporary jobs. Since after two years temporary employees by law became permanent, with mandated benefits and protections, companies often dismissed workers before two years were up. South Korea lagged behind in social welfare benefits. The ROK in the 2000s was spending only 10 percent of its annual budget on social welfare, the lowest of the thirty OECD nations and only half as much as the second-lowest, Mexico.[27] Focused on economic growth, the state gave less priority to social welfare needs. Kim Dae Jung had promised radical increases in what he called "productive welfare," but the IMF financial crisis and the prevalence of neoliberal free-market thinking in the governing circles meant that this promise was not kept. In 2000, the government implemented the National Basic Livelihood Security System, in which everyone below poverty would receive financial benefits. The catch was that they had to prove they were unable to receive support from family, this being unlikely in a society that was so family oriented. So in practice, social support was left to the family, a heavy burden on the poor.

CHANGING GENDER RELATIONS, CHANGING FAMILIES

Family remained a central unit of society, as reflected in the welfare policies that still expected family members to take care of each other, in the corporate culture in which the *chaebŏls* that dominated the country were still family enterprises, and in the nearly obsessive focus on educating family members. In fact, so strong was the family-centeredness of South Korea's society that some observers have referred to the country as undergoing familial modernization.[28] Yet, perhaps no social changes in South Korea were more dramatic than those concerning gender and family. The legal codes were amended to allow women to head households, inherit property, and initiate divorce, and gender discrimination was legally prohibited by the early 1990s. Enrollment of women in colleges and universities soared past that of men in the 2000s. In 2010, women made up 49 percent of those in master's degree programs and 31 percent in doctorate programs.[29] This was still behind men, but the number of women graduate students had nearly doubled in a decade. Higher education was no longer a finishing school where girls majored in home economics, English, and art. Women, however, still faced discrimination in the workplace and elsewhere. Increasingly educated, organized, and empowered, Korean women were no longer accepting the patriarchal traditions of their society. Women also campaigned against the sex industry that had always been a major employer of women. In South Korea, the double standard prevailed in which it was accepted that married men frequented the "room salons" and other places that employed sex workers but that women who worked there were not virtuous. Under pressure from women's groups, the Kim Dae Jung administration created a Ministry of Gender Equality in 2001, renamed the Ministry of Gender Equality and Family in 2005, to deal with this problem. Women in the 1990s dealt more openly with previously taboo issues such as spousal abuse and sexual harassment. During the military regimes, some women had protested against Japanese sex tourism. After 1990, women's groups refocused on these issues, brought attention to the South Korean government's complicity in making prostitution available in base camps used by American troops in Korea, and in other ways confronted the whole issue of sexual exploitation of women.[30]

From the perspective of South Korea's historical legacy of male domination, the changing role of women was almost revolutionary, yet by most measures Korean women still lagged behind their counterparts in other developed nations. In 2006, women made up only 3 percent of executives in companies of over 1,000 employees; major corporations such as Samsung had only 12 women out of 1,300 officers and managers; Hyundai Motors and POSCO had no women in top positions. Women made 50 percent less than men, and the gap actually widened between 2000 and 2005.[31] In one international study in 2014, only 2 out of 142 countries where sufficient data was available had a wider wage gap between men and women. The gender gap in wages was not only greater than in all Western countries but in most other Asian countries as well.[32] Women did make some progress in politics, although here too they lagged behind their sisters in most industrial states. Still, the change in politics was impressive. In 1992, only 1 percent of the members of the National Assembly were women; by 2015, 16 percent were, but eighty-three countries had a higher percentage of parliamentarians.[33] In the spring of 2006, Han Myung-suk (Han Myŏng-suk) (1944–) became the first female prime minister and in 2013 Park Geun Hye became the first woman president.

Korean women typically married at the age of twenty-nine and had their first baby at thirty. Many were not marrying at all; it was estimated in 2013 that 15 percent of all women would remain single. Child-rearing and working at home were major burdens; a study showed that wives devoted five times as much of their time to these tasks as husbands.[34]

Another break with ancient tradition was ending the prohibition in the Civil Code against people marrying who shared the same surname and ancestral home. Most Koreans share one of a small number of family names, nearly half named Kim, Lee (or Yi or Rhee), or Park (or Pak). The surnames were broken down into clans who shared the same ancestral home and reputed ancestral descent. Members of some clans, such as the Gimhae Kim, the Miryang Park, and the Chŏnju Lee, had hundreds of thousands of members—there were 1.5 million members of Gimhae Kim—creating hardship for young people sharing a remote and theoretical ancestry who happened to fall in love. Marriages between them were not recognized, and their children were regarded as illegitimate. A court ruling declared this law unconstitutional in 1997, and in 2002 after lobbying by reformers, the National Assembly formally repealed it.

A truly unprecedented change in Korea's social history was the rise in the divorce rate. Up through the 1980s, divorce brought great shame and was uncommon, but by 1990 this had begun to change. Between 1995 and 2005 the divorce rate tripled. By 2005, the rate was 2.6 divorces per 1,000 people, a little higher than Japan's 2.3 or the European Union average of 1.8, although less than the U.S. rate of 4.0 per 1,000. Many women were opting out of marriage. In one survey of college women, a third said they did not want to get married.[35] For men the problem was not enough women. This was the product of Korean preferences for sons. In the 1980s and 1990s the use of sonograms resulted in increased abortion of female infants. The result was that there were more boys than girls. The imbalance reached a peak in the in the early 1990s when there were 117 baby boys per 100 girls, one of the highest ratios in the world. That surplus of boys began to be a serious problem in the early twenty-first century. However, in the 2000s the gap between male and female births narrowed to just slightly above the natural ratio of 105 males to 100 females. The use of sonograms resulted in similar sexual imbalances in China, India, Vietnam, and other nations. South Korea was the first Asian nation to show this sharp reversal, partly due to government measures in 1991 restricting the practice of sonograms by medical personnel. But public awareness of the problem and changing attitudes also contributed. Many Koreans began to value daughters, often seeing them as caregivers in their old age. Surveys in the early twenty-first century suggested that the age-old preference for sons over daughters no longer prevailed.

Families themselves were changing. In 2007, the average household contained only 2.8 members, half the size of a generation earlier. A quarter of Korean households were headed by women. While still uncommon, this was no longer a rarity. According to one poll in 2007, one in six single women said they would be happy to have children without having husbands.[36] Even adoptions were becoming more common. Because Korean culture placed such emphasis on bloodlines, it was rare to adopt children. As a result, agencies sprang up after the Korean War to arrange for adoption to the United States and Europe. Embarrassingly for many, Korea continued to be a source of adoptees for Westerners at the start of the twenty-first century. This was beginning to change, although slowly. Koreans were also showing more acceptance of gay and lesbian relations, and sexual diversity in general. Still, in some ways South Koreans were socially conservative. In international surveys, they were less likely to approve of cohabitation without marriage or believe that people can be happy without marrying than people in most Western nations or in other developed Asian nations such as Japan and Taiwan.

ETHNIC HOMOGENEITY AND MULTICULTURALISM

South Korea's low birthrate contributed to one of the most radical changes in Korean society in centuries—the end of ethnic homogeneity. A factor contributing to this was the shortage of women due to the preference for males. This hit rural men hard. Few young women wanted to live on a farm, and with the supply of marriage-age men greater than that of women they were able to avoid doing so. Consequently, many rural men sought wives from abroad. By 2006, more than a third of male farmers married foreign women, mostly Chinese and Vietnamese, but also from other Asian countries such as the Philippines and Uzbekistan. According to the National Statistical Office in Seoul, marriage to foreigners accounted for 13 percent of all marriages in 2005; more than 70 percent were between Korean men and women from other Asian countries. According to one study, by 2020 Kosians (bi-ethnic children) would make up one-third of children born in South Korea.[37] In a homogeneous society such as Korea this was a startling statistic. Public awareness of the idea of interethnic and interracial marriage and the implications for what it meant to be Korean was highlighted by the visit of Hines Ward, a Korean-speaking American football hero whose parents were a Korean mother and a black American father, and by a popular TV drama, *The Bride from Hanoi*.

Another development ending the nation's homogeneity was the influx of migrant workers from poorer Asian nations—including Bangladesh, China, Nepal, the Philippines, and Mongolia. They numbered 400,000 in 2007, half undocumented. They were often treated harshly, doing what Koreans called "3-D" jobs, dirty, difficult, and dangerous. The influx of foreign workers began in the 1990s and increased in the 2000s. Finding immigration procedures cumbersome, many employers hired workers on tourist visas, which they overstayed, hence over half the foreign labor force was in the country illegally and subject to exploitation. In 2004, the government introduced an Employment Permit System to make it easier for businesses to legally bring in foreign workers. While these were all temporary workers, the threat of severe labor shortages in the future meant that a permanent non–ethnic Korean population was very likely to be another challenge to the conception of Koreans as constituting a "pure-blooded" nation.

In the 2010s educators began to deal with the fact that many schoolchildren were from ethnically diverse backgrounds. Multiculturalism became a major topic for educators, government officials, and academics as the country began to prepare for the new reality that it was no longer a highly homogeneous society.

Meanwhile as more non–ethnic Koreans moved into the country, some Koreans continued to emigrate. The South Korean government estimated in 2013 that there were about 7.0 million Koreans and people of Korean descent living overseas. This included the 2.5 million Koreans living in China, many in the border areas of Manchuria, where they formed the Yanbian Autonomous Region. About 900,000 lived in Japan, where in contrast to the economically successful Chinese minority they were hindered by discrimination. A half-million lived in the states of the former Soviet Union. There were nearly 2.1 million Korean Americans in the United States. These had become very successful immigrants, with one of the highest education and income levels of any ethnic group. About 200,000 Koreans or people of Korean descent lived in Canada, 150,000 in Australia, 80,000 each in the Philippines and Vietnam, and 50,000 in Brazil. Smaller numbers were scattered throughout Europe, Asia, and South America.[38]

Almost everywhere, Korean immigrants prospered. Many of these were truly international Koreans who were bilingual or multilingual and sometimes went back and forth between Korea and their adopted home. These included businesspeople, scientists, and technicians who were sometimes lured back to South Korea for high-paying jobs. Emigration became significant with the easing of restrictions on emigration by the ROK government after 1970 and peaked in the 1980s. Economic prosperity and political stability resulted in a decline in numbers after 1990; however, many Koreans were still attracted by economic opportunities and a chance for a better or more promising lifestyle for themselves or their children. Many were simply joining family members who had emigrated earlier; some were students who went abroad for study and then accepted job offers there, or romantics seeking a new adventure in a new land. Many Koreans had family members and close friends overseas whom they visited. This only added to the increasing internationalism of Korean society.

FACING HISTORY AND PRESERVING HERITAGE

As the society underwent rapid change, the South Korean government became concerned about maintaining its cultural heritage. In 1962, it passed a Cultural Properties Protection Law patterned after a similar law in Japan. In 1972, a Cultural and Arts Promotion Law gave further financial support to preserving the nation's architecture and maintaining arts and crafts. Various structures were assigned as cultural treasures, and certain individuals skilled in traditional handicrafts, art, and music traditions were named "living cultural treasures" and supported, with the idea that they would train others to pass on their skills. The government established the Academy of Korean Studies in 1979 devoted to studying and preserving the past. The public also developed a keen interest in the past. Historical novels were popular, as were historical dramas on television. Major classics from the past were translated into modern Korean, and *p'ansori*, a traditional dramatic form, had a revival. By the 2000s the middle class, especially the upper-middle class, began to take a deeper interest in their cultural heritage. Traditional furniture, the *ondol* floor-heating system, Korean patterns and decorations, craft items, and even traditional hearty peasant foods became fashionable. The fact that these Korean products were often more expensive than foreign imports or more modern ones may have added to their desirability.[39]

Koreans also began to deal with their troubled recent past. One of the most interesting developments in coming to terms with the past was the Truth and Reconciliation Commission that President Roh Moo-hyun had established in 2005. With 15 commissioners and a staff of 239, it investigated political movements under Japanese colonial rule and all acts of political violence, terrorism, and human rights violations in Korea from 1945 to the democratization of the country in the late 1980s. Although the Roh Moo-hyun government may have had some political motives, seeking to discredit conservative opposition figures with links to past military regimes, the commission was nevertheless an experiment in coming to terms with the past that was unprecedented in East Asia.

Writers dealing with the country's recent history found a large audience for their works. Pak Kyŏng-ni (1926–2008), in her popular twenty-one-volume, 9,000-page saga *T'oji* (*The Earth*) (1969–1994), traced the history of Korea from 1860 to 1945 through four generations of what had been originally a wealthy landowning family from southern Korea. Cho Chŏng-nae (1943–), in his popular ten-volume novel *T'aebak Mountains* (1983), examined the partisans in southern Korea from 1945 to 1953. Sin Kyŏng-suk (1963–), in her novel *Solitary Room* (*Wae Ttan Bang*) (1995), drew upon her own experience growing up during the years of military rule and rapid urbanization. Her novel *Please Look After Mom* (*Ŏmma-rŭl Put'akhae*) (2009) was an international best seller. The emotionally charged Kwangju Incident was explored in Im Ch'ŏl-u's (1954–) novel *Spring Days* (*Bom Nal*) (1998).

At the start of the twenty-first century, many Korean writers were moving away from ideological and political issues, dealing either with more universal themes such as sexual orientation and the limitations of consumer society or with fantasy. Kim Yŏng-ha (1968–) looked beyond Korea for subject matter. His *Dark Flower* (*Kŏmŭn Kkot*) (2007) chronicles Korean immigrants in Mexico in the early twentieth century. Pak Min-kyu (1968–) populated his novels such as *Earth Hero Legend* (2003) with characters from computer games and animation, while breaking grammatical and stylistic conventions. Kim Ae-ran (1980–), in her *Tallyŏra Abi* (*Father Keep Running*) (2005), deals with those on the margins of Korea's competitive, consumer society in a cheerful and accepting manner. Many younger readers have turned to Internet novels and *manhwa* (manga). Facing this phenomenon, some established literary figures have experimented with online novels, including internationally recognized Hwang Sŏk-yong (1943–), with his successful *Dog's Supper Star* (*Kaebap Paragi Pyŏl*) (2008). Celebrating the 100th anniversary in 2008 of the first modern play, *Silver World* (*Ŭnsegye*), Korean theater was also becoming more universal in its themes and global in its activities.

While Koreans were taking an interest in their cultural heritage, they were not only embracing contemporary culture but also becoming a dynamic exporter of it, a phenomenon called the "Korean Wave" (*Hanryu*). Korean movies and television programs in the early 2000s not only regained a domestic audience that had long preferred foreign entertainment, especially Hollywood movies, but they also became popular in China, Japan, and Southeast Asia. The TV serial melodrama *Winter Sonata* began airing in Japan in 2003, where it became a huge hit. Hundreds of thousands of Japanese fans came to visit the film site, and a photo book of lead actor Bae Yong Joon (Pae Yong-jun) sold 100,000 copies at $160 each. Korean movie directors Im Kwŏn-t'aek, Yi Ch'ang-dong, Bong Joon-ho (Pong Chun-ho), and Park Chan-wook (Pak Ch'an-uk) have received critical acclaim, and Kim Ki Duk (Kim Ki-dŏk) has attracted some attention in international film festivals. Big-budget films such as the spy thriller *Shiri* by the director Kang Je-Gu (Kang Che-gyu) were box-office hits in much of Asia.

Korean popular music, or "K-pop," became a major export. Largely the product of three big entertainment companies—S.M., YG, and JYP—that recruited potential talented children and trained them with military efficiency, these K-pop groups, such as Girls' Generation were extremely popular throughout Asia and further abroad. Korean TV dramas and pop singers had become extraordinarily popular across the Pacific Rim and Asia, where they displaced the position of pop culture dominance held by the Americans for decades. Their popularity spread beyond Asia to the Middle East and Latin America. By the time the pop singer Psy's (Ssai or Pak Chae-sang) (1977–) "Gangnam Style" video became a global phenomenon in late 2012, South Korea had become second only to the United States as an exporter of entertainment. The government played an important role in this achievement. It helped to promote movies by passing the Motion Picture Promotion Law of 1995, which provided state subsidies to Korean filmmakers. In 1999, a Basic Law for Culture Industry Promotion was enacted to assist film and television producers. A more important factor contributing to this boom in pop culture was the repeal of restrictions limiting imports of foreign films, music, videos, and comic books, especially those from Japan. It was feared that the country's domestic entertainment industry could not compete with that of its former colonial ruler. In the late 1990s, when the policy was liberalized, the flood of Japanese popular culture imports acted instead as a great stimulus to South Korea's creative youth. Perhaps the most successful cultural exports were South Korean TV dramas. So popular were they in Asia that governments in some countries such as China and Vietnam moved toward imposing quotas on them to protect their own less popular television industry. *The Jewel in the Palace* (*Tae Chang Kŭm*), for example, a series loosely based on a Chosŏn-era woman physician, became the number-one rated show in almost every country along the Pacific Rim of Asia and some beyond. It was estimated in 2007 that 60 percent of the entire adult population of Iran tuned in to it, and it was a big hit in other countries from Russia to Mexico.

NEW CRISES AND NEW PROBLEMS

In the early twenty-first century, Koreans were living in a new globalizing era and were becoming a cosmopolitan people. From a country once labeled the "hermit kingdom," Koreans now traveled across the world in large numbers. Spending time abroad was becoming a routine part of a college education, and an overseas vacation was now becoming something that the average South Korean could afford. In 2013, by one estimate 240,000 South Koreans were studying in foreign countries, and thousands were working in business.[40] There were also thousands of Korean missionaries active in countries from Africa to China. Korea was emerging out of its historical obscurity. Samsung, LG, and Hyundai were internationally known brands, taekwondo (t'ae kwŏndo) was practiced everywhere and was an Olympic sport, and then there was Korean pop culture, which had an enormous audience in Asia and parts of the Middle East and Latin America. Notably, a Korean, Ban Ki Moon (Pan Ki-mun) (1944–), was elected secretary-general of the United Nations in 2006.

But the very degree to which South Korea was connected to the world made it vulnerable to developments beyond its control. This became clear during 2008 and 2009, when the country became caught in the worldwide financial meltdown. In 2009 the economy contracted by 0.8 percent. By the end of the year it was showing a robust recovery fueled by export growth, low interest rates, and government stimulus measures. Its growth rate from 2009 to 2014 remained a modest 3 percent, higher than average for a developed country but very modest by past standards. South Korea's membership in the new G-20 group of the world's major economic powers established in 2008, and its hosting of the G-20 summit in November 2010 symbolized its importance in the world. The country sought to move from manufacturing to a knowledge-based and service-sector economy. Representative of this was the construction of Songdo International Business District forty miles (sixty-five kilometers) southwest of Seoul. Begun in the 2000s and slated for completion by 2018, Songdo was to be a high-tech, eco-friendly Smart City, and an international business, financial, and tourist area. By 2015 it boasted a brand-new skyline and was the center of the United Nations Climate Fund Office. Yet, the country's dependence on manufacturing for export earnings, its rigid labor market, and most of all its aging population were causes for concern. Even more troubling for the nation's long-term future was the prospect of having to deal with, and perhaps absorb, a failed North Korean state.

KOREA IN GLOBAL PERSPECTIVE: SOUTH KOREA'S PLACE IN THE WORLD

A status-conscious society, South Koreans could look at their place in the world with some contentment. In 2015, they ranked about twelfth or thirteenth in GNP. Although the country's economic growth was slowing down, it was still an economic powerhouse. Its firms included the two top makers of DRAM chips in the world, three of the world's biggest shipbuilders, two of the largest consumer electronics manufacturers, the third-largest steel producer, and the fourth-largest automaker. The $1.5 trillion economy was the fourth largest in Asia after China, Japan, and India. With a population not likely to grow beyond its 50 million, in fact scheduled to decline after 2018, the total size of the economy was likely to be overtaken by much more populous nations—Indonesia, Mexico, Vietnam, perhaps eventually nations such as Pakistan or Nigeria. But it was less likely that any of these other developing nations would match South Korea in living standards for a long time. It had a per capita income in 2015 that placed it on par with the countries of Western Europe, and the economy was still growing at a faster rate than most developed nations, if not as fast as previously or as fast as China or India. By 2013, South Korea had one of the world's lowest infant mortality rates, and the average life span of its people at 81.1 was above the OECD average of 80.1.[41] Education levels and standards of learning were among the highest in the world.

In 2015 South Koreans ranked first in the percentage of twenty-five- to thirty-four-year-olds with university degrees. South Korea had the highest percentage of homes with broadband Internet access. South Korea was famously referred to the "world's most wired nation" by the Western media. Broadband service rates were the second lowest in the world. And the country was now a major exporter of popular culture, its fashions imitated in other Asian nations. Still there was progress to be made in improving the quality of life. The country lagged behind most developed nations in parks and recreational facilities. South Koreans worked longer hours than any other developed country—18 percent above the OECD average in 2013.[42] And there was still a small stream of South Koreans seeking a better life abroad. South Koreans had made many achievements in education, but few of their universities ranked among the top 100 in most international surveys. And not a single South Korean scientist had earned a Nobel Prize. While its pop entertainers were internationally known, Korean artists, architects, and writers, with a few exceptions, were still not well known outside their country.

South Korea's place in modern world history was an example of how a poor nation can climb out of poverty and develop stable political institutions accountable to the people, without jettisoning too many of its cultural traditions and without losing its strong sense of national and cultural identity. It followed a path influenced by the one Japan had taken, and in turn, it influenced other developing nations such as China. Koreans may have helped in providing an answer to the question that historians have asked and many in the non-Western world worried about: Does modernization mean Westernization? Koreans have created what is by most measures a modern society (two versions of it if North Korea is included) while not losing touch with their cultural heritage or becoming Westerners.

The struggle to become a strong and rich nation, however, was not a smooth one. The South Korean people went through terrible tragedies from the Korean War to Kwangju, worked in appalling industrial complexes for incredibly long hours, went through the confusion of a rapidly changing society, and made mistakes along the way. The several million who left after the loosening of emigration restrictions in the late 1960s to seek a better life abroad were a testimony to the hardships that seemed too great for many. And in contrast to their many accomplishments, there was the failure to achieve national unity. The unresolved conflict with North Korea has left a sense of frustration and anxiety about the future. Most South Koreans no longer fear a military threat from the North, but instead worry about the possibility of chaos in the event of the DPRK's collapse. They worry about how to bridge the economic and cultural gap with their fellow Koreans, and they are pained at the hunger, human rights abuses, and suffering the people in the North are experiencing. The hope of reformers in the late nineteenth century to see their country survive intact as a progressive member of the modern world has not yet been fulfilled.

Kim Dae Jung, from *Prison Writings*

"A Father's Guilt"

November 24, 1980

To my dear son Hong-up,

I feel a heavy weight as I think of you—a feeling of guilt. Though you have passed the age of thirty, because of your father your hopes for marriage have twice been destroyed and you have not been able to find a job in the business world, where you have always wanted to work. It is not just that I have been unable to help you; I have repeatedly been an obstacle to your happiness and future. How could my heart not ache? And when I see how you persevere without any sign of resentment, I feel even more distressed. I pray to God for your future happiness. I can only hope that the bitter experiences you have undergone will become an asset to you in the future.[43]

"For Life in the Twenty-first Century"

September 23, 1981

In the twenty-first century there will be political and social changes that simply cannot be imagined at this juncture. It does not seem likely, however, that there will emerge a regimented society in which humans are destroyed by the machine and held at bay in slavery such as Aldous Huxley envisioned in his *Brave New World*. I believe it to be much more likely instead that an era of popular freedom and justice will come into being, an age in which, for the first time in our history, human beings will be able to maximize use of their personal characteristics and abilities under conditions of equality of education and a secure economic life. It goes without saying that this will require our efforts and sacrifice, especially for posterity.[44]

"The Strengths and Shortcomings of Our Nation"

September 30, 1981

With love and respect to you and my beloved children:

Because my August letter did not reach you, I asked the prison authorities for permission to write another. . . .

In my letter of the 23d, I wrote about the history of mankind, but today I want to jot down some observations on the strength and shortcomings of our nation, based on my reading of our own history. Our greatest strength has been the astounding ability to maintain independence for 1,300 years—from the time of unification under Silla until the Japanese occupation in 1910. This record is unparalleled in world history. . . .

We tend to treat any signs of dependency on foreign powers as shameful. But one American scholar who has the benefit of an objective broad view of world history has commented that such a tendency in Korea reflects the prudent wisdom to survive when faced with the pressure of the Continental powers. Even though our nation formally adapted to foreign influences, our people have stoutly preserved their identity. Despite the overwhelming influence of Chinese civilization, for example we have retained unique characteristics in our culture. We have kept a distinct life-style in such things as clothing, food, language, and shelter and have completely prevented the penetration and domination by the notorious overseas Chinese. . . .

We also have to acknowledge our ancestors for their intense desire for learning. Although we belong to the hemisphere of Chinese civilization, we do not by any means lag behind China in terms of our levels of education and culture. Such a tradition of independence has given us the resourcefulness to join the ranks of middle-tier nations, such as Hong Kong, Taiwan, and Singapore, all of which are also located within the sphere of Chinese influence. . . .

We have shortcomings, however, that stand in rather shameful contrast to our strengths. First, our political culture is narrow-minded and lacking in magnanimity. . . .

Second, although our nation has distinguished itself in preserving its fundamental attributes, it is quite lacking in progressive tendencies. Our history abounds in conclusive proofs. For example, King Changsu of Koguryo moved the capital from Kungnaesoong, located across the Yalu, to Pyongyang, which is on the peninsula. When Silla unified the peninsula, it voluntarily relinquished the eastern half of the Manchurian lands to the north of Taedong River and would not budge an inch northward in the location of the traditional capital city of Kyongju. Finally, even though Yi Sung'gye participated personally in the northward policy of the Koryo dynasty in its last years, he moved the capital south of Kaesong, misled as he was by the superstition against the north.

In spite of the fact that our country faces the ocean on three sides, we have refused almost completely to recognize this reality. This is why we have been bothered so persistently by the Japanese. If we were to try to identify the great navigators or others engaged in maritime activities, Chang Po-go from the late Silla period is about the only one that comes to mind. . . .

Third, we can take note of the formalist tendencies of our nation. We are so concerned with formal appearances that we quite disregard practical benefits, while our excessive sensitivity to the issue of losing face often leads us to pretensions that we cannot sustain and ultimately to waste. This sort of formalism only aggravates bureaucratic abuses and serves as a major suppressant of creativity.[45]

—from *Prison Writings*

NOTES

1. Chong-Sik Lee and Hyuk-sang Sohn, "South Korea in 1993: The Year of Great Reform, *Asia Survey* 34, no. 1 (January/February, 1994): 1–9.
2. Young Whan Kihl, *Transforming Korean Politics: Democracy, Reform, and Culture* (Armonk, NY: M.E. Sharpe, 2005), 120.
3. B. C. Koh, "South Korea in 1995: Tremors of Transition," *Asia Survey* 36, no. 1 (January/February, 1996): 53–60.
4. B. C. Koh, "South Korea in 1996: Internal Strains and External Challenges," *Asia Survey* 37, no. 1 (January/February, 1997): 1–9.
5. Tong Whan Park, "South Korea in 1998: Swallowing the Bitter Pills of Restructuring," *Asia Survey* 39, no. 1 (January/February, 1999): 133–39.
6. Yong-Chool Ha, "South Korea in 2001: Frustration and Continuing Uncertainty," *Asia Survey* 42, no. 1 (January/February, 2002): 56–66.
7. "Joong Ang Ilbo Chief Questioned," *Korea Herald*, March 5, 2008.
8. "Lee Hit over Grand Daughter's U.S. Birth," *Korea Times*, July 25, 2002.
9. Hong Yung Lee, "South Korea in 2003: A Question of Leadership?" *Asia Survey* 44, no. 1 (January/February, 2004): 130–38.
10. John Lie and Myoungkyu Park, "South Korea in 2005: Economic Dynamism, Generational Conflicts, and Social Transformations," *Asia Survey* 46, no. 1 (January/February, 2006): 56–62.
11. "Roh Urges Newspapers to Be More Responsible," *Korea Times*, May 31, 2005.
12. John Lie and Andrew Eungi Kim, "South Korea in 2008: Scandals and Summits," *Asia Survey* 48, no. 1 (January/February 2008): 116–23.
13. Hyung Gu Lynn, *Bipolar Orders: The Two Koreas Since 1989* (Halifax, NS: Fenwood, 2007), 47.
14. Sunhyuk Kim, "Civil Society in Democratizing Korea," in *Korea's Democratization*, Samuel S. Kim, ed. (Cambridge: Cambridge University Press, 2003), 81–106.
15. James A. Foley, "'Ten Million Families': Statistic or Metaphor?" *Korean Studies* 25, no. 1 (January 2001): 108.
16. Andrei Lankov, "The Legacy of Long-Gone States: China, Korea and the Koguryo," *Japan Focus*, October 2006.
17. Uk Heo and Terrence Roehig, *South Korea's Rise: Economic Development, Power and Foreign Relations* (Cambridge, UK: Cambridge University Press, 2014), 172.
18. *Korea Herald*, May 27, 2014.
19. *Jungang Korea Daily*, October 17, 2014.
20. "The 54th Parallel," *The Economist*, October 26, 2013, 8.

21. "President Calls for Proactive Measures to Reduce Fertility Rate," *Korea Herald*, June 2, 2015.

22. Organization for Economic Cooperation and Development (OECD), *Education at a Glance: OECD Indicators*, (Paris: Organization of Economic Cooperation and Development, 2014).

23. Pearson Educational Services, "Index of Cognitive Skills and Educational Attainment," (London: Pearson Educational Services, 2014). Retrieved from: http://thelearningcurve.pearson.com/index/index-ranking.

24. "Roh's Aide Tried to Cover Up Diploma Forgery," *Korea Times*, August 24, 2007; John Lie and Andrew Eungi Kim, "South Korea in 2008: Scandals and Summits," *Asia Survey* 48, no. 1 (January/February 2008): 116–23.

25. World Bank, "Gini Index," http://data.worldbank.org/indicator/SI.POV .GINI. Accessed June 26, 2015.

26. *Chosŏn ilbo*, January 28, 2015.

27. Young Soo Park, "Comparative Perspectives on the South Korean Welfare System," *Japan Focus*, May 5, 2008.

28. Chang Kyung-Sup, *South Korea under Compressed Modernity: Familial Political Economy in Transition* (London: Routledge, 2010).

29. J. Ahn, "Analysis of women doctorates entering the labor market in Republic of Korea," in Hyunjoon Park and Kim Kyung-keum, eds., *Korean Education in Changing Economic and Demographic Contexts*, (New York: Springer, 2014): 59-76.

30. Moon, Katharine H. S., "South Korean Movements against Militarized Sexual Labor," *The Journal of Asian Studies* 39, no. 2 (March-April, 1999): 473–500.

31. "Gender Gap Widens Over 50% at Large Firms," *Korea Herald*, September 21, 2005.

32. World Economic Forum, *The Global Competitiveness Report, 2014*, available at: http://reports.weforum.org/global-gender-gap-report-2014/rankings (accessed June 4, 2015).

33. *Women in Parliaments* (IPU, 2015), http://www.ipu.org/wmn-e/classif.htm. Accessed June 26, 2015.

34. "Women in South Korea: A Pram Too Far," *The Economist*, October 26, 2013, 9–11.

35. "One in Three Korean Women Reject Motherhood," *Korea Herald*, March 23, 2006.

36. "Social Changes Lead to Various Types of Family," *Korea Times*, October 31, 2007.

37. Andrew Eungi Kim and John Lie, "South Korea in 2006: Nuclear Standoff, Trade Talks, and Population Trends," *Asia Survey* 47, no. 1 (January/February, 2007): 52–57.

38. Republic of Korea, Ministry of Foreign Affairs, "States of Compatriots Overseas," (Seoul: Ministry of Foreign Affairs, 2013) http://www.index.go.kr/potal/main/EachDtlPageDetail.do?idx_cd=1682. Accessed June 6, 2015.

39. Hagen Koo, "The Changing Faces of Inequality in South Korea in the Age of Globalization," *Korean Studies* 31 (2007): 1–18.

40. Karen Fischer, "For Some Foreign Students U.S. Education Is Losing Its Attraction," *New York Times*, May 25, 2014, http://www.newyorktimes.com. Accessed June 13, 2015.

41. Organization for Economic Cooperation and Development, *Health at a Glance 2013*, http://www.oecd.org/health/health-systems/health-at-a-glance.htm. Accessed June 4, 2015.

42. OECD, StatsExtract, 2014, https://stats.oecd.org/Index.aspx?DataSet Code=ANHRS. Accessed June 4, 2015.

43. Kim Dae Jung, *Prison Writings*, Choi Sung-il and David R. McCann, translators (Berkeley: University of California Press, 1987), 4.

44. Kim Dae Jung, *Prison Writings*, 76–77.

45. Kim Dae Jung, *Prison Writings*, 79–84.

Conclusion

Korea's past century, its intensive colonial occupation, its arbitrary division, and most striking of all, the radically different trajectories pursued by the two halves, is without a comparable example in modern history. No modern nation ever developed a more isolated and totalitarian society than North Korea, nor such an all-embracing family cult. No society moved more swiftly from extreme poverty to prosperity and from authoritarianism to democracy than South Korea. Modern history offers no other example of such an ancient, homogeneous society growing so far apart in such a short span of time. By the early twenty-first century the border separating the two Koreas marked a boundary between two lifestyles and living standards more sharply divergent than any border in the world.

Yet due to their common historical inheritance, the two Koreas share many features. Both have been driven by a passionate Korean nationalism. While nationalism has been a globally dominant force in shaping societies, few developing nations have had such a long history as a clearly defined political and cultural entity. As the centuries-old political system crumbled along with the Sino-centric world with which it was associated, members of the educated elite grappled with new forms of identity. They began examining their state and its place in the modern global community; in the process, they gave birth to modern Korean nationalism. This new sense of being part of a Korean nation quickly took root among the general population. A powerful ethnic nationalism emerged in the first half of the twentieth century, unencumbered by racial or linguistic minorities, regional separatism, or strong sectarian identities. Colonialism assisted

301

in this process, since the harsh and intrusive nature of Japanese rule in this ethnically homogenous society contributed to a collective sense of victimization. Both North and South Korea were able to draw upon this Korean nationalism to mobilize their populations for state-directed goals.

Both Koreas are products of the highly turbulent middle third of the twentieth century. The mass uprooting of the Korean people caused by wartime Japan's mobilizations, the dislocations that followed division, and the Korean War all helped to shake up society and break up traditional, rigid class lines, making society more fluid, more open to change and mobility. In North Korea, that social mobility was initially revolutionary, but then that society began to rigidify as a new hierarchical social order emerged. The social revolution in South Korea was at first less marked, as old elites consolidated power, but the Korean War, land reform, mass education, and rapid industrialization established a semimeritocracy, provided many avenues for upward mobility, and created a new middle-class society. In both cases the social upheavals eased the task of pursuing development agendas.

The two states were shaped by the unique geopolitical situation of Korea. The modest-sized Korean peninsula is almost completely encircled by three of the most formidable states in history: China, Russia, and Japan. Korea has no neighbors its own size. With the American occupation of Japan in 1945, Korea acquired a fourth powerful neighbor: the United States. Each of these much more populous and powerful states intervened and occupied at least part of Korea in the century after the country was forced to open its doors to the world. Korea could only survive and flourish as an independent entity by skillfully playing the surrounding great powers off one another or seeking one as a protector. Each of the Koreas after 1945 sought two of these powers for economic support and military protection, not without considerable ambivalence and prickliness. The fear of foreign domination and the frustrations of dependency partly account for the intensity of Korean nationalism and the determined efforts of the North and the South to acquire military and economic strength.

The ROK and the DPRK have also been shaped by Korea's long history of centralized, bureaucratic rule. During the Chosŏn period, 1392–1910, an elaborate system of government was administered from the capital down to the county level. There was little local autonomy. The colonial administration reinforced this pattern, with the state organs penetrating to the township and village level. It was also more authoritarian and militarized than the dynastic state, and it introduced the practice of mass mobilization to achieve state goals. Both Koreas, consequently, were highly centralized states. In North Korea everything was decided from the center, from the allocation of resources for industry to the food and clothing rations issued through the public distribution system. There was a complete absence of provincial autonomy or culture. South Korea also had little local authority. Until the local autonomy laws of the early 1990s, the Ministry of the Interior appointed all local officials from governors to local mayors, the Ministry of Education imposed uniform and detailed regulations on every local school, and there were no local police forces or any other significant administrative organ that was not directed from Seoul. The centralized nature of both states is reflected in their capitals. Pyongyang totally dominates North Korea, it is where all the members of the elite live, and although the size has been kept to a modest 2–2.5 million by strict internal migration controls, it is still much larger than any other city in the country. Seoul, lacking such internal migration controls, grew into a megacity with a population that has reached 10 million, more than 20 million if the suburban "satellite cities" are included, two-fifths of the country's total. It is the largest industrial center, the financial hub, and the political capital. It is also the educational center, with all the best universities located there, and the cultural and intellectual center.

Both Koreas have pursued policies of economic nationalism in which the state directs the economy using centralized planning. This was in part a legacy of the colonial economic experience, the logical outcome of centralized bureaucratic states, and the influence of the Soviet model in North Korea—which in turn influenced South Korea. The goals of the governments in both Koreas remained similar: to make their states strong and independent through economic development. Both were able to tap into a strong sense of national pride to mobilize the population for these aims. The slogan of Meiji Japan after 1868, "rich nation, strong military," could have very well been the motto of the DPRK under Kim Il Sung or the ROK under Park Chung Hee. Both Koreas motivated their populations by appealing to the same sense of ethnic-racial nationalism. This mind-set became increasingly explicit in the North from the 1970s, eventually replacing Marxism-Leninism as the dominant ideology.

Yet the shared inheritance of the two Koreas led them onto different paths. North Korea pursued a model of development that proved to be an economic and historical dead end. The desire to be self-sufficient, to be free from foreign domination despite its precarious geopolitical terrain and modest size, had disastrous consequences for the North. It could not flourish in a world dominated by global capitalism. Attempts by Kim Il Sung, Kim Jong Il, and Kim Jong Un to do so began to resemble the futile efforts at isolation pursued more than a century earlier by the Taewŏn'gun.

South Korea's more chaotic but more pluralistic society proved more successful in bringing prosperity if not self-sufficiency. This was in part because its economic and political links to the United States and Japan proved more effective in developing its economy. Here the crucial role of the United States needs to be acknowledged. The American legacy in modern Korea is an ambiguous one. Despite the important influence that American missionaries had as agents of modernization in the late nineteenth and early twentieth centuries, the U.S. government was largely indifferent to Korea, willing to let it become part of the Japanese Empire. When the United States did actively intervene in Korean affairs, the result was catastrophic, since it was the United States that was initially responsible for the division. The American military intervention in the Korean War turned what would have been a short if nasty civil war into a three-year global conflict that devastated the country and left it divided. Washington tolerated military governments, American firms took advantage of the suppression of labor movements, and the U.S. military presence may have contributed to the tensions between the two Koreas. Yet South Korea enormously benefited by the U.S. involvement. The United States opened its markets to Korean exports and poured in development aid. Its universities educated many tens of thousands of Koreans. It plugged Korea into global society and provided the security needed to attract foreign investment. And for all its tolerance of military rulers, the United States acted as a check on authoritarianism, allowing space for a pluralistic society to grow. North Korea, by contrast, had no similar external check on the ambitions and visions of its authoritarian leaders, and the regime effectively eliminated any element of pluralism.

None of this detracts from the strengths of South Korean society, which made possible its transition to developed status in just several decades. South Korean leaders, while sometimes brutal, corrupt, and self-serving, also made many wise choices, sometimes against American advice. The South Korean people endured many hardships and made many sacrifices, and they were able to draw upon many resources from their cultural heritage and recent history. Their preoccupations with educational attainment, pursuit of status, sense of national purpose, and openness to change were all crucial elements. Especially important was the Korean tradition of looking outside their society for examples of excellence and then trying to emulate them. Tragically, although North Korea shared the same historical inheritance and its people exhibited the same sense of hard work and national purpose, the interplay of historical contingency and policy choices brought about very different outcomes.

The great tragedy of modern Korean history has been the nation's division. In the nearly seven decades since the two states were created, the Koreans have continued to think of themselves as one people. Almost universally, the division of the country has been regarded as "unnatural" and unification at some point inevitable. However, seven decades after the country was partitioned, there was no obvious path to reunification. Nor was it clear just how far the two Koreas have pulled apart and become not only two states but also two cultures. Only if and when the two Koreas become one nation-state will we be able to truly comprehend the significance of this division and the insights into history it provides; and only then will the hopes of Koreans to create a unified modern nation be fulfilled.

Appendix
Romanization

The Korean language has a rather complex sound system that has posed challenges to romanization. This book follows the McCune-Reischauer system that is used by the Library of Congress and with minor variations in most scholarly English language texts. Below is a basic guide to the pronunciation of the McCune-Reischauer system used in this book. *Note:* The Korean sound system is very different than in English so the equivalents below are only rough approximations.

CONSONANTS

ch is as in English but unaspirated, sounding a bit more like a j
ch' is pronounced as in English but more aspirated
k as in English but unaspirated, sounding a bit like a hard g
k' as in English but more aspirated
kk a very tense unaspirated k sound
l as initial l in English, never as a final l such as in well
p as in English but unaspirated and sounding a bit like a b
p' as in English but more aspirated
pp a very tense unaspirated p sound
s softer than an English s, but if followed by i pronounced as sh
ss more tense than an English s
t as in English but unaspirated, sounding a bit like a d
t' more aspirated than in English
tt a tense unaspirated t

tch a tense unaspirated ch sound
Other consonants are pronounced more or less as they are in English.

VOWELS

a as the a in father
ae a bit like the a in cat
e roughly as in get
i between the i of tin and the ee of teen
o as in hope
ŏ between the sound of u in fun and the aw in fawn
oe roughly as "way"
u as the u in tune
ŭ similar to the oo in book
ŭi sometimes as in eh

REVISED ROMANIZATION

In 2000 the South Korean government adopted a new official Revised
Romanization that is also coming into use. The following list shows some
of the differences.

McCune-Reischauer	*Revised Romanization*
ch	j
ch'	ch
k	g
k'	k
p	b
p'	p
t	d
t'	t
ŏ	eo
ŭ	eu

In Revised Romanization hyphens between syllables in names are op-
tional. Many users of McCune-Reischauer also delete hyphens between
syllables in names although they are used in this book.

The following list presents some names and terms written in (1) Mc-Cune-Reischauer, (2) Revised Romanization, and (3) the Korean alphabet.

ch'ŏnmin	cheonmin	천민
Chosŏn	Joseon	조선
Han'gŭl	Hangeul	한글
kisaeng	gisaeng	기생
Kim Pu-sik	Gim Bushik	김부식
Koryŏ	Goryeo	고려
kwagŏ	gwageo	과거
Paekche	Baekje	백제
p'ansori	pansori	판소리
Silla	Silla*	신라
Tan'gun	Dangun	단군
T'oegye	Toegye	퇴계
yangban	yangban*	양반
Yi Sŏng-gye	Yi Seonggye	이성계

*Some Korean names and terms are spelled identically in McCune-Reischauer and Revised Romanization.

Glossary of Korean Words

amhŭkki "dark period" (of colonial rule)
bunka seiji "culture policy" (of colonial administration)
chaebŏl corporate conglomerate in South Korea
Charyŏk kaengsaeng "relying on own strength"
Ch'inaehan Chidoja "Dear Leader" (Kim Jong Il)
Chinbo-dang Progressive Party, another name for Kaehwa-dang
choktae kyech'ŭng "hostile" class in North Korean society
Ch'ŏllima mythical flying horse; movement to speed up productivity in North Korea
ch'ŏmin "mean people" term for low status or outcaste groups
chŏngbo unit of land (approximately 2.5 acres or 1 hectare)
Chōsen Sōtokufu Government-General of colonial Korea
Chosŏn (Chinese: Chaoxian) lit. "Land of the Morning Calm," name of an early kingdom and of the Korean state from 1392–1910
Chosŏn Minjujuŭi Inmin Konghwaguk Democratic People's Republic of Korea (official name of North Korea since 1948)
chuch'e see *juche*
chuch'e sasang *juche* thought
chungin "middle men," a subelite class of technical specialists in Chosŏn
haeksim kyech'ŭng "core class" or loyal class in North Korean society
Hallyu (hanryu) "Korean Wave," the fad for Korean popular culture in Asia during the late 1990s and 2000s
Han'guk Korea, most commonly used term for Korea in South Korea
han'gŭl the indigenous Korean alphabet (lit. "Korean writing")

hanmun   Chinese characters, also called *hanja*
hwan   unit of currency (in South Korea)
hwan'gap   sixtieth birthday celebration
hyŏnji chido   "on the spot guidance"
hyŏpdonghwa   "cooperativization," a North Korean term for collectivization of agriculture
ilmyŏn kŏnsŏl, ilmyŏn kukpang   "construction on the one hand, national defense on the other"
inminban   neighborhood associations in North Korea
inmin wiwŏnhoe   people's committees
iyong husaeng   "enriching the well-being of the people by taking advantage of the useful"
juche (chuch'e)   North Korean ideology based on the thought of Kim Il Sung, sometimes translated "self-reliance"
Kaehwa-dang   Enlightenment Party
kinrōtai   student labor groups
kisaeng   female entertainers
kongdori   factory boy
kongsuni   factory girl
Koryŏ   name of Korean state 935–1392, another name for Korea
Kosian   bi-ethnic child
kun   administrative subdivision of province often translated as county
Kun'guk Kimuch'ŏ   Deliberative Council
kusadae   save-our-company group
kwalliso   North Korean political prisoner camps
kyorin   neighborly relations (Japanese term)
manhwa   Korean comic book or manga
minjok   people or nation
minjok chisang, kukka chisang   "nation first, state first"
minjung   "the masses" or "the people"
mip'ung yangsok   "laudable customs and conduct"
na sŏn   "four lines" military policy in North Korea
namjon yŏbi   revere men, despise women
Nissen yūwa   "Harmony between Japan and Korea"
No (Roh) sa mo   gathering of those people loving Roh
nosukja   unemployed, homeless workers
ondol   style of heated floors in Korean houses
pando   lit. "half island," peninsula
panmal   Korean speech style for addressing inferiors
p'ansori   distinctive Korean form of folk tales presented by a singer/dancer accompanied by a drummer
Pulgŭn Ch'ŏngnyŏn Kŭnwidae   Young Red Guards
p'umassi-ban   mutual aid teams (North Korea)

sadaejuŭi "flunkyism" or the blind subservience to a great power
Saemaŭl new village
samuwŏn term for white-collar workers in North Korea
Seimu Sōkan Director-General of Administration
sŏdang village schools (written differently in Chinese characters)
Sŏhak "Western Learning," Korean term for Christianity
sŏngbun grades into which society is divided (North Korea)
sŏn'gun "Military First" policy of North Korea
Sōtoku Governor-General (of colonial Korea)
sukpak kŏmyŏl midnight home visits in North Korea
Taehan Cheguk Empire of Korea
Taehan Min'guk Republic of Korea (Official name of South Korea since 1948)
tanballyŏng order to cut off topknots
tōkan resident-general
t'ongch'i chagŭm "governing fund'
Tonghak "Eastern Learning," nineteenth-century religious movement
T'ongni Kimu Amun Office for the Management of State Affairs
t'ongyo kyech'ŭng "wavering" class in North Korean society
ŭibyŏng "righteous armies," resistance bands during the Japanese invasions of Korea
Widaehan Chidoja "Great Leader" (used for Kim Jong Il)
Widaehan Ryŏngdoja "Great Leader" (term used for Kim Jong Il)
Widaehan Suryŏngnim "Great Leader" (Kim Il Sung)
wŏn unit of currency
yangban lit. "two sides," the aristocratic elite of Korea
yuilsasangch'egye Monolithic Ideological System of thought in North Korea
yusin "revitalization"
zaibatsu Japanese industrial-financial conglomerates

Annotated Selected Bibliography

Amsden, Alice. *Asia's Next Giant: South Korea and Late Industrialization*. New York: Oxford University Press. 1989.

A favorable examination of South Korea's economic development. Now a bit dated but still useful.

Armstrong, Charles K. *The North Korean Revolution, 1945–1950*. Ithaca, NY: Cornell University Press, 2003.

An important study of the formation of the early North Korean state based on documents captured during the Korean War. The author persuasively argues that the North Korean government developed into a nationalist regime from its early days.

Armstrong, Charles K. *Tyranny of the Weak: North Korea and the World, 1950–1992*. Ithaca, NY: Cornell University Press, 2013.

An excellent history of North Korea's foreign relations.

Atkins, E. Taylor. *Primitive Selves: Koreana in the Japanese Colonial Gaze, 1910–1945*. Berkeley, CA: University of California Press, 2010.

A study of Japanese interest in things Korean and how it helped shape both perceptions and policy toward Korea during the colonial period.

Brandt, Vincent. *A Korean Village between Farm and Sea*. Cambridge, MA: Harvard University Press, 1971.

An anthropological study of a South Korean village just before the country's economic transformation. A fascinating glimpse into rural Korea.

Brazinsky, Gregg. *Nation Building in South Korea: Koreans, Americans, and the Making of Democracy*. Chapel Hill: University of North Carolina Press, 2007.

An important study of the contributions of the United States in the evolution of South Korean democracy. Indispensable for understanding the political development of South Korea.

Buzo, Adrian. *The Guerilla Dynasty: Politics and Leadership in the DPRK 1945–1994*. Sydney: Allen & Unwin, 1999.

A readable, reliable study of North Korea under Kim Il Sung.

————. *The Making of Modern Korea: A History*. London: Routledge, 2002.

An often insightful political history of North and South Korea from 1910 to 2000.

Caprio, Mark. *Japanese Assimilation Policies in Colonial Korea, 1910–1945*. Seattle: University of Washington Press, 2009.

Places colonial Korea in the larger context of colonialism, finding that the Japanese carried policies drawn from German and French cultural assimilationist practices that were almost doomed to failure.

Chen, Jian. *China's Road to the Korean War: The Making of the Sino-American Confrontation*. New York: Columbia University Press, 1994.

Useful work for understanding the reasons for China's intervention into the Korean War.

Cho, S. S. *Korea in World Politics 1940–1950: An Evaluation of American Responsibility*. Berkeley: University of California Press, 1967.

A still-valuable study of diplomacy and politics during this period.

Choi, Hyaewol. *Gender and Mission Encounters in Korea: New Women, Old Ways: Seoul-California Series in Korean Studies*. Berkeley, CA: University of California Press, 2009.

Traces the genealogy of modern womanhood in the encounters between Koreans and American Protestant missionaries in the early twentieth century.

Chung, Young-Iob. *Korea under Siege, 1876–1945: Capital Formation and Economic Transformation*. New York: Oxford University Press, 2006.

An important but demanding economic history of Korea from the nineteenth century to the end of colonial rule.

Clark, Donald N. *Living Dangerously in Korea: The Western Experience, 1900–1950*. Norwalk, CT: Eastbridge, 2003.

An interesting account of the foreign community in Korea in the first half of the twentieth century focusing on the American missionaries.

————, ed. *The Kwangju Uprisings: Shadows Over the Regime in South Korea*. Boulder, CO: Westview Press, 1988.

An examination of this bloody and tragic South Korean political uprising.

Clifford, Mark. *Troubled Tiger: Businessmen, Bureaucrats, and Generals in South Korea*. Armonk, NY: M.E. Sharpe, 1994.

Written by a journalist who covered Korea, it gives a somewhat dark picture of South Korea's economic miracle, emphasizing government-corporate collusion and corruption.

Conroy, Hilary. *The Japanese Seizure of Korea, 1868–1910*. Philadelphia: University of Pennsylvania Press, 1960.

A controversial study of the Japanese takeover of Korea, now a bit dated.

Cumings, Bruce. *Korea's Place in the Sun: A Modern History*. Updated edition. New York: W.W. Norton and Company, 2005.

An engagingly written, if somewhat opinionated, history of modern Korea by one of the most prominent American historians of Korea.

————. *The Origins of the Korean War*. Vol. 1, *Liberation and the Emergence of Separate Regimes, 1945–1947*. Princeton, NJ: Princeton University Press, 1981.

———. *The Origins of the Korean War.* Vol. 2, *The Roaring of the Cataract, 1947–1950.* Princeton, NJ: Princeton University Press, 1990.

These two volumes are an important study of Korea in the five years before the Korean War. Some of the author's arguments have been undermined by more recent evidence, but this is still valuable as a source of information on Korean political developments prior to the war. The first volume includes an especially valuable detailed study of South Korean politics immediately after liberation.

Cwiertka, K. J. *Cuisine, Colonialism and Cold War: Food in Twentieth-Century Korea.* London: Reaktion Books, 2012.

Interesting and often insightful study of food culture in twentieth-century Korea.

Deuchler, Martina. *Confucian Gentlemen and Barbarian Envoys: The Opening of Korea, 1875–1885.* Seattle: University of Washington Press, 1977.

A reliable diplomatic study of the first decade after South Korea was "opened."

Duus, Peter. *The Abacus and the Sword: The Japanese Penetration of Korea, 1895–1910.* Berkeley: University of California Press, 1995.

A study of Japanese politics and diplomacy behind Japan's annexation of Korea by a prominent historian of Japan.

Eckert, Carter J. *Offspring of Empire: The Koch'ang Kims and the Origins of Korean Capitalism.* Seattle: University of Washington Press, 1991.

An important study of the colonial origins of Korea's industrialization focusing on one of Korea's influential entrepreneurial families. Argues for the importance of the colonial period in understanding South Korea's economic development.

Eckert, Carter J., Ki-baik Lee, Young Ick Lew, Michael Robinson, and Edward W. Wagner. *Korea Old and New: A History.* Cambridge: Korea Institute, Harvard University, 1990.

A standard, now a little dated, one-volume history of Korea from earliest times to the late 1980s.

Em, Henry H. *The Great Enterprise: Sovereignty and Historiography in Modern Korea.* Durham, NC: Duke University Press, 2013.

A mostly too-theoretical work aimed at scholars, but important for its insights.

Flake, L. Gordon, and Scott Snyder, eds. *Paved with Good Intentions: The NGO Experience in North Korea.* Westport, CT: Praeger, 2004.

Several essays by aid workers active in North Korea during the famine. Contains many interesting insights.

French, Paul. *North Korea: The Paranoid Peninsula.* New York: St. Martin's Press, 2005.

One in a growing body of literature on North Korea. Generally reliable, with an emphasis on economics.

Gradjanzev, Andrew H. *Modern Korea.* New York: Institute of Pacific Relations and John Day Company, 1944.

A survey of Korea under colonial rule with many statistics that is still a valuable source. The well-informed author's identity remains a mystery.

Gragert, Edwin H. *Landownership under Colonial Rule: Korea's Japanese Experience, 1900–1935*. Honolulu: University of Hawaii Press, 1994.

An important study of landownership during colonial times.

Haggard, Stephan, and Marcus Noland. *Famine in North Korea: Markets, Aid, and Reform*. New York: Columbia University Press, 2007.

The best study to date of this tragic episode in Korean history, with some insights into North Korea under Kim Jong Il.

Halliday, Jon, and Bruce Cumings. *Korea: The Unknown War*. New York: Pantheon Books, 1988.

A popular and critical history, the basis for a PBS documentary.

Han, Sung-joo. *The Failure of Democracy in South Korea*. Berkeley: University of California Press, 1974.

An important analytical study of the short-lived experiment in parliamentary government during the Second Republic, 1960–1961.

Harrington, Fred Harvey. *God, Mammon, and the Japanese: Dr. Horace N. Allen and Korean-American Relations, 1884–1905*. Madison: University of Wisconsin Press, 1944.

Examines the career of an influential American in late Chosŏn Korea.

Henderson, Gregory. *Korea: The Politics of the Vortex*. Cambridge, MA: Harvard University Press, 1968.

Although now dated, it is still a provocative and at times insightful history of South Korea in the first two decades after World War II.

Henry, Todd A. *Assimilating Seoul: Japanese Rule and the Politics of Public Space in Colonial Korea, 1910–1945*. Berkeley, CA: University of California Press, 2014.

This study of public spaces in Seoul provides insights and anecdotes into the complex nature of Japanese colonial rule.

Heo, Uk, and Terrence Roehig. *South Korea's Rise: Economic Development, Power and Foreign Relations*. Cambridge, UK: Cambridge University Press, 2014.

A study of South Korea's emergence as an active player in international affairs since the 1980s as a result of its rise as an economic power.

Hicks, George. *The Comfort Women: Japan's Brutal Regime of Enforced Prostitution in the Second World War*. New York: W.W. Norton, 1995.

The first major work in English on this controversial topic.

Hulbert, Homer B. *The Passing of Korea*. Reprint [1906]. Seoul: Yonsei University Press, 1969.

This is a generally sympathetic account by an American missionary in Korea. Despite the prejudices and limitations of the author, it is worth reading for his firsthand accounts of events and life in Korea at the end of the Chosŏn dynasty.

Jager, Sheila Miyoshi. *Brothers at War: The Unending Conflict in Korea*. New York: W.W. Norton, 2013.

Views the Korean War from the civil war of 1948–1950, to the international conflict from 1950–1953, to the global Cold War from 1953, to a more local conflict of the late 1960s.

Kang, Chol-Hwan, *The Aquariums of Pyongyang: Ten Years in the North Korean Gulag*. Yair Reiner, trans. New York: Basic Books, 2001.

The firsthand account of a survivor of the North Korean prison system and an international best seller. It gives a glimpse into this dark and little-known aspect of the DPRK.

Kihl, Young Whan. *Transforming Korean Politics: Democracy, Reform, and Culture.* Armonk, NY: M.E. Sharpe, 2005.
A study of the geopolitics of the two Koreas.

Kim, Alexander Joungwon. *Divided Korea: The Politics of Development 1945–1972.* Cambridge, MA: East Asian Research Center, Harvard University Press, 1975.
Still a good analysis of Korean politics from liberation to Yushin.

Kim, Byung-Kook, Ezra Vogel, and Jorge I. Dominguez, eds., *The Park Chung Hee Era: The Transformation of South Korea.* Cambridge, MA: Harvard University Press, 2011.
One of several collections of essays reexamining South Korea under Park Chung Hee. These essays tend to emphasize Park Chung Hee's positive achievements in overseeing the economic development of the country.

Kim Choong Soon. *The Culture of Korean Industry: An Ethnography of Poongsan Corporation.* Tucson: University of Arizona Press, 1992.
A case study of a medium-size South Korean industry during the years of rapid industrialization.

Kim, C. I. Eugene, and Han-kyo Kim. *Korea and the Politics of Imperialism: 1876–1910.* Berkeley: University of California Press, 1967.
Provides a detailed factual account of the international diplomacy and great-power maneuvering during this period.

Kim, Dong-no, John B. Duncan, and Kim Do-hyung, eds. *Reform and Modernity in the Taehan Empire.* Seoul: Jimoondang, 2006.
Nine essays by Korean and American scholars.

Kim, Eun Mee. *Big Business, Strong State: Collusion and Conflict in South Korean Development, 1960–1990.* Albany: State University of New York Press, 1997.
A useful account of big conglomerates and the state in South Korea's economic development, accessible to the general reader.

Kim, Janice C. H. *To Live to Work: Factory Women in Colonial Korea, 1910–1945.* Stanford, CA: Stanford University Press, 2009.
Offers an account of the popular expansion of gender, labor, and political consciousness among working women in colonial Korea.

Kim, Key-Hiuk. *The Last Phase of the East Asian World Order.* Berkeley: University of California Press, 1980.
One of the most detailed and best analyzed accounts of the diplomacy and politics surrounding the opening of Korea.

Kim, Richard. *Lost Names: Scenes from a Korean Boyhood.* Berkeley: University of California Press.
A semiautobiographical novel providing a vivid picture of life during the last years of colonial rule.

Kim, Sebastian C. H., and Kirsteen Kim. *A History of Christianity.* Cambridge, UK: Cambridge University Press, 2015.
A comprehensive and balanced study of Christianity in Korea from sixteenth century to 2010s. Especially useful for understanding the role of Christianity in South Korea after 1945.

Kim, Suzy. *Everyday Life in the North Korean Revolution. 1945–1950.* Ithaca, NY: Cornell University Press, 2013.
Study focusing on one county in North Korea during the formative years of that state.

Koo, Hagen. *Korean Workers: The Culture and Pattern of Class Formation*. Ithaca, NY: Cornell University Press, 2001.
An important study of the South Korean working class.

Lancaster, Lewis R., and Richard K. Payne. *Religion and Society in Contemporary Korea*. Berkeley: University of California Press, 1997.
Ten essays on the topic of religion in modern South Korea—includes studies of shamanism, Buddhism, and Christianity.

Lankov, Andrei. *From Stalin to Kim Il Sung: The Formation of North Korea, 1945–1960*. New Brunswick, NJ: Rutgers University Press, 2002.
An insightful political history of early North Korea by one of the best-informed scholars writing on that country.

———. *North of the DMZ: Essays on Daily Life in North Korea*. Jefferson, NC: McFarland & Company Inc., 2007.
A series of essays, many on North Korea, by a leading historian of that country. Provides the best summary of North Korean society available in English with many valuable insights. Highly recommended for anyone interested in North Korea.

———. *The Real North Korea: Life and Politics in the Failed Stalinist Utopia*. Oxford: Oxford University Press, 2013.
A highly readable summary of the North Korean history with a focus on recent years.

Larsen, Kirk W. *Tradition, Treaties, and Trade: Qing Imperialism and Chosŏn Korea, 1850–1910*. Cambridge, MA: Harvard University Press, 2008.
Well-written revisionist study of this period. Argues that Qing was an imperial power using modern diplomacy, international law, telegraphs, and steamboats to aggressively assert itself in Korea.

Lee, Chung-shik. *Park Chung-Hee: From Poverty to Power*. Palos Verdes, CA: KHU Press, 2012.
Traces the personal background of Park Chung Hee up to his seizure of power in 1961.

Lee, H. B. *Korea: Time, Change, and Administration*. Honolulu: East-West Center Press, 1968.
This is still a useful introduction to the bureaucratic culture of South Korea.

Lee, Hong Yung, and Clark W. Sorensen, editors. *Colonial Rule and Social Change in Korea 1910–1945*. Seattle: University of Washington Press, 2013.
A collection of essays incorporating recent scholarship on the colonial period.

Lee, Hy-Sang. *North Korea: A Strange Socialist Fortress*. Westport, CT: Praeger, 2001.
One of a number of useful studies of North Korea. This and many similar books are likely to become outdated if and when North Korea becomes more accessible to scholars.

Lee, Jungsoo. *The Partition of Korea after World War II: A Global History*. New York: Palgrave Macmillan, 2006.
An important recent study of the diplomacy around the division of Korea that makes use of Soviet archival material. Argues that there is no evidence that the Soviet Union immediately after the war had a set plan to create a separate state in the north.

Lee, Namhee. *The Making of Minjung: Democracy and the Politics of Representation in South Korea*. Ithaca, NY: Cornell University Press, 2007.

Examined the place of the *minjung* movement in the country's transformation from an authoritarian to a more open society.

Lett, Denise P. *In Pursuit of Status: The Making of South Korea's "New" Urban Middle Class*. Cambridge, MA: East Asian Research Center, Harvard University Press, 1998.

An insightful study of the emergence of South Korea's new middle class and the persistence of traditional Confucian values and attitudes.

Li, M. *The Yalu Flows: A Korean Childhood*. East Lansing: Michigan State University Press, 1956.

A very readable autobiography providing a glimpse into Korea under Japanese colonialism.

Lie, John. *Han Unbound: The Political Economy of South Korea*. Stanford, CA: Stanford University Press, 1998.

A readable and insightful history of the economic and social transformation of South Korea after 1945.

Lowe, Peter. *The Origins of the Korean War*. New York: Longman, 1986.

A solid, standard history.

Lynn, Hyung Gu. *Bipolar Orders: The Two Koreas since 1989*. Halifax, NS: Fenwood, 2007.

An insightful sketch of contemporary Korean history.

MacDonald, D. S. *The Koreans: Contemporary Politics and Society*. Boulder, CO: Westview Press, 1990.

A basic introduction to South Korea of the 1980s.

McNamara, Dennis L. *The Colonial Origins of Korean Enterprise, 1910–1945*. Cambridge, UK: Cambridge University Press, 1990.

Focuses on Min Tae-sik and his brother Min Kyu-sik, who controlled Hanil bank and its successor in 1931 Tongil Bank; Pak Hŭng-sik of the Hwasin Chain Stores Company; and the brothers Kim Sŏng-su and Kim Yŏn-su, leading manufacturers.

Moon, Seungsook. *Militarized Modernity and Gendering Citizenship in South Korea*. Durham, NC: Duke University Press, 2005.

Moon, Yumi. *Populist Collaborators: The Ilchinhoe and the Japanese Colonization of Korea, 1896–1910*. Ithaca, NY: Cornell University Press, 2013.

A reexamination of the role of the Ilchinhoe in the Japanese takeover of Korea. Provides some interesting analyses of gender and the militarization of South Korean culture.

Myers, Brian. *Han Sŏrya and North Korean Literature: The Failure of Socialist Realism in the DPRK*. Ithaca, NY: Cornell University Press, 1994.

Examines the career of North Korea's most prominent writer with insights into the early years of the Kim Il Sung regime.

———. *The Cleanest Race: How North Koreans See Themselves—And Why It Matters*. Brooklyn, NY: Melville House, 2010.

A provocative examination of North Korea's worldview based primarily on examination of North Korean literature and other internal publications. A highly readable, fascinating, and important, if controversial, work.

Myers, Ramon H., and Mark R. Peattie, eds. *The Japanese Colonial Empire, 1895–1945*. Princeton, NJ: Princeton University Press, 1984.
Contains some useful essays on colonial Korea.

Nahm, Andrew C. *Korea: Tradition and Transformation*. Elizabeth, NJ: Hollym International, 1988.
A good introduction to Korean history, especially modern Korean history, now becoming a bit dated.

Nam, Hwasook Nam. *Building Ships, Building a Nation: Korea's Democratic Unionism under Park Chung Hee*. Seattle: University of Washington Press, 2009.
A case study of shipyard labor unionism in the 1960s; places the 1980s democratization within the context of earlier labor activism.

Natsios, Andrew S. *The Great North Korean Famine*. Washington, DC: United States Institute of Peace Press, 2001.
Contains some eyewitness accounts of the famine in North Korea.

Nelson, Laura C. *Measured Excess: Status, Gender, and Consumer Nationalism in South Korea*. New York: Columbia University Press, 2000.
A mixture of personal accounts and scholarly analysis of how the increasing affluence of South Korea is impacting society, especially how it is shaping the identities of women.

Oberdorfer, Donald. *The Two Koreas: A Contemporary History*. New York: Basic Books, Revised Edition, 2013.
A very readable work on recent politics and foreign affairs by a veteran journalist.

Ogle, George E. *South Korea: Dissent within the Economic Miracle*. Atlantic Highlands, NJ: Zed Books, 1990.
An important study of labor and political dissent by someone with firsthand knowledge of the topic.

Oh, Kongdan, and Ralph C. Hassig. *North Korea: Through the Looking Glass*. Washington, DC: Brookings Institution Press, 2000.
Readable study of North Korea.

Osgood, C. *The Koreans and Their Culture*. New York: Ronald Press, 1951.
Anthropological study done in the late 1940s with good insights into Korean culture on the eve of the Korean War.

Palmer, Brandon. *Fighting for the Enemy: Koreans in Japan's War, 1937–1945*. Seattle: University of Washington Press, 2013.
Interesting study of Koreans who fought in the Japanese imperial forces.

Park, Albert L. *Building Heaven on Earth: Religion, Activism and Protest in Japanese Occupied Japan*. Honolulu: University of Hawaii Press, 2015.
A recent examination of the Korean religious response to modernization and rapid change under colonial rule.

Park, Chung Hee. *The Country, The Revolution and I*. Seoul: Hollym Corporation, 1970.
President Park Chung Hee's justification for his rule. Worth reading for the insights it brings into the thinking and aims of his regime.

Park, Han S. *North Korea: The Politics of Unconventional Wisdom*. Boulder, CO: Lynne Rienner, 2002.
One of a number of useful studies of North Korea.

Park, Soon-won. *Colonial Industrialization and Labor in Korea: The Onoda Cement Factory*. Cambridge, MA: Harvard University Press, 1999.

This book is a study of labor relations and the first generation of skilled workers in colonial Korea, a subject crucial to the understanding of modernization in twentieth-century Korea.

Robinson, Michael E. *Cultural Nationalism in Colonial Korea, 1920–1925*. Seattle: University of Washington Press, 1988.

This monograph introduced the concept of "cultural nationalism." It is indispensable for understanding the rise of modern Korean nationalism.

———. *Korea's Twentieth-Century Odyssey*. Honolulu: University of Hawaii Press, 2007.

Excellent survey of modern Korean history, especially useful on the colonial period.

Schmid, Andre. *Korea Between Empires, 1895–1919*. New York: Columbia University Press, 2002.

An important if challenging work of intellectual history. Argues for the beginnings of modern Korean nationalism in the emergence of a community of educated Korean readers of journals and newspapers.

Shin, Gi-Wook. *Ethnic Nationalism in Korea: Genealogy, Politics, and Legacy*. Stanford, CA: Stanford University Press, 2006.

A sophisticated analysis of the emergence of Korean national identity from the end of the nineteenth century to contemporary North and South Korea.

———. *Peasant Protest and Social Change in Colonial Korea*. Seattle: University of Washington Press, 1996.

An important study of social and economic history in colonial Korea.

Shin, Michael D. et al., eds. *Korean History in Maps: From Prehistory to the Twenty-first Century*. Cambridge, UK: Cambridge University Press, 2014.

Beautifully produced maps accompanied by illustrations and short but informative texts. An excellent reference work for anyone interested in Korean history.

Soh, C. Sarah. *The Comfort Women: Sexual Violence and Postcolonial Memory in Korea and Japan*. Chicago: University of Chicago Press, 2008.

An important study of this controversial subject by an anthropologist. Examines how the comfort women found themselves victimized by Japanese colonialism and Korean patriarchy.

Stueck, W. *The Korean War: An International History*. Princeton, NJ: Princeton University Press, 1995.

A standard work by a noted historian.

Suh, Dae-sook. *Kim Il Sung: A Biography*. Honolulu: University of Hawaii Press, 1989.

The standard biography of Kim Il Sung by a leading authority on North Korea and Korean Communism.

———. *The Korean Communist Movement, 1918–1948*. Princeton, NJ: Princeton University Press, 1967.

Although somewhat dated, still a useful source for understanding the development of Korean Communism.

Suh, Jae-Jung, ed. *Truth and Reconciliation in South Korea: Between the Present and Future of the Korean Wars.* London: Routledge, 2014.

Five essays on the attempt to cope with South Korea's troubled recent past.

Tudor, Daniel and James Pearson. *North Korea Confidential: Private Markets, Fashion Trends, Prison Camps, Dissenters and Defectors.* Tokyo: Tuttle, 2015.

Highly readable introduction to the politics, economy, and everyday life of North Korea aimed at the general reader.

Wada Haruki. *The Korean War: An International History.* Lanham, MD: Rowman & Littlefield, 2014.

A recent work by one of Japan's leading scholars on North Korea. Provides greater role of the dynamics within Korea than in many English-language histories of the Korean War.

Wells, Kenneth M. *New God, New Nation: Protestants and Self-Reconstruction Nationalism in Korea, 1896–1937.* Honolulu: University of Hawaii Press, 1990.

A study of the role of Korean Christians in the emergence of nationalism.

———, ed. *South Korea's Minjung Movement: The Culture and Politics of Dissidence.* Honolulu: University of Hawaii Press, 1995.

Nine essays essential for understanding this important political and intellectual movement in South Korea.

Woo, Jung-en. *Race to the Swift: State and Finance in the Industrialization of Korea.* New York: Columbia University Press, 1991.

One of the best studies of South Korea's economic takeoff.

Yoo, Theodore Jun. *The Politics of Gender in Colonial Korea: Education, Labor, and Health, 1910–1945.* Berkeley, CA: University of California Press, 2008.

A clearly written examination of how the roles and attitudes of many Korean women underwent radical transformation during the Japanese colonial period. Contains an excellent summary of gender relations in premodern and early modern Korea.

Young, Carl F. *Eastern Learning and the Heavenly Way: The Tonghak and Ch'ŏndogyo Movements and the Twilight of Korean Independence.* Honolulu: University of Hawaii Press, 2014.

A recent study of the Tonghak and its successor the Ch'ŏndogyo.

Zhang, Shu Guang. *Mao's Military Romanticism: China and the Korean War, 1950–1953.* Lawrence: University of Kansas Press, 1995.

Provides some insights into China's role in the Korean War.

Index

Abe Nobuyuki, 96
Academy of Korean Studies, 291
aging population, 283
Agreed Framework, 242, 247
agriculture: during colonial rule, 76–77; North Korea, 132, 133, 240, 246, 256 (*see also* famine); South Korea, 176–177
Allen, Horace, 25, 43
American-Soviet Joint Commission, 101
An Chung-gŭn, 40, 52
Andong Kim, 14
Anglo-Japanese Alliance, 37
anti-Americanism, 222–223
art: North Korea, 144; South Korea, 228–229; assimilation, policy of Japanese, 51, 82–83, 86–88
axis of evil, 247

Bae Yong Joon (Pae Yong-jun), 292
Ban Ki Moon (Pan Ki-mun), 293
"base" ("mean") people, 31, 75
"Bean Controversy," 27
birthrate: North Korea, 145; South Korea, 188, 280–281
Black Comrades Society, 62

Bonesteel, Charles, 94
Bong Joon-ho (Pong Chun ho), 192
Britain, 12, 18, 36, 40, 94, 101, 114
Brown Memorandum, 180
Buddhism, 3, 5, 13, 138; Burma, bombing incident, 154, 155
business in South Korea. *See* chaebŏls; economic development

Cairo Declaration, 194
Campaign for National Protection Corps of Industrial Workers (Sanpō), 72
Carter, Jimmy, visit to North Korea, 236, 237
"Case of 105 Persons," 153
Catholicism. *See* Christianity
centralization, 302
Ch'a Ch'i-ch'ŏl, 207
Ch'ae Che-gong, 13
chaebŏls, 183–184, 191, 192, 266, 267, 275, 276, 286
Chaebŏl Specialization Act, 266
Chamint'u, 224
Chang Chiyŏn (Chang Chi-yŏn), 145
Chang In-hwan, 40
Chang Myŏn, 169, 170, 171, 173, 201

325

About the Author

Michael J. Seth is professor of East Asian and world history at James Madison University in Harrisonburg, Virginia. He received his PhD from the University of Hawaii and his MA and BA from the State University of New York at Binghamton. Dr. Seth has lived and worked in South Korea, is the author of *Education Fever: Society, Politics and the Pursuit of Schooling in South Korea* (2002), and is the editor of the *Routledge Handbook of Modern Korean History* (2016).